Lecture Notes in Computer Science   8928

Commenced Publication in 1973
Founding and Former Series Editors:
Gerhard Goos, Juris Hartmanis, and Jan van Leeuwen

More information about this series at http://www.springer.com/series/7412

Lourdes Agapito · Michael M. Bronstein
Carsten Rother (Eds.)

Computer Vision – ECCV 2014 Workshops

Zurich, Switzerland, September 6–7 and 12, 2014
Proceedings, Part IV

 Springer

Editors
Lourdes Agapito
University College London
London
UK

Carsten Rother
Technische Universität Dresden
Dresden
Germany

Michael M. Bronstein
University of Lugano
Lugano
Switzerland

Videos to this book can be accessed at
http://www.springerimages.com/videos/978-3-319-16219-5

ISSN 0302-9743   ISSN 1611-3349   (electronic)
Lecture Notes in Computer Science
ISBN 978-3-319-16219-5   ISBN 978-3-319-16220-1   (eBook)
DOI 10.1007/978-3-319-16220-1

Library of Congress Control Number: 2015933663

LNCS Sublibrary: SL6 – Image Processing, Computer Vision, Pattern Recognition, and Graphics

Springer Cham Heidelberg New York Dordrecht London

Printed on acid-free paper

Springer International Publishing AG Switzerland is part of Springer Science+Business Media
(www.springer.com)

Foreword

Welcome to Zurich !

As you know, the European Conference on Computer Vision is one of the top conferences on computer vision. It was first held in 1990 in Antibes (France) with subsequent conferences in Santa Margherita Ligure (Italy) in 1992, Stockholm (Sweden) in 1994, Cambridge (UK) in 1996, Freiburg (Germany) in 1998, Dublin (Ireland) in 2000, Copenhagen (Denmark) in 2002, Prague (Czech Republic) in 2004, Graz (Austria) in 2006, Marseille (France) in 2008, Heraklion (Greece) in 2010, and Firenze (Italy) in 2012. Many people have worked hard to turn the 2014 edition into as great a success. We hope you will find this a mission accomplished.

The Chairs have decided to adhere to the classical single-track scheme. In terms of the time ordering, we have decided to largely follow the Firenze example (typically starting with poster sessions, followed by oral sessions), which offers a lot of flexibility to network and is more forgiving for the not-so-early-birds and hardcore gourmets.

A large conference like ECCV requires the help of many. They made sure you again get a full program including the main conference, tutorials, workshops, exhibits, demos, proceedings, video streaming/archive, and web descriptions. We want to cordially thank all those volunteers! Please have a look at the conference website to see their names (http://eccv2014.org/people/). We also thank our generous sponsors. You will see their logos around at several occasions during the week, and also prominently on the ECCV 2014 website (http://eccv2014.org/). Their support has been vital to keep prices low and to enrich the program. And it is good to see such level of industrial interest in what our community is doing!

Please do not forget to take advantage of your free travel pass. It allows you to crisscross our splendid city with its fabulous public transportation.

We hope you will enjoy ECCV 2014 to the full.

Also, willkommen in Zürich!

September 2014

Marc Pollefeys
Luc Van Gool

Preface

Welcome to the Workshop proceedings of the 13th European Conference on Computer Vision, held during September 6–12, 2014 in Zurich, Switzerland. We are delighted that the main ECCV 2014 was accompanied by 28 workshops.

We received 38 workshop proposals on diverse computer vision topics. The evaluation process was not easy because of the high quality of the submissions, and the final 28 selected workshops complemented the main conference program. Nearly all of the workshops were running for a full day, with the exception of two half-day workshops and one two-day workshop. In the end, the addressed workshop topics constituted a good mix between novel current trends and traditional issues, without forgetting to address the fundamentals of the computational vision area.

We would like to thank all the Workshop Organizers for their hard work and for making the workshop sessions a great success. We hope that participants enjoyed the workshops, together with the associated papers included in these volumes.

Kind regards / mit freundlichen Grüßen,

November 2014

Michael M. Bronstein
Lourdes Agapito
Carsten Rother

Organization

General Chairs

Luc Van Gool   ETH Zurich, Switzerland
Marc Pollefeys   ETH Zurich, Switzerland

Program Chairs

Tinne Tuytelaars   Katholieke Universiteit Leuven, Belgium
Bernt Schiele   MPI Informatics, Saarbrücken, Germany
Tomas Pajdla   Czech Technical University Prague,
                                   Czech Republic
David Fleet   University of Toronto, Canada

Local Arrangement Chairs

Konrad Schindler   ETH Zurich, Switzerland
Vittorio Ferrari   University of Edinburgh, UK

Workshop Chairs

Lourdes Agapito   University College London, UK
Carsten Rother   Technische Universität Dresden, Germany
Michael M. Bronstein   University of Lugano, Switzerland

Tutorial Chairs

Bastian Leibe   RWTH Aachen, Germany
Paolo Favaro   University of Bern, Switzerland
Christoph H. Lampert   IST, Austria

Poster Chair

Helmut Grabner   ETH Zurich, Switzerland

Publication Chairs

Mario Fritz   MPI Informatics, Saarbrücken, Germany
Michael Stark   MPI Informatics, Saarbrücken, Germany

Demo Chairs

Davide Scaramuzza   University of Zurich, Switzerland
Jan-Michael Frahm   University of North Carolina at Chapel Hill, USA

Exhibition Chair

Tamar Tolcachier   University of Zurich, Switzerland

Industrial Liason Chairs

Alexander Sorkine-Hornung   Disney Research Zurich, Switzerland
Fatih Porikli   ANU, Australia

Student Grant Chair

Seon Joo Kim   Yonsei University, Korea

Air Shelters Accommodation Chair

Maros Blaha   ETH Zurich, Switzerland

Website Chairs

Lorenz Meier   ETH Zurich, Switzerland
Bastien Jacquet   ETH Zurich, Switzerland

Internet Chair

Thorsten Steenbock   ETH Zurich, Switzerland

Student Volunteer Chairs

Andrea Cohen   ETH Zurich, Switzerland
Ralf Dragon   ETH Zurich, Switzerland
Laura Leal-Taixé   ETH Zurich, Switzerland

Finance Chair

Amael Delaunoy   ETH Zurich, Switzerland

Conference Coordinator

Susanne H. Keller   ETH Zurich, Switzerland

Workshop Organizers

W01 - Where Computer Vision Meets Art (VISART)

Gustavo Carneiro   The University of Adelaide, Australia
Alessio Del Bue   Italian Institute of Technology, Italy
Joao Paulo Costeira   Instituto Superior Tecnico, Lisbon, Portugal

W02 - Computer Vision in Vehicle Technology with Special Session on Micro Aerial Vehicles

David Geronimo   KTH, Sweden
Friedrich Fraundorfer   Technische Universität München
Davide Scaramuzza   University of Zurich, Switzerland

W03 - Spontaneous Facial Behavior Analysis

Guoying Zhao   University of Oulu, Finland
Stefanos Zafeiriou   Imperial College London, UK
Matti Pietikäinen   University of Oulu, Finland
Maja Pantic   Imperial College London, UK

W04 - Consumer Depth Cameras for Computer Vision

Andrea Fossati   ETH Zurich, Switzerland
Jürgen Gall   University of Bonn, Germany
Miles Hansard   Queen Mary University London, UK

W05 - ChaLearn Looking at People: Pose Recovery, Action/Interaction, Gesture Recognition

Sergio Escalera   Computer Vision Center, UAB and University
                                        of Barcelona, Catalonia, Spain
Jordi González   Universitat Autònoma de Barcelona and Computer
                                        Vision Center, Catalonia, Spain
Xavier Baró   Universitat Oberta de Catalunya and Computer
                                        Vision Center, Catalonia, Spain
Isabelle Guyon   Clopinet, Berkeley, California, USA
Jamie Shotton   Microsoft Research Cambridge, UK

W06 - Video Event Categorization, Tagging, and Retrieval toward Big Data

Thomas S. Huang	University of Illinois at Urbana-Champaign, USA
Tieniu Tan	Chinese Academy of Sciences, China
Yun Raymond Fu	Northeastern University, Boston, USA
Ling Shao	University of Sheffield, UK
Jianguo Zhang	University of Dundee, UK
Liang Wang	Chinese Academy of Sciences, China

W07 - Computer Vision with Local Binary Patterns Variants

Abdenour Hadid	University of Oulu, Finland
Stan Z. Li	Chinese Academy of Sciences, China
Jean-Luc Dugelay	Eurecom, France

W08 - Reconstruction Meets Recognition Challenge (RMRC)

Nathan Silberman	New York University, USA
Raquel Urtasun	University of Toronto, Canada
Andreas Geiger	MPI Intelligent Systems, Germany
Derek Hoiem	University of Illinois at Urbana-Champaign, USA
Sanja Fidler	University of Toronto, Canada
Antonio Torralba	Massachusetts Institute of Technology, USA
Rob Fergus	New York University, USA
Philip Lenz	Karlsruher Institut für Technologie, Germany
Jianxiong Xiao	Princeton, USA

W09 - Visual Object Tracking Challenge

Roman Pflugfelder	Austrian Institute of Technology, Austria
Matej Kristan	University of Ljubljana, Slovenia
Ales Leonardis	University of Birmingham, UK
Jiri Matas	Czech Technical University in Prague, Czech Republic

W10 - Computer Vision + ONTology Applied Cross-disciplinary Technologies (CONTACT)

Marco Cristani	University of Verona, Italy
Robert Ferrario	ISTC-CNR, Trento, Italy
Jason Corso	SUNY Buffalo, USA

W11 - Visual Perception of Affordances and Functional Visual Primitives for Scene Analysis

Karthik Mahesh Varadarajan   Technical University of Vienna, Austria
Alireza Fathi   Stanford University, USA
Jürgen Gall   University of Bon, Germany
Markus Vincze   Technical University of Vienna, Austria

W12 - Graphical Models in Computer Vision

Michael Yang   Leibniz University Hannover, Germany
Qinfeng (Javen) Shi   University of Adelaide, Australia
Sebastian Nowozin   Microsoft Research Cambridge, UK

W13 - Human-Machine Communication for Visual Recognition and Search

Adriana Kovashka   University of Texas at Austin, USA
Kristen Grauman   University of Texas at Austin, USA
Devi Parikh   Virginia Tech, USA

W14 - Light Fields for Computer Vision

Jingyi Yu   University of Delaware, USA
Bastian Goldluecke   Heidelberg University, Germany
Rick Szeliski   Microsoft Research, USA

W15 - Computer Vision for Road Scene Understanding and Autonomous Driving

Bart Nabbe   Toyota, USA
Raquel Urtasun   University of Toronto, Canada
Matthieu Salzman   NICTA, Australia
Lars Petersson   NICTA, Australia
Jose Alvarez   NICTA, Australia
Fatih Porikli   NICTA, Australia
Gary Overett   NICTA, Australia
Nick Barnes   NICTA, Australia

W16 - Soft Biometrics

Abdenour Hadid   University of Oulu, Finland
Paulo Lobato Correia   University of Lisbon, Portugal
Thomas Moeslund   Aalborg University, Denmark

W17 - THUMOS Challenge: Action Recognition with a Large Number of Classes

Jingen Liu   SRI International, USA
Yu-Gang Jiang   Fudan University, China
Amir Roshan Zamir   UCF, USA
George Toderici   Google, USA
Ivan Laptev   Inria, France
Mubarak Shah   UCF, USA
Rahul Sukthankar   Google Research, USA

W18 - Transferring and Adapting Source Knowledge (TASK) in Computer Vision (CV)

Antonio M. Lopez   Computer Vision Center and Universitat Autónoma
                                     de Barcelona, Spain
Kate Saenko   University of Massachusetts Lowell, USA
Francesco Orabona   Toyota Technological Institute Chicago, USA
José Antonio Rodríguez   Xerox Research EuroFrance
David Vázquez   Computer Vision Cente, Spain
Sebastian Ramos   Computer Vision Center and Universitat Autónoma
                                     de Barcelona, Spain
Jiaolong Xu   Computer Vision Center and Universitat Autónoma
                                     de Barcelona, Spain

W19 - Visual Surveillance and Re-identification

Shaogang Gong   Queen Mary University of London, UK
Steve Maybank   Birkbeck College, University of London, UK
James Orwell   Kingston University, UK
Marco Cristani   University of Verona, Italy
Kaiqi Huang   National Laboratory of Pattern Recognition, China
Shuicheng Yan   National University of Singapore, Singapore

W20 - Color and Photometry in Computer Vision

Theo Gevers   University of Amsterdam, The Netherlands
Arjan Gijsenij   Akzo Nobel, The Netherlands
Todd Zickler   Harvard University, USA
Jose M. Alvarez   NICTA, Australia

W21 - Storytelling with Images and Videos

Gunhee Kim   Disney Research, USA
Leonid Sigal   Disney, USA
Kristen Grauman   University of Texas at Austin, USA
Tamara Berg   University of North Carolina at Chapel Hill, USA

W22 - Assistive Computer Vision and Robotics

Giovanni Maria Farinella	University of Catania, Italy
Marco Leo	CNR- Institute of Optics, Italy
Gerard Medioni	USC, USA
Mohan Triverdi	UCSD, USA

W23 - Computer Vision Problems in Plant Phenotyping

Hanno Scharr	Forschungszentrum Jülich, Germany
Sotirios Tsaftaris	IMT Lucca, Italy

W24 - Human Behavior Understanding

Albert Ali Salah	Boğaziçi University, Turkey
Louis-Philippe Morency	University of Southern California, USA
Rita Cucchiara	University of Modena and Reggio Emilia, Italy

W25 - ImageNet Large-Scale Visual Recognition Challenge (ILSVRC2014)

Olga Russakovsky	Stanford University, USA
Jon Krause	Stanford University, USA
Jia Deng	University of Michigan, USA
Alex Berg	University of North Carolina at Chapel Hill, USA
Fei-Fei Li	Stanford University, USA

W26 - Non-Rigid Shape Analysis and Deformable Image Alignment

Alex Bronstein	Tel-Aviv University, Israel
Umberto Castellani	University of Verona, Italy
Maks Ovsjanikov	Ecole Polytechnique, France

W27 - Video Segmentation

Fabio Galasso	MPI Informatics Saarbrücken, Germany
Thomas Brox	University of Freiburg, Germany
Fuxin Li	Georgia Institute of Technology, Germany
James M. Rehg	Georgia Institute of Technology, USA
Bernt Schiele	MPI Informatics Saarbrücken, Germany

W28 - Parts and Attributes

Rogerio S. Feris	IBM, USA
Christoph H. Lampert	IST, Austria
Devi Parikh	Virginia Tech, USA

Contents – Part IV

W26 - Non-rigid Shape Analysis and Deformable Image Alignment

W22 - Assistive Computer Vision and Robotics (ACVR)

Snippet Based Trajectory Statistics Histograms for Assistive Technologies

Ahmet Iscen[1,3]([⊠]), Yijie Wang[2], Pinar Duygulu[1], and Alex Hauptmann[2]

[1] Bilkent University, Ankara, Turkey
ahmet.iscen@bilkent.edu.tr
[2] Carnegie Mellon University, Pittsburgh, PA, USA
[3] Inria Rennes, Rennes, France

Abstract. Due to increasing hospital costs and traveling time, more and more patients decide to use medical devices at home without traveling to the hospital. However, these devices are not always very straight-forward for usage, and the recent reports show that there are many injuries and even deaths caused by the wrong use of these devices. Since human supervision during every usage is impractical, there is a need for computer vision systems that would recognize actions and detect if the patient has done something wrong. In this paper, we propose to use Snippet Based Trajectory Statistics Histograms descriptor to recognize actions in two medical device usage problems; inhaler device usage and infusion pump usage. Snippet Based Trajectory Statistics Histograms encodes the motion and position statistics of densely extracted trajectories from a video. Our experiments show that by using Snippet Based Trajectory Statistics Histograms technique, we improve the overall performance for both tasks. Additionally, this method does not require heavy computation, and is suitable for real-time systems.

Keywords: Assisted living systems · Medical device usage · Action recognition

1 Introduction

Understanding, predicting, and analyzing people's actions can be a challenging task not only for computers, but also for humans. Even though there have been many breakthrough work in the domain of human action recognition, a significant amount of this research is about recognizing ordinary actions from movies [13] or sports [19]. Most of these solutions can be extended to introduce solutions that may have a more direct impact in our lives. Some of these applications can include video surveillance, anomaly detection, and daily activity analysis.

In this paper, we focus on assistive systems on home medical device usage, more specifically, infusion pump and inhaler usage. Infusion pumps are used to deliver fluid and medication into a patient's body, and inhaler devices are used for asthma therapy. Due to increasing costs, more and more patients decide to use these devices at home to save money and time. However, with lack of

© Springer International Publishing Switzerland 2015
L. Agapito et al. (Eds.): ECCV 2014 Workshops, Part IV, LNCS 8928, pp. 3–16, 2015.
DOI: 10.1007/978-3-319-16220-1_1

Fig. 1. Our task is to detect activities for medical device usage, more specifically for infusion pump and inhaler devices. An example of infusion pump usage is shown on the first row, and inhaler usage is shown on the second row. There are recordings from 3 different camera angles for infusion pump usage.

experience and failure to follow instructions, personal usage of these devices may be ineffective, or even worse, cause fatal problems. In fact, U.S. Food and Drug Administration reported 56,000 incidents between 2005 and 2009, including deaths and injuries, caused by infusion pump usage [8].

With the advancements in computer vision, and impracticality of having a supervisor controlling the correct medical device usage of the patient every time they need to use it, there is a clear need for assistive systems to detect flaws and mistakes during the usage, and report it to the patient. Nevertheless, compared to a typical video analysis system, there may be some limitations of such system. One example is that it must be a real-time system which can detect actions on the fly. Another challenge is that, some actions may only consist of little movements by certain part of the body. This is especially true for infusion pump usage.

On contrary, as such methods are developed for a specific purpose, we can make some assumptions when developing a new method. As an example, we can assume that the camera will usually record the patient from a certain perspective, therefore certain actions may happen in specific positions. In fact, Cai *et al.* make use of this information to detect actions for infusion pump usage [2]. Another assumption we can make is that there most likely will not be a camera motion when the patient performs an action, as the patient is always expected to be seated when the usage takes place.

In this paper, we use Snippet Based Trajectory Statistics Histograms technique [10] to detect actions for assistive system applications. This descriptor encodes the position and movement statistics of a motion, which makes it a suitable candidate for this application due to the aforementioned assumptions. Also, because of their simplicity, it is possible to implement and use them in real time applications. Note that the proposed method only needs RGB videos rather than the depth information which is regularly used for such applications [2,29]. We believe that, although the depth information of a video is extremely useful for detecting some actions, an ordinary patient may not always have an access to a device with such capability. Therefore, we propose to investigate a method which would only use RGB video, and no depth information at all.

2   Related Work

Activity recognition has always been a well studied topic in computer vision. Even though most of the work focuses on finding "ordinary" actions [1], applying them to the medical device usage or other assistive living applications may not always be straight-forward. For example, dense trajectories method [27] by Wang *et al.* works very well for recognizing complex activities, however in this work we show that the simpler Snippet Based Trajectory Statistics Histograms method outperforms it for the medical device usage applications.

Some of the research for activity recognition focuses on applications involving daily activities. One of these applications is anomaly detection, which can be used for surveillance or assistive technologies. Roshtkari *et al.* [22] detects anomalous behaviors by utilising a hierarchical codebook of dense spatio-temporal video volumes. Unusual events are formulated as a sparse coding problem in [33]. Another interesting direction about unusuality detection is learning the crowd behavior [20], and then detecting anomaly as outliers [24]. Ziebart *et al.* predicts people's future locations [34] and Kitani *et al.* [12] forecasts human actions by considering the physical environment. Other works involving daily activities include daily action classification or summarization by egocentric videos [7,14,17], fall detection [15], and classification of cooking actions [11,21,23,26].

Most of the research in assisted living domain requires the use of many different sensors [4,18,28,31]. This kind of setup is usually very costly and not practical for the user. There are also other works that only focus on the use of videos [3]. Fleck and Strasser [9] use cheap smartphone cameras for assisted living monitoring system. Smartphones are also used for obstacle detection for visually impaired people [16,25]. Also, some applications help visually impaired people with their grocery shopping [30], and sonify images for them [32].

Our work is most similar to [2,29], who also analyzes the use of infusion pump and inhaler devices. One of the main differences is that we develop a method only using RGB videos, and not the depth information. Also, unlike [2] we aim for a real-time application which would be able to detect actions rapidly and warn the user if needed.

3   Method

When analyzing the medical device usage, there are two properties that we can make use of; the magnitude of motion and position. Since we can assume that there will not be any camera motion, we can consider all the motion information to be relevant, and do not have to take into account any noisy motion. Also, by assuming that the position of the user will be more or less the same every time, we try to exploit the information about where each action takes place.

3.1   Snippet Based Trajectory Statistics Histograms

Originally introduced to detect unusual actions in videos [10], Snippet Based Trajectory Statistics Histograms method encodes the position and motion information in small intervals. The visualization of the algorithm is shown on Figure 2.

It is built on dense sampling technique introduced by Wang *et al.* [27], which is used to produce the original motion trajectories from the video. These trajectories are extracted densely on the grid, and their motion is tracked for every D frames.

Unlike the *trajectory feature* described in [27], which encodes the shape of each trajectory, Snippet Based Trajectory Statistics Histograms encodes the motion information simply by considering their statistical information. That is, for each trajectory T, we only use its length (l), variance along x-axis(v_x), and y-axis (v_y). Length information is used to distinguish between fast and small motions. Since trajectories are tracked for a fixed number of frames, the longer ones correspond to faster motions, whereas the smaller ones correspond to motions without much movement. Additionally, in order to encode the direction and the spatial extension of the motion, variance of motion in x and y coordinates are also used.

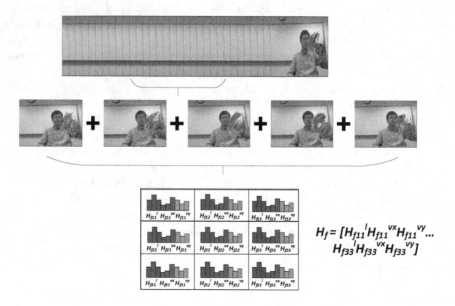

Fig. 2. Visualization of Snippet Based Trajectory Statistics Histograms technique. A small interval of a video is taken, and the motion information is aggregated. A histogram based on the length and the variance statistics of this motion, as well as its spatial location, is created.

In order to aggregate motion statistics along with position, Snippet Based Trajectory Statistics Histograms algorithm finds the average position of each trajectory during D frames which it was tracked for. First, for each trajectory T, we find its average position in x and y coordinates, m_x and m_y respectively, along with its motion statistics. This can be done as follows:

$$m_x = \frac{1}{D} \sum_{t}^{t+D-1} x_t, v_x = \frac{1}{D} \sum_{t}^{t+D-1} (x_t - m_x)^2$$

$$m_y = \frac{1}{D} \sum_{t}^{t+D-1} y_t, v_y = \frac{1}{D} \sum_{t}^{t+D-1} (y_t - m_y)^2, \tag{1}$$

$$l = \sum_{t}^{t+D-1} \sqrt{(x_{t+1} - x_t)^2 + (y_{t+1} - y_t)^2}$$

where l is the length, v_x and v_y are the variance of the trajectory in x and y axes respectively.

To embed the spatial information of the movement, we divide each frame into $N \times N$ spatial grids. Recall that we have already computed the average x and y position m_x and m_y for each trajectory. We assign each trajectory to one of the spatial grids based on their m_x and m_y positions, and for each spatial grid, we create 3 histograms by separately quantizing the l , v_x and v_y values of all the trajectories belonging to that grid into b bins.

For example, let $H_l(t)$ be the frame histogram of length (l) values of all the trajectories which are tracked until frame t. We create this histogram by concatenating b-bin histograms from each spatial bin, such that:

$$H_l(t) = (H_l(t)_{[1,1]}, \ldots H_l(t)_{[1,N]}, \ldots H_l(t)_{[N,N]}) \tag{2}$$

where $H_l(t)_{[i,j]}, 0 \leq i,j \leq N$ contains the b-bin histogram obtained by trajectories whose average position lies in the $[i,j]^{th}$ cell. The same procedure is repeated for the v_x and v_y values of trajectories.

Now that we have the motion statistics of trajectories, they need to be aggregated in order to describe the overall motion in a small interval of the video. This is done by describing all the motion and position statistics in each small interval, which is also referred as *snippets*.

Snippet histograms are calculated for each frame in the video, and they encode the motion before and after the corresponding frame. As an example, for a given snippet size of S all the trajectories that end at frame f are summed, such that:

$$H_f^l = \sum_{t=f-(\|S\|/2)}^{f+(\|S\|/2)} H_l(t) \quad , \quad H_f^{vx} = \sum_{t=f-(\|S\|/2)}^{f+(\|S\|/2)} H_{vx}(t)$$

$$H_f^{vy} = \sum_{t=f-(\|S\|/2)}^{f+(\|S\|/2)} H_{vy}(t)) \tag{3}$$

and we concatenate them to obtain a $3 \times b \times N \times N$ dimensional histogram for each frame f in the end:

$$H_f = [H_f^l, H_f^{vx}, H_f^{vy}] \tag{4}$$

3.2 Why Snippet Based Trajectory Statistics Histograms

Our goal is to detect actions for medical device usage. We propose to use Snippet Based Trajectory Statistics Histograms method for this domain for a few properties which we believe would be handled by Snippet Based Trajectory Statistics Histograms.

First of all, we know that the camera will be standing still and looking over the patient from a certain angle during the usage. Therefore, certain actions will always occur in certain spatial positions of the frame, since the position of each user will more or less be the same. Because Snippet Based Trajectory Statistics Histograms divides the spatial coordinate into grids, and creates a separate histogram for each grid, we believe that it will help us to distinguish similar actions taking place in different positions.

Secondly, medical device usage may involve very fast actions, such as *shaking* and very slow actions, such as *opening a cap*. By exploiting the statistical information of trajectories, such as the length and the variance of the trajectory motion, Snippet Based Trajectory Statistics Histograms would enable the system to distinguish fast actions from slow actions.

Lastly, due to the simplicity and easiness of the implementation, Snippet Based Trajectory Statistics Histograms can be suitable for real-time applications. In fact, the major overhead of execution is to generate initial trajectories using the dense trajectory method [27], but this can be sped up easily by downsampling the sizes of frames. Once we have the initial trajectories, Snippet Based Trajectory Statistics Histograms requires only a few fast calculations.

4 Experiments

We conduct our experiments for two different scenarios, inhaler device and infusion pump device usage. In this section, we first describe the datasets we used for each task, and explain our results.

4.1 Implementation Details

For our implementation of Snippet Based Trajectory Statistics Histograms for medical device usage, we extract initial snippets for $D = 15$ frames. Then, we find Snippet Based Trajectory Statistics Histograms in $N \times N$ spatial grid where $N = 3$, and quantize length and variance information into $b = 5$ bins. Therefore, we have $3 \times 5 \times 3 \times 3 = 135$ dimensional descriptors in the end. The size of each snippet is $S = 10$ frames.

4.2 Baseline

We compare Snippet Based Trajectory Statistics Histograms with other trajectory-based descriptors, such as Trajectory Shape Descriptor [27], histograms of oriented gradients (HOG) [5], histograms of optical flow (HOF) [13], and motion boundary histograms (MBH) [6]. We quantize the other descriptors with bag-of-words using a dictionary of size $k = 100$.

4.3   Inhaler Usage

Dataset: Inhaler Dataset [29] has 77 RGB and depth video recordings of users using GlaxoSmithKline Inhalation Aerosol device. The user performs inhaler usage operation while sitting 50-70 cm in front of the camera. The dataset has 4 different action classes, *shaking*, where the user shakes the inhaler device, *position checking*, where the user puts the device about 2 inches in front of his or her mouth, *inhaling* and *exhaling*. However, since *inhaling* and *exhaling* actions cannot be detected visually, and need additional features such as audio, we do not evaluate them. We use recall, precision, and F-score measures for the evaluation of performance in this dataset.

(a) shaking   (b) position checking   (c) inhaling

Fig. 3. Some of the actions in the Inhaler Dataset. Although *shaking* and *position-checking* actions can be detected visually, *inhaling* and *exhaling* actions do not have any visual cues and require other modalities such as audio. Therefore, we do not include these two actions in our experiments.

Results: Our first set of experiments for this dataset with the Snippet Based Trajectory Statistics Histograms is for the *shaking action*. Before we make any comparisons, we need to decide what we consider as a correct detection. We introduce the *overlap ratio* threshold t, which is the ratio of overlap in terms of frames between the detected action and the ground truth. If the detection and the ground truth has a greater overlap than t, then we consider it as a match.

As we see in Figure 4, the performance remains the same until $t = 0.5$. This is also a reasonable threshold value for evaluation. Therefore, we set the overlap ratio threshold $t = 0.5$, and conduct experiments to compare Snippet Based Trajectory Statistics Histograms with other trajectory based descriptors.

Table 1 shows the comparison of trajectory shape, HOG, HOF and MBH features from [27], with Snippet Based Trajectory Statistics Histograms descriptors. Our method has the highest overall F-score, having a perfect 100% precision score. The second-best performing descriptor is HOF, which is not a surprise, because it also mostly encodes the flow information and not the appearance information. If we analyze the shaking action, such as the examples shown in Figure 5, we see that it produces fast and long trajectories. Therefore, it is expected that these descriptors perform very well for this task.

Our second set of experiments is done for *position checking*. Note that we have no ways of checking the correct distance between the inhaler and the mouth

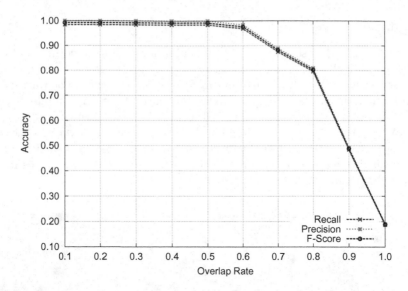

Fig. 4. The effect of overlap rate threshold. Based on this figure, we choose $t = 0.5$ as the overlap rate in our experiments.

Table 1. Comparison of Snippet Based Trajectory Statistics Histograms with other trajectory based descriptors for the *shaking* action of Inhaler Dataset. Trajectory scores are the same as those reported in [29].

	Trajectory	HOG	HOF	MBH	Snippet Hist
Recall	95.31	50.00	**100.00**	87.50	98.44
Precision	91.04	22.70	91.43	71.79	**100.00**
F-score	93.13	31.22	95.52	78.87	**99.21**

Fig. 5. Regardless of whichever direction user shakes the inhaler device, we get many long trajectories as the result.

simply by using the RGB camera, we just try to see if we can detect this action by the user's motion.

As shown in Table 2, position checking performance is nowhere close to that of [29], which uses the face detector and depth information. However, our goal

Table 2. Comparison of position checking action results. Although RGB-based descriptors are nowhere close to the depth video performance in [29], Snippet Based Trajectory Statistics Histograms still perform better than other trajectory-based descriptors.

	Trajectory	HOG	HOF	MBH	Snippet Hist	Depth
Recall	8.82	8.82	13.24	10.29	30.88	**90.30**
Precision	17.07	12.77	16.36	24.24	18.46	**78.80**
F-score	11.63	10.43	14.63	14.45	23.11	**84.20**

Fig. 6. Position checking is a more subtle action than shaking. The user may slowly or suddenly move the device towards his or her face. As a result, we get trajectories of varying lengths for this action.

of this experiment was not to try to improve their result, but rather to compare Snippet Based Trajectory Statistics Histograms with other trajectory-based features. We can see that the Snippet Based Trajectory Statistics Histograms still has the best F-score when compared with the other descriptors, though it is really low.

One of the reasons for such a low score for trajectory-based features in this task is that the motion of moving the inhaler device towards the mouth differs significantly from user to user. Some users move it suddenly, resulting in long trajectories, whereas others move it very subtly, as shown in Figure 6. Therefore, we must make use of depth, face and other information in this task, as done in [29].

4.4   Infusion Pump

Dataset: Pump Dataset [2] consists of different users using Abbot Laboratories Infusion Pump device. Each user is asked to perform the operation multiple times, and they may or may not follow the correct order of operation. The dataset is annotated with 7 action classes. There are three different cameras recording each user synchronously from the side, above and front of the user. The dataset has both RGB and depth videos of these recordings, however we only make use of the RGB videos in this paper.

(a) front	(b) side	(c) above

Fig. 7. Example of extracted trajectories for the same frame. We can see more motion information from the cameras positioned above and side, compared to the camera positioned in front of the user

Table 3. Results for Pump Dataset. The accuracy performance for each camera is reported separately, and the best performance among three cameras is reported under the *fusion* column.

Actions	Trajectory				HOG			
	front	side	above	fusion	front	side	above	fusion
Turn the pump on/off	65.40	65.40	67.30	67.30	67.13	58.82	72.32	72.32
Press buttons	56.23	63.32	71.11	71.11	56.92	66.78	74.74	74.74
Uncap tube end/arm port	51.04	67.13	63.15	67.13	52.25	70.07	65.74	**70.07**
Cap tube end/arm port	51.04	57.61	66.44	66.44	55.88	68.51	59.34	68.51
Clean tube end/arm port	53.29	58.65	56.57	58.65	56.40	63.32	63.32	63.32
Flush using syringe	47.58	64.53	60.90	64.53	57.27	61.59	77.68	77.68
Connect/disconnect	48.79	56.23	62.63	62.63	54.33	67.47	64.71	67.47
Average	53.34	61.84	64.01	65.40	57.17	65.22	68.26	70.59

Actions	HOF				MBH			
	front	side	above	fusion	front	side	above	fusion
Turn the pump on/off	67.99	65.74	76.99	**76.99**	69.20	68.17	74.91	74.91
Press buttons	45.67	61.59	74.22	74.22	57.44	66.26	72.84	72.84
Uncap tube end/arm port	42.56	59.69	65.57	65.57	57.09	70.07	69.20	**70.07**
Cap tube end/arm port	52.08	72.32	59.52	72.32	52.42	72.84	69.20	**72.84**
Clean tube end/arm port	52.25	62.63	67.13	**67.13**	55.71	56.23	66.78	66.78
Flush using syringe	49.13	73.88	70.59	73.88	54.67	71.80	68.69	71.80
Connect/disconnect	57.27	53.11	60.73	60.73	52.94	71.11	70.59	71.11
Average	52.42	64.14	67.82	70.12	57.06	68.09	70.32	71.48

Actions	Snippet Based Trajectory Statistics Histograms			
	front	side	above	fusion
Turn the pump on/off	75.26	69.03	75.09	75.26
Press buttons	68.34	70.93	76.12	**76.12**
Uncap tube end/arm port	67.13	64.19	67.30	67.30
Cap tube end/arm port	54.33	70.59	66.44	70.59
Clean tube end/arm port	55.02	66.78	65.40	66.78
Flush using syringe	64.01	73.18	82.01	**82.01**
Connect/disconnect	54.33	72.66	72.15	**72.66**
Average	62.63	69.62	72.07	**72.96**

4.5   Results

In order to show the effect of each camera, we report scores separately for each camera in Table 3, as well as taking the best result among 3 cameras and reporting it under the *fusion* column. One of the points that we can observe from these results is that the camera from *above* seems to work better for trajectory-based features than the others. This can be explained by the fact that there are more movements when looked from above compared to side or front during the infusion pump usage (see Figure 7). Since these descriptors depend on trajectories of motion, they work better when there is more motion on camera. Compared to other descriptors, Snippet Based Trajectory Statistics Histograms slightly have better performance in this task.

As our last experiment on Infusion Pump Dataset, we train a temporal model based on the order of actions in the training set. It has been shown that this approach improves performance for daily-action recognition applications [7, 11]. We follow the method introduced in [11], and simply train a 2nd-order Markov Chain using the order of operations in order to store the temporal sequence information of the actions.

Table 4. Comparison of temporal sequence model used with different descriptors. We also compare our results with the *ROI-BoW* method introduced in [2]. For this experiment, we only report the best result obtained among 3 cameras for each method.

Actions	Trajectory	HOG	HOF	MBH	Snippet Hist	ROI-BoW
Turn the pump on/off	91.52	91.52	90.83	92.39	**97.23**	89.40
Press buttons	79.93	80.28	80.10	79.76	83.91	**88.33**
Uncap tube end/arm port	84.26	85.64	83.56	85.47	**91.35**	65.41
Cap tube end/arm port	84.26	83.91	83.91	84.26	**89.45**	44.55
Clean tube end/arm port	70.24	73.18	77.51	74.05	75.78	**92.02**
Flush using syringe	88.75	88.24	88.06	87.20	92.56	**94.80**
Connect/disconnect	90.14	90.31	88.24	90.14	**92.73**	53.35
Average	84.16	84.73	84.60	84.75	**89.00**	75.41

Based on Table 4, we see that the temporal sequence model has improved the results dramatically. It performs much better than *ROI-BoW* introduced in [2] when used with Snippet Based Trajectory Statistics Histograms. This shows us that the temporal sequence information can be used successfully for medical device usage as well.

5   Conclusion

In this paper we apply Snippet Based Trajectory Statistics Histograms to recognize actions in medical device usage. Our experiments show that they can be used successfully in this domain. This is especially evident for actions with fast motions, such as the *shaking* action. In addition to having a good performance, they do not require any heavy computation and can be easily used for real-time applications. For Infusion Pump Dataset, we also show that storing the sequence information of actions improves the results dramatically when used with Snippet Based Trajectory Statistics Histograms. These results encourage us to believe that the use of medical devices at home can be regulated with the help of technology, saving patients from injuries or fatal incidents.

Acknowledgement. This material is based in part upon work supported by the National Science Foundation under Grant No. IIS-1251187. This paper is also partially supported by TUBITAK grant number 112E174.

References

1. Aggarwal, J., Ryoo, M.S.: Human activity analysis: A review. ACM Computing Surveys (CSUR) **43**(3), 16 (2011)
2. Cai, Y., Yang, Y., Hauptmann, A.G., Wactlar, H.D.: A cognitive assistive system for monitoring the use of home medical devices. In: Proceedings of the 1st ACM international workshop on Multimedia indexing and information retrieval for healthcare. pp. 59–66. ACM (2013)
3. Cardinaux, F., Bhowmik, D., Abhayaratne, C., Hawley, M.S.: Video based technology for ambient assisted living: A review of the literature. Journal of Ambient Intelligence and Smart Environments **3**(3), 253–269 (2011)
4. Crispim-Junior, C.F., Bremond, F., Joumier, V., et al.: A multi-sensor approach for activity recognition in older patients. In: The Second International Conference on Ambient Computing, Applications, Services and Technologies-AMBIENT 2012 (2012)
5. Dalal, N., Triggs, B.: Histograms of oriented gradients for human detection. In: CVPR (2005)
6. Dalal, N., Triggs, B., Schmid, C.: Human detection using oriented histograms of flow and appearance. In: Leonardis, A., Bischof, H., Pinz, A. (eds.) ECCV 2006. LNCS, vol. 3952, pp. 428–441. Springer, Heidelberg (2006)
7. Fathi, A., Farhadi, A., Rehg, J.M.: Understanding egocentric activities. In: IEEE International Conference on Computer Vision (ICCV), pp. 407–414. IEEE (2011)
8. FDA: White paper: Infusion pump improvement initiative (2010). http://www.fda.gov/medicaldevices/productsandmedicalprocedures/GeneralHospitalDevicesandSupplies/InfusionPumps/ucm205424.htm
9. Fleck, S., Straßer, W.: Smart camera based monitoring system and its application to assisted living. Proceedings of the IEEE **96**(10), 1698–1714 (2008)
10. Iscen, A., Armagan, A., Duygulu, P.: What is usual in unusual videos? trajectory snippet histograms for discovering unusualness. In: CVPR 2014 2nd Workshop on Web-scale Vision and Social Media (VSM)
11. Iscen, A., Duygulu, P.: Knives are picked before slices are cut: recognition through activity sequence analysis. In: Proceedings of the 5th international workshop on Multimedia for cooking & eating activities. pp. 3–8. ACM (2013)
12. Kitani, K.M., Ziebart, B.D., Bagnell, J.A., Hebert, M.: Activity forecasting. In: Fitzgibbon, A., Lazebnik, S., Perona, P., Sato, Y., Schmid, C. (eds.) ECCV 2012, Part IV. LNCS, vol. 7575, pp. 201–214. Springer, Heidelberg (2012)

13. Laptev, I., Marszalek, M., Schmid, C., Rozenfeld, B.: Learning realistic human actions from movies. In: 2008 IEEE Conference on Computer Vision and Pattern Recognition. CVPR 2008, pp. 1–8. IEEE (2008)
14. Lu, Z., Grauman, K.: Story-driven summarization for egocentric video. In: 2013 IEEE Conference on Computer Vision and Pattern Recognition (CVPR), pp. 2714–2721. IEEE (2013)
15. Mubashir, M., Shao, L., Seed, L.: A survey on fall detection: Principles and approaches. Neurocomputing **100**, 144–152 (2013)
16. Peng, E., Peursum, P., Li, L., Venkatesh, S.: A smartphone-based obstacle sensor for the visually impaired. In: Yu, Z., Liscano, R., Chen, G., Zhang, D., Zhou, X. (eds.) UIC 2010. LNCS, vol. 6406, pp. 590–604. Springer, Heidelberg (2010)
17. Pirsiavash, H., Ramanan, D.: Detecting activities of daily living in first-person camera views. In: 2012 IEEE Conference on Computer Vision and Pattern Recognition (CVPR), pp. 2847–2854. IEEE (2012)
18. Rashidi, P., Mihailidis, A.: A survey on ambient-assisted living tools for older adults. IEEE journal of biomedical and health informatics **17**(3), 579–590 (2013)
19. Rodriguez, M., Javed, A., Shah, M.: Action mach: a spatio-temporal maximum average correlation height filter for action recognition. In: 2008 IEEE Conference on Computer Vision and Pattern Recognition. CVPR 2008, pp. 1–8. IEEE (2008)
20. Rodriguez, M., Sivic, J., Laptev, I.: Analysis of crowded scenes in video. Intelligent Video Surveillance Systems pp. 251–272
21. Rohrbach, M., Amin, S., Andriluka, M., Schiele, B.: A database for fine grained activity detection of cooking activities. In: 2012 IEEE Conference on Computer Vision and Pattern Recognition (CVPR), pp. 1194–1201. IEEE (2012)
22. Roshtkhari, M.J., Levine, M.D.: Online dominant and anomalous behavior detection in videos. In: CVPR (2013)
23. Spriggs, E.H., De La Torre, F., Hebert, M.: Temporal segmentation and activity classification from first-person sensing. In: 2009 IEEE Computer Society Conference on Computer Vision and Pattern Recognition Workshops, CVPR Workshops 2009, pp. 17–24. IEEE (2009)
24. Sun, X., Yao, H., Ji, R., Liu, X., Xu, P.: Unsupervised fast anomaly detection in crowds. In: ACM MM (2011)
25. Tapu, R., Mocanu, B., Bursuc, A., Zaharia, T.: A smartphone-based obstacle detection and classification system for assisting visually impaired people. In: 2013 IEEE International Conference on Computer Vision Workshops (ICCVW), pp. 444–451. IEEE (2013)
26. Tenorth, M., Bandouch, J., Beetz, M.: The tum kitchen data set of everyday manipulation activities for motion tracking and action recognition. In: 2009 IEEE 12th International Conference on Computer Vision Workshops (ICCV Workshops), pp. 1089–1096. IEEE (2009)
27. Wang, H., Kläser, A., Schmid, C., Liu, C.L.: Dense trajectories and motion boundary descriptors for action recognition. IJCV (2013)
28. Wang, Q., Shin, W., Liu, X., Zeng, Z., Oh, C., AlShebli, B.K., Caccamo, M., Gunter, C.A., Gunter, E.L., Hou, J.C., et al.: I-living: An open system architecture for assisted living. In: SMC, pp. 4268–4275 (2006)
29. Wang, Y., Hauptmann, A.: An assistive system for monitoring asthma inhaler usage. In: CMU-LTI-14-002 Technical Report (2014)
30. Winlock, T., Christiansen, E., Belongie, S.: Toward real-time grocery detection for the visually impaired. In: 2010 IEEE Computer Society Conference on Computer Vision and Pattern Recognition Workshops (CVPRW), pp. 49–56. IEEE (2010)

31. Wood, A., Stankovic, J.A., Virone, G., Selavo, L., He, Z., Cao, Q., Doan, T., Wu, Y., Fang, L., Stoleru, R.: Context-aware wireless sensor networks for assisted living and residential monitoring. IEEE Network **22**(4), 26–33 (2008)
32. Yoshida, T., Kitani, K.M., Koike, H., Belongie, S., Schlei, K.: Edgesonic: image feature sonification for the visually impaired. In: Proceedings of the 2nd Augmented Human International Conference, p. 11. ACM (2011)
33. Zhao, B., Fei-Fei, L., Xing, E.P.: Online detection of unusual events in videos via dynamic sparse coding. In: CVPR (2011)
34. Ziebart, B.D., Ratliff, N., Gallagher, G., Mertz, C., Peterson, K., Bagnell, J.A., Hebert, M., Dey, A.K., Srinivasa, S.: Planning-based prediction for pedestrians. In: IROS (2009)

Combining Semi-autonomous Navigation with Manned Behaviour in a Cooperative Driving System for Mobile Robotic Telepresence

Andrey Kiselev$^{(\boxtimes)}$, Annica Kristoffersson, and Amy Loutfi

Örebro University, örebro, Sweden
{andrey.kiselev,annica.kristoffersson,amy.loutfi}@oru.se

Abstract. This paper presents an image-based cooperative driving system for telepresence robot, which allows safe operation in indoor environments and is meant to minimize the burden on novice users operating the robot. The paper focuses on one emerging telepresence robot, namely, mobile remote presence systems for social interaction. Such systems brings new opportunities for applications in healthcare and elderly care by allowing caregivers to communicate with patients and elderly from remote locations. However, using such systems can be a difficult task particularly for caregivers without proper training. The paper presents a first implementation of a vision-based cooperative driving enhancement to a telepresence robot. A preliminary evaluation in the laboratory environment is presented.

Keywords: Human-robot interaction · Mobile robotic telepresence · Teleoperation · User interfaces

1 Introduction

Mobile Remote Presence (MRP) [1] is an emerging field of assistive robotics which aims to bring mobile robots equipped with certain telepresence and teleoperation capabilities into domestic environments. The main goal of those systems is to allow rich natural human-human interactions from distant locations. Many systems are now available for research and some are already commercial products. The application domains of such systems may vary and define the appearance and functionality of a particular robot to certain degree. [2] provides an overview of modern MRP systems for different applications.

One of the important application domains for MRP systems is healthcare and elderly care, where telepresence robots can be profitable [3] and contribute to prevention of problems related to loneliness and social isolation [4]. At the same time, with the spread of the technology into consumer fields, scientists and developers are facing problems related to the nature of end-users who may have no proper skills, knowledge and experience on using such systems and who cannot be exposed to extensive training which is normally acceptable in other application domain for telepresence and teleoperation. Particularly, previous research

© Springer International Publishing Switzerland 2015
L. Agapito et al. (Eds.): ECCV 2014 Workshops, Part IV, LNCS 8928, pp. 17–28, 2015.
DOI: 10.1007/978-3-319-16220-1_2

has shown that some novice users of MRP system can experience high workload even in a relatively simple driving task [5]. This actually might leave no room for actual interaction between local and remote people diminishing the utility of such solutions [6].

The problem of high mental workload during driving/piloting tasks has been previously studies in automotive industry [7], aviation [8] and related fields. However, in a vast majority of cases, it is possible or assumed to be possible to overcome the problem the problem with training and experience [9], [10]. Unfortunately, it is not always possible to use extensive training for those who operate telepresence robots in domestic environments as the type of end-users are diverse and the care structures may not be suitable to enable this type of training. Another possible solution to coping with inexperienced users is to provide certain semi-autonomous functions that can predict and avoid possible hazardous situations. Such systems are growing rapidly for example in automotive industry [11] [12].

One important function is to avoid collisions and utilizing various sensors and processing techniques to detect possible collisions. For example, [13] presents a system for real-time obstacle and lane detection in a structured environment based on stereoscopic cameras, [14] proposes the fusion algorithm for combining stereo vision and laser scanner data, [15] introduces the system for safe car navigation using multiple sensors and software algorithms, [16] describes the system for collision-free navigation for humanoid robot using laser range finder and camera, [17] investigates the effectiveness and drivers' acceptance of collision avoidance system. For MRP systems, a good balance between autonomous functions and manual driving is needed. Pilots must be able to not only use video-conferencing, but also to express behaviours through the mobile robot. For example, during the conversation the remote user might want to nod using the robot camera, or screen tilt function or to show impatience by slightly rotating left-right. This basic problem can be found in many different domains. Particularly, [18] and [19] discuss the problem of balanced control for urban search and rescue (USAR) robots, a constrained-based method for vehicle semi-autonomous operation is presented in [20], shared control for robots is discussed in [21]. Different operation modes for cooperative control are shown in [22].

In this paper we present an image-based system for drivable area discovery and collision avoidance for telepresence robot which implements the cooperative control paradigm in a parallel mode in combined case [22]. The system only uses the video stream from the robot to find drivable areas based on floor samples. The current paper is based on the previous research reported in [23].

The rest of the paper is organized as follows: Section 2 depicts our cooperative driving system along with the drivable area discovery algorithm. First tests are described in Section 3. The paper is concluded by Section 4.

2   Semi-autonomous Cooperative Driving

When mobile robots are used in indoor environments and especially in homes of older adults, there are certain considerations that must be taken into account.

First of all, the safety aspect of a fully autonomous domestic robot might be questionable [24]. And this need special attention concerning that MRP systems naturally have human in the loop in most of cases, which makes the entire system even more complicated.

Another important aspect of a telepresence robot is its ability to keep the balance between autonomy or semi-autonomy with a possibility for human users to express behaviours through the robot as briefly mentioned in Section 1. It is important to understand that a MRP system is not only a video-conferencing system on wheels. Its ability to mediate user's statements through body language is also important. In this light, our proposed system attempts to combine robot's semi-autonomy with a possibility for manned behaviours. We use parallel shared cooperation control to combine manned driving performed by an operator with an autonomous collision avoidance algorithm.

2.1 System Architecture

The system which we use for this study is the Giraff MRP system [25]. It is a split system in which there are two essential components: the Giraff robot and pilot interface called Giraff Pilot. Since both parts of the system are actually PCs running Windows®OSs, and several levels of API are currently available for developers, there are several possibilities to inject drivable area discovery algorithm into the basic system. Currently, all semi-autonomous driving functions are implemented on the side of pilot. There are advantages and drawbacks of such solution in comparison to the robot-side implementation of collision avoidance. There are two factors which influence the decision on pilot side implementation:

- When all processing is done on the pilot side, there is no dependency on the robot itself. Thus, the tests can be carried out with different robots and in case of lacking computational resources, a pilot side computer's performance can be increased in an easy way.
- The problem of synchronization under conditions of variable control latency is also eliminated. The control latency of the system depends on many factors and cannot be easily controlled except the case when there is a direct network connection between the robot and the pilot. Performing all processing on the same side eliminates the need of synchronization.

The downsides of this decisions are the reduced quality of the video stream (frames may contain compression artefacts) and a varying framerate.

2.2 Image-Based Drivable Area Discovery

The current implementation of the drivable area discovery algorithm is based on a combination of image thresholding in HSV-space [26] and flood filling. Thus, the method only uses the robot's camera for drivable area discovery. In this paper, the algorithm is called "image-based" because the whole processing is done from scratch on each frame and there is not between-frame persistence of the discovered drivable area.

While the work presented here could utilize similar or better such as depth sensors, various laser range finders or a combination of techniques, our motivation to only use images provided by the onboard camera is driven by the intent to use a standard platform with no hardware modification, to reduce overall system cost and to ease portability to other robotic platforms.

Method. The frames received from the robot have the resolution of *640 X 480 px* at the rate of *15-25 FPS*. Therefore, our goal was to develop an algorithm simple enough to be able to process frames in real time using a standard office PC for pilot. The full processing chain for the algorithm is shown in Fig. 1.

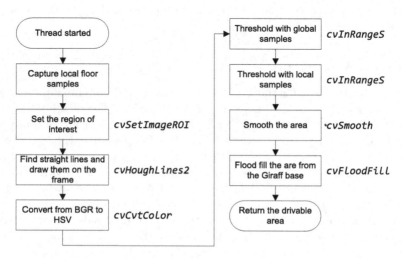

Fig. 1. Algorithm of the frame processing. Note that global floor samples are being loaded outside the frame processing.

The algorithm uses samples of known surfaces called *"floor samples"* to discover the drivable area from frames. There are two kinds of floor samples used by algorithms. First, global floor samples are those which are previously known to belong to floor surfaces allowed to drive. Those floor samples come from initial teaching and experience. Additionally, local floor samples are taken from each frame to allow traversal of unknown surfaces further algorithm learning. Pilot users can choose to store recently taken local floor patterns into the permanent database. Local floor samples are taken in front and on both sides of the robot's base. The actual capturing area is shown on Fig. 2. In the preparation phase, additionally to selecting the region of interest, the Canny edge detection and Hough transform [27] is applied to find any long straight lines and draw them back to the frame. This is done to emphasize the margins between segments of the frame (e.g. floor and wall) which may have not significantly different color to be found by thresholding, but the margin can be still extracted by edge detection and Hough transform.

Fig. 2. Sampling area (white) in front of the robot's base used to take local floor samples

After that, the frame is converted into HSV color space and thresholding is performed using the global floor samples loaded from the library and local floor samples taken in front of the robot.

After the main plugin loop received any discovered drivable area, it attempts to avoid possible collisions or to minimize impact. The algorithm for collision avoidance is shown of Fig. 3.

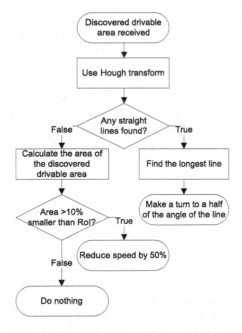

Fig. 3. Algorithm for collision avoidance

The proposed system implements the cooperative control paradigm in a parallel mode in combined case. Therefore, the user input is modified by the system to avoid obstacles if there are any in the drivable area. As it can be seen from Fig. 3, the system attempts to find two types of obstacle. First, it the drivable area is fully cut by some straight line (like from the wall or furnitures), the collision avoidance algorithm attempts to make a turn to avoid collision. Then, if the drivable area contains some obstacle, but no straight line is found, the system reduces the current speed.

Implementation. All image processing is done on the pilot side. Giraff Pilot plugin API [25] was used to embed the code into the basic Giraff Pilot software. Development is accomplished in Java, using JavaCV[1] [29] computer vision library.

Giraff Pilot plugin API offer two interfaces: 1. GiraffViewPlugin interface, which allows to access the video stream received from the robot and manipulate the video stream on the user interface; 2. GiraffDrivePlugin interface, which extends the previous one with hardware access and driving capabilities. The latter is used in this study.

Essentially, the Cooperative Driving plugin replaces the original driving UI in that sense that it implements all basic robot driving functions. but also incorporates cooperative driving and collision avoidance parts.

When the pilot application starts it also loads and instantiates all available plugins. The cooperative driving plugin is designed in a way to also load all dependencies during this stage to avoid any delays if the plugin is actually selected and started by users. Then, during the call when the plugin is actually started by user it identifies available CPU cores and memory and starts processing each new frame in a new thread. The framerate of the video stream received from the robot depends on many factors, such as selected resolutions, network conditions, available PC resources, etc. The plugin attempts to use maximum available CPU cores and starts processing each frame, but may skip some frames if the received framerate is too high in comparison to computational resources available.

3   Preliminary Evaluation

Two variations of the visualization method were developed and incorporated into the Giraff pilot software. They are shown on Fig. 4 and Fig. 5. On the user interface, the main video area shows the video stream received from the robot along with some overlays containing important information (resolution and framerate, rotation and back up buttons, battery status), a driving line (green on both screens) and a drivable area discovery visualization. The driving is done with a mouse. Our previous research [30] shows that using projected image which corresponds to the real robot's size in user interface can assist novice users to drive in narrow passages. This was used for the second visualization method shown in Fig. 5. At the same time, the interface with round shape visualization

---

[1] JavaCV is a wrapper library for OpenCV [28] library.

Fig. 4. Pilot interface with round shape drivable area visualization

Fig. 5. Pilot interface with a corridor-like drivable area visualization

helps users to identify obstacles in the sides of the robot. Nevertheless, the drivable area discovery and obstacle avoidance algorithms behind both visualization methods are identical and use the same region of interest to cope with obstacles in front and on the sides of the robot.

Some examples of drivable area discovery is shown in Fig. 6. In the case (b) the collision avoidance algorithm extracts the straight line in the drivable area (shadow of the bed) and attempts to turn left to avoid front collision. Of course, this implementation of collision avoidance inevitably falls into a local minima, for example, in the corner of the room, which was observed during the trials. On other cases no long enough straight lines is found and the system reduces the forward speed. Fig. 6d shows the work of the drivable area discovery in a fast motion when the robot is being rotated. It can be clearly seen that there is a gap between the margin of the extracted drivable area and the actual obstacle[2] caused by the frame processing lag. In this test the system was trained and used both local floor samples along with the previously captured and stored global samples. The video demonstration of this test is available also in [23]. In another

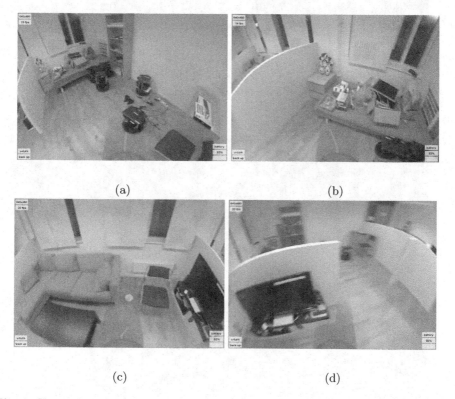

(a)   (b)

(c)   (d)

Fig. 6. Examples of drivable area discovery in a lab environment with wooden floor pattern

---

[2] The robot is rotated clockwise at a rotation speed of 60 degrees/s

test, the robot was put into an environment with a coloured and reflective floor without any global samples to work with (see Fig. 7). Here, several issues with the drivable area discovery system were discovered. First, the system is not capable to cope with light *blobs* (see Fig. 7b and Fig. 7c). This is due to a restriction in the algorithm which does not permit to classify overexposed segments as drivable. This limitation does not also allow the robot to traverse the overexposed area in Fig. 7d. One possible way to address the issue with light blobs in the future is to track them in motion according to the robot's actual speed.

Another issue seen in Fig. 7c is the margin between two different areas. Although both areas are classified as drivable according to the local floor samples captured in both areas, the margin between them is still considered as an obstacle due to the straight line detection stage. In both tests, the pilot software was run

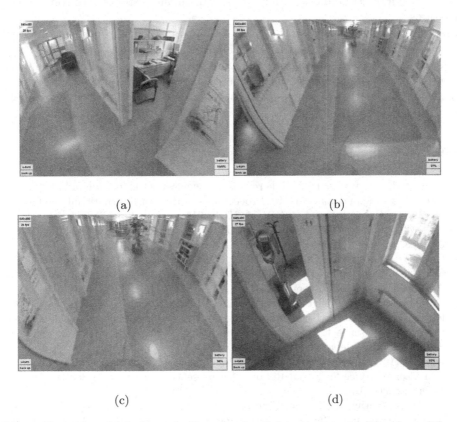

(a)   (b)

(c)   (d)

Fig. 7. Examples of drivable area discovery in a lab environment with coloured floor

on an average laptop PC[3] using Oracle®Java[TM]SE Runtime Environment 1.7.0. In this configuration, the average measured performance was 18.7 FPS (average frame processing time is $\mu = 53.4ms$, $\sigma = 10.0ms$).

---

[3] Intel®CORE[TM]i5-2520M@2,50GHz,   Intel®HD   Graphics,   4.0GB   RAM, Windows®7 x64.

4   Discussion and Future Work

This paper outlines an attempt to incorporate active collision avoidance into a teleoperated mobile robot. This issue is currently well known and recent research shows rapid development of new technologies and their application in automotive industry. However, it appears quite a new and different problem for teleoperation and mobile robotic telepresence in particular when users have different level of immersion and depth perception.

There are two main directions of future work. First of all, the system reported in this paper was primarily developed for conducting studies in the HRI field. Specifically, the possible difference in technology perception and pilots' self confidence depending on the system autonomous behaviour is of a particular interest. We are also interested in evaluating semi-autonomous systems in conversational situations.

At the same time, reliability of the system must be improved in order to allow more complicated experimental scenarios and thorough evaluations. The currently used drivable area discovery algorithm does not guarantee stable work on surfaces with complex patterns. To overcome this limitation, another or additional methods must be implemented. Such methods can be based for example Local Binary Patterns [31] or Gabor filters [32].

References

1. Beer, J.M., Takayama, L.: Mobile remote presence systems for older adults: acceptance, benefits, and concerns. In: Proceedings of the 6th International Conference on Human-Robot Interaction HRI 11. HRI 2011, pp. 19–26. ACM (2011)
2. Kristoffersson, A., Coradeschi, S., Loutfi, A.: A Review of Mobile Robotic Telepresence. Advances in Human-Computer Interaction **2013**, 1–17 (2013)
3. Gandsas, A., Parekh, M., Bleech, M.M., Tong, D.A.: Robotic telepresence: profit analysis in reducing length of stay after laparoscopic gastric bypass. Journal of the American College of Surgeons **205**(1), 72–77 (2007)
4. Coradeschi, S., Kristoffersson, A., Loutfi, A., Von Rump, S., Cesta, A., Cortellessa, G., Gonzalez, J.: Towards a methodology for longitudinal evaluation of social robotic telepresence for elderly. In: Proceedings of the HRI 2011 Workshop on Social Robotic Telepresence, pp. 1–7 (2011)
5. Kiselev, A., Loutfi, A.: Using a Mental Workload Index as a Measure of Usability of a User Interface for Social Robotic Telepresence. Workshop in Social Robotics Telepresence (2012)
6. Lee, M.K., Takayama, L.: Now, i have a body. In: Proceedings of the 2011 annual conference on Human factors in computing systems - CHI 2011, p. 33. ACM Press, New York (2011)
7. Engström, J., Johansson, E., Östlund, J.: Effects of visual and cognitive load in real and simulated motorway driving. Transportation Research Part F: Traffic Psychology and Behaviour **8**(2), 97–120 (2005)
8. Hankins, T.C., Wilson, G.F.: A comparison of heart rate, eye activity, EEG and subjective measures of pilot mental workload during flight. Aviation space and environmental medicine **69**(4), 360–367 (1998)

9. Parasuraman, R., Riley, V.: Humans and Automation: Use, Misuse, Disuse, Abuse. Human Factors: The Journal of the Human Factors and Ergonomics Society **39**(2), 230–253 (1997)
10. Patten, C.J.D., Kircher, A., Ostlund, J., Nilsson, L., Svenson, O.: Driver experience and cognitive workload in different traffic environments. Accident Analysis & Prevention **38**(5), 887–894 (2006)
11. Vlassenroot, S., Broekx, S., Mol, J.D., Panis, L.I., Brijs, T., Wets, G.: Driving with intelligent speed adaptation: Final results of the Belgian ISA-trial. Transportation Research Part A: Policy and Practice **41**(3), 267–279 (2007)
12. Urmson, C., Anhalt, J., Bagnell, D., Baker, C., Bittner, R., Clark, M.N., Dolan, J., Duggins, D., Galatali, T., Geyer, C., Gittleman, M., Harbaugh, S., Hebert, M., Howard, T.M., Kolski, S., Kelly, A., Likhachev, M., McNaughton, M., Miller, N., Peterson, K., Pilnick, B., Rajkumar, R., Rybski, P., Salesky, B., Seo, Y.W., Singh, S., Snider, J., Stentz, A., Whittaker, W.R., Wolkowicki, Z., Ziglar, J., Bae, H., Brown, T., Demitrish, D., Litkouhi, B., Nickolaou, J., Sadekar, V., Zhang, W., Struble, J., Taylor, M., Darms, M., Ferguson, D.: Autonomous driving in urban environments: Boss and the Urban Challenge. Journal of Field Robotics **25**(8), 425–466 (2008)
13. Bertozzi, M., Broggi, A.: GOLD: a parallel real-time stereo vision system for generic obstacle and lane detection. IEEE transactions on image processing : a publication of the IEEE Signal Processing Society **7**(1), 62–81 (1998)
14. Labayrade, R., Royere, C., Gruyer, D., Aubert, D.: Cooperative Fusion for Multi-Obstacles Detection With Use of Stereovision and Laser Scanner. Autonomous Robots **19**(2), 117–140 (2005)
15. Aufrère, R., Gowdy, J., Mertz, C., Thorpe, C., Wang, C.C., Yata, T.: Perception for collision avoidance and autonomous driving. Mechatronics **13**(10), 1149–1161 (2003)
16. Maier, D., Stachniss, C., Bennewitz, M.: Vision-Based Humanoid Navigation Using Self-Supervized Obstacle Detection. International Journal of Humanoid Robotics **10**(02), 1350016 (2013)
17. Itoh, M., Horikome, T., Inagaki, T.: Effectiveness and driver acceptance of a semi-autonomous forward obstacle collision avoidance system. Proceedings of the Human Factors and Ergonomics Society **3**, 2091–2095 (2010)
18. Wegner, R., Anderson, J.: Balancing robotic teleoperation and autonomy for urban search and rescue environments. In: Tawfik, A.Y., Goodwin, S.D. (eds.) Canadian AI 2004. LNCS (LNAI), vol. 3060, pp. 16–30. Springer, Heidelberg (2004)
19. Doroodgar, B., Ficocelli, M., Mobedi, B., Nejat, G.: The search for survivors: Cooperative human-robot interaction in search and rescue environments using semi-autonomous robots. In: 2010 IEEE International Conference on Robotics and Automation, pp. 2858–2863. IEEE (May 2010)
20. Anderson, S.J., Karumanchi, S.B., Iagnemma, K., Walker, J.M.: The intelligent copilot: A constraint-based approach to shared-adaptive control of ground vehicles. IEEE Intelligent Transportation Systems Magazine **5**(2), 45–54 (2013)
21. Law, C.K.H., Xu, Y.: Shared control for navigation and balance of a dynamically stable robot. Proceedings - IEEE International Conference on Robotics and Automation **2**, 1985–1990 (2002)
22. Yokokohji, Y., Ogawa, A., Hasunuma, H., Yoshikawa, T.: Operation modes for cooperating with autonomous functions in intelligent teleoperation systems. In: Proceedings - IEEE International Conference on Robotics and Automation, vol. 3, pp. 510–515. IEEE (1993)

23. Kiselev, A., Mosiello, G., Kristoffersson, A., Loutfi, A.: Semi-autonomous Cooperative Driving for Mobile Robotic Telepresence Systems. In: Proceedings of the 2014 ACM/IEEE International Conference on Human-robot Interaction. HRI 2014, 104. ACM New York (2014)
24. International Organization for Standartization: ISO 13482:2014 Robots and robotic devices - Safety requirements for personal care robots (2014)
25. Giraff Technologies AB: Giraff Technologies AB (2013)
26. Joblove, G.H., Greenberg, D.: Color Spaces for Computer Graphics. SIGGRAPH Comput. Graph. **12**(3), 20–25 (1978)
27. Stockman, G., Shapiro, L.G.: Computer Vision, 1st edn. Prentice Hall PTR, Upper Saddle River (2001)
28. Bradski, G.: The OpenCV Library. Dr. Dobb's Journal of Software Tools (2000)
29. Bytedeco: JavaCV (2014)
30. Mosiello, G., Kiselev, A., Loutfi, A.: Using Augmented Reality to Improve Usability of the User Interface for Driving a Telepresence Robot. Paladyn, Journal of Behavioral Robotics **4**(3), 174–181 (2013)
31. Ojala, T., Pietikainen, M., Maenpaa, T.: Multiresolution gray-scale and rotation invariant texture classification with local binary patterns. IEEE Transactions on Pattern Analysis and Machine Intelligence **24**(7), 971–987 (2002)
32. Fogel, I., Sagi, D.: Gabor filters as texture discriminator (1989)

Associating Locations Between Indoor Journeys from Wearable Cameras

Jose Rivera-Rubio$^{(\boxtimes)}$, Ioannis Alexiou, and Anil A. Bharath

Imperial College London, London, UK
jose.rivera@imperial.ac.uk

Abstract. The main question we address is whether it is possible to crowdsource navigational data in the form of video sequences captured from wearable cameras. Without using geometric inference techniques (such as SLAM), we test video data for its location-discrimination content. Tracking algorithms do not form part of this assessment, because our goal is to compare different visual descriptors for the purpose of location inference in highly ambiguous indoor environments. The testing of these descriptors, and different encoding methods, is performed by measuring the positional error inferred during one journey with respect to other journeys along the same approximate path.

There are three main contributions described in this paper. First, we compare different techniques for visual feature extraction with the aim of associating locations between different journeys along roughly the same physical route. Secondly, we suggest measuring the quality of position inference relative to multiple passes through the same route by introducing a positional estimate of ground truth that is determined with modified surveying instrumentation. Finally, we contribute a database of nearly 100,000 frames with this positional ground-truth. More than 3 km worth of indoor journeys with a hand-held device (Nexus 4) and a wearable device (Google Glass) are included in this dataset.

1   Introduction

There is increasing interest in technologies that perform the indoor localisation of a user with respect to his or her surroundings. Many of the applications of such a technology are in commerce, allowing mobile devices, such as smartphones, to be more context-aware. However, there are many assistive contexts in which accurate user localisation could have a strong role to play. These include the ability of a user to request assistance in a public space, allowing him or her to be found, and guidance or assistance directed towards them. A more general and wide-ranging possibility is the use of computer vision to contribute to the guidance of an individual. With the emergence of wearable cameras, the potential contributions of computer vision to the navigational context, particularly for visually-impaired users, is enormous. This work explores a complementary approach to visual localisation than using geometric and Simultaneous Localization and Mapping (SLAM)-based techniques. Location is inferred through answering

© Springer International Publishing Switzerland 2015
L. Agapito et al. (Eds.): ECCV 2014 Workshops, Part IV, LNCS 8928, pp. 29–44, 2015.
DOI: 10.1007/978-3-319-16220-1_3

visual queries that are submitted against the paths of other users, rather than by explicit map-building or geometric inference. This mimics current hypotheses about at least one component of localisation in mammalian vision, where different localisation mechanisms are thought to co-exist; see, for example, the review article by Hartley and others [7]. We test the ability to localise from visual content – not self-motion – in a new dataset of *visual paths* [18], containing more than 3 km of video sequences in which ground-truth is acquired using modified surveying equipment. The dataset can be used to assess localization accuracy using any number of techniques that involve vision, including SLAM. The results suggest that, even without tracking, good localization of a user, even in ambiguous indoor settings, can be captured. The application to wearable camera technology – whereby image cues are harvested from volunteered journeys, then used to help other users of the same space – is the eventual goal of this work, a natural extension to recently reported approaches based on harvesting environmental signals [28].

2   Related Work

2.1   Early Findings in Robotics

Early work by Matsumoto *et al.* [14] suggested the concept of a "view-sequenced route representation" in which a robot performed simple navigation tasks by correlating current views to those held in a form of training database. Similar ideas can be seen on the work by [15], using the difference between frames of detected vertical lines to estimate changes in position and orientation. Their results were constrained to controlled robot movement, and therefore arguably of limited applicability to images obtained from human self-motion. Tang *et al.* also used vertical lines as features [24], but from from omni-directional cameras; their technique relied on estimating positional differences between playback and training sequences to achieve robot navigation. Tang introduced odometers as well, therefore fusing vision with self-motion sensing. This is, in fact, what one might expect a working system to do. However, fusing sensor data makes it difficult to really assess and tune the contribution of individual sensing cues, particularly one as complex as vision, where several visual processing strategies could be applied: optic flow, feature detection and tracking, stereo, etc.

2.2   Emerging Methods

The mapping of outdoor navigational routes has progressed rapidly in the past 2 decades, with satellite-based positioning and radio-strength indicators providing high-quality navigation capability over scales of around 10 m or less. In an *indoor* context, localization technology is in its infancy [17,21,28]. For indoor localization, there has been remarkable work from Google and crowdsourced sensor information and maps [9]. The potential to use retrieval-based visual localization systems, such as the proposed by the NAVVIS team, are relatively

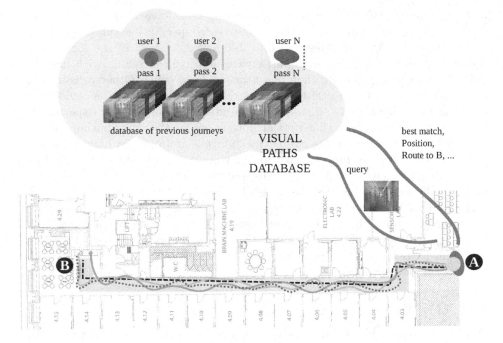

Fig. 1. A sample path (Corridor 1, C1) illustrating the multiple passes through the same space. Each of these passes represents a sequence that is either stored in a database, or represents the queries that are submitted against previous journeys. In the assistive context, the user at point A could be a blind or partially sighted user, and he or she would benefit from solutions to the association problem of a query journey relative to previous "journey experiences" along roughly the same path, crowdsourced by N users that may be sighted.

computationally intensive, but provide a source of data that is often neglected in human navigation systems. Nevertheless, the NAVVIS team demonstrated that estimating the position of a robot was possible, and provided a dataset acquired from a camera-equipped robot with ground truth [8]. They also expanded early work on visual localization based on SIFT descriptors [16] to one that uses a Bag-of-Features. This is an important step, as it allows scalable operation in larger datasets, or a subset of data to be cached on a smartphone or wearable device for low-latency operation during active navigation [19,20].

2.3   Biological Motivation

Over the past 40 years, research into mammalian vision has uncovered remarkable details about the way in which neurons in the brain respond to the environment of an animal. One of the areas known to be strongly associated with memory is also implicated in localization: the hippocampus. Evidence suggests that there are at least three sources of explicit localization encoding in hippocampal cells. For example in rodents, cells have been found to display elevated firing rates when the animal is in specific locations within an environment, but the responses fall into different "features" of the location of the animal. Some cells appear to participate in a joint encoding, with individual cells responding to more than one location (grid cells). Other cells appear to use various cues to localise themselves relative to boundaries, as evidenced by firing rates that encode "distance to boundary". From detailed experiments in insect vision, we know that optical flow is one of the contributing sources of such information, and quite similar mechanisms are found in higher animals [11]. The third type of hippocampal localization cell motivates this work: hippocampal place cells [7]. These cells display elevated firing when an animal is in a specific location, and they can also be found in humans [3]. To be clear, each cell that is characterised as a place cell has the property that it displays significantly elevated firing rates *only* when an animal is in a particular spatial location. The nature of these experiments cannot rule out the possibility that such cells participate in a joint encoding, but the "simplistic" view of place cells is "one-cell, one-location".

2.4   This Work

Our usage context is related to aspects of previous work, but is motivated by the idea that there are significant opportunities to use computer vision in assistive contexts. Whilst often considered power and compute intensive compared to other sources of sensor data, visual data is almost singularly rich in the navigation context. There are only a few examples of its use in assistive technology, where techniques such as ultrasound, intelligent canes and standard localization technologies are dominant. However, due to the emergence of wearable cameras and highly connected devices that can process video data efficiently (e.g. general purpose graphics processors, embedded on phones), the opportunity to harness visual data for navigation is very attractive.

The dominant technique for localization and mapping in computer vision is SLAM. However, we consider that the convergence of crowdsourcing approaches to "map out" physical spaces is not supported by this technique. In other words, the approaches we can use with crowdsensing of *signal* data to learn navigational routes has not been applied to *visual* data. Of course, in using visual information, one would certainly seek to support it with other forms of sensor such as Received Signal Strength Indication (RSSI) data, magnetometers, and tracking algorithms [17,19,20]. However, in *assessing* and evaluating its performance, it is hard to isolate factors that affect the quality of visual information when it is included as part of a sensor fusion approach. Thus, we focus in this work on purely visual methods, with the purpose of teasing out aspects of the algorithms that represent, in a location-specific way, the location of a person with a camera.

The first step in doing this is, therefore, to a) collect data that allows us to determine how plausible it is to infer the location of one user relative to others that have made the same journey using visual data *alone*; b) apply matching techniques between data sets, treating some video data as a "journey" database, and other data as one or more queries. The general principle of the data acquisition takes the form of experiments in which ground-truth is measured using modifications to fairly standard surveying equipment. We now describe this more fully.

3   The Dataset

In order to allow different approaches to be compared, and as a community resource to develop this technique, the *RSM dataset* is made publicly available at http://rsm.bicv.org [18].

3.1   Existing Datasets

Datasets for evaluating visual localization methods have historically been tied to specific publications and their function was often limited to demonstrate the performance of particular metrics. This has led to a number of datasets that were difficult to adapt to new work, or simply impossible to use because they were never released to the community.

Historical Datasets. Early work described in Section 2.1 used custom-planned datasets for their specific evaluation objectives. This led to datasets [14, 15, 24] containing very short sequences, of few meters of length, that could not be used to assess localization performance at human scale.

SLAM datasets and the NAVVIS Dataset. SLAM datasets, found in the robotics community, have a variety of scopes and recorded distances: large indoor spaces [23], outdoor itineraries [1], and up to the scale of a few km car ride [22]. They are also heterogeneous in terms of the precision and nature of the ground truth: some use GPS, others the Microsoft Kinect to capture depth [23], while others use the Vicon motion capture system. While the ground truth is often precise (up to the level of GPS, Kinect or Vicon precision), these have usually targeted outdoor comparisons; indoor comparisons focused at geometric reconstruction or pose estimation rather than localisation.

To the best of our knowledge, with the exception of NAVVIS, SLAM datasets have had rather restricted distances, not addressing real-world navigation on the scale of buildings. The NAVVIS project described in Section 2.2 first introduced a more generalistic dataset that could evaluate visual localization and navigation at human scale for robotic applications. Our proposed dataset takes the evaluation and the principle closer to the assistive context than the robot-centric approach of the NAVVIS team: our data and evaluation context introduces the particularities of human motion, both from hand-held and a wearable camera.

3.2   Visual Paths

We define a "visual path" as the video sequence captured by a moving person in executing a journey along a particular physical path. For the construction of our dataset, the *RSM dataset of visual paths*, a total of 60 videos were acquired from 6 corridors of a large building. In total, 3.05 km of data is contained in this dataset at a natural indoor walking speed. For each corridor, ten passes (i.e. 10 separate visual paths) are obtained; five of these are acquired with two different devices with 30 videos each. One device was a LG Google Nexus 4 phone running Android 4.4.2. The video data was acquired at approximately 24-30 fps at two different resolutions, 1280 × 720 and 1920 × 1080 pixels. The second device was a Google Glass (Explorer edition) acquiring at a resolution of 1280 × 720, and at a frame rate of 30 fps. Table 1 summarizes the acquisition. As can be seen, the length of the sequences varies within some corridors, due to a combination of different walking speeds and/or different frame rates. Lighting also varied, due to a combination of daylight/night-time acquisitions, and occasional prominent windows that represent strong lighting sources in certain parts of some corridors. Changes were also observable in some videos from one pass to another, due to the presence of changes and occasional appearance from people. In total, more than 90,000 frames of video are labelled with positional ground-truth in a path relative manner. The dataset is publicly available for download at http://rsm. bicv.org [18].

3.3   Ground Truth Acquisition

A surveyor's wheel (Silverline) with a precision of 10 cm and error of ±5% was used to record distance, but was modified by wiring its encoder to a Raspberry Pi running a number of measurement processes. The Pi was synchronised to network time enabling synchronisation with timestamps in the video sequence. Because of the variable-frame rate of acquisition, timestamp data from the video was used to align ground-truth measurements with frames. This data was used to access the accuracy of associating positions along journeys through frame indexing and comparison.

4   Retrieval Methods for Visual Localisation

We include results from unmodified, widely-used frame and sequence-based descriptor implementations reported in the image and video categorization and retrieval literature. We also implemented our own methods for greater control of parameter tuning and a more consistent comparison of the possible choices of spatial derivatives, temporal derivative/smoothing and spatial pooling. We describe the two classes of methods as "standard" and "projective"; the latter refers to the fact that our implementations are all performed by linear projections onto spatial weighting functions, and are created by a cascade of convolution operations, followed by spatial sub-sampling.

4.1   Standard Methods

Keypoint based SIFT (KP_SIFT). The original implementation of Lowe's SIFT descriptor follows the identification of interesting points, each with assigned

Table 1. A summary of the dataset with thumbnails

Photo		Length (m)			No. of frames		
		Avg	Min	Max	Avg	Min	Max
C1		57.9	57.7	58.7	2157	1860	2338
C2		31.0	30.6	31.5	909	687	1168
C3		52.7	51.4	53.3	1427	1070	1777
C4		49.3	46.4	56.2	1583	1090	2154
C5		54.3	49.3	58.4	1782	1326	1900
C6		55.9	55.4	56.4	1471	1180	1817
Total		3.042 km			90,302 frames		

intrinsic scales and orientations within the image that are likely to be stable, known as the "SIFT keypoints" [13]. This is widely used across many computer vision applications from object recognition to motion detection and SLAM. We used the standard implementation from VLFEAT to compute $\nabla f(x, y; \sigma)$ where $f(x, y; \sigma)$ represents the scale-space embedding of image $f(x, y)$ within a Gaussian scale-space at scale σ. We also filtered out small local maxima in scale-space. The resulting descriptors are sparsely spread through each video frame.

Dense SIFT (DSIFT). The Dense-SIFT [12,25] descriptor is a popular and fast alternative to keypoint based SIFT. This DSIFT descriptor was calculated by dense sampling of the smoothed estimate of $\nabla f(x, y; \sigma)$. We used dense SIFT from VLFEAT toolbox using $\sigma = 1.2$, with a stride length of 3 pixels. This process yielded around $2,000$ descriptors per frame, each describing a patch of roughly 10×10 pixels in the frame. Spatial scale is fixed with this approach, though the descriptor structure is otherwise the same as for the sparse keypoints.

HOG3D. The **HOG 3D** descriptor (HOG3D) [10] was introduced with the aim of extending the very successful two-dimensional histogram of oriented gradients technique [5], to space-time fields, in the form of video sequences. HOG 3D seeks computational efficiencies by smoothing using box filters, rather than Gaussian spatial or space-time kernels. This allows three-dimensional gradient estimation across multiple scales using *integral video* representations, a direct extension of the integral image idea [27]. The gradients from this operation are usually performed across multiple scales. We used the dense HOG 3D option from the implementation of the authors, and the settings yielded approximately 2,000, 192-dimensional descriptors per frame of video.

4.2 Projective Descriptors

This grouping of descriptors is based on distinct implementations of spatial and/or temporal filtering. In this sense, there are exact or minor variations on the gradient-based methods considered in the previous section. However, what is common to all of the methods below is that the initial filtering is converted into descriptors using projections against spatial weighting functions, one for each descriptor element. This approach is similar to a soft-histogram approach, but allows greater flexibility in tuning the bin weightings.

Single Frame Gabor descriptors (SF_GABOR). This is an odd-symmetric Gabor-based descriptor. For this, we used 8-directional spatial Gabor filters previously tuned on PASCAL VOC data [6] in order to encode the image gradient field. Each filtering operator produces a filtered image plane, denoted $\mathbf{G}_{k,\sigma}$. Spatial pooling of these image planes was performed by the spatial convolution $\mathbf{G}_{k,\sigma} * \Phi_{m,n}$. $\Phi_{m,n}$ represent *spatial pooling functions* that are generated by spatial sampling of the function:

$$\Phi(x, y; m, n) = e^{-\alpha \left[\log_e \left(\frac{x^2 + y^2}{d_n^2} \right) \right]^2 - \beta |\theta - \theta_m|} \tag{1}$$

We used $\alpha = 4$ and $\beta = 0.4$ in our implementation. The values of m and n were selected to "collect" filtered image data over 8 angular regions and with the weighting roughly peaking around distances $d_1 = 0.45$ and $d_2 = 0.6$ away from the centre of each pooling region, for a total of 17 pooling regions across each of the eight filtering channels. In the $(m = 0)$ central region, there is no angular variation. The resulting fields – one field for each pooling region for each directional channel – are sub-sampled to produce dense 136-dimensional descriptors, each representing a 10×10 image region, yielding approximately 2,000 descriptors per image frame when the result of the convolution is sub-sampled. The pooling regions are illustrated in Fig. 2.

Space-time Gabor (ST_GABOR) Functions have been used in activity recognition, structure from motion and other applications [2]. We performed convolution between the video sequence and three one-dimensional Gabor functions along each spatial dimension i.e. x or y, or along t. The one-dimensional convolution is crude, but appropriate if the videos have been spatially smoothed. The spatial extent of the Gabor was set to provide one cycle of weight oscillation over roughly a 5 pixel distance, both for the x and y spatial dimensions. The filter for the temporal dimension used a wavelength of around 9 frames. We also explored symmetric Gabor functions, but found them less favourable.

After performing three separate filtering operations, each pixel of each frame is assigned a triplet of values corresponding to the result of each filtering operation. The three values are treated as being components of a 3D vector. Over a spatial extent of around 16×16 pixels taken at the central frame of the 9-frame support region, these vectors contribute weighted votes into descriptor bins according to their azimuth and elevations, with the weighting being given by the length of the vector. This is similar, but not identical, to the initial stages of the HOG3D filter. Pooling is then performed using the spatial lobe pattern illustrated in Fig. 2. Each frame had approximately 2,000, 221 dimensional ST_GABOR descriptors.

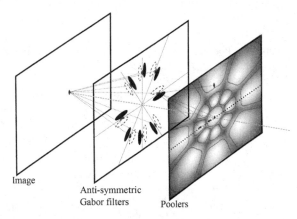

Image

Anti-symmetric
Gabor filters   Poolers

Fig. 2. This illustrates the nature of the spatial pooling used in the projective descriptors. The regions are produced from Eq. 1, generating non-negative spatial filters that collect (pool) filtered data over a 10×10 pixel region. Because of the spatial symmetry, the masks can be applied to the Gabor filtered video frame outputs by spatial convolution. These regions were obtained as a result of optimisation of parameters of Eq. 1 using a metric similar to mean absolute precision (mAP).

Space-Time Gaussian. This descriptor consisted of spatial derivatives in space, combined with smoothing over time (**ST_GAUSS**). In contrast to the strictly one-dimensional filtering operation used for the ST_GABOR descriptor, we used two 5×5 gradient masks for the x and y directions based on derivatives of Gaussian functions, and an 11-point Gaussian smoothing filter in the temporal direction with a standard deviation of 2. 8-directional quantization was applied to the angles of the gradient field, and weighted voting with the gradient magnitude was used to populate the bins of a 136-dimensional descriptor. Like the ST_GABOR descriptor, the pooling regions were as shown in Fig. 2. The number of descriptors produced was equivalent to the other methods described for patch-based indexing.

5   Evaluation Framework

5.1   BOVW Pipeline

In order to test the ability to localise position based on the visual structure of either a short sequence of frames or individual frame information, we adopted a retrieval structure for efficient mapping of the visual descriptors, sparsely or densely populating an image, into a single frame or vignette-level representation. The approach is based on fairly standard retrieval architectures used for image categorization – the Bag-of-Visual Words (BOVW)– and is illustrated in Figure 3.

For the vector quantization, hard assignment (HA) was used to encode each descriptor vector by assignment to a dictionary entry. The data set was partitioned by selecting $M - 1$ of the M video sequences of passes through each

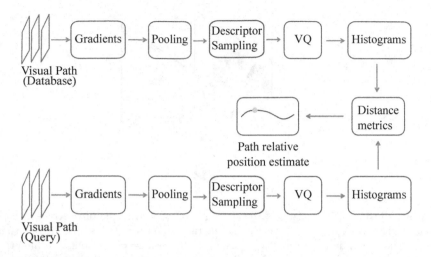

Fig. 3. Video sequences from wearable and hand-held cameras are processed using a customized BOVW pipeline. Variants of the gradient operators, pooling operators, quantization and distance metrics are described in Section 4.

possible path. This ensured that queries were *never* used to build the vocabulary used for testing the localization accuracy. The dictionary was created by applying the k-means algorithm on samples from the video database. We fixed the dictionary size to 4,000 (clusters, words); this allows comparison with the work of others in related fields, such as [4].

The resulting dictionaries were then used to encode the descriptors, both those in the database and those from queries. The frequency of occurrence of atoms was used to create a histogram of visual words "centered" around each frame of the video sequence (visual path) in a database, and the same process was used to encode each possible query frame from the remaining path. Histograms were all L_2-normalized.

5.2 Localization Using "kernelized" Histogram Distances

Once histograms had been produced, a kernelized-version in [26] of a distance measure in 4,000-dimensional space was used to compare the similarity of histograms in a query frame with the database entries. A variety of kernel functions exist, such as the popular Hellinger kernel, but we found the χ^2 best for this problem. For a random subset of the $M - 1$ videos captured over *each* path in the dictionary, the query is generated from the remaining journey. Each query frame, H_q, results in $M - 1$ separate comparison vectors, each containing the distance of each frame to the query. We identified the best matching frame, $\hat{m}$ from pass $\hat{p}$ across all of the $M - 1$ vectors. This is done using:

$$L(\hat{p}, \hat{f}) = \arg \max_{p,f} \{K_D(H_q, H_{p,f})\} \tag{2}$$

$H_{p,f}$ denotes the series of normalized histogram encodings, indexed by p drawn from the $M - 1$ database passes, and $\hat{f}$ denotes the frame number within that pass. K_D denotes so-called "kernelized" distance measure [26]. The estimated "position" of a query, L, was that corresponding to the best match given by Eq. 2; this position is always relative to that of another journey along roughly the same route; the accuracy and repeatability of this in associating location between passes was evaluated using distributions of location error distributions and area-under-curve criteria derived from these distributions.

5.3 Measurements of Performance

We quantify the accuracy of being able to associate *locations* along physical paths in corridors within the dataset described in Section 3. By permuting the paths that are held in the database and randomly selecting queries from the remaining path, we were able to obtain the error in localization. Repeated runs with random selections of groups of frames allowed variability in these estimates to be obtained, including that due to different paths being within the database. To estimate these distributions, we measured the absolute error in localization as a distance, ϵ, relative to route ground truth, summarizing this as estimates of $P(\epsilon < x)$. For this, we used the ground-truth information acquired as described in Section 3.

5.4 Cumulative Distribution Functions

In Fig. 5, we compare the error distributions of all techniques. In Figs. 4(a) to 4(b), we provide separate assessments of the *variability* in error distribution when 1 million permuted queries are performed by cycling through 1,000 permutations of 1,000 randomly selected queries. This Monte-Carlo approach to testing accuracy allows the stability of approaches to be assessed. The graphs here suggest high reproducibility of retrieval performance (small shaded areas between lower and upper traces of each graph). All the results were generated with videos resized down to 208×117 pixels; these are also supplied with the dataset.

5.5 Area-Under-Curve Comparisons

We calculated the average absolute positional error (in m) and the standard deviation of the absolute positional errors (Table 2). All queries were again performed by adopting the leave-one-out strategy, but because of the high repeatability of results (as seen in Fig. 4), we did not apply random frame-level sampling. Standard deviations of the absolute error distribution are also provided. Table 2 also provides the area-under-curve (AUC) values obtained from the CDFs of Fig. 4.

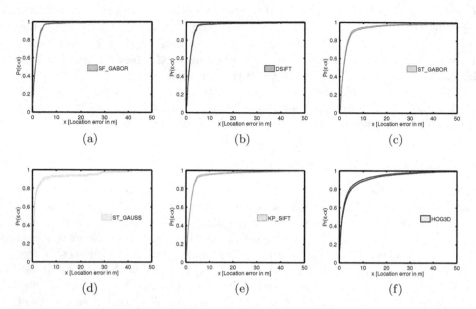

Fig. 4. Comparison between the error distributions obtained with the different methods. Note the high reproducibility of the performance results. The origin of the variability within each curve is explained in Section 5.4.

6   Results

One of the clear distinctions that we found, whether we used standard methods or the projective version of descriptors, is that single frame methods worked better than multiple-frame methods. This can be seen by comparing the top and bottom rows of Table 2. The results show that localization is achieved with

Table 2. Summaries of average absolute positional error and standard deviation of positional errors for different descriptor types. μ_ϵ is the average absolute error, and σ_ϵ is the standard deviation of the error, both in metres. Top: single frame methods. Bottom: spatio-temporal methods.

Method	Error summary (m)		AUC (%)	
	μ_ϵ	σ_ϵ	Min	Max
SF_GABOR	**1.59**	0.11	96.11	**96.39**
DSIFT	1.62	0.11	95.96	96.31
KP_SIFT	2.14	0.17	94.58	95.19
ST_GAUSS	**2.11**	0.24	94.82	**95.57**
ST_GABOR	2.54	0.19	93.90	94.44
HOG3D	4.20	1.33	90.89	91.83

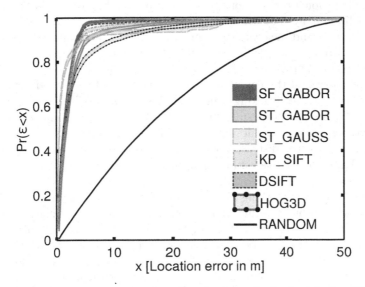

Fig. 5. Comparison between the error distributions obtained with the different methods. The results for a random frame test (RANDOM) were introduced as a "sanity check".

high accuracy in terms of CDF and AUC without a large difference between the applied methods, despite the big diversity in their complexity. Absolute errors show significant differences between methods, with average absolute errors in the range of 1.5 m to 4.20 m. Single frame methods (SF_GABOR, KP_SIFT and DSIFT) perform slightly better than spatio-temporal ones. This is not surprising, as the spatio-temporal methods might be too affected by the self motion over fine temporal scales.

In spite of using image retrieval methods in isolation, this performance is in the range of methods reviewed in Section 2 that include tracking, other sensors or estimate motion. We emphasise that no tracking was used in estimating position: this was deliberate, in order that we could assess performance in inferring location from the visual data fairly. Introducing tracking will, of course, improve localization performance, and could reduce query complexity. Yet, tracking often relies on some form of motion model, and for pedestrians carrying or wearing cameras, motion can be quite unpredictable.

7   Conclusion

We have presented several contributions in the topic of indoor localization using visual path matching from wearable and hand-held cameras. We provide an evaluation of six local descriptor methods: three custom designed and three standard image (KP_SIFT and DSIFT) and video (HOG3D) matching methods as baseline. These local descriptions follow a standard bag-of-words and kernel encoding pipeline before they are evaluated with the ground truth. The code for the local descriptors and the evaluation pipeline is available on the web page [18]. We also make available a large dataset with ground truth of indoor journeys to complete the evaluation framework.

The results show that there is significant localization information in the visual data even without using tracking, and that errors as small as 1.5 m can be achieved. We have split the results in two: a) Absolute positional errors that help to discern between image description methods and assess their localization capabilities; and b) error distributions that can be used to build a model for inclusion in a Kalman or particle filtering approach that is appropriate for human ambulatory motion.

We plan to introduce tracking as part of our future work and make use of the error distributions to build human motion models. There are, of course, numerous other enhancements that one could make for a system that uses visual data; integration of data from other sensors springs to mind, such as inertial sensing, magnetometers and RSSI. Although the fusing of independent and informative data sources leads to improvements in performance, we would argue that the methods applied to infer location from each information source should be rigorously tested, both in isolation and as part of an integrated system. This will ensure that real-world systems perform well in standard use, but are also somewhat robust to the sensor failure. With their very good standalone performance, we anticipate that using vision and associating the journeys of several users through their visual paths could play an important role in localization.

References

1. Bosse, M.: Simultaneous Localization and Map Building in Large-Scale Cyclic Environments Using the Atlas Framework. The International Journal of Robotics Research **23**(12), 1113–1139 (2004)
2. Bregonzio, M.: Recognising action as clouds of space-time interest points. IEEE Conference on Computer Vision and Pattern Recognition (CVPR) pp. 1948–1955 (June 2009). http://ieeexplore.ieee.org/lpdocs/epic03/wrapper.htm? arnumber=5206779
3. Burgess, N., Maguire, E.A., O'Keefe, J.: The human hippocampus and spatial and episodic memory. Neuron **35**(4), 625–641 (2002)
4. Chatfield, K., Lempitsky, V., Vedaldi, A., Zisserman, A.: The devil is in the details: an evaluation of recent feature encoding methods. In: Procedings of the British Machine Vision Conference 2011 (1), 76.1-76.12 (2011). http://www.bmva.org/ bmvc/2011/proceedings/paper76/index.html
5. Dalal, N., Triggs, B.: Histograms of Oriented Gradients for Human Detection. IEEE Computer Society Conference on Computer Vision and Pattern Recognition (CVPR 2005) 1, 886–893 (2005). http://ieeexplore.ieee.org/lpdocs/epic03/ wrapper.htm?arnumber=1467360
6. Everingham, M., Gool, L., Williams, C.K.I., Winn, J., Zisserman, A.: The Pascal Visual Object Classes (VOC) Challenge. International Journal of Computer Vision **88**(2), 303–338 (2009). http://www.springerlink.com/index/10.1007/s11263-009-0275-4

7. Hartley, T., Lever, C., Burgess, N., O'Keefe, J.: Space in the brain: how the hip-pocampal formation supports spatial cognition. Philosophical Transactions of the Royal Society B: Biological Sciences **369**(1635), 20120510 (2014)
8. Huitl, R., Schroth, G.: TUMindoor: An extensive image and point cloud dataset for visual indoor localization and mapping. In: International Conference on Image Processing (2012). http://ieeexplore.ieee.org/xpls/abs_all.jsp?arnumber=6467224
9. Kadous, W., Peterson, S.: Indoor maps: the next frontier. In: Google IO (2013)
10. Kläser, A., Marszalek, M., Schmid, C.: A spatio-temporal descriptor based on 3D-gradients. In: British Machine Vision Conference. pp. 995–1004 (2008). http://eprints.pascal-network.org/archive/00005039/
11. Layton, O.W., Browning, N.A.: A Unified Model of Heading and Path Perception in Primate MSTd. PLoS Computational Biology **10**(2), e1003476, February 2014. http://dx.plos.org/10.1371/journal.pcbi.1003476
12. Lazebnik, S., Schmid, C., Ponce, J.: Beyond bags of features: Spatial pyramid matching for recognizing natural scene categories. In: Computer Vision and Pattern Recognition. vol. 2, pp. 2169–2178. IEEE (2006)
13. Lowe, D.G.: Distinctive image features from scale-invariant key-points. International journal of computer vision **60**, 91–110 (2004). http://www.springerlink.com/index/H4L02691327PX768.pdf
14. Matsumoto, Y., Inaba, M., Inoue, H.: Visual navigation using view-sequenced route representation. In: International Conference on Robotics and Automation, pp. 83–88. No., April 1996. http://ieeexplore.ieee.org/xpls/abs_all.jsp?arnumber=503577
15. Ohno, T., Ohya, A., Yuta, S.: Autonomous Navigation for Mobile Robots Referring Pre-recorded Image Sequence. In: IEEE/RSJ International Conference on Intelligent Robots and Systems. IROS 1996. vol. 2, pp. 672–679. IEEE (1996). http://ieeexplore.ieee.org/lpdocs/epic03/wrapper.htm?arnumber=571034
16. Park, S., Jung, S., Song, Y., Kim, H.: Mobile robot localization in indoor environment using scale-invariant visual landmarks. In: 18th IAPR International Conference in Pattern Recognition, pp. 159–163 (2008). http://www.eurasip.org/Proceedings/Ext/CIP2008/papers/1569094833.pdf
17. Quigley, M., Stavens, D.: Sub-meter indoor localization in unmodified environments with inexpensive sensors. In: Intelligent Robots and Systems, pp. 2039–2046. IEEE, October 2010
18. Rivera-Rubio, J., Alexiou, I., Bharath, A.A.: RSM dataset (2014). http://rsm.bicv.org
19. Schroth, G., Huitl, R.: Mobile visual location recognition. IEEE Signal Processing Magazine, 77–89, July 2011. http://ieeexplore.ieee.org/xpls/abs_all.jsp?arnumber=5888650
20. Schroth, G., Huitl, R.: Exploiting prior knowledge in mobile visual location recognition. In: IEEE ICASSP, pp. 4–7 (2012). http://ieeexplore.ieee.org/xpls/abs_all.jsp?arnumber=6288388
21. Shen, G., Chen, Z., Zhang, P., Moscibroda, T., Zhang, Y.: Walkie-Markie: Indoor Pathway Mapping Made Easy. In: 10th USENIX Symposium on Networked Systems Design and Implementation (NSDI 13) USENIX, pp. 85–98 (2013). http://research.microsoft.com/en-us/um/people/moscitho/Publications/NSDI_2013.pdf
22. Simpson, R., Cullip, J., Revell, J.: The Cheddar Gorge Data Set (2011)
23. Sturm, J., Engelhard, N., Endres, F., Burgard, W., Cremers, D.: A benchmark for the evaluation of rgb-d slam systems. In: Proc. of the International Conference on Intelligent Robot Systems (IROS), October 2012

24. Tang, L., Yuta, S.: Vision based navigation for mobile robots in indoor environment by teaching and playing-back scheme. In: International Conference on Robotics and Automation, pp. 3072–3077 (2001). http://ieeexplore.ieee.org/xpls/abs_all.jsp?arnumber=933089
25. Vedaldi, A., Fulkerson, B.: VLFeat: An Open and Portable Library of Computer Vision Algorithms (2008). http://www.vlfeat.org/
26. Vedaldi, A., Zisserman, A.: Efficient additive kernels via explicit feature maps. IEEE Transactions on Pattern Analysis and Machine Intelligence (2010)
27. Viola, P., Jones, M.: Robust real-time object detection. International Journal of Computer Vision, pp. 1–25 (2001). http://www.staroceans.net/documents/CRL-2001-1.pdf
28. Wang, H., Sen, S., Elgohary, A., Farid, M., Youssef, M.: Unsupervised Indoor Localization. In: MobiSys. ACM (2012). http://synrg.ee.duke.edu/papers/unloc.pdf

Smart Camera Reconfiguration in Assisted Home Environments for Elderly Care

Krishna Reddy Konda, Andrea Rosani,
Nicola Conci, and Francesco G.B. De Natale

Department of Information Engineering and Computer Science,
University of Trento, Via Sommarive 9, 38123 Trento, Italy
andrea.rosani@unitn.it

Abstract. Researchers of different fields have been involved in human behavior analysis during the last years. The successful recognition of human activities from video analysis is still a challenging problem. Within this context, applications targeting elderly care are of considerable interest both for public and industrial bodies, especially considering the aging society we are living in. Ambient intelligence (AmI) technologies, intended as the possibility of automatically detecting and reacting to the status of the environment and of the persons, is probably the major enabling factor. AmI technologies require suitable networks of sensors and actuators, as well as adequate processing and communication technologies. In this paper we propose an innovative solution based on a real time analysis of video with application in the field of elderly care. The system performs anomaly detection and proposes the automatic reconfiguration of the camera network for better monitoring of the ongoing event. The developed framework is tested on a publicly available dataset and has also been deployed and evaluated in a real environment.

Keywords: Elderly care · Real time video analysis · Automatic camera reconfiguration

1 Introduction

In the society of the developed countries there is the evidence that the number of elderly people, is rapidly increasing with respect to the past, also due to an longer life expectancy. Normal life activity becomes somehow difficult while aging, thus resulting a parameter to be monitored in order to infer the health status of a person [14, 24].

Moreover, the analysis of human behavior can detect remarkable situations where people need immediate assistance to avoid major risks and severe injuries.

Notwithstanding the effort of researchers in the direction of behavior understanding, a complete and reliable description of the ongoing situation using only sensors analysis is still a challenging task.

Activities and behaviors can be detected using different approaches, and video analysis is often used among them [6] because in many situation cameras

© Springer International Publishing Switzerland 2015
L. Agapito et al. (Eds.): ECCV 2014 Workshops, Part IV, LNCS 8928, pp. 45–58, 2015.
DOI: 10.1007/978-3-319-16220-1_4

are already present in the site for security reasons and, if not, because of the low cost of installation and maintenance. Compared to other sensing techniques, video cameras have the advantage of not being intrusive and burdensome like wearable sensors, and they are usually more precise than ambient sensors.

Thanks to the advances in video signal processing technology and the increasing computer power available, video analysis can provide significant information for this purpose including location, posture, motion, interaction with objects, people, and environment [3].

In this paper we present a framework for elderly care using the information coming from the video motion flow directly from streaming in the compressed domain, prior to decoding. The proposed technique is able to detect events directly and to perform camera reconfiguration in order to focus the attention on the occurring event. This allows for a very fast and robust detection of the event, with the possibility of real-time processing of the information and early alerting.

For testing purposes we considered the event "fall" [17,26] as a remarkable example of a situation where there is the need of an immediate assistance. The *fall* can be described as a sudden event, which takes place in about half a second. Such a sudden event usually creates large variations in terms of pixel intensities and visual features. In addition to detection of falls, obtaining a better view of the person involved in the accident would help in taking the most appropriate action. To this extent, we propose a unique system, capable of detecting falls and also to reconfigure the camera network in real-time, in order to achieve a more accurate information of the event. Video analysis is performed by completely operating in H.264 [25] compressed domain, while reconfiguration is achieved by automatically modifying the Pan-Tilt-Zoom (PTZ) parameters of the camera.

2 State of the Art

2.1 Camera Reconfiguration

Research on camera reconfiguration is in a nascent stage. Micheloni et al. summarized the current state of the research in [16]. More in general, camera reconfiguration is performed with respect to a specific task. One of the earliest works to consider PTZ cameras is [18], where PTZ cameras are specifically used for tracking. In another paper Quaritsch et al. [20] utilize multiple cameras and reconfiguration to achieve better tracking. Scotti et al. [23] utilize a PTZ camera along with an omnidirectional camera, in order to achieve tracking of objects at higher resolution. Another work, which utilizes a combination of omni directional and PTZ cameras for tracking is presented in [5], where the authors approach the problem in terms of spatial correlation, in order to map the targets across two types of cameras.

2.2 Ambient Assisted Living and Fall Detection

During the last years, there has been an increasing amount of technologies dedicated to the care of the elderly, usually grouped under the umbrella of

"Ambient Intelligence". These technologies span from a variety of sensors and analysis techniques to infer the performed activity [21]. Recently, the research community developed solutions based on video analysis and computer vision systems with promising results. However, to reach maturity, several challenges still need to be faced, including the development of systems that are robust in the real-world and are accepted by users [4]. One of the major objective of Ambient Intelligence is to provide safety to the monitored people, especially those who need more attention. To this extent, the detection of falls represents a remarkable situation, where the automatic detection of the event can activate an early alert to relatives and caregivers.

Fall detection is apparently a simple task; however, a person can fall from walking or standing or while moving inside home or in a hospital. A common situation is the fall from standing on support, like ladders as an example, that could cause severe injuries and needs in many cases an immediate intervention from the carers. Moreover, especially in the care of elderly or impaired people, the falls from sleeping or lying in a bed and falls from sitting on a chair should be carefully addressed [17].

The use of cameras in home care and assistive infrastructures has widely increased, thanks to the little invasiveness (especially if compared to wearable sensors), and also because of the higher precision when compared to ambient technologies [10]. The fall detection system can be arranged with one or multiple cameras, involving also moving devices [17]. Spatio temporal analysis has been studied in [1,22], where shape modeling is performed to detect the event. Inactivity/change of shape using the information built in contextual models can be exploited to analyze human behavior and detect anomalies [11,19]. In this context an analysis in the compressed domain is considered by the authors in [15], combining global motion estimation and local motion clustering. Also posture has been used for fall detection in [9], with very high accuracy, using posture maps learned on a set of training sequences. Head position analysis has been instead considered for a three dimensional environment. The principle that considers faster vertical motion than horizontal during a fall event is applied. Thresholds should be introduced to distinguish falls from other events [12].

Although a lot of effort has been spent in the design of fall detection systems, there is plenty of room for efficient and robust development in this research direction, to achieve real time analysis, a fundamental step to achieve an effective action in case of need.

3   Motivation and Contribution

As can be noticed from the state of the art, algorithms for fall detection operate in many cases in the pixel domain, whereas most of the surveillance cameras only provide the video in the compressed domain. In order for these algorithms to be applied, the video has to be decoded, introducing an additional processing layer. Furthermore, most algorithms are not operating in real time, barely reaching 20-25 frames per second on a PC-based platform, which hampers the ability of their deployment in real scenarios. In order to respond to this need, especially in case of elderly care, it is necessary to develop low-complexity algorithms, which can deployed directly in the DSP (Digital Signal Processor) onboard of the camera and possibly in the compressed domain, thus dropping the need for decoding. In this paper we present an algorithm which completely operates in the compressed H.264 [25] domain and that requires a negligible complexity, hence it can be deployed on DSP (or similar) processor. Fall detection and reconfiguration is achieved by proposing a generic entropy measure derived using the distribution of the motion field extracted from the compressed video bit stream.

4 Framework Description

4.1 Motion Descriptors

In order to measure and monitor the movement of the objects in the camera view, we propose a descriptor based on the disorder, or entropy, of the motion vectors of the video. The standard for video coding H.264, as most of its predecessors, achieves compression through a block-based algorithm, where blocks have variable size from 4×4 to 16×16 pixels [25]. Motion vectors are calculated for individual blocks in order to remove the temporal redundancy of the video. The distribution of the motion vectors throughout the frames gives us a very accurate insight about the analytics of the video, since it tends to exhibit more disorder whenever there is any moving object in the video frame.

Fig. 1. Motion vectors extracted from a frame of the fall dataset. The red arrows highlight the regions in which the motion field exhibits strong disorder.

An example is shown in Figure 1, and represents a frame in a fall sequence captured from a static camera; motion vectors are overlaid on the picture. As can be seen, the motion vectors show a zero value along most of the video frame, as it is expected in case of moving camera. However, the motion vectors distribution at the edges of the person about to fall tends to have higher disorder. We propose to exploit this aspect in order to measure the amount of information in the video frame and also to use it for the detection of fall events.

4.2   Motion Entropy Measure

As mentioned in the previous section, we choose to operate in the compression domain to achieve real time operational capabilities. Motion vectors are chosen as the main features for analysis, as they are immune to changes in bit-rate and quantization parameters (QP) of the encoded H.264 video stream. The disorder in the motion field represents the information content in the video. In H.264, standard motion vectors are computed at 4×4 and the block size is based on the observed variance. Each motion vector consists of two components representing distances in pixels along X and Y direction from the best match found in the reference frame. In this context we represent the pixel difference along X and Y as $MV_x(i,j)$ and $MV_y(i,j)$, respectively, where i and j represent the location of a 4×4 block in the video frame. After reading the motion vectors from the H.264 stream, we group $MV_x(i,j)$ and $MV_y(i,j)$ into a 8×8 matrix, therefore each of these blocks represents the motion vectors of a region corresponding to an area of 32×32 pixels. On these super-blocks the 8×8 DCT (Discrete Cosine Transform) is performed according to Eqs. (1) and (2).

$$MD_x^{(c,d)}(a,b) = [\frac{1}{4} \sum_{a=0}^{7} \sum_{b=0}^{7} MV_x[(c-1)*8+a,(d-1)+b] * \cos \frac{(2a+1)*\pi}{16} * \cos \frac{(2b+1)*\pi}{16}]$$

(1)

$$MD_y^{(c,d)}(a,b) = [\frac{1}{4} \sum_{a=0}^{7} \sum_{b=0}^{7} MV_y[(c-1)*8+a,(d-1)+b] * \cos \frac{(2a+1)*\pi}{16} * \cos \frac{(2b+1)*\pi}{16}]$$

(2)

After the transform, each block describes the motion pattern of the 32×32 pixel region in X and Y directions, respectively, which becomes our motion descriptor. In the equations (c,d) represent the block location of 32×32 pixels in the frame, (a,b) represent the location of the 4×4 block within the 32×32 block.

The choice for a block size of 32×32 pixels is made to ensure minimum variability of motion vectors which occurs in the case of 16×16 mode in H.264 bit stream. The result is a 2D DCT transform of 8×8 blocks of motion vectors. Inferring from the properties of the DCT transform we can notice that DC values $MD_x^{(c,d)}(0,0)$, $MD_y^{(c,d)}(0,0)$ represent the localized global motion and AC coefficients represent the variation in motion vectors. The frequency of variation increases as we move towards the bottom-right corner. We propose to accumulate the AC coefficients to arrive at a measure of motion disorder. However, higher frequencies represent more disorder in comparison to the lower ones, hence the accumulation has to be done in a weighted manner. This is exactly the opposite of what happens in image and video compressions, where lower frequencies are usually more important. Therefore, we calculate the entropy values along X and Y as E_X and E_Y from the equations Eq. (3) and Eq. 4, respectively.

$$E_X(c,d) = \sum_{a=0}^{7} \sum_{b=0}^{7} MD_x^{(c,d)}(a,b) * [2^{a-8} + 2^{b-8}]$$

(3)

$$E_Y(c,d) = \sum_{a=0}^{7} \sum_{b=0}^{7} MD_y^{(c,d)}(a,b) * [2^{a-8} + 2^{b-8}] \tag{4}$$

The aggregated entropy gives us a generalized measure of information present in the video frame in case of P (predicted) macroblocks for which the motion vectors exist. However in presence of very rapid motion, which cannot be covered by motion search algorithm of the H.264, the macro blocks are typically classified as *intra*. In order to calculate the entropy measure for these blocks we utilize the number of bits that a particular macro block requires. As we know by definition, the H.264 encoder is basically a sparse encoder which assigns a variable number of bits to every macro block based on its information content. Such an assumption is perfectly valid according to Shannon's information theory.

The entropy measures that we use in the proposed method are reported hereafter:

$$E_X(c,d) = K_x * N_b(c,d) \tag{5}$$

$$E_Y(c,d) = K_y * N_b(c,d) \tag{6}$$

$$G_{XY} = \sum_{c=0}^{\frac{Width}{32}} \sum_{d=0}^{\frac{Height}{32}} [E_X(c,d) + E_Y(c,d)] \tag{7}$$

where K_x and K_y are weighting factors and $N_b(c,d)$ is the numbers of bits for that particular macro block.

4.3   Object Detection and Segmentation

E_X and E_Y are the measure of the extent of disorder for $MV_x(i,j)$ and $MV_y(i,j)$ in case of P macro blocks, and they are considered as measure of information for intra macro blocks. Since we have defined a quantitative measure for the disorder, we now have to identify the blocks, which have high E_X and E_Y. Initially both E_X and E_Y across the frame are contributing to obtain a frame level metric for disorder, as shown in Eq (7). Then the steps shown in Algorithm 1 are followed.

The algorithm iteratively checks the values for E_X and E_Y for each block against the threshold, which varies from 100% to 50% of their respective mean values. If both conditions are met, the block is selected as a contour block and its contribution $(E_X + E_Y)$ is accumulated. The algorithm is terminated when the ratio between the disorder of the contour region and G_{XY} reaches the value K, or in case the adaptive threshold decreases beyond 0.5. In this way only the blocks with significant motion along X and Y are identified. The value of K is a user-defined parameter, and determines the size of the contour around the moving object. High values will result in extended contours around the moving objects, while low values will shrink the thickness of the contour around the object. This parameter is data dependent and should be adjusted to fit the scenario requirements.

---

input : Entropy Measures E_X and E_Y
input : Global Disorder Measure G_{XY}
input : Segmentation Measure K
output: Contour region CR

E_X ;   % Variation metric for MV_x

E_Y ;   % Variation metric for MV_y

G_{XY} ;   % Combined measure of disorder for whole frame

$CR = \phi$;   % Union of contour blocks

C = 1 ;   % Gradient
Buffer = 0 ;   % buffer variable
while Buffer $<=$ K $* G_{XY}$ **do**
  for $i \leftarrow 1$ **to** $\frac{width}{32}$ **do**
    for $j \leftarrow 1$**to** $\frac{Height}{32}$ **do**
      if $E_X(i,j) >$ C $*$ mean(E_X)&&$E_Y(i,j) >$ C $*$ mean(E_Y)&&Buffer $<=$ K $* G_{XY}$ **then**
        $CR = CR \bigcup$ Region (i,j) ;
        Buffer = Buffer + E_X (i,j)+E_X (i,j) ;
      end
    end
  end
  C = C $- 0.1$;
  if C $<= 0.5$ **then**
    Break ;
  end
end
Return CR;

Algorithm 1. Identification of contour blocks

To further refine the extracted information, a 3×3 majority filter is applied across the whole frame; blocks having at least 4 neighbouring blocks, labeled as showing a high level of disorder, are classified as part of the moving objects.

5   Proposed Method

5.1   Fall Detection

In the section above we have defined the motion descriptors and their usage for moving objects detection and segmentation. We approach fall detection in a similar manner. Fall detection can be described as a sudden event, which causes rapid variation of video features in the temporal domain. In line with this observation, the unified entropy measure defined earlier, also exhibits large values and also strong variations across the frames, in presence of the fall.

In order to identify potential candidate frames for the occurrence of fall, we discard the frames which have lower entropy. Lower entropy frames typically do not contain any object motion, hence the likelihood of occurrence of the fall in these frames is almost negligible. After selecting the frames with higher entropy with a cut off, which is specific to camera orientation and illumination conditions, we further analyze these frames for the detection of the fall. Figure 2 (a) shows the movement of centroid of the person per frame. As we can see, during the fall the velocity of centroid dramatically increases and then goes to zero.

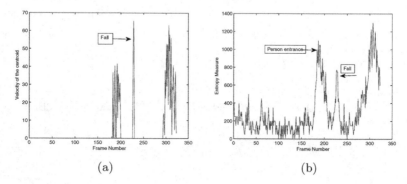

(a)   (b)

Fig. 2. (a) Velocity of the centroid of the person per frame. (b) Variation of entropy and the events as marked using ground truth.

Another feature that characterizes a falling event, is the sudden change in location and motion orientation of the centroid over a very short number of frames. In order to further refine the accuracy of the prediction, we also consider that after the fall occurs, the amount of motion reduces, there by decreasing the entropy measure defined in the previous section. Figure 2 (b) illustrates the variation of entropy. We can notice that any sudden event results in a spike in the entropy plot, followed by a decrease of the values after the fall.

5.2   Algorithm

Let the frame at the time instant i for a given video stream from a camera be F_i, then the entropy measure of that frame is given by $E(F_i)$ and the centroid of the segmented person as a pixel location in a video is given by $C(F_i)$, and the distance traveled by the centroid (or velocity per frame) is given by:

$$V(F_i) = Euclidean(C(F_i), C(F_{i-1})) \qquad (8)$$

The proposed algorithm is shown in Figure 3. As mentioned in the previous paragraphs, we first check for the high variance in the entropy measure, the velocity of the moving object. After that we check for sudden drop of entropy in the neighborhood to check for the fall. Thresholds $Th1$, $Th2$ and $Th3$ depend on the mean and variance of entropy and velocity. The main purpose of these thresholds is to detect the peaks that occur in the entropy measure and also to

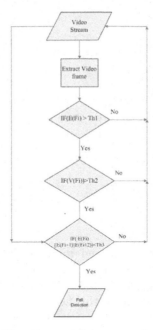

Fig. 3. Flow chart of the proposed algorithm

detect the peak changes in velocity of the centroid. Ideally, any value falling above the mean of the entropy and velocity should be considered; however, background noise also contributes significantly to motion entropy and is largely dependent on the deployed environment.

5.3   Reconfiguration

Reconfiguration of the camera is triggered by the fall detection algorithm mentioned in the above sections. The basis for reconfiguration is the fallen person. The main aim of the reconfiguration of the camera is to get the best possible view of the subject. In order to do so, we adjust the camera parameters in such a manner that the person to be observed falls at the centre of the image plane. Further precaution is also taken so that the person does not fill the entire image plane of the camera. This can be achieved in most PTZ cameras by specifying the particular area in a video frame, by using the available CGI (Commond Gateway Interface) commands. In this scenario, the segmented object is selected as the area of interest. Cameras automatically adjust alignment at the midpoint of the area specified. After the reconfiguration is complete in order to make the person fully visible, the new parameters of the camera are set using the subject segmentation information. This helps understanding the reason of fall and further monitoring of the person after the fall, that is especially relevant for elderly people living alone and monitored for their care.

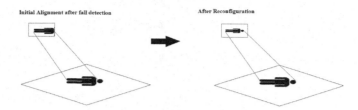

Fig. 4. Reconfiguration of the camera carried out to guarantee full visibility of the subject of interest

6   Evaluation

In order to demonstrate the utility and robustness of the algorithm, we first evaluate the performance of the fall detection algorithm by testing it against the reference fall detection dataset published by the University of Montreal [2], widely used to validate algorithms in this field.

To show the reconfiguration capability, we deployed a set up in a real environment and observe its performance during the occurrence of fall. To this extent we used two cameras "Sony SNC-EP521 indoor", day/night, with PTZ. These IP cameras are equipped with a 36x optical zoom allowing operators to cover large, open areas and zoom in for detailed close-up shots. Panning can span from 0 to 340 degrees, with max 105 degrees tilt, and their configuration can change using built in network commands. The cameras have been installed in our Department facility, and falling events have been recorded thanks to the collaboration of volunteers.

6.1   Fall Detection

Since the algorithm operates in the compressed domain, we had to convert all the videos in the dataset [2] into the H.264 format using the JM H.264 reference encoder [13], at the frame rate of 25 frames per second. The thresholds necessary for a proper operation of the algorithm are learned for each camera and are maintained constant for that particular camera for all scenarios. Fall is defined as an event lasting 5-10 seconds, starting from the momentary stop by the subject just before the fall and ending with a motion less layover of the subject. The total number of correct fall detections, as compared to the ground truth, are deemed as true positives (TP), while false detections are termed as false positives (FP). Finally, true falls which have been skipped by the detector are termed as false negatives (FN). The results obtained for the video dataset are given in Table 1 in terms of Precision, Recall and F-Measure. A comparison with respect to the state of the art techniques is provided in 2. As can be seen, the fall detection algorithm performs reasonably well especially given the fact that it operates in real time. The algorithm fails to detect the falls, when the subject is very far

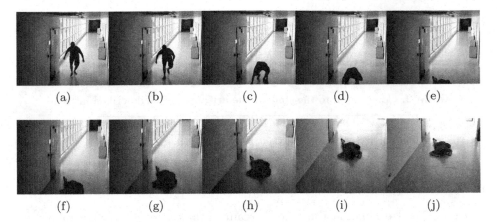

Fig. 5. Fall detection and subsequent reconfiguration of the camera for better view

away from the camera and subsequently the motion entropy generated by the subject is very low. In such scenario noise becomes dominant thereby causing false detections. Another scenario where the algorithm fails is in case of actions, which correspond to bending down on the floor etc. However, since we also took into consideration the momentary fall entropy, just after the fall most of such false detections have been resolved.

6.2 Comparison

Our algorithm completely operates in the compressed domain. Hence it has the advantage of being very light in terms of computational and memory requirements. Nevertheless it compares very well with the other pixel domain state of the art fall detection methods as we can see from the table 1. Our method also provides a significant improvement with respect to other compressed domain methods like [15]. Most of these methods rely on the segmentation of moving object and the trajectory of its centroid, and also include other features like velocity of centroid. Present algorithm also uses these aspects, but it turns out to be more robust as it also exploits the motion disorder as one of the factors to determine fall detection. Furthermore, the compressed domain method presented in [15] uses AC and DC coefficients along with motion vectors to achieve object segmentation, which are heavily dependent on the quantization parameter used for encoding the video bit stream. The proposed method, instead is entirely based on motion vectors, which are independent with respect to changes in QP. In terms of complexity our solution offers the lowest complexity of all compressed domain methods as it operates at the level of 32×32 blocks, and the number of operations required for processing one frame are 5.2K, 16K, 48K, 106K computations for CIF, VGA, HD, full HD resolutions, respectively.

Table 1. Performance of the algorithm on the dataset [2]

Precision	Recall	F-Measure
0.89	0.86	0.88

Table 2. Comparison to the state of the art approaches described in [10]

	Our method	K-NN	C4.5	SVM	Bayes	Feng et. all
Sensitivity	0.86	0.75	0.85	0.95	0.80	0.98

6.3 Reconfiguration

In case of real evaluation the video stream obtained from the camera has a resolution of 720 × 576 pixels and a frame rate of 25 frames per second. The H.264 bit stream obtained from the camera is encoded in the baseline profile. In order to access the Network Abstraction Layer (NAL) packets from the camera we have used the functions available in the *ffmpeg* library [8]. Fall detection and moving object segmentation are implemented using the motion vectors extracted from the H.264 (JM 18.6 version) decoder [13]. In order to control the camera automatically the *curl* library functions [7] are adopted. The whole set up is implemented on an Intel i5 processor, 3.10 GHz.

Fall detection and subsequent reconfiguration is shown in Figure 5. As we can see from the images, fall of the person occurs towards the end of the image in one of the frames. However, camera instantly reconfigures to bring back the view of the fallen person. This shows that the algorithm works in real time and is robust enough to work in tricky illumination conditions.

7 Conclusions

In this paper we proposed a framework for elderly care for behavior anomaly detection from video. The analysis is performed using the information coming from the video motion flow, directly from streaming, without decoding. This allows the real time analysis of the event, introducing the possibility of implementing the proposed solution directly on-board of cameras. The described technique has been tested on a publicly available dataset, verifying its ability in detecting fall events, and compared with state of the art methods. Moreover it has been tested on a set-up developed by authors, where, besides the fall detection only, it has been proved its capability in performing real-time camera reconfiguration, in order to focus the attention of the vision system on the fallen person. The proposed framework is an instrument able to preserve the privacy of the persons monitored, since no information should be decoded and transfered before an event is detected.

References

1. Anderson, D., Keller, J.M., Skubic, M., Chen, X., He, Z.: Recognizing falls from silhouettes. In: Engineering in Medicine and Biology Society, 2006. EMBS 2006. In: 28th Annual International Conference of the IEEE, pp. 6388–6391. IEEE (2006)
2. Auvinet, E., Rougier, C., Meunier, J., St-Arnaud, A., Rousseau, J.: Multiple cameras fall dataset. DIRO-Université de Montréal, Tech. Rep 1350 (2010)
3. Borges, P., Conci, N., Cavallaro, A.: Video-based human behavior understanding: A survey. IEEE Transactions on Circuits and Systems for Video Technology **23**(11), 1993–2008 (2013)
4. Cardinaux, F., Bhowmik, D., Abhayaratne, C., Hawley, M.S.: Video based technology for ambient assisted living: A review of the literature. Journal of Ambient Intelligence and Smart Environments **3**(3), 253–269 (2011)
5. Chen, C.H., Yao, Y., Page, D., Abidi, B., Koschan, A., Abidi, M.: Heterogeneous fusion of omnidirectional and ptz cameras for multiple object tracking. IEEE Transactions on Circuits and Systems for Video Technology **18**(8), 1052–1063 (2008)
6. Climent-Pérez, A., Flórez-Revuelta, F., Chaaraoui, F.: A review on vision techniques applied to human behaviour analysis for ambient-assisted living. Expert Systems with Applications **39**(12), 10873–10888 (2012)
7. Open source multiple contributions, O.S.: Command line tool for transferring data with url syntax, March 2014. http://curl.haxx.se/
8. Open source multiple contributions, O.S.: Trans standard multimedia framework for media manipulation, March 2014. http://www.ffmpeg.org/
9. Cucchiara, R., Grana, C., Prati, A., Vezzani, R.: Probabilistic posture classification for human-behavior analysis. IEEE Transactions on Systems, Man and Cybernetics, Part A: Systems and Humans **35**(1), 42–54 (2005)
10. Feng, W., Liu, R., Zhu, M.: Fall detection for elderly person care in a vision-based home surveillance environment using a monocular camera. Signal, Image and Video Processing, pp. 1–10 (2014)
11. Foroughi, H., Aski, B.S., Pourreza, H.: Intelligent video surveillance for monitoring fall detection of elderly in home environments. In: 2008 11th International Conference on Computer and Information Technology. ICCIT 2008, pp. 219–224. IEEE (2008)
12. Hazelhoff, L., Han, J., de With, P.H.N.: Video-based fall detection in the home using principal component analysis. In: Blanc-Talon, J., Bourennane, S., Philips, W., Popescu, D., Scheunders, P. (eds.) ACIVS 2008. LNCS, vol. 5259, pp. 298–309. Springer, Heidelberg (2008)
13. HHI.: H.264 reference decoder from heinrich hertz institute, January 2014. http://iphome.hhi.de/suehring/tml/
14. Katz, S., Downs, T.D., Cash, H.R., Grotz, R.C.: Progress in development of the index of adl. The gerontologist **10**(1 Part 1), pp. 20–30 (1970)
15. Lin, C.W., Ling, Z.H.: Automatic fall incident detection in compressed video for intelligent homecare. In: 2007 Proceedings of 16th International Conference on Computer Communications and Networks. ICCCN 2007, pp. 1172–1177. IEEE (2007)
16. Micheloni, C., Rinner, B., Foresti, G.L.: Video analysis in pan-tilt-zoom camera networks. IEEE Signal Processing Magazine **27**(5), 78–90 (2010)
17. Mubashir, M., Shao, L., Seed, L.: A survey on fall detection: Principles and approaches. Neurocomputing **100**(0), 144–152 (2013). (Special issue: Behaviours in video)

18. Murray, D., Basu, A.: Motion tracking with an active camera. IEEE Transactions on Pattern Analysis and Machine Intelligence **16**(5), 449–459 (1994)
19. Nait-Charif, H., McKenna, S.J.: Activity summarisation and fall detection in a supportive home environment. In: 2004 Proceedings of the 17th International Conference on Pattern Recognition. ICPR 2004. vol. 4, pp. 323–326. IEEE (2004)
20. Quaritsch, M., Kreuzthaler, M., Rinner, B., Bischof, H., Strobl, B.: Autonomous multicamera tracking on embedded smart cameras. EURASIP Journal on Embedded Systems **2007**(1), 35–35 (2007)
21. Rashidi, P., Mihailidis, A.: A survey on ambient-assisted living tools for older adults. IEEE journal of biomedical and health informatics **17**(3), 579–590 (2013)
22. Rougier, C., Meunier, J., St-Arnaud, A., Rousseau, J.: Fall detection from human shape and motion history using video surveillance. In: 21st International Conference on 2007 Advanced Information Networking and Applications Workshops, AINAW'07. vol. 2, pp. 875–880. IEEE (2007)
23. Scotti, G., Marcenaro, L., Coelho, C., Selvaggi, F., Regazzoni, C.: Dual camera intelligent sensor for high definition 360 degrees surveillance. IEE Proceedings-Vision, Image and Signal Processing **152**(2), 250–257 (2005)
24. Van Kasteren, T., Englebienne, G., Krse, B.: An activity monitoring system for elderly care using generative and discriminative models. Personal and Ubiquitous Computing **14**(6), 489–498 (2010)
25. Wiegand, T., Sullivan, G.J., Bjontegaard, G., Luthra, A.: Overview of the h. 264/avc video coding standard. IEEE Transactions on Circuits and Systems for Video Technology **13**(7), 560–576 (2003)
26. Yu, X.: Approaches and principles of fall detection for elderly and patient. In: 2008 10th International Conference on e-health Networking, Applications and Services. HealthCom 2008, pp. 42–47, July 2008

W23 - Computer Vision Problems
in Plant Phenotyping

3-D Histogram-Based Segmentation and Leaf Detection for Rosette Plants

Jean-Michel Pape and Christian Klukas[✉]

Department of Molecular Genetics, Leibniz Institute of Plant Genetics and Crop
Plant Research (IPK), Corrensstrasse 3, 06466 Gatersleben, Germany
{pape,klukas}@ipk-gatersleben.de

Abstract. Recognition and segmentation of plant organs like leaves is
one of the major challenges in digital plant phenotyping. Here we present
a 3-D histogram-based segmentation and recognition approach for top
view images of rosette plants such as *Arabidopsis thaliana* and tobacco.
Furthermore a euclidean-distance-map-based method for the detection
of leaves and the corresponding plant leaf segmentation method were
developed. An approach for the detection of optimal leaf split points for
the separation of overlapping leaf segments was created. We tested and
tuned our algorithms for the Leaf Segmentation Challenge (LSC). The
results demonstrate that our method is robust and handles demanding
imaging situations and different species with high accuracy.

Keywords: 3-D Histogram thresholding · Euclidean distance map ·
Graph analysis · Leaf counting · Leaf segmentation

1 Introduction

The analysis of digital images is an important task in plant phenotyping to
evaluate plant parameters in a non-invasive fashion. A wide variety of different
screening systems with varying requirements for the image analysis have been
developed and are in part commercially available. Fully automated systems for
phenotyping try to establish constant environments for image acquisition, but
due to the high costs, space requirements and installation effort of those systems the utilization of more flexible ad-hoc installations would often be desirable. The demanding non-constant imaging situations with respect to varying
plant background and fluctuating illumination cause similar problems for image
analysis as field-based imaging. Challenging are big differences in image-quality
like image resolution and lightning conditions, which need to be handled by
image-processing algorithms. Improvements in these areas would allow an easier
monitoring of plant growth in non-automated greenhouses and would also be
useful for improved image-based field-phenotyping solutions.

State of the Art Software. A comprehensive overview about phenotyping software can be found at http://www.plant-image-analysis.org/. There are a various

© Springer International Publishing Switzerland 2015
L. Agapito et al. (Eds.): ECCV 2014 Workshops, Part IV, LNCS 8928, pp. 61–74, 2015.
DOI: 10.1007/978-3-319-16220-1_5

number of applications which support fully automated or semi-automated plant image analysis, especially for rosette plants, as described in [14],[16],[7],[2],[5] and [4]. Some tools already provide general pipelines for shoot analysis and different plant species including the possibility for rosette plant analysis [8]. In most biological experiments which are designed to be analyzed by automated imaging solutions the growth conditions are modified in comparison to normal field and greenhouse growth. For example, instead of soil, nutrient solutions are used for root phenotyping, special carrier systems, and different pot soil covering solutions are used in automated greenhouses. One of the goals of these modifications is to ensure homogeneous imaging conditions in respect to image quality. However, to reduce effort and costs for setting up high-throughput phenotyping experiments, it is desirable to handle even disturbed images by image analysis tools. Image analysis frameworks such as ImageJ and Fiji include state of the art image processing algorithms which can be utilized for algorithm and plugin development [13], [12]. To enhance the robustness of segmentation approaches, besides color features also texture features can be utilized [15], additionally active contours are used to improve segmentation [10]. Active Contours are also used for leaf shape classification [3]. Nevertheless, including these algorithms and methods in a framework which is applicable for high-throughput analysis proves to be challenging due to the storage and processing requirements and the need for processing plant identifiers and meta-data.

2 Methods

The main steps of our method are depicted in figure 1. After image acquisition the pre-processing procedures are performed. Based on the training data two 3-D color-histograms for foreground and background data are calculated. These are used in the segmentation phase to separate the testing image set into foreground and background. The segmentation results are further processed in the feature extraction phase to detect the leaf segments. This involves the detection of leaf center points and skeleton generation. Skeleton-points with minimal distance to the background are starting points for the calculation of split lines. These lines are used as borders during segmentation of overlapping leaves. In a last step the separated leaves are labeled by a region-growing algorithm. Our method development are related to a dataset provided through the Leaf Segmentation Challenge (LSC) of the Computer Vision Problems in Plant Phenotyping (CVPPP 2014) workshop organized in conjunction with the 13th European Conference on Computer Vision (ECCV) [11]. The dataset is used for testing our methods, further details are provided in the results section.

2.1 Image Acquisition

Our segmentation approach requires plant images and manually labeled images as input for the training phase. Within the Leaf Segmentation Challenge (LSC) a comprehensive set of image and label data (ground-truth data) has been made

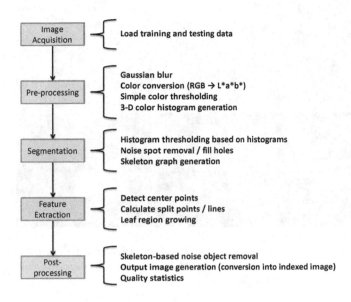

Fig. 1. Method overview, main pipeline steps based on the traditional image processing pipeline

available. Three training datasets were provided: Two *Arabidopsis thaliana* plant image datasets with 95 (A1) and 31 (A2) images, and one dataset consisting of 27 tobacco plant images (A3) (fig. 2). The datasets A1 and A2 are similar with respect to their image quality (resolution A1: 500×530 px, A2: 530×565 px). A1 includes more artifacts, e.g. moss. The background and lightning conditions are homogeneous. In opposite, the dataset A3 has a much better image quality (resolution 2448×2048 px), but the background and lightning conditions are very in-homogeneous, also the plant is not strictly located in the image center and other plants are partially visible at the image borders, parts of some of the plants are cut off at the image borders.

2.2 Pre-processing

L*a*b* Color Space Conversion. All RGB images are converted into the L*a*b* color space (color components are normalized and discretized between 0 - 255). Using L*a*b* channels as features for segmentation has some advantages over using the RGB color space. In comparison to the RGB color space the L*a*b* color components are better suited to separate foreground and background, also the color components are less correlated to each other [1].

Simple Color Thresholding. To prevent influences of very dark and very bright pixels to the training data, a color thresholding is applied. These pixels with a

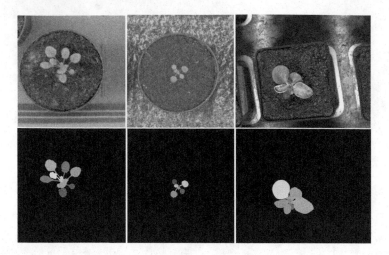

Fig. 2. Example training images from datasets A1, A2 and A3 (left, middle, right). Top - RGB images, bottom - provided ground-truth label images, representing desired optimal thresholding and leaf segmentation results.

L-value near the white and black point are mostly the result of an overexposure, reflections or shadows and include no reasonable color information.

Creation of Color Cubes. The segmentation approach based on a supervised classification in foreground and background orientated on the kernel density estimation approach. Therefore a 3-D histogram creation for all training images (including labeled images) from a given dataset A1, A2 and A3 are processed individually. Each pixel from the training image is categorized into foreground or background by inspecting the provided label data. The corresponding L*a*b* pixel color values are used as indices for the 3-D histogram cubes. For each pixel the corresponding histogram bin is incremented. During this procedure a over-all foreground and background 3-D histogram is accumulated. To improve the robustness of the thresholding approach, all input images for the cube calculation were filtered in the pre-processing phase by a Gaussian blur operation.

2.3   Segmentation

As described in Kurugollu et al. a simple histogram thresholding for each channel would result in a partitioning of the 3-D histogram into rectangular regions [9] with non-optimal results. For this reason a direct look-up in the 3-D histogram cubes instead of (multiple) one-dimensional color component thresholds are used. The cubes act as a look-up table which stored the classification probabilities for each color feature. The indices for look-up of the histogram values belonging to particular pixel color, are again based on the discretized L*a*b* color values. For color values not present in the training data, the histogram values are zero. In such a case the surrounding of the particular histogram cell is considered by calculating down-sampled cubes, containing the average of multiple adjacent cells. The histogram values are interpreted as probabilities and the pixels are assigned to foreground if the corresponding cube contains a higher value than the cell of the background cube.

As the color information is not sufficient to separate the image error-free, the results still include noise and artifacts. As shown in figure 3, it becomes obvious that a simple multiple histogram thresholding would not result in a good segmentation quality, especially the foreground and background components in the A3 dataset contain many overlapping areas.

To handle this disturbances a connected components detection is performed to delete artifacts with an area below a certain threshold. Background areas within the filled image area are also investigated according to their size, and filled, if they fall below a certain threshold. Morphological operations are used to smooth the object borders. In case of the A3 images, plants are not strictly located at the center of the image and other plant parts protrude into the image from the side. Therefore, all foreground parts which are connected to the border are removed (e.g. leaves from neighbor plants), except if this removal operation would remove the largest connected component.

Remaining large greenish objects within the image are further evaluated in the post-processing phase, once structural shape information (needed for the leaf segmentation), is available.

2.4 Feature Extraction

The segmentation results serve as input for the leaf detection. Especially the leaves of the *Arabidopsis thaliana* plants are considered as compact objects which only partly overlap. In the corresponding euclidean distance map (figure 4 top right) the leaf center points appear as peaks. Before calculating the distance map a morphological erode operation is performed for a improved separation of leaves. The Euclidean distance map (Edm) is processed by a maximum search. The result is shown in the bottom left of figure 4. Slightly overlapping leaves are in still detected separately. In cases where overlapping leaves form a single compact object this approach may fail to detect specific leaves. Finally, a skeleton image is calculated for the subsequent analysis steps.

Graph Representation. The plant leaves are mostly connected with each other (either overlapping or connected by the plant center). To detect split points for leaf-separation, a graph structure for efficient traversal of the plant mask image skeleton is generated (see fig. 5). Before generating the graph, values of the calculated euclidean distance map are mapped on the skeleton image. The result image is used for creation of the skeleton graph: Leaf center points, skeleton end-points and skeleton branch-points are represented as nodes in the graph. Edges are created if the according image points are connected by the skeleton. Additionally, a list of the positions and minimal distances of each particular edge segment is saved as an edge-attribute. This list is used to detect the exact positions of the leaf split points.

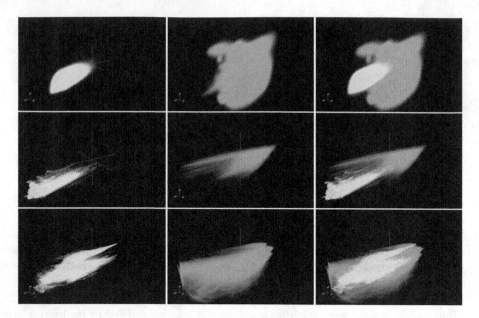

Fig. 3. Accumulated foreground (green) and background (blue) probabilities, stored in 3-D histogram cubes derived from all images of the three training datasets (A1 in first line, A2 second line, A3 third line). For illustration the cube cell values were normalized between 0 - 255 and converted to 8-bit grayscale TIFF images and then visualized using ParaView [6]. Afterwards the values were mapped to green (foreground) and blue (background) color table (left and middle of the image, combined view in the third column). Light colors indicates low values (and thus a low probability) and saturated colors indicate high values. L*a*b* color axes: z-axis: L-value, x-axis: a-value, y-axis: b-value.

Split Point and Split Lines Estimation. To separate all leaves from each other, all paths between the leaves are investigated using the corresponding graph structure. The minimum distance points (points where the distance to the image background is minimal) between any two leaf center point nodes are determined by investigating the path edges minimum distance attributes and saved as leaf split points. The according edges are removed from the graph structure. This procedure continues until all leaf center point nodes in the graph are disconnected from each other. Based on the calculated split points the exact split lines are needed to separate overlapping leaves (see fig. 6). For each split point the nearest background point is searched. The second coordinate of the split line is searched at the opposite position relative to the split point (a background pixel near the opposite point but with minimum distance to the split point). After the split line estimation a region filling, considering the segmentation result and the split line positions is performed starting from the leaves center points. The result represents the leaf labels.

Fig. 4. Segmentation result (top left), distance map (top right), distance map with highlighted peaks, which serve as leaf center points (bottom left) and skeleton image (bottom right)

Fig. 5. Derived graph from leaf center points and skeleton image

2.5   Post-processing

During the segmentation phase only color and size information is considered for artifact removal. For the A3 dataset including large greenish noise objects, the structural information from the skeleton and graph structure is evaluated. The average distance from node to node is calculated for each connected component. While the shape of plant objects is relatively compact the noise objects contain many skeleton branch points. Therefore, the average distance for noise objects is small. To increase the difference of this property for plant and noise objects

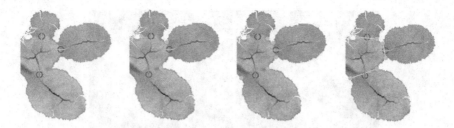

Fig. 6. Example for split point and split line estimation. For illustration the euclidean distance map derived skeleton is mapped on the segmented plant image (gray values indicate the euclidean distance to the background). (from left to right) Identified split points, detected start points for split line detection (nearest outline points to the individually split point), corresponding endpoints for split lines, resulting split lines.

the distance is scaled according to the average distance of the object relative to the image center. Objects at the image border are then more likely removed.

The last step of the workflow includes the output image generation (labeled result images) and the measurement of quality statistics based on the provided evaluation functions.

3   Implementation

Our approach is implemented in Java, taking advantage of its platform independence and the availability of numerous libraries like ImageJ and Fiji. As shown in figure 7, the pipeline consists of four main blocks. The provided training images and their labels are used to calculate the foreground and the background 3-D color histogram cubes. These cubes are then used in a first segmentation phase to process the provided testing images and extract the foreground and background. The segmentation result is used to detect leaves by detecting leaf center points and the corresponding split points and split lines based on distance map and skeleton calculation. In the last step the region growing algorithm labels each leaf region.

Pipeline Parameters. Besides the trained 3-D histogram cubes several parameters influence the segmentation and leaf detection. Individually for the three datasets well suited parameter values were selected. Depending on the dataset noise level in the pre-processing according blurring factors, noise removal and gap fill size limits for disconnected components were determined. The segmentation results were further improved by introduction of a weighting factor in order to increase the probability for detection of foreground pixels. This way the plant is better recognized, additionally introduced noise objects are removed if they fall below the noise area limit or during the post-processing based on their irregular shape.

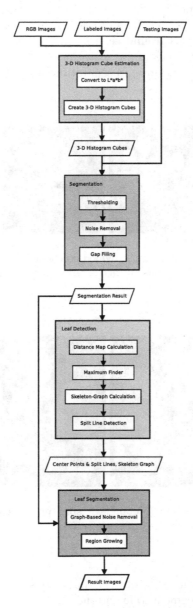

Fig. 7. Design of the implemented processing pipeline. Green: training phase including the histogram estimation for foreground and background. Brown: segmentation and noise removal. Orange and Blue: Extraction of features for.

4   Results and Discussion

Training Results. The images (fig. 8 and fig. 9) show the result of different pipeline-steps. Table 1 contains the statistical results of the leaf area labeling (column 1), foreground/background separation (column 2) and leaf detection (average absolute and mean errors per image in column 3 and 4) of the training data. The foreground and background separation of the three datasets is nearly optimal (97.4 - 99.7%).

Fig. 8. From left to right: input image, provided image label, segmentation result, color coded difference image (yellow - false positive, red - false negative)

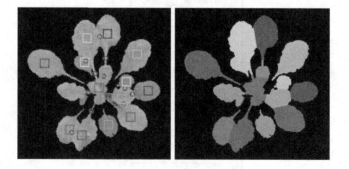

Fig. 9. Left: Leaf center points (rectangles), split points (blue circles), split lines (orange lines). Right: Result of the leaf segmentation.

Testing Results. The result for the testing data are shown in table 2. The foreground and background segmentation and the leaf labeling was performed mostly successfully with similar results as for the training data (fig. 10).

For the testing phase three datasets, belonging to the training data without the according ground-truth images have been provided by the organizers of the Leaf Segmentation Challenge. The test data images for A1 (33) and A2 (9) are very similar to the training data, the 56 A3 test images show more differences to the training data in respect to the imaging background and plant colorization.

Table 1. Results of the evaluation of the training data. BestDice: Quality of the individual leaf segmentation. FGBGDice: Quality of the foreground and background separation. AbsDiffFGLabels: Average absolute difference of the number of the detected leaves. DiffFGLabels: Average difference of the detected number of leaves. For all values the standard derivation is indicated. Calculation details are described in [11].

	BestDice [%]	FGBGDice [%]	AbsDiffFGLabels	DiffFGLabels
A1	74.2 (±7.7)	97.4 (±1.8)	2.6 (±1.8)	-1.9 (±2.5)
A2	80.6 (±8.7)	99.7 (±0.3)	0.9 (±1.0)	-0.3 (±1.3)
A3	61.8 (±19.1)	98.2 (±1.1)	2.1 (±1.7)	-2.1 (±1.7)
all	73.5 (±11.5)	98.0 (±1.9)	2.2 (±1.7)	-1.7 (±2.3)

Table 2. Statistical evaluation results provided by the Leaf Segmentation Challenge board, based on the submitted image analysis results for the testing-dataset

	BestDice [%]	FGBGDice [%]	AbsDiffFGLabels	DiffFGLabels
A1	74.4 (±4.3)	97.0 (±0.8)	2.2 (±1.3)	-1.8 (±1.8)
A2	76.9 (±7.6)	96.3 (±1.7)	1.2 (±1.3)	-1.0 (±1.5)
A3	53.3 (±20.2)	94.1 (±13.3)	2.8 (±2.5)	-2.0 (±3.2)
all	62.6 (±19.0)	95.3 (±10.1)	2.4 (±2.1)	-1.9 (±2.7)

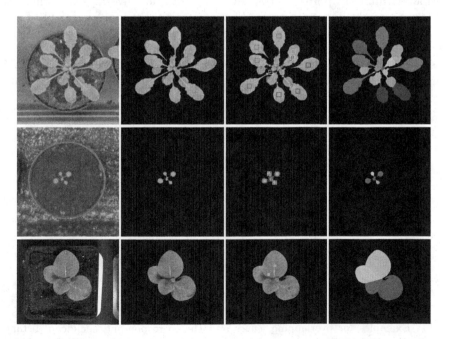

Fig. 10. Example results from the evaluation-phase. From left to right: input image, segmentation result, detected leaf center points, labeled leaves. Test-images from top to bottom: plant 87 from dataset A1, plant 10 from set A2 and plant 47 from set A3.

Overall, the results of the test data are similar to those of the training data. Problematic for segmentation was discoloration of some of the images in the A3 dataset. In one case the whole (very small plant) was removed completely, as the cut-off value for the size of noise objects was tuned for the smallest plants in the training dataset and proved to be too high for the testing-data. The quality of our segmentation approach depends on the homogeneity of the training data in comparison to the testing data. The training dataset needs to be representative, it would desirable to improve the interpolation of missing points (determination of probabilities for unknown color values) in the histogram cubes. The current scale space method is an inaccurate approximation, a better option would have been a blurring operation in the 3-D space.

In the segmentation example for A1 it is noticeable that the petioles are missing in some images for some leaves. An explanation could be that the color of these thin areas is similar to the moss and other background parts in the A1 dataset.

A remaining challenge is the recognition of very small leaves and leaves which overlap strongly. Figure 11 shows some examples for the leaf center point detection based on the euclidean distance map and maxima detection. In addition, the leaf segmentation could perform better at leaf borders which overlap. Due to current implementation issues regarding the discretization of the distance map, the split lines sometimes don't directly connect points of minimal distance. In addition, within our approach, it is not clear which leaf overlaps the other and therefore a straight line is constructed for separation. By analyzing the leaf area next to the line and the borders of the leaves in the surrounding, a better fitting curve could be estimated. The average leaf count results are too low for all three datasets (DiffFGLabel-values of -1.8 for A1, -1.0 for A2 and -2.0 for A3). This is mainly caused by very small leaves which are located at the center of the plant, these leaves are not detected as they don't appear as peaks in the distance map.

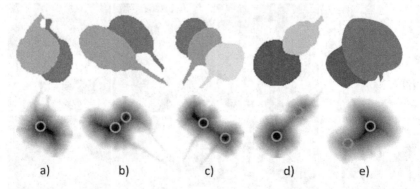

a)   b)   c)   d)   e)

Fig. 11. Examples for overlapping leaves and the corresponding euclidean distance map with detected maxima. a) - d) Examples for arabidopsis, e) example for tobacco. Correctly identified are b), d) and e), too few maxima are observed in case a) and c). The distance map is not fine granular enough in these cases.

The leaf segmentation for the tobacco images of the A3 dataset performs comparably worst (BestDice values of 53% in A3 versus 74 and 77% for A1 and A2). The leaves of the tobacco plants have a different shape than the *Arabidopsis thaliana* plants. In later development stages the leaf overlap becomes so large that our detection of peaks in the distance-maps fails to recognize those plant structures.

5   Conclusions

The leaf separation approach was developed for compact leaf shapes as found in *Arabidopsis thaliana*. Leaves of tobacco plants are not as well separated from each other, while the developed approach still works for tobacco plants.

The calculation of color cubes using the L*a*b* color space proved to be a very good basis for foreground/background separation of images which are not too different from the training data. We also developed a way for the detection of leaf center points using a distance map, and an approach for separation of leaf segments, by calculating split lines.

It is conceivable to use this approach in the future within a semi-automated segmentation method, outside of this specific Leaf Segmentation Challenge. The representative training data could be created by the user by marking image regions belonging to foreground and background. In addition, the leaf segmentation approach could be improved by a shape-adjusting component.

Acknowledgments. This work was supported by the Leibniz Institute of Plant Genetics and Crop Plant Research and by the German Plant Phenotyping Network which is funded by the German Federal Ministry of Education and Research (grant no. 031A053B).

References

1. Bansal, S., Aggarwal, D.: Color image segmentation using cielab color space using ant colony optimization. International Journal of Computer Applications **29**(9), 28–34 (2011)
2. Bours, R., Muthuraman, M., Bouwmeester, H., van der Krol, A.: Oscillator: A system for analysis of diurnal leaf growth using infrared photography combined with wavelet transformation. Plant methods **8**(1), 29 (2012)
3. Cerutti, G., Tougne, L., Vacavant, A., Coquin, D.: A parametric active polygon for leaf segmentation and shape estimation. In: Bebis, G., et al. (eds.) Advances in Visual Computing. LNCS, vol. 6938, pp. 202–213. Springer, Heidelberg (2011)
4. De Vylder, J., Vandenbussche, F., Hu, Y., Philips, W., Van Der Straeten, D.: Rosette tracker: an open source image analysis tool for automatic quantification of genotype effects. Plant physiology **160**(3), 1149–1159 (2012)
5. Green, J.M., Appel, H., Rehrig, E.M., Harnsomburana, J., Chang, J.F., Balint-Kurti, P., Shyu, C.R.: Phenophyte: a flexible affordable method to quantify 2d phenotypes from imagery. Plant methods **8**(1), 45 (2012)
6. Henderson, A., Ahrens, J., Law, C.: The ParaView Guide. Kitware, Clifton Park (2004)

7. Ispiryan, R., Grigoriev, I., zu Castell, W., Schffner, A.R.: A segmentation procedure using colour features applied to images of arabidopsis thaliana. Functional Plant Biology **40**, 1065–1075 (2013)
8. Klukas, C., Chen, D., Pape, J.M.: Integrated analysis platform: An open-source information system for high-throughput plant phenotyping. Plant physiology **165**(2), 506–518 (2014)
9. Kurugollu, F., Sankur, B., Harmanci, A.E.: Color image segmentation using histogram multithresholding and fusion. Image and vision computing **19**(13), 915–928 (2001)
10. Minervini, M., Abdelsamea, M.M., Tsaftaris, S.A.: Image-based plant phenotyping with incremental learning and active contours. Ecological Informatics (2013)
11. Scharr, H., Minervini, M., Fischbach, A., Tsaftaris, S.A.: Annotated image datasets of rosette plants. Tech. rep. (2014). http://juser.fz-juelich.de/record/154525
12. Schindelin, J., Arganda-Carreras, I., Frise, E., Kaynig, V., Longair, M., Pietzsch, T., Preibisch, S., Rueden, C., Saalfeld, S., Schmid, B., et al.: Fiji: an open-source platform for biological-image analysis. Nature methods **9**(7), 676–682 (2012)
13. Schneider, C.A., Rasband, W.S., Eliceiri, K.W., Schindelin, J., Arganda-Carreras, I., Frise, E., Kaynig, V., Longair, M., Pietzsch, T., Preibisch, S., et al.: 671 nih image to imagej: 25 years of image analysis. Nature methods **9**(7) (2012)
14. Tessmer, O.L., Jiao, Y., Cruz, J.A., Kramer, D.M., Chen, J.: Functional approach to high-throughput plant growth analysis. BMC systems biology **7**(Suppl 6), S17 (2013)
15. Valliammal, N., Geethalakshmi, S.: Leaf image segmentation based on the combination of wavelet transform and k means clustering. International Journal of Advanced Research in Artificial Intelligence **1**(3), 37–43 (2012)
16. Walter, A., Scharr, H., Gilmer, F., Zierer, R., Nagel, K.A., Ernst, M., Wiese, A., Virnich, O., Christ, M.M., Uhlig, B., et al.: Dynamics of seedling growth acclimation towards altered light conditions can be quantified via growscreen: a setup and procedure designed for rapid optical phenotyping of different plant species. New Phytologist **174**(2), 447–455 (2007)

Representing Roots on the Basis of Reeb Graphs in Plant Phenotyping

Ines Janusch[1]([✉]), Walter G. Kropatsch[1], Wolfgang Busch[2],
and Daniela Ristova[2]

[1] Institute of Computer Graphics and Algorithms,
Pattern Recognition and Image Processing Group,
Vienna University of Technology, Vienna, Austria
{ines,krw}@prip.tuwien.ac.at
[2] Gregor Mendel Institute of Molecular Plant Biology,
Austrian Academy of Sciences, Vienna, Austria
{wolfgang.busch,daniela.ristova}@gmi.oeaw.ac.at

Abstract. This paper presents a new representation for root images based on Reeb graphs. The representation proposed captures lengths and distances in root structures as well as locations of branches, numbers of lateral roots and the locations of the root tips. An analysis of root images using Reeb graphs is presented and results are compared to ground truth measurements. This paper shows, that the Reeb graph based approach not only captures the characteristics needed for phenotyping of plants, but it also provides a solution to the problem of overlapping roots in the images. Using a Reeb graph based representation, such overlaps can be directly detected without further analysis, during the computation of the graph.

Keywords: Root representation · Root structure analysis · Topological graphs · Reeb graphs · Graph-based shape representation

1 Introduction

While hidden from view, plant roots represent a significant portion of the plant body and are of crucial importance for plant growth and productivity. For phenotyping of roots characteristics such as the number of branches, position of branches, branching angles and the length of roots are analyzed. These characteristics can be captured based on root images and represented using graphs. An important property of root image representations, besides capturing the needed characteristics, is to handle common problems that may occur for the root images, as for example overlaps of roots in the image.

Topological graphs capture branching points and endpoints of roots as nodes in the graph, while the edges in the graphs represent the root's connectivity. Root properties as the number of branches (primary root and lateral roots), length of individual branches or branching angles are therefore obtained as well.

© Springer International Publishing Switzerland 2015
L. Agapito et al. (Eds.): ECCV 2014 Workshops, Part IV, LNCS 8928, pp. 75–88, 2015.
DOI: 10.1007/978-3-319-16220-1_6

Such topological graphs are for example the medial axis based graphs which were introduced by Blum in [2] (further description by Lee in [10]). Another type of topological graphs are Reeb graphs (for example described by Biasotti et al. in [1]). Topology studies properties of space that are preserved under continuous deformation (these are for example stretching or bending). Therefore, topological properties are for example connectedness and continuity. In comparison, geometry analyzes properties as for example the shape of an object (contour, corners), its size or relative positions. While two shapes may be different regarding geometry (as are for example a square and a circle) these two shapes may be identical regarding topology (here both the square and the circle form one connected component).

For plant phenotyping based on root images a topological analysis of these images possesses advantages over a geometric analysis as roots may transform non-rigidly. Roots may for example bend around an obstacle when growing or they may be be rearranged or bended when grown in soil but taken out of the soil for an image. Such actions change the shape of the root and thus its geometric properties. In contrast the roots' connectedness and branching structure, thus its topological properties, are not affected by these actions. Due to this invariance of the topological characteristics to actions as rearranging of roots or bending around an obstacle, these properties provide a stable representation of root images. Such a representation allows for comparison of roots on different days of growth or of different plants on the same day. The approach presented in this paper utilizes these advantages and is therefore based on a topological image analysis and representation.

A medial axis based graph representation is a common representation of root images based on topological graphs. Leitner et al. for example show an analysis of root systems based on a medial axis approach [11]. Galkovskyi et al. as well rely on a medial axis approach to derive a root skeletonization [6]. Iyer-Pascuzzi et al. use the medial axis to compute root lengths [8].

However, this paper presents an automatic image analysis based on Reeb graphs. A first attempt to use Reeb graphs to represent root structures was presented in [9]. Within the scope of this paper, we show that the properties needed in plant phenotyping (length and angles of branches, numbers of branches, etc.) are captured using a Reeb graph based representation of root images. Furthermore, we show that, compared to a medial axis, Reeb graphs possess the ability of solving the problem of overlaps of lateral roots of one plant without additional post-processing. Using a Reeb graph such overlaps can be detected and resolved immediately. Reeb graphs therefore not only provide a simple solution to the problem of overlapping branches but they first of all provide a representation of root images that captures the characteristics needed in plant phenotyping, while at the same time being invariant to continuous deformations and handling the problem of overlaps.

This paper is structured as follows: the dataset as well as the analyzed properties are presented in Section 2. A theoretical introduction to Reeb graphs is given in Section 3 and the actual approach is described in Section 4, while Section 5 discusses the results. Section 6 concludes the paper.

2   Dataset

For this dataset roots of the plant *Arabidopsis thaliana*, a model organism in plant sciences [7], were grown and imaged on day 7 and day 10 of their growth period.

The plants were grown on a plate of 0.2 Murashige and Skoog (MS) basal media (0.2 MS), with 1% sucrose as a carbon source and pH=5.7 for 7 days. Each plate holds 20 plants, five seeds for any of the four genotypes: Columbia (Col-0), Landsberg erecta(Ler-1), Fei-0 and Bch-1. An example image of such a plate is shown in Figure 1.

After these 7 days of growth, the roots were transferred to plates with a medium of different hormone treatments and were imaged on the following three days. The following hormone treatments were tested: 3-Indolacetic acid (auxin, IAA), Kinetin (cytokinin, CK), Abscisic acid (ABA) and IAA and CK combined. A similar dataset setup is for example described by Ristova et al. in [12].

he approach presented in this paper was evaluated on 66 plants on day 7 and day 10 (132 root images) out of a dataset of 160 plants (320 root images).

On the dataset the following measurements were performed and are available as ground truth: primary root length on the transfer day, day7 (P1); primary root length growth after three days from the transfer day, day 10 (P2); lateral root numbers in day 10 (LR#), length of primary root between first and last lateral root for the day 10 (R) and average lateral root length for the day 10 (LRl), and primary root length on day 10 (P).

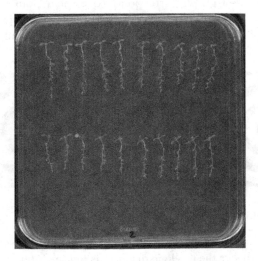

Fig. 1. Dataset example image: *Arabidopsis thaliana* roots on day 10, under IAA treatment

The ground truth measurements were obtained using Fiji (Image J) by drawing on the original images and extracting the length values.

3   Reeb Graphs and Related Morse Theory

The analysis of the presented dataset is based on Reeb graphs. These graphs are named after the French mathematician Georg Reeb and are based in Morse theory [3]. Reeb graphs describe the topological structure of a shape (e.g. 2D or 3D content) as the connectivity of its level sets [5]. A shape is analyzed according to a Morse function to derive a Reeb graph. Two common Morse functions were tested and used for our data:

- Height Function:
  The height function in 2D is defined as the function f that associates for each point $p = (a, b)$ of a function $f(x, y)$ the value b as the height of this point p: $f(x, y) \mapsto y$.
- Geodesic Distance:
  The geodesic distance is defined as the shortest distance in a curved space or a restricted area measured between two points of this area or space.

A comparison of the function values generated by these two Morse functions is shown in Figure 2. Figure 2a shows the input image, the Morse function values are shown in Figure 2b for the height function and respectively Figure 2c for the geodesic distance. Here the function values vary strongly for these two Morse functions. However, for a shape, for which changes in topology appear in a mainly vertical direction, both height function and geodesic distance (with the source pixel set in the topmost pixel line) will result in similar function values.

The nodes of a Reeb graph correspond to critical points computed on a shape according to a Morse function. At critical points the topology of the analyzed shape changes, thus the number of connected components in the level-set

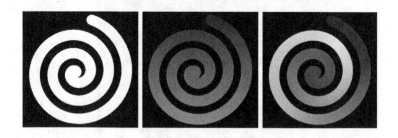

(a) spiral image   (b) height function (c) geodesic distance

Fig. 2. Example images for the two Morse functions: the height function is computed top-down, the seed point for the geodesic distance is in the center of the topmost pixel line of the foreground. Red indicates high function values, blue low function values.

changes. At regular points the topology remains unchanged. Edges connecting critical points describe topological persistence.

A point (a, b) of a function $f(x, y)$ is called a *critical point* if both derivatives $f_x(a, b)$ and $f_y(a, b)$ are equal 0 or if one of these partial derivatives does not exist. Such a critical point p is called degenerate if the determinant of the Hessian matrix at that point is zero, otherwise it is called non-degenerate (or Morse) critical point [14].

According to Morse theory Reeb graphs are defined in the continuous domain as follows:

A smooth, real-valued function $f : M \rightarrow \mathbb{R}$ is called a Morse function if it satisfies the following conditions for a manifold M with or without boundary:

- *M1*: all critical points of f are non-degenerate and lie inside M,
- *M2*: all critical points of f restricted to the boundary of M are non-degenerate,
- *M3*: for all pairs of distinct critical points p and q, $f(p) \neq f(q)$ must hold [4].

Although originally defined for the continuous domain, Reeb graphs have been extended to the discrete domain. For the definition of a discrete Reeb graph, we need to define connective point sets and level-set curves first:

- Two point sets are connected if there exists a pair of points (one point of each point set) with a distance between these two points below a fixed threshold.
- If all non-empty subsets of a point set, as well as its complements, are connected, such a point set is called *connective*.
- A group of points that have the same Morse function value and that form a connective point set, is called a *level-set curve* [16].

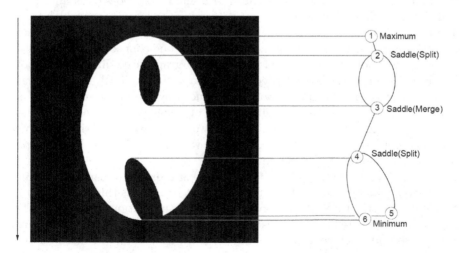

Fig. 3. Reeb graph according to height function and the geodesic distance (here they generate identical critical points), computed for the white foreground region

The nodes in a discrete Reeb graph represent level-set curves, the edges connect two adjacent level-set curves, therefore the underlying point sets are connected [16].

In 2D three types of nodes in a Reeb graph correspond to critical points: minima, maxima or saddles [4]. We will further distinguish saddle nodes of type split (increase in the number of connected components) and merge (reduction in the number of connected components). Minimum and maximum nodes are of degree 1 (one adjacent node in the graph), saddle nodes are of degree 3 (3 adjacent nodes in the graph). An example Reeb graph containing all possible types of nodes is shown in Figure 3. The nodes in this graph correspond to the critical points of two Morse functions: the height function as well as the geodesic distance both result in this set of nodes.

4   Reeb Graphs in Plant Phenotyping

The methods presented in this section requires a pre-segmented image as an input. Therefore an image segmentation is done as a first pre-processing step. The segmentation is based on the approach presented by Slovak et al. [13]. The transition between shoots and roots is found based on the color information.

The Reeb graphs are computed for the segmented images based on the geodesic distance inside the region of the root (foreground). For each foreground pixel the distance to one predefined source pixel is computed as the chessboard distance. This source pixel is located at the transition between shoots and roots, therefore at the top of the root. Thus, there is only one node of type maximum in a Reeb graph based on the geodesic distance which is the source pixel. Minimum nodes (root tips) are found as the position of a maximal geodesic distance in a branch (local maxima). Saddle points are determined as locations at which foreground parts with the same geodesic distance to the source pixel are split in two connected components or are merged from two into one connected component.

he so found nodes are connected in the Reeb graph according to the root region. For the root dataset evaluated in this paper, a modified approach was used to connect the nodes. Due to noise introduced by the image segmentation the roots of this dataset show a high number of nodes (for example 56 nodes for the root in Figure 6). As in this dataset we only deal with primary roots and lateral roots that do not further branch, we can modify the Reeb graph computation as described in Algorithm 1.

For two nodes (accordingly two critical points) at the same distance (the same Morse function value) a unique Reeb graph cannot be built as this configuration contradicts condition three of the conditions of Morse functions (condition $M3$ in Section 3). Therefore for two nodes at the same geodesic distance (chessboard distance) a second distance measurement, the Euclidean distance is used for the decision.

Algorithm 1. Reeb graph computation

---

connect maximum node to the split saddle node of the smallest geodesic distance
for each split saddle node **do**
    look for closest split node in each branch (s_1, s_2);
    look for most distant minimum node in each branch (m_1, m_2);
    if $m_1 < m_2$ **then**
        connect current split saddle node s_c to m_1 and s_2.
        if distance between s_c and m_1 < 10 pixel **then**
            discard connection again.
        end if
    else
        connect current split saddle node s_c to m_2 and s_1.
        if distance between s_c and m_2 < 10 pixel **then**
            discard connection again.
        end if
    end if
end for

The approach described in Algorithm 1 results in a graph for which every minimum node (root tips) represents the end point of a lateral root, respectively the primary root and every saddle node of type split represents the start point of a lateral root. The maximum node represents the start point of the root.

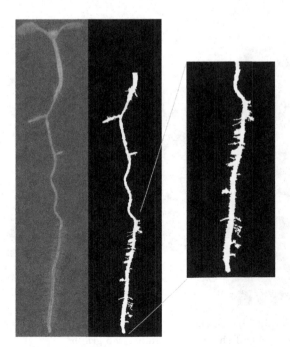

Fig. 4. Segmentation artefacts due to root hairs

Based on a such a Reeb graph the measurements described in Section 2 can be done based on the geodesic distance values of the individual nodes. The segmentation that is done as pre-processing step introduces artefacts as for example frayed borders (see Figure 4). For these artefacts spurious branches (additional lateral roots) may be added to the graph. Therefore a simple graph pruning is used and branches that are shorter than 10 pixels are discarded. This length was determined empirically to minimize the number of discarded true branches (false negatives) as well as the number of accepted false branches (false positives).

An example for such a Reeb graph computed on a root image is shown in Figure 6 in Section 5.

The Reeb graph based approach as presented above provides some advantages when compared to a medial axis based representation:

– Detection of Overlaps:
  Due to the projection of the 3D root shape to a 2D image, roots of one plant may overlap in the image. In a graph such an overlap introduces a cycle. For a cycle in the graph a saddle node of type merge is introduced in the Reeb graph (see node number 3 in Figure 3). Based on this particular node, the overlap can be automatically detected in a Reeb graph. To resolve such an overlap, the merge node can be doubled and each node can be connected to one of the adjacent nodes at higher distances. For correct connections the continuity of the direction of growth of a root can be considered. Figure 5 shows an example image (from a different dataset) for such an overlap, the merge node is highlighted in red.

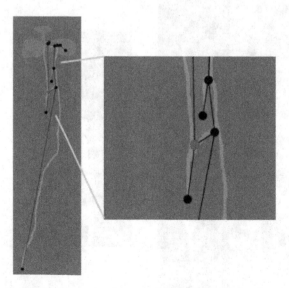

Fig. 5. An overlap of branches in the root image introduces a cycle in the graph and therefore a merge node (highlighted in red) in a Reeb graph

For a medial axis based graph an overlap is not detected automatically. It may be found looking for cycles in the graph. Since the medial axis has no explicit start point of the root, there is no order induced by distances from the start point. Consequently the crossing of two root branches cannot be resolved as simple as in the Reeb graph.

– Length Measurement:
For a Reeb graph based on a geodesic distance with the source pixel located at the transition between shoots and roots, the geodesic distance provides an implicit measurement of length. The geodesic distance for an endpoint of a root (a minimum node in the Reeb graph) correlates with the length (in pixels) between the source point and this endpoint. Therefore the length between the top of the root and a tip of the root can be easily measured. In the same way the length of lateral roots can be measured as the length between the corresponding saddle node (branching point) and the minimum node (tip of root) which is the difference of their distances to the source pixel.

Such a measurement is not implicitly given by a medial axis based representation, but needs to be computed based on the skeleton. Here the length can be obtained as the number of skeleton pixels between two nodes. A weighted approach (as for example discussed in [15]) that considers different weights for 4- and 8-connected pixels may further be used for a better approximation of the actual root length.

– Analysis of Root Structure:
Due to the different types of nodes in a Reeb graph, numbers of lateral roots can be counted simply as the number of minimum nodes in the graph. Furthermore locations of branches can be easily found as they are represented by saddle nodes of type split.

5   Results on the Dataset

For the evaluation of the approach introduced in Section 4 the method presented is tested on the dataset described in Section 2. For this data ground truth measurements are available and are compared with the results obtained by the Reeb graphs. A subset of 66 of the 160 plants in the dataset was used for the evaluation. For the rest of the dataset the image segmentation was either not available or the quality of the segmentation was too low (for example the primary root was not segmented as foreground in the segmentation image). Therefore these images could not be used in the evaluation of the presented approach.

Figure 6 shows an example for a Reeb graph computed on a root image of the dataset. The branching points indicating the branching positions of lateral roots as well as the tips of the individual roots are represented by nodes in the graph while the edges represent the root structure. According to the ground truth this root has eight lateral roots, the Reeb graph based approach detects

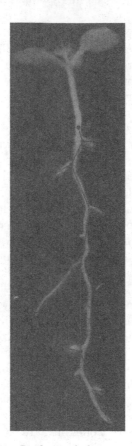

Fig. 6. Resulting Reeb graph for root 29_06 on day 10

six lateral roots only, as the two additional roots are too short. Therefore they are discarded as spurious branches.

The number of lateral roots can be determined based on the number of nodes representing branching points or on the number of nodes representing root tips. For the Reeb graph based on the geodesic distance measurements of length can be computed directly on the Morse function value as the geodesic distance with the source pixel set to the start of the root (at the transition between roots and shoots) measures the distance inside the root region to this source pixel. This distance corresponds to the intrinsic length in pixel between the top of the root and any position along the root. When measuring the length of roots one possible option is to measure the Euclidean distance between the start point of the root (top of root or branching point for lateral roots) and the endpoint of the root (tip of the root). However, for the Euclidean distance curvature of the root is not taken into account. For the geodesic distance the length is measure inside the root region, and curvature is included in the length. Therefore the geodesic distance measurement approximates the actual root length better.

Table 1. Comparison of average measurements according to ground truth and to Reeb graphs for the subset of 66 plants of the dataset described in Section 2. The mean deviation of the Reeb graph measurements from the ground truth is shown as well. The abbreviations of the measured characteristics are described in Section 2.

Comparison of Measurements - Dataset			
Characteristic	Average Ground Truth	Average Reeb Graph	Mean Deviation from GT
P1 in mm	17.0416	17.2670	0.6893
P in mm	21.7741	23.0805	1.8149
LR#	7 (7.4545)	7 (7.3333)	2 (1.7880)
R in mm	11.2849	12.4798	2.6220
LRl in mm	0.8631	0.6582	0.2902

For the root images of the dataset evaluated in this paper, a ruler was imaged with the plants to use as a reference measurement. Therefore the computed geodesic distances in pixels were converted to millimeters to compare them to the ground truth measurements.

Table 1 shows an overview of the Reeb graph based measurements compared to the ground truth. While Table 2 shows detailed results for a selection of eight root images of the dataset and the corresponding ground truth. The measurements shown in these tables are:

- **P1:** length of primary root on day 7
- **P:** length of primary root on day 10
- **LR#:** number of lateral roots on day 10
- **R:** length of primary root between first and last lateral root on day 10
- **LRl:** average length of lateral roots on day 10

In general, the length measured for the primary roots according to the Reeb graphs is longer than the ground truth length. The ground truth measurements were done manually by drawing on the root image, while the Reeb graph measurements are based on the geodesic distance (from an automatically detected start point) measured on a segmented image. Differences in the measured length may therefore arise due to the position of the automatically (based on color information) detected start point and due to the image segmentation. The average length measurements for the set of 66 plant images in Table 1 show that the Reeb graph based measurements approximate the ground truth measurements for day 7 well (difference of 0,23mm). The difference in the measurements for day 10 is larger (difference of 1,31mm). As the length according to the Reeb graph representation is measured as the geodesic distance between the top of the root and the tip of the root, curvature is taken into account by this measurement. The roots on day 7 grow in a mainly vertical direction. The older roots on day 10 show more deviation from the vertical direction of growth, they are more likely to bend. As this length due to bending is directly captured by the geodesic distance, the lengths obtained by this measurement are in general longer.

While the automatically measured lengths of the primary roots match the ground truth well, the other characteristics such as the number of lateral roots or

Table 2. Comparison of individual measurements according to ground truth and to Reeb graphs for eight plants of the dataset described in Section 2

Comparison of Measurements - Individual Plants						
Root	Type	P1 in mm	P in mm	LR#	R in mm	LRl in mm
29_04	GT	17.6445	18.0255	9	15.0199	0.4929
	RG	17.8814	18.0297	5	10.9534	0.3771
29_05	GT	17.6670	18.1525	9	16.9672	0.6830
	RG	18.2839	18.6017	8	16.6525	0.4396
29_06	GT	11.7433	11.5993	8	10.9051	0.8901
	RG	12.8602	12.5000	6	10.4873	0.7521
29_07	GT	12.8270	13.0810	9	12.4460	0.6670
	RG	12.2034	13.3729	8	11.2288	0.6674
29_11	GT	20.3030	21.0058	10	18.6270	0.7612
	RG	20.8475	23.1992	8	14.9364	0.5826
29_14	GT	17.1027	17.7546	9	14.2071	0.8852
	RG	18.4958	18.6017	8	14.6186	0.5244
29_19	GT	21.5053	21.8101	14	18.3642	0.5056
	RG	21.3347	20.0847	11	15.2331	0.5104
29_20	GT	27.4320	27.3558	15	21.8863	0.5904
	RG	26.5890	25.6992	10	17.0339	0.4788

the average length of the lateral roots vary from ground truth to Reeb graph measurements. This difference in the measurements is based on the pre-processing steps needed for the automatic Reeb graph analysis. The ground truth measurements were done on the original root image, while the Reeb graph measurements were done on a segmented image. Lateral roots may be missing in this segmentation, just as segmentation artefacts may be classified as lateral roots. Especially root hairs introduce segmentation artefacts, that resemble small lateral roots and that may be mistaken as roots in the Reeb graph approach. Because of segmentation artefacts, a graph pruning approach was applied to discard small spurious branches. True lateral roots may be discarded by this procedure in case they resemble spurious branches (length shorter than 10 pixels).

Table 2 shows detailed individual results for eight plants to provide a direct comparison of ground truth and Reeb graph based measurements. For each of the four genotypes in the dataset two plants were selected for this subset and all eight plants were grown on the same plate (with IAA and CK treatment). Plant 04 and 05 are of type Bch-1, plant 06 and 07 of type Fei-0, plant 11 and 14 are of type Col-0 and plant 19 and 20 are of type Lan.

In case a shorter length is measured for the primary root on day 10 compared to day 7 (as it is for example the case for plant 20 in Table 2), this is a measurement error, due to differently detected start points of the roots on these two days.

As shown for the overall results of the dataset, the length measurements for the primary roots based on the Reeb graphs approximate the human ground truth. The number of lateral roots in the ground truth and the Reeb graph representations differ for all of these eight plants. This is caused by the image segmentation and graph pruning needed for the Reeb graph based approach.

6 Conclusion

The approach presented in this paper builds a Reeb graph representation based on the geodesic distance for a pre-segmented root image. Measurements regarding lengths or numbers of roots can be derived directly from the graph. Which is not as easily possible for a medial axis approach, as distances between nodes are not stored as function values in a medial axis representation. Another advantage of Reeb graphs is the automatic detection of overlapping branches in the root image, as such an overlap introduces a cycle in the graph and therefore a particular node in a Reeb graph.

However, a Reeb graph representation, as well as a medial axis representation uses a segmented image as its input. The segmentation that is done as a pre-processing step is on the one hand likely to introduce noise and artefacts which may be represented as root structure in the graphs. On the other hand actual parts of the root may be lost during the segmentation process. The quality of a graph representation based on a segmented image depends on the segmentation. Reeb graphs just as well as medial axis representations need a segmentation that does not introduce noise and segmentation artefacts as frayed borders, that resemble small branches of the roots.

Graph representations are suitable for branching structures as roots. Especially Reeb graphs are able to capture the characteristics needed for phenotyping of plants. However the true bottleneck of such an approach is the segmentation. The graph representation can only provide reliable results for a correct segmentation.

Acknowledgments. We thank the anonymous reviewers for their constructive comments.

References

1. Biasotti, S., Giorgi, D., Spagnuolo, M., Falcidieno, B.: Reeb graphs for shape analysis and applications. Theoretical Computer Science **392**(1–3), 5–22 (2008)
2. Blum, H.: A Transformation for Extracting New Descriptors of Shape. In: Wathen-Dunn, W. (ed.) Models for the Perception of Speech and Visual Form, pp. 362–380. MIT Press, Cambridge (1967)
3. Bott, R.: Lectures on Morse theory, old and new. Bulletin of the American Mathematical Society **7**(2), 331–358 (1982)
4. Doraiswamy, H., Natarajan, V.: Efficient algorithms for computing Reeb graphs. Computational Geometry **42**(6–7), 606–616 (2009)
5. EL Khoury, R., Vandeborre, J.P., Daoudi, M.: 3D mesh Reeb graph computation using commute-time and diffusion distances. In: Proceedings SPIE: Three-Dimensional Image Processing (3DIP) and Applications II. vol. 8290, pp. 82900H–82900H-10 (2012)

6. Galkovskyi, T., Mileyko, Y., Bucksch, A., Moore, B., Symonova, O., Price, C., Topp, C., Iyer-Pascuzzi, A., Zurek, P., Fang, S., Harer, J., Benfey, P., Weitz, J.: GiA roots: software for the high throughput analysis of plant root system architecture. BMC Plant Biology **12**(1), 116 (2012)
7. Hayashi, M., Nishimura, M.: Arabidopsis thaliana - a model organism to study plant peroxisomes. Biochimica et Biophysica Acta (BBA) - Molecular. Cell Research **1763**(12), 1382–1391 (2006)
8. Iyer-Pascuzzi, A.S., Symonova, O., Mileyko, Y., Hao, Y., Belcher, H., Harer, J., Weitz, J.S., Benfey, P.N.: Imaging and analysis platform for automatic phenotyping and trait ranking of plant root systems. Plant Physiology **152**(3), 1148–1157 (2010)
9. Janusch, I., Kropatsch, W.G., Busch, W.: Reeb graph based examination of root development. In: Proceedings of the 19th Computer Vision Winter Workshop, pp. 43–50 (Febraury 2014)
10. Lee, D.T.: Medial axis transformation of a planar shape. IEEE Transactions on Pattern Analysis and Machine Intelligence. **PAMI**–4(4), 363–369 (1982)
11. Leitner, D., Felderer, B., Vontobel, P., Schnepf, A.: Recovering root system traits using image analysis exemplified by two-dimensional neutron radiography images of lupine. Plant Physiology **164**(1), 24–35 (2014)
12. Ristova, D., Rosas, U., Krouk, G., Ruffel, S., Birnbaum, K.D., Coruzzi, G.M.: Rootscape: A landmark-based system for rapid screening of root architecture in arabidopsis. Plant Physiology **161**(3), 1086–1096 (2013)
13. Slovak, R., Göschl, C., Su, X., Shimotani, K., Shiina, T., Busch, W.: A scalable open-source pipeline for large-scale root phenotyping of Arabidopsis. The Plant Cell Online (2014)
14. Stewart, J.: Calculus. Cengage Learning Emea, 6th edition. international met edn (February 2008)
15. Vossepoel, A., Smeulders, A.: Vector code probability and metrication error in the representation of straight lines of finite length. Computer Graphics and Image Processing **20**(4), 347–364 (1982)
16. Werghi, N., Xiao, Y., Siebert, J.: A functional-based segmentation of human body scans in arbitrary postures. IEEE Transactions on Systems, Man, and Cybernetics, Part B: Cybernetics **36**(1), 153–165 (2006)

Visual Object Tracking for the Extraction of Multiple Interacting Plant Root Systems

Stefan Mairhofer[1,3]([✉]), Craig J. Sturrock[1,2], Malcolm J. Bennett[1,2], Sacha J. Mooney[1,2], and Tony P. Pridmore[1,3]

[1] Centre for Plant Integrative Biology, University of Nottingham, Nottingham, UK
stefan.mairhofer@nottingham.ac.uk
[2] School of Biosciences, University of Nottingham, Nottingham LE12 5RD, UK
[3] School of Computer Science, University of Nottingham, Nottingham NG8 1BB, UK

Abstract. We propose a visual object tracking framework for the extraction of multiple interacting plant root systems from three-dimensional X-ray micro computed tomography images of plants grown in soil. Our method is based on a level set framework guided by a greyscale intensity distribution model to identify object boundaries in image cross-sections. Root objects are followed through the data volume, while updating the tracker's appearance models to adapt to changing intensity values. In the presence of multiple root systems, multiple trackers can be used, but need to distinguish target objects from one another in order to correctly associate roots with their originating plants. Since root objects are expected to exhibit similar greyscale intensity distributions, shape information is used to constrain the evolving level set interfaces in order to lock trackers to their correct targets. The proposed method is tested on root systems of wheat plants grown in soil.

Keywords: Multiple object tracking · Root system recovery · Plant interaction · X-ray micro computed tomography

1 Introduction

Image analysis methods have become an inherent part of many plant biological studies, assisting researchers in extracting and processing information implicit in collected image data. The focus can vary from specific plant organs [6, 22] to whole individual plants [3]. In this work we are interested in the below-ground portion of the plant, its root system. It has been shown that plants rely on their roots for water and nutrient uptake, which largely determine their performance and development [15]. We focus on the analysis of multiple interacting plants, as their root systems can facilitate either cooperative or competitive interactions. This is provided, for instance, by influencing the composition of the bacterial flora in the rhizosphere, which may positively affect the nutrient availability, or by competing for (limited) resources [26].

When roots are to be examined, they are usually either destructively removed from their environment [31] or grown in artificial media [5], which may alter their

© Springer International Publishing Switzerland 2015
L. Agapito et al. (Eds.): ECCV 2014 Workshops, Part IV, LNCS 8928, pp. 89–104, 2015.
DOI: 10.1007/978-3-319-16220-1_7

natural growth behaviour due to the lack of complex biological, chemical and physical properties usually found in soil [10]. An alternative solution that allows roots to be imaged in soil is given by X-ray micro computed tomography (μCT), which is becoming increasingly accessible [19]. An additional advantage to its non-disruptive characteristic [35] is the acquisition of three-dimensional volumetric image data, which allows a more accurate quantification of root system traits. Plant root systems are complex, highly branched structures, composed of many individual roots of varying size. Recovering the fine and complex structure from μCT image data presents a challenging problem in image analysis. The process is complicated by the highly heterogeneous growth environment, composed of minerals, soil particles, organic matter, water and air filled pores.

In this work we present a visual object tracking framework that allows the extraction of interacting plant root systems from their soil environment. A given data volume can be horizontally sliced into thin cross-sections to obtain a stack of images. Using a level set method guided by a greyscale intensity distribution model, it is possible to **identify the boundaries of root cross-sections** in each image. When traversing these images in sequence, root objects will appear at slightly different positions due to the root's slanted growth through the soil environment. The architectural structure of plant root systems is found by **following individual root cross-sections** through a sequence of image slices. This is achieved using an adaptive appearance model of the target and readjusting the interface of the level set function to the new location and outline of the root object. In the presence of multiple root systems, multiple trackers can be used but **root cross-sections need to be distinguished from one another** in order to allow the correct labelling of different plants. However, because all root objects are likely to have similar greyscale intensity values, their appearance models can be expected to be similar or even identical. If two or more independently tracked targets interact, their trackers can easily drift away to the object that best fits the model [12]. This can often result in an uncontrolled behaviour in which trackers switch their targets or trackers follow the same target while losing hold of others. In case of root extraction, this can lead to root cross-sections being assigned to incorrect root systems. To address the problem, a shape constraint is added to the evolving interface of the level set function during the period of target interaction.

In what follows we give a brief overview of related work on the extraction of root-structure-like networks with focus on X-ray CT (Section 2) and give a detailed description of our proposed method (Section 3). The extraction method is first applied to volume data of individual and then of multiple interacting root systems of winter wheat Cordiale (*Triticumaestivum L.*) (Section 4), followed by discussion and conclusions (Section 5).

2   Related Work

Using a high energy X-ray CT scanner, Heeraman et al. [9] endeavoured to image and quantify the root system of plants grown in sand culture. With this they were

among the first who showed that roots can be separated from non-root material
on a computational basis and not just by human assumption of the presence of
roots. A number of voxels were manually selected to define groups of different
components (air, roots, sand). These were tested for normality and used to sta-
tistically classify the remaining voxels to one of these groups. The method does
not guarantee connectivity and outlier voxels can easily be assigned to incorrect
components. Seeking to advance imaging and analysis procedures, Lontoc-Roy
et al. [14] presented methods and results obtained using X-ray CT for soil-root
studies. Roots were segmented from the images by choosing visually a lower
and upper threshold value. The resulting segmentation included primarily larger
roots. In a second step, an iterative three-dimensional region growing method
was used, appending voxels that are connected to the initial extraction, but
which also fall within a second, wider, threshold boundary. A similar approach
is reported by Perret et al. [20]. To extract the root system from the growth
media, a predefined threshold boundary was applied after which a 26-neighbour
connectivity constraint was imposed. While this guarantees connectivity of the
root system, thresholding only gives satisfactory results if the greyscale values of
different components do not overlap, in our experience this is often not the case.
In the work presented by Pierret et al. [21], image slices were first segmented
using a combination of thresholding and a top-hat filter [18]. By superimposing
two consecutive images, extracted root cross-sections were tested for continuity
while roughly defining the roots' skeleton. Since elliptical objects were prone
to artefacts, they were ignored in the analysis, which had the disadvantage of
missing out horizontally growing roots. The authors were aware of this limitation, but considered it a reasonable compromise, leaving the method useful
for preliminary investigations. Quantification was made based on the extracted
skeletons. To overcome the limitation of thresholding for overlapping greyscale
intensity distributions, Kaestner et al. [11] applied a non-linear diffusion filter
multiple times with different parameters to smooth out the texture of the sand
matrix. As a result, the intensity distribution of root material was shifted to the
tail of the sand distribution, making Rosin's unimodal thresholding algorithm
applicable [24]. To remove misclassified voxels, a dilation by reconstruction operation [33] was applied to eliminate speckles while at the same time preserving
thin root segments and enforcing connectivity of the root system. Filtering the
data does not always result in the distribution of root material being shifted to
the tail of the background distribution. The effect depends on the condition and
composition of the soil matrix. Even though the methods presented by Pierret
et al. [21] and Kaestner et al. [11] make use of thresholding to perform an initial crude segmentation, additional rules are applied to help decide whether an
extracted object reflects the characteristics of a root segment.

Using an electron beam X-ray CT scanner, Sonka et al. [30] presented in
their work a method able to identify airway trees in lungs, which, compared
to plant root systems, share a similar structure. Analogous to the method presented by Lontoc-Roy et al. [14], a conservative threshold was chosen for a three-
dimensional region-growing to recover the primary tree of the airway structure
without the fine segments of smaller diameter. To enhance the fine details of

small airways, the image was scaled by a factor of 2 and enhanced using a top hat transform [29]. Using edge-based region-growing, the enhanced image was segmented into airways, vessels and background corresponding to dark, bright and intermediate greyscale values. A rule-based analysis using prior knowledge of the anatomical structure of airways and their relationship with pulmonary vascular trees, was used to refine the segmentation. Although prior knowledge of root system structures could be useful in their recovery, linking root segments to their environment is not straightforward. An alternative method for the extraction of airways from electron beam X-ray CT image data, was presented by Aykac et al. [1], whose method is based on mathematical morphology which was also a key component in Kaestner et al.'s presented method [11]. A greyscale morphological reconstruction was used to identify local minima in cross-sectional images, which correspond to potentially fine airway segments. The image was then thresholded using a relative value that lies between the minimum and maximum greyscale values. This process was repeated a number of times using different sized morphological structure elements. The union of all candidate regions found were used for reconstructing the airway tree. While using morphological operations can enhance fine details in the image data, it cannot completely overcome the limitations of threshold based segmentation. In addition to methods based on region growing [30] or mathematical morphology [1], solutions were proposed that use a tracing strategy [32].

This was also found to be successful in the extraction of three-dimensional and root-structure-like networks outside of X-ray CT imaging. Flasque et al. [7] for instance, used magnetic resonance angiography (MRA) for imaging cerebral blood vessels and developed a centreline tracing based method for their extraction. The centreline was traced stepwise, with successive points being estimated by searching within an orientated parallelepiped around previously identified points. Rules, like the definition of a maximum allowed curvature, were imposed for each search area. Such a rule-based concept allows the specification of a profile that is based on prior knowledge. To deal with the detection of junctions or branches, the number of entry and exit points along the surface of each parallelepiped is noted. By the definition of a continuous vessel, a parallelepiped must have exactly one entry and exit point. If more than one exit point is detected, then the presence of a junction is assumed, for which a new starting point is created. In a final step, all traced centreline points are connected using B-spline curves. A common problem when tracing centrelines is the possibility of loops being formed due to interactions with other vessels or irregularities in the image data. An alternative approach was presented by Wilson and Noble [34]. To extract the vascular network from the image data, an adaptive expectation maximization (EM) algorithm was presented that recursively divides the volume into smaller sub-volumes on which a localised segmentation was performed. The identified parameters for the distributions within a sub-volume, give indications of which tissues are present, and as such 'special' cases were applied for the classification of voxels. Variation in signal intensity is only expected for arteries, but not for the cerebrospinal fluid and brain tissue. In this the data differs from soil-root samples, where the soil environment is found to be highly hetero-geneous. Other complex root-structure-like networks are found, for instance, in neuronal arborescences [17].

3   Method

In this section we give a detailed description of the proposed extraction tech-nique, beginning with the extraction of a single individual root system, assuming that all root cross-sections belong to the same plant. We introduce each of the components and how they are integrated into the tracking framework. A collision detection mechanism is then added to identify the interaction of multiple tar-gets, to which a shape constraint is imposed, allowing the extraction of multiple interacting plant root systems. The objectives of the work reported here are to:

- identify the boundaries of root cross-sections
- track individual root cross-sections
- keep root cross-sections arising from different plants separate

3.1   Object Boundary Detection

We adopt the level set framework [28] to search for the boundaries of root cross-sections. We aim at finding the interface

$$C\left(t\right) = \left\{ \left(x, y\right) \middle| \varPhi_{x,y,t} = 0 \right\}$$ (1)

of a time-dependent function $\varPhi_{x,y,t}$ that separates an object consisting of compa-rable intensity values from its heterogeneous background. The interface of $\varPhi_{x,y,t}$ can be implicitly propagated solving a partial differential equation

$$\frac{\partial \varPhi_{x,y,t}}{\partial t} + F\left|\nabla \varPhi_{x,y,t}\right| = 0$$ (2)

which can be approximated and rewritten using a finite forward difference scheme in time

$$\frac{\varPhi_{x,y}^{t+1} - \varPhi_{x,y}^{t}}{\Delta t} + F\left|\nabla_{x,y}\varPhi_{x,y}^{t}\right| = 0$$ (3)

giving a general formulation of the time-discretized level set method, with F being a speed function that defines the motion of the front over time t. One possible way to find the boundary of an arbitrary object is to define a speed function that stops at high image gradients. A solution based on the formula-tion presented in [16] was tested, but failed to correctly identify root objects: blurred and low contrast boundaries are common in CT data. A solution is there-fore proposed that evolves a level set function guided by a greyscale intensity distribution model. Assuming we have the greyscale intensity values of a known root object, we use a kernel density estimator to build a statistical probability density function, which we will refer to as our root appearance model p_m

$$p_m(x) = \frac{1}{nh} \sum_{i=0}^{n} K\left(\frac{x - x(i)}{h}\right) \qquad (4)$$

where n is the number of data points, h the bandwidth and K a Gaussian smoothing kernel $K(x) = \frac{1}{\sqrt{2\pi}} e^{-\frac{1}{2}x^2}$. Using the Jensen-Shannon (JS) divergence [13] as given in Equation 5, we compute the distance between a probability density function p_f estimated around the interface of the level set function and our known root model p_m.

$$JS(p_f, p_m) = H(w_1 p_f + w_2 p_m) - w_1 H(p_f) - w_2 H(p_m) \qquad (5)$$

where H is the Shannon entropy function and calculated as in Equation 6. w_1 and w_2 are two weighting parameters $w_1, w_2 \geq 0, w_1 + w_2 = 1$ to balance the contribution of the two statistical probability density functions and useful for conditional probability studies where the weighting parameters represent prior probabilities. In our case, however, we set $w_1 = w_2 = 0.5$.

$$H(p) = -\sum_{i=0}^{n} p_i \, log_b(p_i) \qquad (6)$$

The JS divergence is a non-negative and symmetric dissimilarity measure, bounded by $[0, log_b 2]$. Using a logarithm of base 2 results in a distance that is measured within $[0, 1]$, where 0 is considered a complete match between two probability density functions. The higher the value of the JS divergence the lower is the probability that the data come from the same distribution. These and the fact that the dissimilarity measure is not constrained by the number of samples and their shape of the distribution, makes the JS divergence a good choice in our application. Given the above definitions, we can now build them into a level set framework

$$\Phi_{x,y}^{t+1} = \Phi_{x,y}^{t} + \Delta t \left[-(\alpha) \left(JS_{\beta\vee} \nabla^+ + JS_{\beta\wedge} \nabla^- \right) + (1-\alpha)(\kappa) \right] \qquad (7)$$

where $JS_{\beta\vee} = max(\lceil \beta - JS \rceil, 0)$ and $JS_{\beta\wedge} = min(\lfloor \beta - JS \rfloor, 0)$ are the propagation forces, with $\beta \in [0, 1]$ defining the acceptance distance of the JS divergence between model and data distribution. $\alpha \in [0, 1]$ is a weighting parameter between the propagation force and the curvature dependency $\kappa = \nabla \cdot \frac{\nabla \Phi_{x,y}^t}{|\nabla \Phi_{x,y}^t|}$ of the front. The numerical solution requires choosing the correct difference scheme that propagates information in the direction upwind to the moving interface. This is achieved through $\nabla^+ = \sqrt{max(D^{-x,y}, 0)^2 + min(D^{+x,y}, 0)^2}$ in case of an expanding force and similarly through $\nabla^- = \sqrt{max(D^{+x,y}, 0)^2 + min(D^{-x,y}, 0)^2}$ for a contracting force, where $D^{+x} = \frac{\Phi_{x+\Delta x, y, t} - \Phi_{x,y,t}}{\Delta x}$ is the forward difference operator and $D^{-x} = \frac{\Phi_{x,y,t} - \Phi_{x-\Delta x, y, t}}{\Delta x}$ the backward difference operator. The level set framework is implemented using the narrow band strategy [4] for increased efficiency and the fast sweeping method [36] for re-initialisation. Figure 1 shows a cross-sectional image in which root objects are identified and separated from their complex and heterogeneous soil environment using the above described method.

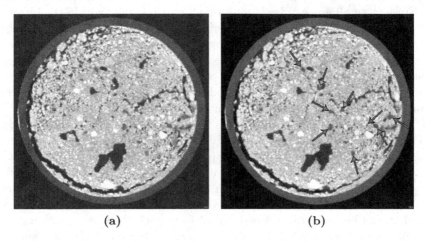

Fig. 1. Cross-sectional image of (a) raw data and (b) with identified root objects

3.2   Tracking Root Objects

Target objects are selected for tracking by the user manually setting seed points in the first (top) image in the stack. An initial root appearance model is built for each target from the greyscale intensity values within a 5 pixel radius. The seed points also mark the initial interface of the propagating level set function, which is evolved until the root object boundaries are identified. Since a level set function can implicitly represent multiple interfaces, a classical two-pass connected component algorithm [23] is used to assign a label to each object. Labels are propagated when constructing the narrow band around an interface and it is therefore possible to evolve the level set function using different appearance models for each root object. This means that we do not have a single model that represents all the root objects in a plant at the same time, but several models that are generated, each representing a single target (root segment).

Once the boundaries of root objects are identified, the aim is to track target objects through a sequence of horizontal slices, or images, thereby building up a three-dimensional segmentation of the root system. Due to the high resolution of X-ray μCT data, we assume that corresponding root locations in consecutive images partially overlap, and that their greyscale intensity distributions vary smoothly. Some variation is to be expected due to the heterogeneous environment of different density materials and unevenly distributed water content in the soil throughout the sample and the root system, which can vary the overall estimated attenuation of the voxel data. Therefore, as root objects are followed through the image sequence, their assigned root model distribution must be updated to adapt to their changing appearance. This is done by re-computing the root appearance model from the greyscale intensity values enclosed by each of the converged interfaces of the level set function.

Updating the root model is an inevitable step, yet it conceals potential problems. Noise or small areas of background might be included within the interface and so contribute to its probability density function. These errors can accumulate and result in a model that is no longer an appropriate representation of a tracked root object. Therefore, to reduce the potential of model drift, we use a complex Fourier shape descriptor [8] to compare the shape of a root object in pairs of consecutive images and only update the root appearance model when the sum of squared differences of their filtered and normalised power spectra is below a given threshold.

A root system is composed of several branching roots. Splitting of a root boundary as it branches throughout the image stack is implicitly dealt with by the level set's ability to adapt to changing topologies. As the level set interface evolves from one state to another it can split into multiple disjoint interfaces. When a target object separates, the level set evolves based on the same root model, but will become two independent objects with their own updating root appearance model after proceeding to the next image slice. Figure 2 shows a sequence of cross-sectional images in which root objects are followed.

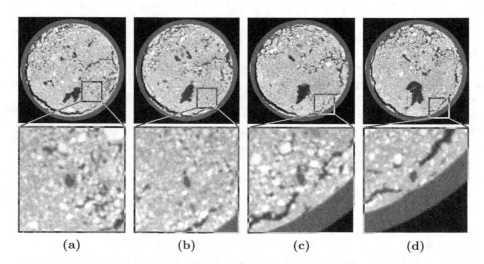

(a)   (b)   (c)   (d)

Fig. 2. Sequence of cross-sectional images with target objects highlighted and followed shown at an interval of every 40 image slices

3.3 Multiple Interacting Objects

To extract multiple root systems, a level set tracker is initialised to each plant and their level set functions evolved simultaneously. In this work we adopt the concept of multiple level set functions as presented in [27]. Let Φ_A^t and Φ_B^t be two level set functions and their interfaces occupy two different regions at time step t. The level set functions evolve separately, based on their individual root appearance models, resulting in a temporary state of Φ_A^* and Φ_B^*. Φ_A^* and Φ_B^* are then combined to obtain the level set functions Φ_A^{t+1} and Φ_B^{t+1} at time $t+1$. The combination of the temporary level set functions depends on whether or not the interface of A can penetrate the interface of B, or vice versa, and as such pushes back the adjacent interface. Assuming that A can penetrate B, but B cannot penetrate A, then the new level set function at time step $t+1$ will be updated accordingly:

$$\Phi_A^{t+1} = \Phi_A^*$$
$$\Phi_B^{t+1} = \max\left(\Phi_B^*, -\Phi_A^*\right) \tag{8}$$

This example should make it easy to understand how interacting level set fronts can be controlled and how this can be modified to define similar rules such that during an encounter of two level set fronts, neither is allowed to penetrate the other. This will stop them from advancing further and give an exact partition of the two regions at the front of collision. The mechanism of multiple fronts can be easily extended to any number of level set functions using the same principles of combination. Each evolving front in the set must be compared to all other level set functions of the same set. This easily allows identification of any collisions between interfaces and determination of which of the level set functions interact. Figure 3 shows three different scenarios where two level set functions (front A (red) and front B (blue)) are evolved until their fronts interact with each other, at which point different combination rules are applied. This is a key element in the extraction of multiple interacting root systems, but not sufficient to allow separation of interacting root systems. While the combination rules allow individual trackers to be separated, the true boundary between touching root cross-sections remains unknown. Although level set functions can penetrate each other's interface, there is no definition given yet of when these rules are to be applied. For this, shape information is used to estimate the boundary of root objects and so to find the intersecting front between them.

While tracking target objects through the image stack, their shape is noted and used to control appearance model updates. We can, therefore, easily recall an object's outline and store the most recent shape information before the interaction with other objects. This information is kept until the interaction ceases. Let $U = \{u_i | i = 1..N_u\}$ be a set of data points along the outline of a stored shape and $V = \{v_i | i = 1..N_v\}$ be a set of data points along a level set's interface. The rotation matrix $\mathbf{R}$ and the translation matrix $\mathbf{T}$ are sought to minimise the root mean squared distance between U and V and therefore to find the best alignment of the two point sets. This can be achieved using the iterative closest point (ICP) algorithm [2]. By calculating the centre of mass μ_u and μ_v of the two point clouds, it is possible to determine the cross-covariance matrix $cov_{uv} = \frac{1}{N_u}\sum_{i=1}^{N_u}[(u_i - \mu_u)(v_i - \mu_v)^\mathsf{T}]$ for U and V. Using the cyclic components $a = (A_{23}, A_{31}, A_{12})$ of a matrix $\mathbf{A} = cov_{uv} - cov_{uv}^\mathsf{T}$ allows the definition of a 4×4 matrix $\mathbf{Q}$

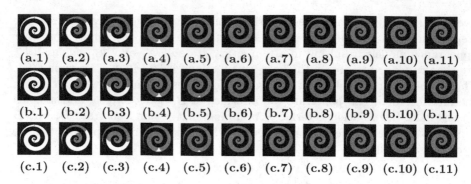

(a.1)   (a.2)   (a.3)   (a.4)   (a.5)   (a.6)   (a.7)   (a.8)   (a.9)   (a.10) (a.11)

(b.1)   (b.2)   (b.3)   (b.4)   (b.5)   (b.6)   (b.7)   (b.8)   (b.9)   (b.10) (b.11)

(c.1)   (c.2)   (c.3)   (c.4)   (c.5)   (c.6)   (c.7)   (c.8)   (c.9)   (c.10) (c.11)

Fig. 3. Two level set function A (red) and B (blue) interacting with each other, where (a) front A penetrates front B, (b) front B penetrates front A and (c) neither A or B is penetrated

$$\mathbf{Q}_{4\times4} = \begin{pmatrix} tr(cov_{uv}) & \boldsymbol{a}^{\mathsf{T}} \\ \boldsymbol{a} & cov_{uv} + cov_{uv}^{\mathsf{T}} - tr(cov_{uv})\mathbf{I}_3 \end{pmatrix} \tag{9}$$

The eigenvector $\boldsymbol{r} = (q_1 \quad q_2 \quad q_3 \quad q_4)$ of the matrix $\mathbf{Q}$ with the maximum eigenvalue is used to define the rotation matrix $\mathbf{R}$

$$\mathbf{R} = \begin{pmatrix} q_1^2 + q_2^2 - q_3^2 - q_4^2 & 2(q_2q_3 - q_1q_4) & 2(q_2q_4 + q_1q_3) & 0 \\ 2(q_2q_3 + q_1q_4) & q_1^2 + q_3^2 - q_2^2 - q_4^2 & 2(q_3q_4 - q_1q_2) & 0 \\ 2(q_2q_4 - q_1q_3) & 2(q_3q_4 + q_1q_2) & q_1^2 + q_4^2 - q_2^2 - q_3^2 & 0 \\ 0 & 0 & 0 & 1 \end{pmatrix} \tag{10}$$

The vector $\boldsymbol{t} = (\boldsymbol{\mu}_v - \mathbf{R}\boldsymbol{\mu}_u)$ is used to define the translation matrix $\mathbf{T}$

$$\mathbf{T} = \begin{pmatrix} 1 & 0 & 0 & t_1 \\ 0 & 1 & 0 & t_2 \\ 0 & 0 & 1 & t_3 \\ 0 & 0 & 0 & 1 \end{pmatrix} \tag{11}$$

The ICP algorithm is initialised by setting the rotation and translation matrices equal to the identity matrix $\mathbf{R} = \mathbf{T} = \mathbf{I}$ and begins by identifying for each point $\boldsymbol{u} \in U$ the best match with the shortest distance $d(\boldsymbol{u}, V) = min_{v \in V} \|\boldsymbol{v} - \boldsymbol{u}\|$. This step can be efficiently performed using a k-d tree [25]. With the set of matching pairs as input, the best registration is calculated using the quaternion-based least square method, determining $\mathbf{R}$ and $\mathbf{T}$ which are then applied to U. The whole process is repeated iteratively, finding new matching points and their transformation, until the change in mean squared error falls below a given threshold.

When the interfaces of two level set functions collide, and each is made impenetrable, race conditions are generated, as illustrated in Figure 4. This, however, can be solved using shape constraints. The ICP algorithm, as described above, is used to find the best alignment of the stored shape to the evolving interface. This leaves each point within the interface in one of two possible states: it is

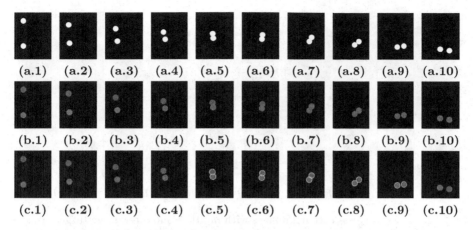

Fig. 4. Two colliding target objects; (a) raw data, (b) extracted using the conventional level set tracking approach and (c) combined with the ICP algorithm during the period of contact (5-9)

either outside or inside of its aligned region. Let $S = \{S_1..S_n\}$ be the enclosed areas of each aligned shape to its corresponding level set function, $L = \{\Phi_1..\Phi_n\}$ be the set of level set functions at time t and $L^* = \{\Phi_1^*..\Phi_n^*\}$ the set of their temporary states, then the final value of the level set function Φ_i^{t+1} at time step $t + 1$ and position p is updated accordingly

$$
\Phi_i^{t+1} = \begin{cases} \Phi_i^* & \text{if } (p \in S_i) \wedge (p \notin \{S \backslash S_i\}) \\ \max(\Phi_i^*, -\{L_j | p \in S_j\}) & \text{if } (p \in S_i) \wedge (p \cap \{S \backslash S_i\} \neq \emptyset) \\ \max(\Phi_i^*, -\{L^* \backslash \Phi_i^*\}) & \text{if } (p \cap S_i = \emptyset) \end{cases} \quad (12)
$$

A particular benefit of this solution is that, while it constrains the movement of the front, the selected root object is not required to maintain the registered shape. This allows the detection of lateral roots, since a level set function can still evolve beyond the aligned region. At the same time it prevents the path of a level set function being blocked by faster evolving level sets and allows their interface to be penetrated so that control over its target is maintained. The effect of adding shape constraints to the level set functions is illustrated in Figure 4. Figure 5 shows a sequence of images in which tracked root cross-sections interact with each other.

4   Experiment

Winter wheat Cordiale (*Triticumaestivum L.*) were grown in columns of 30mm and 60mm in diameter filled with soil. Two each of the four 30mm columns were filled with loamy sand and clay loam. The 60mm column was filled with loamy sand. The soil was air-dried and sieved to <2mm. The seeds were germinated in Petri dishes on wet filter papers, covered with an aluminium foil to shield them

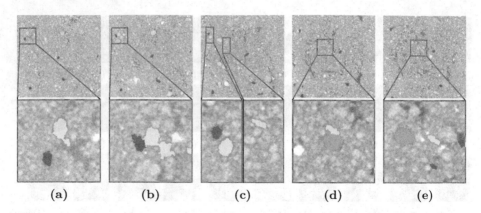

(a)   (b)   (c)   (d)   (e)

Fig. 5. Sequence of cross-sectional images with multiple and interacting target objects highlighted and followed shown at an interval of every 20-40 image slices

from sunlight, and planted after two days. A single seed was placed in each of the 30mm columns, while three seeds were placed 10mm to 15mm apart from each other in the 60mm column. The plants grew in environmental controlled growth rooms with 16/8 hours light cycle at a temperature of 23/18 degree Celsius and were scanned ten days after germination. The water status of the samples at the point of imaging was approximately at field capacity.

The imaging device used in this experiment was a Nanotom (Phoenix X-ray/GE Measurement & Control Systems) X-ray μCT scanner. The scan for the 30mm columns was performed at 120keV and 250μA, taking 1,200 projections at an exposure time of 750ms, using a signal averaging of 3 and 1 skipping per projection. A 0.1mm Cu filter was used to harden the beam. Samples were placed 200mm away from the X-ray gun, resulting in a volume with resolution of 25.0μm voxel size and an image stack of 1,400×1,400×2,200 voxels. The scan for the 60mm column was performed at 130keV and 200μA, taking 1440 projections at an exposure time of 1,000ms, using a signal averaging of 4 and 1 skipping per projection. A 0.2mm Cu filter was used to harden the beam. The sample was placed 220mm away from the X-ray gun, resulting in a volume with resolution of 27.5μm voxel size and an image stack of 2,100×2,100×2,260 voxels. The acquired volume data was saved to a stack of 8-bit images. The tracking framework proposed here was used to recover the root systems from the image data. Seed points were selected manually in the first image of each stack to mark target objects and to initialise separate trackers to each of the root systems.

Figure 6 shows the rendered images of the extracted root systems of the individually grown wheat plants. After scanning the samples with X-ray μCT, they were root-washed free of soil, placed on a water tray and imaged with a flatbed scanner at 400dpi. The two-dimensional images are shown as reference to the extracted data. The figures in comparison show that the overall architecture of the root systems has been captured successfully. It has been proven to be difficult to recover all of the fine lateral roots of the root system at this resolution

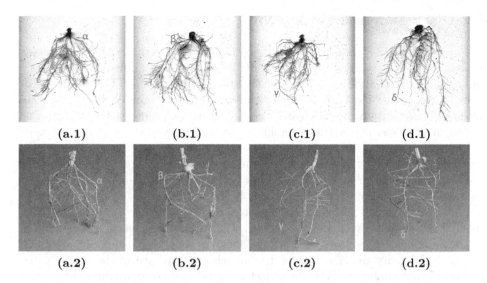

Fig. 6. Extracted root systems of wheat grown in (a-b) loamy sand and (c-d) clay loam, (x.1) imaged for comparison with a flatbed scanner and (x.2) the rendered root systems extracted from X-ray μCT data using α, β, γ and δ for alignment reference. The root systems in (x.1) once extracted from the soil, lost their three-dimensional geometry information, while still preserved in (x.2)

of scanning. While some might not be visible in the image data, due to their small size, others might be present, but not necessarily shown as connected due to disruptions caused by small image irregularities. The extracted root systems from the sample of multiple interacting plants are shown in Figure 7, highlighting each of the three root systems separately in a different colour.

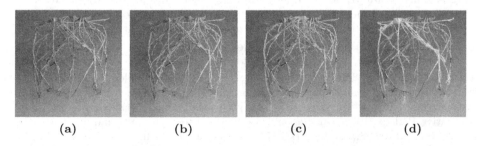

Fig. 7. Extracted root systems of multiple interacting wheat plants (a) all together, (b) highlighted first, (c) second and (d) third root system

5   Discussion and Conclusions

We have presented a visual object tracking framework for the extraction of plant root systems grown in soil from X-ray μCT volume data, allowing the recovery of both individual and multiple interacting plant root systems. The method proposed here uses a modified level set framework that is guided by a greyscale intensity distribution model to find the boundaries of root cross-sections. The appearance model is updated to adapt to variations in the greyscale intensity values of the target object. The interface of a level set function is continuously readjusted to locate the new position and outline of the target objects in subsequent images. After following root cross-sections through the image stack, the extracted information is used to reassemble the complete root system of a plant.

In the presence of multiple root systems, multiple trackers are deployed, but need to be able to keep their targets distinguished from each other. This is challenging since root cross-sections are likely to share similar, if not identical, greyscale intensity distributions and hence the appearance model used by the trackers is not enough to keep the objects separate. Shape constraints are therefore added when objects interact, and help lock the trackers to their correct targets.

The method proposed here was tested on root systems of winter wheat Cordiale (*Triticumaestivum L.*), using data showing individual as well as multiple interacting root systems. Results show that the proposed technique can successfully recover and separate plant roots from each other and therefore increase the likelihood of the assigned roots belonging to the originating plant.

As more mature plant root systems are examined, larger columns are needed to provide enough space for the root system to explore the soil environment. When using larger samples, scan resolution will be compromised, resulting in more disjoint root segments. While at present an adaptive appearance model is used by the tracking framework, its motion model is still very simplistic, relying on the assumption that root cross-section will partially overlap in consecutive images. This assumption might not hold if larger samples are used. Hence a more sophisticated motion model will be required. Another compromise in using larger sample sizes is that more fine lateral roots will become unidentifiable due to the reduction in resolution. These issues will be the subject of future reports.

Acknowledgments. This work was supported by Biotechnology and Biological Sciences Research Council and Engineering and Physical Sciences Research Council Centre for Integrative Systems Biology program funding to the Centre for Plant Integrative Biology; European Research Council Advanced Grant funding to M.J.B., T.P.P., S.J.M., C.J.S., S.M.; BBSRC Professorial Fellowship funding to M.J.B.; Belgian Science Policy Office (grant IAP7/29) funding to M.J.B.; Royal Society Wolfson Research Merit Award to M.J.B.; EU FP7-KBBE-2011-5 project EURoot: Enhancing resource uptake from roots under stress in cereal crops to T.P.P. and M.J.B.

References

1. Aykac, D., Hoffman, E., McLennan, G., Reinhardt, J.: Segmentation and analysis of the human airway tree from three-dimensional X-ray CT images. IEEE Transactions on Medical Imaging **22**(8), 940–950 (2003)
2. Besl, P.J., McKay, N.D.: A method for registration of 3-D shapes. IEEE Transactions on Pattern Analysis and Machine Intelligence **14**(2), 239–256 (1992)
3. Chéné, Y., Rousseau, D., Lucidarme, P., Bertheloot, J., Caffier, V., Morel, P., Belin, Í., Chapeau-Blondeau, F.: On the use of depth camera for 3D phenotyping of entire plants. Computers and Electronics in Agriculture **82**, 122–127 (2012)
4. Chopp, D.L.: Computing minimal surfaces via level set curvature flow. Journal of Computational Physics **106**(1), 77–91 (1993)
5. Clark, R.T., MacCurdy, R.B., Jung, J.K., Shaff, J.E., McCouch, S.R., Aneshansley, D.J., Kochian, L.V.: Three-dimensional root phenotyping with a novel imaging and software platform. Plant Physiology **156**(2), 455–465 (2011)
6. Crowell, S., Falcao, A.X., Shah, A., Wilson, Z., Greenberg, A.J., McCouch, S.R.: High-resolution inflorescence phenotyping using a novel image analysis pipeline, panorama. Plant Physiology (2014)
7. Flasque, N., Desvignes, M., Constans, J.M., Revenu, M.: Acquisition, segmentation and tracking of the cerebral vascular tree on 3D magnetic resonance angiography images. Medical Image Analysis **5**(3), 173–183 (2001)
8. Granlund, G.H.: Fourier preprocessing for hand print character recognition. IEEE Transactions on Computers **C−21**(2), 195–201 (1972)
9. Heeraman, D.A., Hopmans, J.W., Clausnitzer, V.: Three dimensional imaging of plant roots in situ with X-ray computed tomography. Plant and Soil **189**, 167–179 (1997)
10. Hinsinger, P., Gobran, G.R., Gregory, P.J., Wenzel, W.W.: Rhizosphere geometry and heterogeneity arising from root-mediated physical and chemical processes. New Phytologist **168**(2), 293–303 (2005)
11. Kaestner, A., Schneebeli, M., Graf, F.: Visualizing three-dimensional root networks using computed tomography. Geoderma **136**(12), 459–469 (2006)
12. Khan, Z., Balch, T., Dellaert, F.: MCMC-based particle filtering for tracking a variable number of interacting targets. IEEE Transactions on Pattern Analysis and Machine Intelligence **27**(11), 1805–1819 (2005)
13. Lin, J.: Divergence measures based on the shannon entropy. IEEE Transactions on Information Theory **37**(1), 145–151 (1991)
14. Lontoc-Roy, M., Dutilleul, P., Prasher, S.O., Han, L., Brouillet, T., Smith, D.L.: Advances in the acquisition and analysis of CT scan data to isolate a crop root system from the soil medium and quantify root system complexity in 3-D space. Geoderma **137**(12), 231–241 (2006)
15. Lynch, J.P.: Root architecture and plant productivity. Plant Physiology **109**(1), 7–13 (1995)
16. Malladi, R., Sethian, J.A., Vemuri, B.C.: Shape modeling with front propagation: a level set approach. IEEE Transactions on Pattern Analysis and Machine Intelligence **17**(2), 158–175 (1995)
17. Meijering, E.: Neuron tracing in perspective. Cytometry Part A **77A**(7), 693–704 (2010)
18. Meyer, F.: Contrast features extraction. SPIE Milestone Series **127**, 139–145 (1996)
19. Mooney, S.J., Pridmore, T.P., Helliwell, J., Bennett, M.J.: Developing X-ray computed tomography to non-invasively image 3-D root systems architecture in soil. Plant and Soil **352**, 1–22 (2012)

20. Perret, J.S., Al-Belushi, M.E., Deadman, M.: Non-destructive visualization and quantification of roots using computed tomography. Soil Biology and Biochemistry **39**(2), 391–399 (2007)

21. Pierret, A., Capowiez, Y., Moran, C.J., Kretzschmar, A.: X-ray computed tomography to quantify tree rooting spatial distributions. Geoderma **90**(34), 307–326 (1999)

22. Price, C.A., Symonova, O., Mileyko, Y., Hilley, T., Weitz, J.S.: Leaf extraction and analysis framework graphical user interface: Segmenting and analyzing the structure of leaf veins and areoles. Plant Physiology **155**(1), 236–245 (2011)

23. Rosenfeld, A.: Connectivity in digital pictures. Journal of the ACM **17**(1), 146–160 (1970)

24. Rosin, P.L.: Unimodal thresholding. Pattern Recognition **34**(11), 2083–2096 (2001)

25. Rusinkiewicz, S., Levoy, M.: Efficient variants of the ICP algorithm. In: 2001 Proceedings of the Third International Conference on 3-D Digital Imaging and Modeling, pp. 145–152 (2001)

26. Schenk, H.J.: Root competition: beyond resource depletion. Journal of Ecology **94**(4), 725–739 (2006)

27. Sethian, J.A.: Level set techniques for tracking interfaces: Fast algorithms, multiple regions, grid generation and shape/character recognition. In: Proceedings of the International Conference on Curvature Flows and Related Topics, Trento, Italy, pp. 215–231 (1994)

28. Sethian, J.A.: Level Set Methods and Fast Marching Methods: Evolving Interfaces in Computational Geometry, Fluid Mechanics, Computer Vision, and Materials Science.. on Applied and Computational Mathematics, 2nd edn. Cambridge University Press (1999)

29. Sonka, M., Hlavac, V., Boyle, R.: Image Processing, Analysis, and Machine Vision. Chapman and Hall (1993)

30. Sonka, M., Park, W., Hoffman, E.A.: Rule-based detection of intrathoracic airway trees. IEEE Transactions on Medical Imaging **15**(3), 314–326 (1996)

31. Trachsel, S., Kaeppler, S., Brown, K., Lynch, J.: Shovelomics: high throughput phenotyping of maize (Zea mays L.) root architecture in the field. Plant and Soil **341**(1–2), 75–87 (2011)

32. Tschirren, J., Hoffman, E., McLennan, G., Sonka, M.: Intrathoracic airway trees: segmentation and airway morphology analysis from low-dose CT scans. IEEE Transactions on Medical Imaging **24**(12), 1529–1539 (2005)

33. Vincent, L.: Morphological grayscale reconstruction in image analysis: applications and efficient algorithms. IEEE Transactions on Image Processing **2**(2), 176–201 (1993)

34. Wilson, D.L., Noble, J.A.: An adaptive segmentation algorithm for time-of-flight MRA data. IEEE Transactions on Medical Imaging **18**(10), 938–945 (1999)

35. Zappala, S., Helliwell, J.R., Tracy, S.R., Mairhofer, S., Sturrock, C.J., Pridmore, T., Bennett, M., Mooney, S.J.: Effects of X-ray dose on rhizosphere studies using X-ray computed tomography. PloS one **8**(6), e67250 (2013)

36. Zhao, H.: A fast sweeping method for eikonal equations. Mathematics of computation **74**(250), 603–628 (2005)

A Crop/Weed Field Image Dataset for the Evaluation of Computer Vision Based Precision Agriculture Tasks

Sebastian Haug[1]([⊠]) and Jörn Ostermann[2]

[1] Corporate Research, Robert Bosch GmbH, Stuttgart, Germany
sebastian.haug@de.bosch.com
[2] Leibniz Universität Hannover, Hannover, Germany
ostermann@tnt.uni-hannover.de

Abstract. In this paper we propose a benchmark dataset for crop/weed discrimination, single plant phenotyping and other open computer vision tasks in precision agriculture. The dataset comprises 60 images with annotations and is available online (http://github.com/cwfid). All images were acquired with the autonomous field robot Bonirob in an organic carrot farm while the carrot plants were in early true leaf growth stage. Intra- and inter-row weeds were present, weed and crop were approximately of the same size and grew close together. For every dataset image we supply a ground truth vegetation segmentation mask and manual annotation of the plant type (crop vs. weed). We provide initial results for the phenotyping problem of crop/weed classification and propose evaluation methods to allow comparison of different approaches. By opening this dataset to the community we want to stimulate research in this area where the current lack of public datasets is one of the barriers for progress.

Keywords: Computer vision · Phenotyping · Dataset · Precision agriculture · Classification · Bonirob field robot

1 Introduction

Automation in agriculture, intelligent farm management as well as robotic precision agriculture activities require detailed information about the environment, the field, the condition and the phenotype of individual plants. An increase in available data allows more automatic, precise, cost-effective and organic production of crops and vegetables.

Camera sensors and computer vision with machine learning are promising technologies to capture such information and further process it to be able to realize autonomous farming. Combined with field robots such as Bonirob [18] that navigate autonomously in fields [1,9] tasks that are still manual today can be automated. For example, weed control in organic carrot farming is still performed manually and necessary to avoid substantial loss of crop yield.

© Springer International Publishing Switzerland 2015
L. Agapito et al. (Eds.): ECCV 2014 Workshops, Part IV, LNCS 8928, pp. 105–116, 2015.
DOI: 10.1007/978-3-319-16220-1_8

(a) Sample image from dataset.   (b) Field robot used for dataset acquisition.

Fig. 1. Sample image from dataset (a) that was acquired with the autonomous field robot Bonirob (b)

In this paper we consider the use-case of processing top-down looking images of row cultures (organic carrots) with machine vision to capture and extract information that is useful for management and automation of such farming tasks. The image data and annotations made available with this dataset enable the development of solutions for phenotyping problems. Crop / weed discrimination, crop counting, determination of inter-crop spacing or of crop / weed coverage ratios are examples for phenotyping tasks that can be realized and evaluated with this dataset.

From a computer vision perspective the data provided plays an important role: On the one hand the image acquisition process in the agricultural domain is difficult, as it requires complex hardware systems, access to farms and the acquisition must be correctly timed and synchronized to the crop growth cycle (only once a year for many cultures). On the other hand, agricultural experts are needed to define suitable ground truth. That makes this domain different from other problems in computer vision such as object detection in home or street scenes where computer vision researchers can record both data and ground truth more easily themselves. This public dataset allows phenotyping research without the upfront burden of setting up robots, fields and experts.

The dataset comprises field images in top-down view that were acquired with the autonomous field robot Bonirob in an organic carrot farm in 2013 (see Figure 1). All data acquisition was carried out during field tests within the publicly funded project RemoteFarming.1 [3]. The images were captured while the crop was in growth stages where one or more true leaves were present. Some hours after data acquisition the farmer applied manual weed control on this field. Here we consider organic carrots, however similar manual weed control activities are also required for chicory, onions and other cultures. All images are annotated and a ground truth vegetation segmentation mask is available together with crop / weed annotations. Section 3 provides more details about the data, metadata and acquisition conditions.

A concrete example for a phenotyping task which is addressed with this dataset is crop / weed discrimination, for which we provide initial results. A machine vision pipeline is applied and a subset of the images is used together with the ground truth annotations to train a classifier. This classification pipeline is applied to the test images and predicts for each vegetation pixel whether it is part of a crop or weed plant.

To allow comparison of different algorithms we propose evaluation metrics for the vegetation segmentation, plant segmentation and crop / weed discrimination phenotyping tasks.

In summary the contributions of this paper are:

- A dataset of 60 top-down field images of a common culture (organic carrots) with the presence of intra-row and close-to-crop weeds.
- Each image is annotated with a vegetation segmentation mask and crop / weed labels (162 crop plants, 332 weed plants in total).
- The formulation of machine vision and phenotyping problems together with evaluation metrics for future comparison of different approaches.
- Initial results for the crop / weed phenotyping problem of these images.

2   Related Work

In many domains including machine vision, robotics and biology, open datasets are established and play an important role in the scientific community. Public datasets open challenging questions to a wider community and allow direct comparison of different algorithms to the state of the art.

In computer vision there exist many datasets: For example for stereo processing and optical flow, the Middlebury datasets [10,21] and the newer KITTI benchmark [6] are widely used. For image retrieval and object classification larger datasets have been created: For example LabelMe [20], ImageCLEF [16] and the PASCAL VOC challenges [5]. In machine learning datasets play an equally important role and a large collection of datasets is available from UCI [2]. Also in robotics, open and public datasets play a major role and for example allow labs without specific robots to do research. KITTI is a dataset for vision based autonomous driving [7], the RGB-D SLAM dataset [25] is a benchmark dataset for simultaneous localization and mapping with depth based vision sensors. Many more datasets exist in all of these domains.

For phenotyping and agricultural tasks however, the availability of datasets is much more limited. In recent years some datasets in the leaf segmentation and classification domain have been published. Söderkvist's Swedish leaf dataset [23] was one of the first available datasets and contains leaf images of Swedish trees. The Flavia dataset by Wu et al. [26] is a newer popular dataset for leaf classification tasks. Kumar et al. developed a Smartphone application for leaf classification called Leafsnap [13] and published their dataset.

The goal of this paper is to provide a real-world field image dataset to the phenotyping, agricultural vision and robotics community. This enables research on perception for data acquisition or treatment in row cultures, such as carrots in early growth stages.

3   Dataset and Problem Description

Figure 2 displays example images from the dataset together with all annotations. The following section describes the content of the dataset, the acquisition parameters as well as the exact format of the image data and metadata.

(a) Field Image   (b) Vegetation Mask   (c) Crop/Weed Annotation

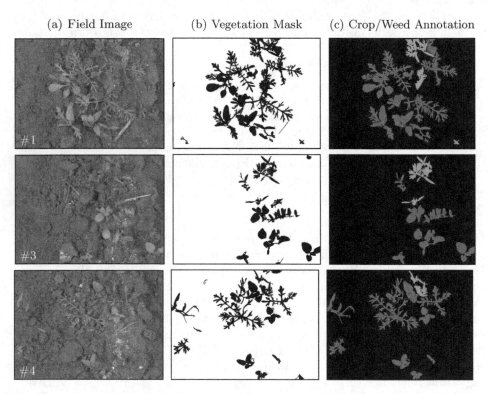

Fig. 2. Sample images from the dataset (a) with ground truth vegetation masks and crop / weed annotations. The annotation images (b) and (c) are supplied for every image of the dataset. Best viewed in color.

3.1   Field Setup and Acquisition Method

The 60 image dataset was captured at a commercial organic carrot farm in Northern Germany in 2013 just before manual weed control was applied. The carrots were grown in single rows on small soil dams. The growth stage of the crop was approximately BBCH $10-20$ (see [15] for a description of the BBCH plant growth stage scale) and a significant amount of close-to-crop and intra-row weeds was present. Figure 3 describes how the images were selected from five sections in the field. In the agricultural application context where a robot drives along rows, the larger 20 image section at the start of the row is designated as training data, the other sections (40 images) are designated as test set and

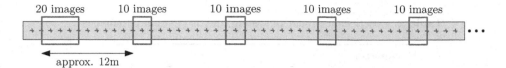

Fig. 3. Schematic overview of a row in the field with annotation of the sections where the dataset images were captured. Near the beginning of the row a section with 20 images was defined; then at a distance of approx. 12 m sections of 10 images each were defined.

Table 1. Extent of the dataset

Parameter	Value
Image count	60
Labeled plant count	494
Labeled crop plant count	162
Labeled weed plant count	332

were spread out across the row to better capture the variability in the field. Subsequent images in the dataset do not overlap and display unique situations to avoid redundant data. Table 1 summarizes the extent of the dataset.

The images were acquired with a camera mounted to the autonomous field robot Bonirob which drove along the carrot row with a speed of ~ 4.5 cm/s. A JAI multi-spectral camera [11] that captures both visible and near-infrared light was used and mounted on the robot. The camera was looking downwards and the area under the robot was shaded and artificially lit to avoid changing lighting conditions. Table 2 describes the camera setup and its configuration. The red (R) and near-infrared (NIR) channels were selected because the spectral characteristics of plants in these channels can be exploited for background removal using vegetation indices [22].

3.2   Dataset and Annotation Format

In addition to the field images the dataset also contains annotations. First, a vegetation mask is provided which masks soil pixels, see Figure 2b. Second, all images were manually annotated by a human expert. The user was asked to mark crop and weed plants / parts with polygons and to assign a type (crop or weed) to each polygon. Note that some areas are not labeled, for example areas with heavy overlap. Figure 2c shows the resulting ground truth crop / weed annotation image when the polygon labels are combined with the vegetation mask. All vegetation pixels that lie inside a polygon inherit the label from the polygon. The label at each pixel is plotted in color code where red denotes weed and green denotes crop. The dataset contains both the polygon information and the crop / weed annotation images as given in Figure 2c. Table 3 summarizes the specific data and file format of the field images and the annotations.

Table 2. Description of camera system and acquisition parameters

Parameter	Value
Camera model	JAI AD-130GE [12]
Image resolution	1296 x 966 pixels
Lens	Fujinon TF15-DA-8
Focal length	15 mm
F-number	4
Mean distance to ground (d)	450 mm
Ground resolution	$\sim$8.95 pixels/mm
Field of view x (at distance d)	$\sim$145 mm
Field of view y (at distance d)	$\sim$108 mm

The vegetation masks were derived using the Normalized Differential Vegetation Index (NDVI) [22] that was calculated from the NIR and R image channel. A threshold in NDVI space was selected using Otsu's method [17] given the training images. Then this threshold value was fixed and used to generate the ground truth masks for all images of the dataset.

The crop / weed annotations are given as image (Figure 2c) and in a data format that contains the list of polygons plus one label per polygon (crop / weed). The polygon data is stored in YAML[1] format, see Listing 1. Each YAML file contains a `filename` field and an `annotation` field in which a list of `points` and `type` entries is stored. The `points` field contains the x and y coordinates of the polygon vertices. The `type` is either crop or weed and defines the plant type.

The crop / weed annotations are also given as polygons because this enables single plant evaluations which are not possible if only an image (Figure 2c) is given. In the annotation image plants of the same type that overlap are no longer separable. Pixels that are covered by more than one polygon with different types are defined as invalid and the plant type is set to unknown.

3.3   How to Get the Dataset

The Crop / Weed Field Image Dataset (CWFID) is available online and can be downloaded from http://github.com/cwfid.

4   Problems and Evaluation Metrics

Field images acquired using a top-down camera system can deliver a lot of information. Nevertheless, their natural setting with different plants growing close together in an unordered scene poses many challenges.

---

[1] YAML is a data serialization standard which aims to be easy to read for humans. Parsers are available for many programming languages. See yaml.org.

Table 3. Description of dataset and annotation format

Data	Description
Field image (Figure 2a)	
Filename	000_image.png
Format	PNG (3 channel), 8 bit
Channels	1 ↦ Red
	2 ↦ Near-Infrared
	3 ↦ Red
Vegetation mask (Figure 2b)	
Filename	000_mask.png
Format	PNG (monochrome), 1 bit
Mapping	Biomass ↦ 0
	Background ↦ 1
Crop / weed annotation image (Figure 2c)	
Filename	000_annotation.png
Format	PNG (3 channel), 8 bit
Channels	1 → 255 if weed at pixel, 0 otherwise
	2 → 255 if crop at pixel, 0 otherwise
	3 → always 0
Crop / weed annotation data (Listing 1)	
Filename	000_annotation.yaml
Format	YAML with list of polygon vertices and labels

From a computer vision point of view, these images can be segmented into background and foreground or on a higher level into different objects (for example rows, plants etc.). Furthermore, classification challenges arise including the classification of individual pixels, connected areas or segmented objects. Additionally, many advanced computer vision techniques such as tracking, optical flow etc. can be used to extract information. Some of these tasks overlap with goals of a phenotyping and agricultural image processing point of view.

In the following we are focusing on these more plant specific tasks and formulate four relevant problems:

1. **Vegetation Segmentation**: A binary mask is desired that masks all background soil and residue pixels [14]. Applying this mask results in a vegetation image where only pixels displaying vegetation are non-zero.
2. **Plant Segmentation**: Individual plants should be segmented in the image. This is challenging because plants in the field are growing close together and overlap between plants occurs.
3. **Plant Classification**: Plants or leaves can be classified. Here the use-case of crop / weed discrimination is considered, which results in a two class classification problem. This can be extended to individual species classification.

Listing 1. Definition of the YAML annotations file

```
filename: 000_image.png
annotation:
- type: weed
  points:
    x: [810.0,  841.0,  846.0,  926.0,  956.0,  1054.0]
    y: [225.0,  234.0,  266.0,  338.0,  408.0,  422.0]
- type: crop
  points:
    x: [1070.0,  1055.0,  980.0,  850.0,  844.0]
    y: [626.0,  722.0,  739.0,  658.0,  730.0]
```

4. **Individual Plant Phenotyping**: From the images also information about the phenotype of individual plants can be obtained [19]: This includes the growth stage, plant stem position, biomass amount, leaf count, leaf area and others. Furthermore, crop / weed coverage ratio, inter crop spacing, crop plant count and other derived measurements are of interest to farmers.

For problems 1-3, we define evaluation metrics that enable comparison of different approaches when using this dataset. The individual plant phenotyping problems crop plant count and crop / weed coverage ratio can be directly compared to values calculated from ground truth. A definition of metrics for the other phenotyping problems is considered future work and probably requires more annotations.

1. For comparison of different vegetation masks we propose to use the Jaccard index as segmentation accuracy measure (as done in the PASCAL VOC challenges [5]), which is defined as intersection over union. This can be expressed in terms of correctly assigned pixels (true positives) and incorrectly assigned pixels (false positives and false negatives):

$$\text{seg. accuracy} = \frac{\text{true pos.}}{\text{true pos.} + \text{false pos.} + \text{false neg.}} \tag{1}$$

A final score is achieved by averaging the segmentation accuracy over all test images.
2. To evaluate plant segmentation results also the Jaccard index is applied, see Equation (1). The predicted segmentation of a plant (consisting of a set of pixels) is compared with the set of vegetation pixels of the plant in the ground truth annotation. The ground truth vegetation pixels for a single plant are derived by selecting only pixels from the vegetation mask that lie inside the ground truth polygon of the plant. To get a final score the Jaccard index is calculated per plant and then averaged over all plants in the test set.
3. For crop / weed or plant classification, we assume that the classification system returns a full image with per-pixel predictions. Then we propose to

compare the predictions and ground truth pixel-wise and to calculate the following metrics per image: Average accuracy, precision, recall and F1-score [24]. For final results, we propose averaging over the test images. If the prediction also outputs scores and not only binary votes a Receiver Operator (ROC) curve should be plotted.

For tasks that require separate training and test data we propose two splits. First, from an agricultural point of view, we propose a sequential split. Images #1 − 20 located at the beginning of the row are used for training and images #21 − 60 for testing (see Figure 3). This is derived from the real world use-case where system set-up is done at the beginning of the field or row and then performance is expected to be stable during operation.

Second, from a computer vision point of view, we propose a random 66 % train and 33 % test split. Fixed indices for one such split are given in that dataset file `train_test_split.yaml`.

5   Initial Results on Crop / Weed Discrimination

Crop / weed discrimination is an important step towards assessment of crop properties and single plant weed control. Once the type and location of for example crop plants is known, further phenotype measurements can be derived.

Here we provide initial results on the crop / weed discrimination problem on this dataset using the machine vision approach from Haug et al. [8]. In the following, the proposed agricultural test train split is chosen. The 20 training images and vegetation masks are used during the training process, which involves feature extraction using a sliding window approach. For each window position center the corresponding ground truth label is extracted from the ground truth crop / weed annotation. Using the training data (feature vectors) with labels, a Random Forest [4] classifier is trained and applied to the test images of this dataset (images #21 − 60). The predictions of the Random Forest classifier are post-processed and the output of the plant classification system is a predicted crop / weed image similar to the ground truth image.

Figure 4 displays the crop / weed predictions next to a ground truth image from the dataset. In both the ground truth image and the predicted image each vegetation pixel is plotted in color code, where red denotes weed and green denotes crop. A border of 40 pixels is masked and was ignored during evaluation, as this approach does not predict the plant type at the edges of the image.

To quantitatively analyze the performance of this approach to crop / weed discrimination, pixel-wise comparison of ground truth image and prediction is applied. Table 4 summarizes the proposed per-pixel metrics averaged over all test images.

(a) Image   (b) Ground truth   (c) Prediction

Fig. 4. Image, ground truth and crop / weed prediction for two test images. Red color denotes weed and green color denotes crop. Best viewed in color.

Table 4. Results of crop / weed classification when comparing per-pixel predictions of test images with the ground truth

Metric	Result
Average Accuracy	85.9 %
Precision	79.6 %
Recall	80.8 %
F1-score	80.2 %

6   Conclusions

This paper proposes a crop / weed field image dataset for phenotyping and machine vision problems in agriculture. Field images of carrots were acquired on a commercial organic farm in early crop growth stage, where close-to-crop and intra-row weeds were present. Such images pose both phenotyping and machine vision related questions that – if solved – allow the automation of manual and cost intense tasks including for example weed control.

The data is fully annotated by experts. Initial results on crop / weed discrimination report an average accuracy and F1-score of 85.9 % and 80.2 % respectively. This indicates that automation of such tasks is probably feasible, however difficult and needs more research.

Finally, we propose evaluation metrics for segmentation and classification tasks to encourage other groups to use this dataset and compare results. We hope that this increases progress in this domain where data acquisition requires extensive setups, experts with agricultural knowledge are needed to generate ground truth and availability of public datasets is very limited.

In the future, this dataset can be enlarged with more images from another field or growth season and additional ground truth can be defined for the individual plant phenotyping problems.

Acknowledgments. The authors thank the following colleagues for their comments and help with the acquisition of the dataset: Wolfram Strothmann, Fabian Sellmann, Arno Ruckelshausen, Susanne Fittje, Frederik Langsenkamp, Maik Kohlbrecher, Dieter Trautz (University of Applied Sciences Osnabrück), Waldemar Bangert, Florian Rahe (Amazone), Andreas Michaels, Slawomir Grzonka, Peter Biber, Hannes Becker, Amos Albert (Bosch).

The project RemoteFarming.1 is partially funded by the German Federal Ministry of Food, Agriculture and Consumer Protection (BMELV).

References

1. Åstrand, B., Baerveldt, A.J.: An agricultural mobile robot with vision-based perception for mechanical weed control. Autonomous Robots **13**(1), 21–35 (2002)
2. Bache, K., Lichman, M.: UCI machine learning repository (2013). http://archive.ics.uci.edu/ml
3. Bangert, W., Kielhorn, A., Rahe, F., Albert, A., Biber, P., Grzonka, S., Haug, S., Michaels, A., Mentrup, D., Hänsel, M., Kinski, D., Möller, K., Ruckelshausen, A., Scholz, C., Sellmann, F., et al.: Field-robot-based agriculture: RemoteFarming. 1 and BoniRob-Apps. VDI. Agricultural Engineering **2013**, 439–446 (2013)
4. Breiman, L.: Random forests. Machine Learning **45**(1), 5–32 (2001)
5. Everingham, M., Van Gool, L., Williams, C.K., Winn, J., Zisserman, A.: The pascal visual object classes (voc) challenge. International Journal of Computer Vision **88**(2), 303–338 (2010)
6. Geiger, A., Lenz, P., Stiller, C., Urtasun, R.: Vision meets robotics: The kitti dataset. The International Journal of Robotics Research **32**(11), 1231–1237 (2013)
7. Geiger, A., Lenz, P., Urtasun, R.: Are we ready for autonomous driving? the kitti vision benchmark suite. In: 2012 IEEE Conference on Computer Vision and Pattern Recognition (CVPR), pp. 3354–3361. IEEE (2012)
8. Haug, S., Michaels, A., Biber, P., Ostermann, J.: Plant classification system for crop/weed discrimination without segmentation. In: 2014 IEEE Winter Conference on Applications of Computer Vision (WACV), pp. 1142–1149. IEEE (2014)
9. Hemming, J., Rath, T.: Computer-vision-based weed identification under field conditions using controlled lighting. Journal of Agricultural Engineering Research **78**(3), 233–243 (2001)
10. Hirschmuller, H., Scharstein, D.: Evaluation of cost functions for stereo matching. In: 2007 IEEE Conference on Computer Vision and Pattern Recognition (CVPR), pp. 1–8. IEEE (2007)
11. JAI: Datasheet: JAI AD-130GE 2 CCD Multi-spectral Camera., Document version: March 2012

12. JAI: User's Manual: JAI AD-130GE 2CCD Multi-Spectral Camera., Document version: 1.1 (2012)
13. Kumar, Neeraj, Belhumeur, Peter N., Biswas, Arijit, Jacobs, David W., Kress, WJohn, Lopez, Ida C., Soares, João V.B.: Leafsnap: A Computer Vision System for Automatic Plant Species Identification. In: Fitzgibbon, Andrew, Lazebnik, Svetlana, Perona, Pietro, Sato, Yoichi, Schmid, Cordelia (eds.) ECCV 2012, Part II. LNCS, vol. 7573, pp. 502–516. Springer, Heidelberg (2012)
14. McCarthy, C., Hancock, N., Raine, S.R.: Applied machine vision of plants: a review with implications for field deployment in automated farming operations. Intelligent Service Robotics **3**(4), 209–217 (2010)
15. Meier, U.: Growth stages of mono-and dicotyledonous plants. BBCH monograph. German Federal Biological Research Centre for Agriculture and Forestry, Berlin (2001)
16. Müller, H., Clough, P., Deselaers, T., Caputo, B., CLEF, I.: Experimental evaluation in visual information retrieval. The Information Retrieval Series 32 (2010)
17. Otsu, N.: A threshold selection method from gray-level histograms. Automatica **11**(285–296), 23–27 (1975)
18. Ruckelshausen, A., Biber, P., Dorna, M., Gremmes, H., Klose, R., Linz, A., Rahe, F., Resch, R., Thiel, M., Trautz, D., et al.: Bonirob - an autonomous field robot platform for individual plant phenotyping. Precision Agriculture **9**, 841 (2009)
19. Ruckelshausen, A., Busemeyer, L., Klose, R., Linz, A., Moeller, K., Thiel, M., Alheit, K., Rahe, F., Trautz, D., Weiss, U.: Sensor and system technology for individual plant crop scouting. In: International Conference on Precision Agriculture (ICPA) (2010)
20. Russell, B.C., Torralba, A., Murphy, K.P., Freeman, W.T.: Labelme: a database and web-based tool for image annotation. International Journal of Computer Vision **77**(1–3), 157–173 (2008)
21. Scharstein, D., Szeliski, R.: A taxonomy and evaluation of dense two-frame stereo correspondence algorithms. International Journal of Computer Vision **47**(1–3), 7–42 (2002)
22. Scotford, I., Miller, P.: Applications of spectral reflectance techniques in northern european cereal production: a review. Biosystems Engineering **90**(3), 235–250 (2005)
23. Söderkvist, O.: Computer Vision Classification of Leaves from Swedish Trees. Master's thesis, Linköping University, Sweden (2001)
24. Sokolova, M., Lapalme, G.: A systematic analysis of performance measures for classification tasks. Information Processing & Management **45**(4), 427–437 (2009)
25. Sturm, J., Engelhard, N., Endres, F., Burgard, W., Cremers, D.: A benchmark for the evaluation of rgb-d slam systems. In: 2012 IEEE/RSJ International Conference on Intelligent Robots and Systems (IROS), pp. 573–580. IEEE (2012)
26. Wu, S.G., Bao, F.S., Xu, E.Y., Wang, Y.X., Chang, Y.F., Xiang, Q.L.: A leaf recognition algorithm for plant classification using probabilistic neural network. In: 2007 IEEE International Symposium on Signal Processing and Information Technology, pp. 11–16. IEEE (2007)

Generation and Application of Hyperspectral 3D Plant Models

Jan Behmann[1]([✉]), Anne-Katrin Mahlein[2], Stefan Paulus[3], Heiner Kuhlmann[3],
Erich-Christian Oerke[2], and Lutz Plümer[1]

[1] Institute of Geodesy and Geoinformation (IGG), Geoinformation,
University of Bonn, Bonn, Germany
behmann@igg.uni-bonn.de
[2] Institute for Crop Science and Resource Conservation (INRES) - Phytomedicine,
University of Bonn, Bonn, Germany
[3] Institute of Geodesy and Geoinformation (IGG), Geodesy,
University of Bonn, Bonn, Germany

Abstract. Hyperspectral imaging sensors have been introduced for measuring the health status of plants. Recently, they have been also used for close-range sensing of plant canopies with a more complex architecture. The complex geometry of plants and their interaction with the illumination scenario severely affect the spectral information obtained. The combination of hyperspectral images and 3D point clouds are a promising approach to face this problem. Based on such hyperspectral 3D models the effects of plant geometry and sensor configuration can be quantified an modeled. Reflectance models can be used to remove or weaken the geometry-related effects in hyperspectral images and, therefore, have the potential potential to improve automated phenotyping significantly.

We present the generation and application of hyperspectral 3D plant models as a new, interesting application field for computer vision with a variety of challenging tasks. The reliable and accurate generation requires the adaptation of methods designed for man-made scenes. The adaption requires new types of point descriptors and 3D matching technologies. Also the application and analysis of 3D plant models creates new challenges as the light scattering at plant tissue is highly complex and so far not fully described. New approaches for measuring, simulating, and visualizing light fluxes are required for improved sensing and new insights into stress reactions of plants.

Keywords: Hyperspectral · 3D scanning · Close range · Phenotyping · Modeling · Sensor fusion

1 Introduction

Hyperspectral images are an important tool for assessing the vitality and stress response of plants [1,2]. In recent time, the sensor technology for hyperspectral

Electronic supplementary material The online version of this chapter (doi:10.1007/978-3-319-16220-1_9) contains supplementary material, which is available to authorized users.

© Springer International Publishing Switzerland 2015
L. Agapito et al. (Eds.): ECCV 2014 Workshops, Part IV, LNCS 8928, pp. 117–130, 2015.
DOI: 10.1007/978-3-319-16220-1_9

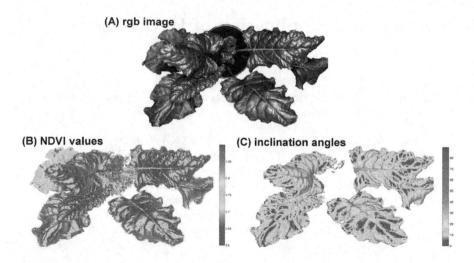

Fig. 1. The effect of plant geometry on spectral characteristics. Displayed is (A) the rgb visualization, (B) the NDVI image with NDVI = (R800-R670)/(R800+R670) and (C) the pixelwise inclination angle in degrees, calculated from depth information projected to the image coordinate system. The low NDVI values on the horizontal leaf parts are caused by the specular reflection and are not related to a lower chlorophyl concentration. Such geometric effects hamper the accurate and reliable interpretation of hyperspectral images.

plant phenotyping has improved in resolution, accuracy, and measurement time and is integrated into phenotyping platforms. However, the spectral signals are influenced by the geometric sensor configuration and the plant geometry. So far, these effects are not considered and also often neglected in data analysis and, therefore, increase the noise level.

Simultaneously, the sensor technology for the assessment of 3D shapes is considerably improving. Today, extremely high accurate sensor systems with high resolution are available [3] and even low cost systems reach usable levels of accuracy [4].

In consequence, combining both data types, the hyperspectral images and the 3D point clouds, to hyperspectral 3D plant models has several advantages. The explanation of various optical effects is given by the geometry. Relating both information types, the cause and the effect, in one spatial model system generates a suitable data base for describing and removing the misleading effects. Furthermore, the mapped geometric and spectral information can be used for an advanced data analysis. The combination of feature sets from both information sources or the calculation of combined features may improve the result quality for tasks like organ segmentation, detection of disease symptoms and assessment of senescence levels.

The generation of hyperspectral 3D plant models is not trivial. It requires suitable sensor techniques and computer vision methods adapted to the plant scenario. An important point is the spatial calibration of hyperspectral cameras, commonly designed as pushbroom cameras with sufficient accuracy. Common calibration routines for pushbroom cameras are not adapted to the close range and to the sensing of plants. The assessment of plant shapes requires 3D imaging techniques that handle the non-regular surface and the non-solid characteristics of the plant architecture.

On the other hand, the analysis of hyperspectral 3D models poses new challenges. The reflectance models (e.g. bidirectional reflectance distribution function (BRDF) [5,6]) are very specific to the sensor type and the plant species. Therefore, these models have to be derived for each individual experiment with sufficient accuracy and reliability. Robust methods have to adapt the correction functions to the new experiment at best from a single hyperspectral 3D plant model. Usually, nearly all combinations of leaf angles and shading situations are included in such a model of a higher plant. Missing data need to be interpolated or derived from prior information.

The hyperspectral 3D plant models supply huge amounts of high-dimensional data that require advanced data analysis methods. The complexity of the analysis with both, spectral and spatial features is higher than by using a homogenous data source. On the one hand, the different data sources partially explain each other. On the other hand, the spectral and geometric information complement each other and provide additional information. Therefore, a suitable data analysis does not simply combine the different features in a single feature vector, but uses the redundancy and complement characteristics for integrated features with more information than provided by a single sensor. Such features may support a human interpretation, but in most cases they will be optimized for a specific task, e.g. the detection of disease symptoms by a specific algorithm.

We present hyperspectral 3D plant models as an integration platform for multiple sensors and models of metabolic processes. Further, geometrically calibrated sensors may be integrated as additional texture layers. In the first part of this paper, we summarize the available sensors and methods for the generation of hyperspectral 3D plant models. In the second part, advantages and potential applications are presented.

The most important challenges for computer vision in this study are specified and highlighted. They refer to different sub-divisions of computer vision and show the diverse interesting aspects of hyperspectral 3D models.

2   Fusion of Hyperspectral and Shape Information

In this section, common sensor systems for spectral and spatial data are introduced. Furthermore, we present an applicable and proven method for the combination of hyperspectral pushbroom cameras and 3D plant models. Combining hyperspectral measurements and geometric information is conducted by assigning the 3D coordinate of the reflecting plant surface point to the recorded spectrum. In a phenotyping context, the geometric flexibility and temporal variability of plants makes it complicated to obtain the required mapping accuracy.

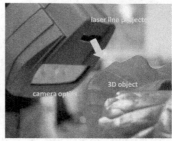

Fig. 2. The used sensors: hyperspectral sensing system including two hyperspectral pushbroom cameras and linear stage and the close range 3D laser scanner using the triangulation principle on a laser line

2.1 Hyperspectral Images

Hyperspectral cameras record the reflected radiation at narrow wavelengths with a high spatial resolution in a defined field of view. Hyperspectral imaging sensors which are used for plant phenotyping are based on different measurement methods. Currently hyperspectral sensors are classified depending on their spatial scale (airborne or close-range sensing), on the spectral resolution (multispectral to hyperspectral) and on the type of detector. The most common measurement principle is the pushbroom camera with a slit spreading up the incoming light of a line into its spectral composition [7]. Other principles like adapting filters are also available but less common. Interesting new developments like the Cubert UHD 185 Firefly (Cubert, Ulm, Germany) combine the advantages of line scanners and spectral filters by projecting a 2D image on a 1D slit. So far, these sensors do not reach the accuracy and resolution of pushbroom sensors.

The hyperspectral pushbroom sensor unit used in this study consists of two line scanners (ImSpector V10 and SWIR-camera, Specim, Oulu, Finland) whose viewing planes are moved across the plant (Fig. 2). The resulting hyperspectral image is represented by a data cube which is spanned by two spatial and one spectral dimension. These hyperspectral data cubes contain a spectral signature from 350 to 2500 nm in narrow wavelength for each pixel. The reflectance of plants in different ranges of the electromagnetic spectrum is driven by multiple interactions; absorption due to leaf pigments in the visible range (400 to 700 nm), scattering of light due to leaf or canopy structure in the near infrared (700 to 1000 nm) and absorption by leaf chemistry in the shortwave infrared (1000 to 2500 nm) [8]. Thus these hyperspectral imaging systems are appropriate to assess subtle differences among different plant phenotypes and the reaction of different genotypes to stress. However, the quality of hyperspectral imaging data depends strongly on the measuring setup. Hereby particularly the arrangement of the sensor to the object and the light source has to be considered.

2.2   Capturing the 3D Shape of Plants

Capturing the 3D geometry of plants is a common technique in plant science and can be applied across various scales like laboratory [9], greenhouse [10] and field [11]. A variety of sensors can be used to acquire the 3D geometry like stereo camera system [12], hyperspectral cameras [13], terrestrial lidar [14], laser triangulation for close-up scanning [3] or structured light approaches [15]. Close-up laserscanning using laser triangulation provides several advantages if highly accurate and resolved 3D images are necessary (Fig. 2). Smallest organs and deformations due to growth in the sub-millimeter range can be monitored on organ level with highest quality [3]. However, this technique is vulnerable to wind and the actor's movement. Scanning results are highly affected by tissue composition, surface property, size and consistence of wax layer and epidermis and the scanner set-up e.g. exposure time and angle of incidence and reflection [3]. Moreover, it is hard to track single organs when e.g. leaves change their position due to growth, the sun movement or stress.

As almost all measuring systems, laserscanning has to deal with a trade-off between measurable volume and resolution. Combinations with position-tracking-devices like lasertracker or articulated measuring arms enable an enlargement of the measurable volume to the size of some meters without loosing the advantage of resolution and accuracy [3]. Thus, laserscanning can be depicted to be method of choice for high precision 3D imaging of plants. Using laser scanned data, algorithms for automated segmentation [16] using geometry-based surface descriptors have been developed that enable an automated parameterization [17].

In this study, a Perceptron laser triangulation scanner (Perceptron Scan Works V5, Perceptron Inc., Plymouth MI, USA) was used (Fig. 2). By coupling with a measuring arm (Romer Infinite 2.0 in 2.8m variant) it provides an occlusion-free option for close-up imaging of plants and a point reproducibility of 0.088 mm. It was chosen due to its high resolution and accuracy and has been successfully applied for 3D imaging of various plants [9,16].

2.3   Generation of Hyperspectral 3D Plant Models

The introduced sensor types record data with differing properties. The 3D sensor records points or other geometric primitives in a 3D coordinate system and the hyperspectral imager records the reflected spectra in a 2D image reference system. The mapping and combination of spectral and geometric information requires that all data is related to a unique coordinate system.

This can be achieved by more than one approach. On the one hand, the hyperspectral camera can be calibrated in the coordinate system of the 3D plant models by corresponding points in the image and the 3D model [18]. Here arises the problem that such corresponding points are not available because the point detectors are not adapted to plant surfaces and, consequently, do not give reliable results. The transfer of algorithms and methods for man-made scenes to short-range plant scenarios is in its early stages and requires further impulses from the domain of computer vision.

The use of a reference object is a more promising approach. The reference object delivers automatically detectable surface points with known position in the coordinate system of the reference object and defines a unique reference coordinate system. As reference object, a composite of two horizontal, parallel planes with a chess pattern texture was used for this study. The extracted image points with corresponding 3D coordinate were used as input for the camera calibration.

The geometric calibration of the camera requires a calibration method and a camera model that corresponds to the measuring principle of the camera. Numerous camera calibration models are available. A pinhole camera can be described by a perspective projection matrix. A pushbroom sensor may be described by the linear pushbroom camera model of [7]. Non-linear deviations, which occur in close-range observations, can not be described by this model and have to be removed in a pre- or post-processing step.

A further challenge for the generation of hyperspectral plant models is the time factor because, in general, the spectral and geometric characteristics are not measured simultaneously. Significant inaccuracies may be caused by the non-solid architecture of the plants. When moved or even after short time in a fixed position the leaves are moving on the millimeter scale. Therefore, both measurements have to be carried out without delay and with great care and patience.

Fig. 3. 3D point cloud with a hyperspectral texture. The left part shows the oblique view and the right part a top view on the textured point cloud of a young sugar beet plant.

If the hyperspectral camera is geometrically calibrated in the reference system, the measured 3D model of the plant needs only to be transformed into the reference system. This approach turns out to deliver accurate and reliable mappings displayed in most of the figures included. The depth information can be projected to the image coordinate system and assigned to the single pixels (Fig. 1 (C)). Alternatively, the hyperspectral image is used as texture for the 3D plant model (Fig. 3 and Fig. 4). Such an enriched model can be termed a hyperspectral 3D plant model.

The generation of a hyperspectral texture of a 3D object is accompanied by a resampling and transformation because the pixel observations are now assigned to vertices of a meshed surface. Normally, resampling incorporates bi-linear or bi-cubic observations. At hyperspectral textures these interpolation techniques are problematic as implausible or non-biological spectra can be generated. Therefore, we used a nearest neighbor assignment and did not re-calculate new spectra.

2.4 Data Set Description

The supplemented data set contains the hyperspectral 3D plant model of a juvenile sugar beet plant generated by the method outlined in section 2.3. The sugar beet plant was observed at an age of 10 weeks by the described 3D laserscanner (section 2.2) and two hyperspectral cameras (section 2.1). The data set is designed as textured point cloud. In the supplementary material a spectrally and spatially sub-sampled version is attached. A larger version of the data set is available at *www.ikg.uni-bonn.de\datasetCVPPP*.

The data set is provided in *.mat*-format accessible directly via Matlab or via import routines for further analysis software. The *.mat*-container contains three variables: the 3D point cloud *coord3*, the visnir texture *visnir* and the swir texture *swir*. Both textures are stored without redundancy resulting in a matrix *spectra* containing the observed spectra and a index vector *index* assigning the spectra to the points of the point cloud by *spectra_pcl = spectra(index, :)*. A function *visualize_hyperspectral_3D_model.m*, that loads the hyperspectral 3D model and visualizes the textured point cloud, is supplied with the data set.

3 Applications of Hyperspectral 3D Plant Models

The resulting hyperspectral 3D model constitutes a new data set with two data channels, one spectral and one spatial, that offers new and challenging applications. The combination of hyperspectral and 3D shape data is particularly suitable because these sensors are well established for phenotyping, observe different characteristics and their analysis benefits from each other. The referenced information channels regards complementary aspects and is therefore suited to reveal new traits. In general, there are two approaches to exploit the new wealth of information. On the one hand, one data channel can be used to explain and remove specific phenomena in the other data channel. On the other other hand, both data channels can be combined in a unique feature space and analyzed in an integrated way. Both approaches require innovative algorithms to exploit their full potential.

3.1 Radiometric Calibration

The intensity of reflected light observed depends significantly on the plant geometry. Under the assumption of a known geometry, various effects can be removed from the observations.

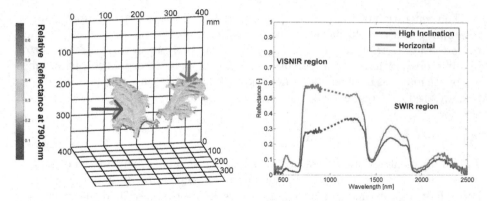

Fig. 4. Hyperspectral 3D plant model integrating the spectral information of two cameras with different spectral range and spatial resolution. In the right part, the combined spectra of the two distinct hyperspectral cameras for two points (marked by a red and blue arrow in the left part) are displayed. The red spectra was reflected by a horizontal leaf part and the blue spectra from a lower leaf with a high inclination angle.

The effects of geometry on the observed spectra can be differentiated into two groups: sensor-related and plant geometry-related effects. The decreasing illumination intensity with increasing distance from the light source, the varying illumination intensity in the field of view of the camera and the varying observations angles as a result of the aperture angle of the camera are effects which depend on the sensor setup. They are static and do not depend on the specific plant geometry. However, they depend only on the location (x, y and z coordinate) where the light is reflected on the plant. Therefore, the modeling of sensor geometry related effects requires the information about the 3D shape of the plant.

The major part of the geometric effects are specific for the single plant geometry and related to the varying observation and illumination angles (Fig. 5). This situation is aggravated by the fact that multiple tissues of a leaf in combination with internal and specular reflection cause a complex reflection function with a "sweet spot" of excessive specular reflection [6]. The most important effects are inclination-dependent (angle between zenith and surface normal) reflection and self-shadowing. Both effects depend, beyond the raw coordinate, on the whole geometry of plant and sensor.

For the description of the geometry-related reflectance dependance a 6D function called bidirectional reflectance function (BRDF, [6]) is used. BRDF models are established for remote sensing applications and are proven to support the extraction of relevant parameters from hyperspectral observations [5]. However, the remote sensing BRDF models are not transferable to the close-range because, in general, they rely on a leaf angle distribution function [19]. This approach is not applicable because a sensor pixel observes a specific area on the leaf surface with an approximately constant leaf angle extractable from the 3D model. Moreover, the BRDF models depend on the plant species [6].

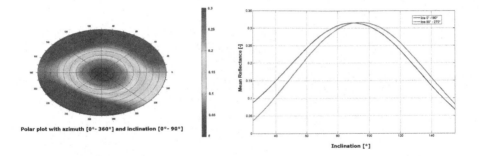

Fig. 5. Relation between the mean reflectance over all wavelength and the local inclination (angle in degrees between zenith and surface normal) extracted from a hyperspectral 3D plant model of a single leaf. The sensor setup uses 6 light spots which illuminate diffusely the plant from zenith direction (Fig. 2).

For phenotyping purposes, the derivation of an BRDF model which is specific for each experiment, including plant species and sensor configuration, is desirable. The efficient and reliable derivation of such scenario-specific light models is an interesting task with high relevance for the computer vision community. First approaches are based on multi-angle goniometer measurements [5] and utilize predefined parametric models [19].

The radiometric calibration requires a light distribution model of the whole sensor system and aims at a improved image quality and an undistorted measurement of plant-physiological characteristics. This approach is common in remote sensing and is included in the process chain of satellite imaging products.

In the close range, the surface is rougher and indirect effects like self shadowing and in-leaf light transport represent a major fraction of the sensed spectral information. The complexity of the observation situation is further enhanced by multi-reflections and light transmissions through the leaves. Illuminated leaves function as light sources with distorted spectra, most probably with a peak in the green region because of absorptions by the leaf chlorophyll. High-performance simulation techniques and hyperspectral ray-tracing methods are requirements to exploit the full potential of the sensor signal [20] and at the same time for the generation of more realistic 3D plant models for virtual reality applications. Therefore, computer vision may contribute an important share to trends in plant science.

3.2 Improved Classification and Segmentation

The segmentation of a plant into its organs is a complex task with high relevance [3]. Plant organs are functional units with specific texture, size and position within the plant. The information about the development of single organs and the retrieval of a single organ within multiple observations is highly relevant for breeding and the quantification of disease effects. The introduced hyperspectral

Fig. 6. Organ segmentation of a vine branch into leaves (green points) and stems (brown points) based on spatial features. Such tasks will benefit from the additional hyperspectral layer because the organs differ clearly in their reflection characteristics.

3D plant models are a suitable data base for organ segmentation as two information sources are already spatially fused. Fig. 6 shows the results of a organ segmentation of a vine branch into leaf tissue and stems.

The expected segmentation improvement will be obtained by the complementary characteristics of the two information types. This kind of fused or integrated analysis corresponds to the human way of observing. The semantic analysis of a scene by humans is based on texture information and the spatial context. Only the combined analysis of multiple information sources ensures highest reliability and recognition quality.

3.3   Spatial Requests

Disease symptoms, senescence processes and growth disorders do not develop uniformly within a plant. In some cases the upper leaves and in some cases the lower leaves are more infested. Also the leaf size and age are important. Currently, hyperspectral images are analyzed with regard to the 2D image, e.g. by the ratio of infested pixels [21]. This two dimensional analysis can be extended to the third dimension by the introduced hyperspectral 3D plant models. The information at which height a symptoms appears or whether leaves of a specific size are infested more often than others is directly available and usable in an automatic way. Furthermore, the 3D model exposes the plant parts with critical geometry supporting complicated reflectance conditions for the hyperspectral images. Such image region may be excluded from further analysis.

On the other hand, the manual analysis of hyperspectral images can be extended by spatial requests and constraints. Investigations on real plants include the observation from different viewing angles. This approach is simulated by the 3D plant model as views from different direction can be simulated. Further scanerios are the fading-out of unimportant background plant parts or the focus on a specific level within the plant. This 3D-shape-sensitive visualization techniques support the explorative investigation of plant characteristics because misleading spatial proximities within the 2D image caused by overlapping leaves and the projection in the image plane are neglected.

3.4   Hyperspectral 3D Plant Models as an Integration Platform

Current phenotyping platforms integrate multiple sensors. These sensors record multiple plant characteristics, each within a distinct geometric reference system and scale. Pointwise measurements are conducted by some chlorophyll fluorescence sensors, gas-based measurements of the metabolism regard the whole plant, pinhole cameras perform a perspective projection of the plants' reflectance characteristics and hyperspectral pushbroom cameras record the reflected light intensities line by line. The 3D shape sensors can be based on multiple measurement principles and determines the point location in its local coordinate system.

So far, the data of all these sensors is recorded, stored and analyzed separately and the results are combined as a description of a plant. This approach is very simple and reliable, as a data integration is not necessary and a sensor failure does not affect the other measurements. However, the recorded signals are not independent but they are caused partly by the same characteristic and, therefore, can be used to explain the observed phenomena. A separated analysis neglects these relations and does not reach the optimal analysis result which can be achieved by an integrated analysis.

Therefore, we propose to use the 3D model of the plant as an integration platform for all measurements conducted at one plant. For this purpose, all sensors have to be defined and calibrated in a unique coordinate system (Fig. 4). The measurements are assigned to the surface part which has been observed and stored with the additional spatial context. This additional effort of calibration and referencing provides directly referenced measurements of all sensors in a unique coordinate system. As in a example, destructive measurements of pigment concentrations at specific leaf points can be stored with relation to the plants' coordinate system. Further developments may enable a growing coordinate systems, the phyto-reference-system, which allows to track symptoms and specific phenomena over time by relating the 3D models of different observation days to each other.

Such plant model can be further enriched by process models to build a functional - structural plant model (FSPM) with additional real measurements [22]. Simulation of nutrient fluxes can be used to predict the development depending on environmental factors. The comparison of simulated and observed plant development will help to improve the growth models and extend the knowledge about the development mechanisms of plants.

The visualization of the generation, degradation and transport of substances within the plant is an interesting field for computer graphic. Particularly the different scales, from single cells to plant or field scale in a unique model, demand both generalizing and specific visualization techniques.

4   Conclusion

We present hyperspectral 3D plant models as a solution approach for the handling of geometrically related sensor signals and the shortcomings of hyperspectral imaging. However, the referenced data channels induce a number of open questions in generation as well as in analysis. The majority of these open tasks can be assigned to the field of computer vision. From the perspective of the computer vision community the combination of hyperspectral and geometric data can be a connecting point to the plant research. Different groups can work on subproblems.

We have identified several tasks for computer vision in the context of hyperspectral 3D models. The generation of hyperspectral 3D models demands for feature descriptor adapted to plant surfaces in 2D images and 3D point clouds. The generated hyperspectral 3D plant models require analysis methods that regard the specific relations between the two data channels. Especially, the high dimensional hyperspectral data contains high levels of redundancy which impairs the results quality. So far, the geometry-based radiometric calibration of hyperspectral plant images is neglected in the close-range. To improve the quality of high dimensional plant phenotyping data the measurement specifications have to be considered in detail, since i.e. spectral signals of plants are influenced by geometric configuration of sensor and illumination and the plant geometry. A combination of hyperspectral imaging with 3D laserscanning allows to model and to remove these effects from the data. It requires hyperspectral, virtual simulation environments integrating hyperspectral raytracing algorithms adapted to plant tissues. Methods for measuring and parameterizing the reflection characteristics of plants are required.

We believe that hyperspectral 3D plant models can significantly improve the phenotyping results and that they are a chance for the computer vision community to face real world problems. We are convinced that the computer vision community can contribute to the solution for the grand challenges facing society. The accelerated breeding and improved precision crop protection substantially contributes to safeguard the food supply while reducing the used resources such as water, fertilizer and pesticides.

References

1. Fiorani, F., Rascher, U., Jahnke, S., Schurr, U.: Imaging plants dynamics in heterogenic environments. Current Opinion in Biotechnology **23**, 227–235 (2012)
2. Mahlein, A.K., Oerke, E.C., Steiner, U., Dehne, H.W.: Recent advances in sensing plant diseases for precision crop protection. European Journal of Plant Pathology **133**(1), 197–209 (2012)
3. Paulus, S., Schumann, H., Leon, J., Kuhlmann, H.: A high precision laser scanning system for capturing 3D plant architecture and analysing growth of cereal plants. Biosystems Engineering **121**, 1–11 (2014)
4. Paulus, S., Behmann, J., Mahlein, A.K., Plümer, L., Kuhlmann, H.: Low-cost 3D systems - well suited tools for plant phenotyping. Sensors **14**, 3001–3018 (2014)

5. Bousquet, L., Lachérade, S., Jacquemoud, S., Moya, I.: Leaf BRDF measurements and model for specular and diffuse components differentiation. Remote Sensing of Environment **98**(2–3), 201–211 (2005)
6. Comar, A., Baret, F., Viénot, F., Yan, L., de Solan, B.: Wheat leaf bidirectional reflectance measurements: Description and quantification of the volume, specular and hot-spot scattering features. Remote Sensing of Environment **121**, 26–35 (2012)
7. Gupta, R., Hartley, R.I.: Linear pushbroom cameras. IEEE Transactions on Pattern Analysis and Machine Intelligence **19**(9), 963–975 (1997)
8. Jacquemoud, S., Verhoef, W., Baret, F., Bacour, C., Zarco-Tejada, P.J., Asner, G.P.: Franois, C., Ustin, S.L.: Prospect + sail models: A review of use for vegetation characterization. Remote Sensing of Environment **113**(suppl. 1), S56–S66 (2009)
9. Wagner, B., Santini, S., Ingensand, H., Gärtner, H.: A tool to model 3D coarse-root development with annual resolution. Plant and Soil **346**(1–2), 79–96 (2011)
10. Hosoi, F., Nakabayashi, K., Omasa, K.: 3-d modeling of tomato canopies using a high-resolution portable scanning lidar for extracting structural information. Sensors **11**(2), 2166–2174 (2011)
11. Omasa, K., Hosoi, F., Konishi, A.: 3D Lidar imaging for detecting and understanding plant responses and canopy structure. Journal of Experimental Botany **58**(4), 881–898 (2007)
12. Biskup, B., Scharr, H., Schurr, U., Rascher, U.: A stereo imaging system for measuring structural parameters of plant canopies. Plant, Cell & Environment **30**(10), 1299–308 (2007)
13. Liang, J., Zia, A., Zhou, J., Sirault, X.: 3d plant modelling via hyperspectral imaging. In: 2013 IEEE International Conference on Computer Vision Workshops (ICCVW), pp. 172–177 (2013)
14. Tilly, N., Hoffmeister, D., Liang, H., Cao, Q., Liu, Y., Miao, Y., Bareth, G.: Evaluation of terrestrial laser scanning for rice growth monitoring. International Archives of the Photogrammetry, Remote Sensing and Spatial Information Sciences, ISPRS Congress, Melbourne, Australia XXXIX, pp. 351–356 (2012)
15. Bellasio, C., Olejníčková, J., Tesa, R., Sebela, D., Nedbal, L.: Computer reconstruction of plant growth and chlorophyll fluorescence emission in three spatial dimensions. Sensors **12**(1), 1052–1071 (2012)
16. Paulus, S., Dupuis, J., Mahlein, A., Kuhlmann, H.: Surface feature based classification of plant organs from 3D laserscanned point clouds for plant phenotyping. BMC Bioinformatics **14**, 238–251 (2013)
17. Schöler, F., Steinhage, V.: Towards an automated 3D reconstruction of plant architecture. In: Schürr, A., Varró, D., Varró, G. (eds.) AGTIVE 2011. LNCS, vol. 7233, pp. 51–64. Springer, Heidelberg (2012)
18. Haralick, B.M., Lee, C.N., Ottenberg, K., Nölle, M.: Review and analysis of solutions of the three point perspective pose estimation problem. International Journal of Computer Vision **13**(3), 331–356 (1994)
19. Jacquemoud, S., Verhoef, W., Baret, F., Bacour, C., Zarco-Tejada, P.J., Asner, G.P., François, C., Ustin, S.L.: Prospect+ sail models: A review of use for vegetation characterization. Remote Sensing of Environment **113**, S56–S66 (2009)

20. Kuester, T., Spengler, D., Barczi, J.F., Segl, K., Hostert, P., Kaufmann, H.: Simulation of multitemporal and hyperspectral vegetation canopy bidirectional reflectance using detailed virtual 3-d canopy models. Geoscience and Remote Sensing **52**(4) (2013)
21. Behmann, J., Steinrücken, J., Plümer, L.: Detection of early plant stress responses in hyperspectral images. ISPRS Journal of Photogrammetry and Remote Sensing **93**, 98–111 (2014)
22. Vos, J., Evers, J., Buck-Sorlin, G., Andrieu, B., Chelle, M., De Visser, P.: Functional-structural plant modelling: a new versatile tool in crop science. Journal of Experimental Botany **61**(8), 2101–2115 (2010)

3D Multimodal Simulation of Image Acquisition by X-Ray and MRI for Validation of Seedling Measurements with Segmentation Algorithms

Landry Benoit[1], Georges Semaan[1], Florence Franconi[2], Étienne Belin[1], François Chapeau-Blondeau[1], Didier Demilly[3], and David Rousseau[4(✉)]

[1] Laboratoire Angevin de Recherche en Ingénierie des Systèmes (LARIS), Université d'Angers, 62 avenue Notre Dame du Lac, 49000 Angers, France
[2] Plateforme d'Ingénierie et d'Analyse Moléculaire (PIAM), Université d'Angers, Angers, France
[3] GEVES, Station Nationale d'Essais de Semences (SNES), rue Georges Morel, 49071 Beaucouzé, France
[4] Université de Lyon, Laboratoire CREATIS; CNRS, UMR5220; INSERM, U1044, Université Lyon 1; INSA-Lyon, 69621 Villeurbanne, France
david.rousseau@univ-lyon1.fr

Abstract. In this report, we present a 3D simulator for the numerical validation of segmentation algorithms for seedling in soil from X-ray or MRI. A 3D simulator of root in elongation is coupled to a simulator of the image acquisition to generate images of simulated seedling associated with a known synthetic ground truth. We detail how acquisition parameters of the seedling and parameters of the imaging systems are estimated and combined to produce realistic images. The resulting simulator is available on line to open the possibility of segmentation challenges with *in silico* validation based on unlimited number of seedling.

Keywords: Seedling monitoring · X-Ray · MRI · 3D simulation

1 Introduction

Plant roots present challenges for computer vision, as they form rich 3D networks inaccessible via visible light imaging. Analysis of these highly complex structures has recently been made possible in 3D and directly in pots with soil by the use of X-Ray computed tomography (X-Ray CT)[1–3] or magnetic resonance imaging (MRI) [4]. In addition, the constitution of roots and soil in terms of atomic number and water composition are often poorly contrasted in X-Ray CT or MRI, making the segmentation of such images also challenging. Accordingly, the segmentation of the roots from X-Ray CT or MRI is currently receiving attention from computer scientists, to develop new algorithms [1–4]. Because of their novelty, these first segmentation algorithms of [1–4] stand as pilot studies and proofs of feasibility. However, the assessment of performance of such image

© Springer International Publishing Switzerland 2015
L. Agapito et al. (Eds.): ECCV 2014 Workshops, Part IV, LNCS 8928, pp. 131–139, 2015.
DOI: 10.1007/978-3-319-16220-1_10

processing tasks is uneasy. Mechanical extraction of the root from the soil for topological comparison is risky since it might damage or destruct the smallest parts of the root system. Also, since X-Ray CT and MRI are rather new as routine tools for plant science, it is complicated to find experts in plant science and radiology to manually segment the root in 3D as commonly done in X-Ray CT and MRI for the segmentation of organs in the biomedical domain. Another approach, usual in the biomedical domain, and here also difficult to transpose to plant science because of the network nature of the roots, is the realization of physical phantoms. In this report, we propose an alternative for the validation of segmentation algorithms from X-Ray CT and MRI with the use of a 3D root simulator coupled to a simulator of the image acquisition to generate 3D stacks of X-ray like or MRI like images of simulated plants associated with a known synthetic ground truth. Such an approach is quite common again in the biomedical domain [5], but has only very recently been introduced to roots [4,6]. The proposed numerical validation method of algorithms for image processing of roots described in Fig. 1 is composed of three stages: A seedling simulator establishes a ground truth. This is followed by an acquired image simulator which generates the images to be processed by the algorithm being tested. At the end, a comparison between the ground truth and the results produced by the algorithm is realized. The imaging system simulated in [6] generates seedling in 2D acquired from backlight with conventional visible imaging. We provide an extension of [6] in 3D and apply it to X-Ray CT and MRI. The monitoring of the elongation of seedling is an important biological task since this elongation corresponds to the so-called heterotrophic growth which is highly correlated with the probability of emergence of the seedling at the surface of the soil. Also, the analysis of movement of the radicle of seedling during the elongation stage has recently been demonstrated to reveale oscillations of the tip of the root. Such findings are of great interest for bio-inspired robotics [7], however, so far the analysis of these oscillatory movements have been demonstrated outside the soil. This adds another motivation for the segmentation of the seedling in the soil and the importance to validate the segmentation algorithms with the simulation approach presented in this report.

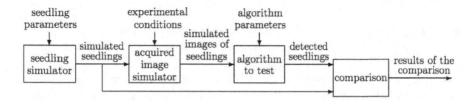

Fig. 1. Principle of the numerical method used to validate image processing algorithms of seedling images. In this report we present the coupling between a 3D seedling simulator with two acquired image simulator: X-ray CT and MRI.

The report is organized as follows. We start with the simulator of seedling and then give the image acquisition simulator used for X-Ray CT and MRI. This is illustrated with simulated images of various plants at the scale of seedlings. We present how simulation tools introduced for the biomedical domain in [5] for X-Ray CT and MRI can be also serve for plants. We eventually discuss possible extensions of this work and provide the address of the on line platform to run our simulator.

2   Seedling Elongation Simulation

Seedling are simulated from the L-system process described in [8] which enables accelerated elaboration of root systems simulated in 3D with no control on root width as shown in Fig. 2. We use the upgraded version of this simulator recently presented in [6] which allows, as visible in Fig. 3, the generation of spherical seeds at initial time and adds control on root width. This seedling simulator is available on line at [9]. This corresponds to the germination and elongation stages of seedling growth occuring for real plants in the soil before the activation of the photosynthesis. The parameters used by this simulator are the size of the seeds, the width of the roots, the number of roots per seedling and the duration of the simulation fixing the overall size of the root system.

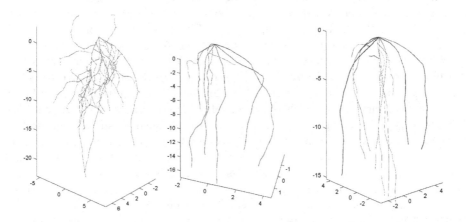

Fig. 2. Three simulated root systems using the generation algorithm described in [8].

3   Image Simulator

The simulation of images of seedling acquired by a specific imaging technique requires the estimation of the physical parameters at the origin of the contrasts in the images produced by this imaging technique. We start with X-Ray CT

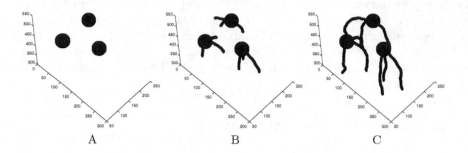

Fig. 3. Three simulated seedlings in phase of elongation from the stage of seeds (A), at 7 days (B), at 14 days (C) with the simulator described in [6] and extended here in 3D. After the initial time the spheres gives rise to the cotyledons and the tubular parts to the radicles of the seedling.

which provides, in first approximation, a contrast of absorbance of X-Ray in the tissue following a Beer-Lambert exponential law as a function of the width x of the sample

$$I(x) = I_0 \exp(-\mu x) \,, \tag{1}$$

with I_0 the intensity of the incident X-Ray beam and μ, expressed in m^{-1}, the absorbance coefficient. With prior knowledge of I_0 and seedling width x, we estimated from the X-Ray 2D projection of Fig. 4 (obtained for a given and fixed beam energy), the absorbance μ in the seedlings, assumed here in first approximation as homogeneous, for various species. We then recorded images of a pot containing only the nutritive substrate where the seedling are to grow. For illustration, two substrates of practical interest were acquired with sand and soil. The resulting tomogram displays complex 3D structures at multiple scales difficult to reproduce with simple statistical models such as surrogates models based on first and second order statistics. Instead, we propose, as in [6] and shown in Fig. 5, an empirical approach by recording a bank of images of real substrate. It is then straightforward to generate, as in Fig. 6, simulation of images of a seedling in substrate by replacing the background of the seedling by the substrate and by simulating the intensity in the seedling from Eq. (1). To appreciate the realism of our simulator, we provide in Fig. 7 two views of a seedling in soil and sand acquired from a real X-Ray system. Fig. 6 and 7 demonstrate that the segmentation of seedling in soil is a difficult problem for plant image analysis. The segmentation of root in soil in X-Ray CT images has been recently solved with an elegant region growing approach based on the Shannon-Jensen divergence [1–3]. The segmentation in these studies is done on adult plants with aerial parts highly contrasted in X-Ray CT. Therefore it is easy to locate the position of the root at the surface of the soil as initiation of the region-growing process. Such an initiation is more difficult to realize automatically or manually when one works

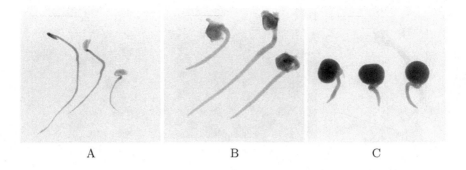

Fig. 4. X-Ray images of *Medicago truncatula* (A), sugar beet (B) and peas (C). The mesurated absorbance of cotyledons is 366±34 m^{-1} for *Medicago truncatula*, 338±27 m^{-1} for sugar beet and 166±12 m^{-1} for Peas. The mesurated absorbance of radicle is 372±74 m^{-1} for *Medicago truncatula*, 428±13 m^{-1} for sugar beet and 271±29 m^{-1} for Peas.

on seeds or seedling buried in the soil. Consequently, the segmentation of X-Ray CT images of seedling in soil stands as an open problem for plant phenotyping that can be tackled with *in silico* validation with the simulation approach with have initiated here.

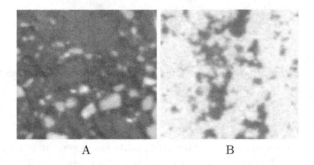

Fig. 5. Two experimentally acquired X-Ray tomography images of substrate for the seedling (A: a pot of soil - B: a pot of sand with water)

We have undertaken the same approach of 3D simulator with MRI that we now describe in a similar way. Basic spin-echo MRI sequences provide a gray level I in the tissue depending on the density of protons DP, relaxation times (T_1, T_2) and acquisition times T_R (repetition time) and T_E (acquisition time) in response to magnetic impulses following

$$I \sim DP \times [1 - \exp((-T_R)/T_1)] \exp((-T_E)/T_2) . \qquad (2)$$

Contrasts in basic spin-echo MRI therefore depends on characteristics (DP, T_1, T_2) and acquisition parameters (T_E, T_R). For illustration, we have estimated

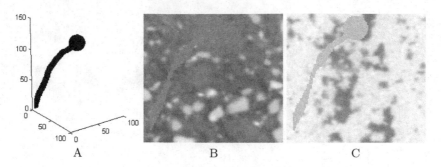

Fig. 6. 3D simulated seedling (A) used as ground truth to simulate the X-Ray CT images of B and C respectively produced with the substrates of Figs. 5A and B

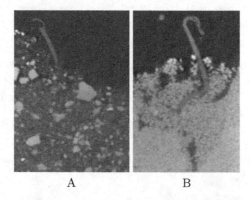

Fig. 7. Two experimentally acquired X-Ray tomography images of wheat seedlings in a pot of soil (A) and in a pot of sand (B)

these parameters modeled as Gaussian distributions in seedlings of wheat buried in sand with water. The corresponding estimates are given in Table 1.

Table 1. Mean m, and standard deviation std for MRI parameters of Eq. (2) estimated from averaging on seedlings of wheat in sand with water. Acquisition realized on a Bruker Advance DRX MRI system (Bruker Biospin SA, Wissembourg, France) in conventional acquisition conditions with a reference 2D spin-echo and a linear sampling process.

Parameters	T1 (in milliseconds)	T2 (in milliseconds)	DP
Water in sand	$m = 2626$; $std = 86$	$m = 17$; $std = 5$	$m = 65912$; $std = 1443$
Cotyledons	$m = 989$; $std = 44$	$m = 17$; $std = 5$	$m = 123187$; $std = 29341$
Radicle	$m = 2235$; $std = 47$	$m = 34$; $std = 1$	$m = 250304$; $std = 5597$

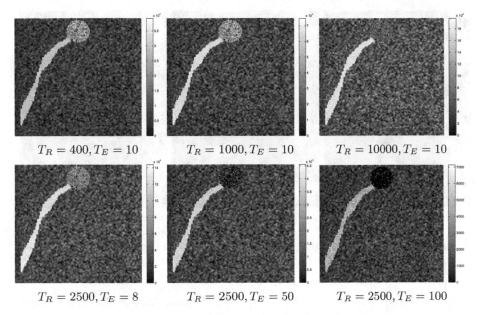

$$T_R = 400, T_E = 10 \qquad T_R = 1000, T_E = 10 \qquad T_R = 10000, T_E = 10$$

$$T_R = 2500, T_E = 8 \qquad T_R = 2500, T_E = 50 \qquad T_R = 2500, T_E = 100$$

Fig. 8. Six MRI images generated from different choices of acquisition parameters (T_R, T_E). The gray scale level is different from one image to another in order to facilitate visualization.

Therefrom, based on the binary masks of simulated seedlings such as those of Fig. 3, we can generate 3D maps of MRI parameters (DP, T_1, T_2) here modeled as Gaussian distribution with mean and standard deviation values taken from Table 1 in the sand (background), the cotyledons (sphere) and the radicle (tubular part). The simulation of 2D spin-echo MRI images can then be obtained from the computation of Eq. (2) for a choice of acquisition parameters (T_R, T_E). This can be done automatically on line with help of the virtual imaging platform VIP [5]. It is then possible to search for optimal acquisition parameters (T_R, T_E) for a given image processing tasks. A very useful simulation tool indeed since the choice of acquisition parameters are usually left to the qualitative empirical expertise of the person in charge of the acquisition but without guarantee of satisfying an optimal criterion on the information to be eventually extracted from the images. As an illustration of the interest of our simulation process, we give in Fig. 8 the MRI images generated from different choices of acquisition parameters (T_R, T_E). To appreciate the realism of our simulator, we provide in Fig. 9 a view of a seedling buried in sand with water acquired from a real MRI system with similar acquisition parameters. Simulation of root systems in MRI were also given in [4], but it is to be noted that the approach was distinct from the one described above. In [4], the MRI signal in the substrate and in the root system is generated with a statistical approach from a Gaussian model in the acquired image I directly (while our Gaussian model lay here on (DP, T_1, T_2)) and tested for various signal to noise ratio (SNR). Here, the proposition is more

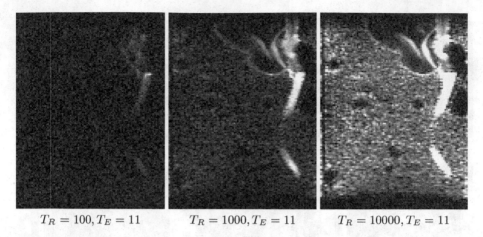

$$T_R = 100, T_E = 11 \qquad T_R = 1000, T_E = 11 \qquad T_R = 10000, T_E = 11$$

Fig. 9. Three images of a seedling of wheat in a pot of sand acquired from a real MRI system with different choices of acquisition parameters (T_R, T_E)

physics-oriented with the simulation of the 2D spin-echo signal which allow to search for the acquisition parameters giving the optimal SNR.

4   Conclusion

We have extended to 3D and multimodality the simulation approach recently introduced in [6] for *in silico* validation of root segmentation algorithms. The simulator in [6] was given in 2D and illustrated with seedling segmentation from visible imaging in backlight mode. Our new simulator can now serve for the validation, with a 3D synthetic ground truth, of root segmentation algorithms applied on 3D images of roots. For illustration here we have generated images of seedlings in substrate of soil or sand. The acquisition parameters for X-Ray CT or MRI in the seedling were considered spatialy homogeneous or distributed following Gaussian distributions. It would however be straightforward to inject more elaborated spatial variation models on larger root systems if a more realistic description is needed. Other perspectives concern the extension to other imaging modalities of interest for root screening. This includes 3D positron emission tomography (PET) which gives access to physiological informations in roots [10]. The estimation of desintegration life-time of biomarkers would have to be undertaken but the virtual imaging platform [5] used in this report for MRI also incorporates PET simulation and could thus still serve to generate simulated images. Also, when the full 3D organization of the roots or the mechanical impact of the soil on the root are not required for the biological purpose, it is possible to lower the cost of the imaging modality and use rhizotron or hydroponic growth in which roots are accessible from conventional visible imaging. These imaging systems however present specificities due to the presence of a nutritive substrate possibly different from the one modeled in [6] and it would also be interesting to extend our simulation approach to these systems.

Acknowledgments. This work received support from the French Government supervised by the "Agence Nationale de la Recherche" in the framework of the program "Investissements d'Avenir" under reference ANR-11-BTBR-0007 (AKER program). Landry BENOIT gratefully acknowledges financial support from Angers Loire Métropole and SNES-GEVES for the preparation of his PhD. Authors thank Lydie Ledroit (INRA) for technical support on seedlings, Karima BOUDEHRI and Laurence LECORRE from SNES-GEVES for X-Ray acquisition on the platform PHENOTIC, Angers, France and Sorina POP from CREATIS, Université Lyon 1, France for introducing to simulation on the platform VIP.

References

1. Mairhofer, S., Zappala, S., Tracy, S., Sturrock, C., Bennett, M., Mooney, S., Pridemore, T.: Rootrak: automated recovery of 3D plant root architecture in soil with X-Ray micro computed tomography using visual tracking. Plant Physiology **158**, 561–569 (2012)
2. Zappala, S., Mairhofer, S., Tracy, S., Sturrock, C., Bennett, M., Pridemore, T., Mooney, S.: Quantifying the effect of soil moisture content on segmenting root system architecture in X-Ray micro-Computed Tomography. Plant and Soil (2013)
3. Mairhofer, S., Zappala, S., Sturrock, C., Bennett, M., Mooney, S., Pridemore, T. Recovering complete plant root system architectures from soil via X-Ray Micro-Computed Tomography. Plant Physiology 359 (2013)
4. Schultz, H., Postma, J., Dusschoten, D., Scharr, H., Behnke, S.: Plant root system from MRI images. Computer Vision, Imaging and Computer Graphics **359**, 411–425 (2013)
5. Glatard, T., Lartizien, C., Gibaud, B.: Ferreira da Silva, G., Cervenansky, F., Alessandrini, M., Benoit Cattin, H., Bernard, O., Camarasu Pop, S.: A virtual imaging platform for multi-modality medical image simulation. IEEE Transactions on Medical Imaging **32**, 110–118 (2013)
6. Benoit, L., Rousseau, D., Belin, E., Demilly, D., Chapeau-Blondeau, F.: Simulation of image acquisition in machine vision dedicated to seedling elongation to validate image processing root segmentation algorithms. Computers and Electronics in Agriculture **104**, 84–92 (2014)
7. Popova, L., Russino, A., Ascrizzi, A., Mazzolai, B.: Analysis of movement in primary maize roots. Biologia **67**, 517–524 (2012)
8. Leitner, D., Klepsch, S., Bodner, G., Schnepf, A.: A dynamic root system growth model based on L-systems. Plant Soil **332**, 177–192 (2010)
9. http://lisabiblio.univ-angers.fr/PHENOTIC/telechargements.html
10. Jahnke, S., Menzel, M.I., Van Dusschoten, D., Roeb, G.W., Bühler, J., Minwuyelet, S., Blümler, P., Temperton, V.M., Hombach, T., Streun, M., Beer, S., Khodaverdi, M., Ziemons, K., Coenen, H.H., Schurr, U.: Combined MRI-PET dissects dynamic changes in plant structures and functions. Plant Journal **59**, 634–644 (2009)

Distortion Correction in 3D-Modeling of Root Systems for Plant Phenotyping

Tushar Kanta Das Nakini and Guilherme N. DeSouza[✉]

Vision-Guided and Intelligent Robotics (ViGIR) Lab,
Electrical and Computer Engineering Department,
University of Missouri, Columbia, USA
DeSouzaG@vigir.org

Abstract. Root Phenotyping is an important tool in predicting the life and growth of plants. Many systems have been developed to automate the process of extracting root traits using 3D imaging system, however, not many of those systems corrected for the distortions that frequently appear during this process. In this paper we present a new method to compensate for light refractions that occur due to hydroponic substrates – gel-based platforms for growing plants. As our results demonstrate, our method provides an accurate 3D point cloud containing the coordinates of the surface of the root system with error smaller than 0.16 mm in average and standard deviation of less than 0.13 mm.

Keywords: Root phenotyping · Gel-based media · Hydroponic substrate · Glass cylinder · Distortion correction · 3D modeling

1 Introduction

Root System Architecture (RSA) is the spatial representation of a plant root system [24]. It plays a vital role in determining the life and growth of plants and hence, it is becoming one of the main focus of Computer Vision (CV) researchers in the field of biology and plant sciences. Indeed, many researchers have long correlated root traits present in the various RSAs to physiological functions of the plant, such as resistance to drought [9,30], carbon allocation [4], phosphorous and nitrogen affinity [5,22,42], nutrient-acquisition capacity, etc. However, due to the practical difficulties in measuring and classifying RSAs, root phenotyping had, at least until recently, received little attention from the CV community. Among these difficulties is the ability to measure root traits without destroying the plants. In that sense, some researchers opted to grow plants in hydroponic substrates– translucent gel-based media [8]. This approach allowed for the inspection of the plant while still inside a cylinder using, for example, simple two-dimensional (2D) imaging. In fact, 2D imaging was not only the first, but it is still likely the most popular tool for studying RSAs [7,23,29]. Unfortunately, while rich in details and extensively exploited, 2D features are quite limited by the possibility of self occlusion in the RSA, the high density of some

© Springer International Publishing Switzerland 2015
L. Agapito et al. (Eds.): ECCV 2014 Workshops, Part IV, LNCS 8928, pp. 140–157, 2015.
DOI: 10.1007/978-3-319-16220-1_11

roots, perspective distortions, etc. For that reason, researchers started to shift their attention to three dimensional (3D) modeling of RSAs [8,18,36]. In that case, however, distortion becomes a major problem, since the refractive nature of light passing through gel-glass media makes it virtually impossible to register raw images obtained from different viewing angles – a required step in any method for 3D modeling.

In this paper, our main goal is exactly to handle distortions caused by the refraction of light during the creation of 3D models of roots. This same distortion problem has been addressed in [39]. However, in that work, the authors assumed the simple case of a spot laser range finder that could move up and down perpendicular to the cylinder vertical axis. Later, in [38], the authors extended that idea to accommodate for a vertical laser stripe. At that time, however, the surface of the media was considered flat and the thickness of the glass was not taken into consideration. In contrast, the main contribution of this research is to provide the first holistic distortion model for 3D imaging of RSA using structure light scanners and a gel-based platform for growing soybean. In summary, here, it will be explained how to achieve clear, undistorted 3D models as the ones shown in Figures 1a-d, as opposed to the 3D models created from distorted data in Figures 1e-h.

(a)   (b)   (c)   (d)

(e)   (f)   (g)   (h)

Fig. 1. 3D Models of four different families of soybean: in (a) - (d) the undistorted models after the proposed corrections; and in (e) - (h) the raw, distorted models

2   Background and Related Works

In the field of computer vision, imaging systems can be classified into two groups: 1) passive; and 2) active sensing. In passive sensing methods, the images are collected from different viewing angles using only the natural ambient lights [12, 21, 25, 27]. Later, those multiple images must be corresponded and *stitched* together to create a single 3D cloud of points. In active sensing, approaches can be divided into three groups depending on the type of sensor used: time-of-flight (ToF) sensors, structured-light scanners (SLS), and resonance sensors [6, 20].

In the first group, ToF, we will find sensors that measure the actual time it takes for the signal to bounce off the object (e.g. sound echoes), or those that instead resort to measuring phase changes in the returned signal to infer the actual distance (e.g most of the sensors with light-spectrum or higher wavelengths). In either cases, ToF sensors are usually quite expensive, and therefore, they lost popularity in the computer vision circles to recent SLS. In this case, a SLS uses an external light or energy source to project fixed or moving patterns or "lighting structures" onto the scene. These patterns deform around the objects indicating their depths, or ranges from the sensor. Examples of SLS's include those using: 1) alternating illuminated-dark stripes; 2) dot patterns (usually in the near IR spectrum); and 3) a moving, thin laser stripe. Early works with SLS's date back to almost forty years ago [1, 2, 16, 41] but they are still popular in newer hardware versions such as the Microsoft Kinect. Finally, the resonance sensors employ strong energy sources – e.g. from X-ray emitters – that penetrate the object causing resonance on the chemical components or particles of the object lying on a plane created by another energy source – e.g. from a magnetic field. The magnetic field is controlled so that the plane is successively moved up or down, *slicing* the object into almost contiguous images.

As with the passive sensing, and despite the quite different principles employed by the active sensing systems, they also require the multiple range images or slices to be registered with one another while creating a single and complete 3D model.

In terms of root phenotyping, imaging systems can be broadly divided into two groups: destructive and non-destructive. In destructive approaches, the roots are quickly excavated, so they can be immediately imaged and analyzed [34]. By doing so, the roots are often damaged and the soils irreparably disturbed, making it impossible to image that same root under the same conditions in the future. On the other hand, in non-destructive methods, the roots are grown in translucent media, which allows for proper imaging systems to continuously create 2D or 3D models for future analysis. In such cases, the plant remains virtually undisturbed and temporal analyses of the root growth and responses to stress are possible.

Typical 3D modeling systems include: 1) structured-light scanners (e.g. laser) and multi-stereopsis based setups [8, 10, 26, 28, 33]; 2) Magnetic Resonance Imaging (MRI) or Nuclear Magnetic Resonance (NMR) [18, 31, 36, 37]; and 4) X-ray Computerized Axial Tomography (CAT) or simply Computerized Tomography (CT) [13, 14, 35].

Most of these systems, e.g. MRI, NMR and CT, are quite expensive and complex in nature. In the original CT technology, for example, the use of cone-shape beams caused the image of the object to become magnified. In order to compensate for this magnification, CT equipment started to use synchrotron emitters, which instead keep the beams almost parallel. In turn, these orthogonal projections cause artifacts in the image which must be eliminated together with other artifacts that also appear due to incomplete sampling of the so-called Radon space [19].

Another problem from which, in this case, all 3D imaging systems for gel-based platforms suffer is image distortion. This distortion is due to the refractive nature of light, or EM waves in general, that bends as it traverses different media. In order to cope with this problem, many researchers have opted to: 1) use optical correction tanks [8,33]; 2) increase the size of the cylinder with respect to the volume of the RSA to minimize the effects of distortion [17,32]; or 3) simply ignore the distortions [10,11,40].

In the case of correction tanks, even though they may indeed eliminate distortion errors, the final setup is quite cumbersome due to the extra tank that needs to be added to the system; the care with its positioning with respect to the root/gel cylinder; and the positioning of the principle axis of the camera perpendicular to the tank surface.

Similarly, the reliance on a small root systems in comparison to the volume of the gel cylinder as a method to minimize distortions is not always possible or easy to achieve. In the case of rice and other cereal grains with small RSAs, this may not represent a problem. However, for soybean, corn and many other plants with larger root systems, making sure that the root is confined to the interior of the cylinder may represent a large waste of gel and the associated increase in the cost for root phenotyping per plant.

In contrast, here we propose a new method for correcting distortion in 3D modeling of root systems inside a gel-based platform. Our system is quite less expensive and comparatively much simpler than other active sensing systems. Also, and possibly more importantly, there are little constraints on the positioning of any of its components – camera, laser emitter, gel cylinder, etc. In fact, both the system's intrinsic and extrinsic parameters are automatically calibrated. That includes, of course, the distortion parameters used later on while imaging a root system. These distortion parameters originate from the many refractions of light from the emitter, through the glass-gel, and back onto the

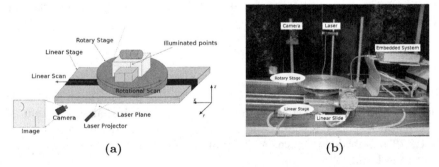

(a)   (b)

Fig. 2. Laser Stripe Structured-Light Scanner: a) Depiction of the principle behind a SLS using a laser stripe: the laser stripe conforms to the contour of the object in the scene, which provides to the camera a measurement of the object's depth and shape; b) Actual system used in this research. Indications of the position of the camera, the position of the laser, the coordinate frames, etc. are superimposed onto the picture.

camera sensor. As our results demonstrate, at the end of the process, our systems provides a 3D point cloud of the surface of the root with error smaller than 0.02mm in average and a standard deviation of less than 0.3mm.

3   Proposed Method

In this work, a structured-light system (SLS) using a laser stripe similar to the one in [28] was employed to image RSAs of plants in a gel-based platform. As pointed out earlier, the proposed system is quite inexpensive while it provides a dense, precise and accurate 3D point cloud. However, as with any other active sensor for the same application, the use of SLS results in distorted models due to the refraction of the light through the various changes of media – air-to-glass, glass-to-gel, and back. These distortions are compensated by the system presented here.

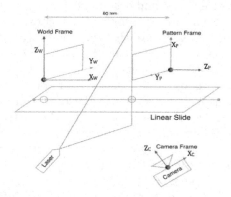

Fig. 3. Details on the SLS and its choices of coordinate frames. The figure shows the World, the Pattern, and the Camera coordinate frames with the actual orientations used in this paper: e.g., the XY plane of the pattern was arbitrarily set parallel to the world YZ plane.

3.1   Hardware Setup

The hardware used in our setup consists of three parts: 1) a laser light source (Lasiris Structured Laser Light, 635nm, 5mW); 2) a firewire camera (Firefly MV FFMV-03M2C); and 3) a linear slide platform with a turn table, both controlled by a TS-7250 embedded device. A sketch and an actual picture of the system is presented in Figure 2.

In this setup, the plane created by the laser source is made approximately perpendicular to the direction of movement of the turn-table platform on the linear slide. As shown in Figure 2b, the liner slide moves along the X-axis and the rotary stage rotates about the Z-axis. The camera is connected to a computer through a firewire port and it is calibrated for the extrinsic and intrinsic parameters by placing a chess board at the origin of the pattern coordinate frame – refer to Figure 3. The calibration of the intrinsic and extrinsic parameter of the camera as well as of its lens distortions are performed using the algorithm described in [28]. Because of this calibration, in the next sections, it will be assumed that the camera lenses produce undistorted 2D images of the scene. The world reference frame, indicated in Figure 3, is the coordinate frame with respect to which the position of the laser, the center of the camera and the position of the axis of the gel cylinder are calibrated.

3.2   Creating 3D Models

In this section, we explain in detail the data acquisition process employed by the SLS; the proposed technique for compensating for distortion due to light refraction; and the process to create the final 3D model.

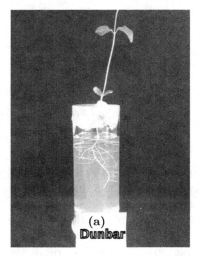

Fig. 4. Image of a root growing inside a gel-based platform

Data Acquisition: First, roots are grown inside the gel cylinder as shown in Figure 4. Then, the gel platform is placed on the linear slide which is moved back and forth for scanning the plant. One complete scan consists of moving the linear slide forward in front of the laser and then backwards to its initial position, followed by a rotation of the turn table by a predefined angle around its vertical axis. This process is repeated until the root is observed from all 360 degrees.

The linear slide has four different phases: 1) Ramp-up, which is when the slide accelerates to reach the desired velocity; 2) Constant-speed, when the slide moves with a constant velocity; 3) Ramp-down, when the slide decelerates to a full stop; and 4) Quick return to origin and rotate the turn-table. As pointed out earlier, the world frame – shown in Figure 3 – is chosen in such a way that the position of the linear slide at the beginning of its constant-speed phase coincides with the origin of the world coordinate frame. Also, at that moment, images of the root are grabbed and stored in sequence, until the linear slide reaches the end of the constant-speed phase. The camera is synchronized with the embedded device that controls the liner slide.

Every image in a scan registers the shape of the laser stripe at a specific position of the linear slide, as illustrated in Figure 2a – i.e. the index j of an image file saved by the system corresponds directly to a position of the linear slide in the X direction of the World coordinate frame. Also, the row value v^j of a pixel on the laser stripe in the image plane j relates to the height of the corresponding point on the object/root – as measured by the Z coordinate in the World frame. Similarly, the column value u^j of that same pixel relates to the depth of the object in space – this time along the Y coordinate in the World frame. In summary, the relation between the image coordinate (u^j, v^j) of a pixel on the laser stripe in the jth image and the corresponding space coordinate (x^j, y^j, z^j) of the object being illuminated by the laser stripe is given by the following equations:

$$\begin{bmatrix} \bar{x}^j \\ \bar{y}^j \\ \bar{z}^j \\ \rho^j \end{bmatrix} = T * \begin{bmatrix} v^j \\ u^j \\ 1 \end{bmatrix}$$

$$\begin{bmatrix} x^j \\ y^j \\ z^j \end{bmatrix} = \begin{bmatrix} \bar{x}^j/\rho^j \\ \bar{y}^j/\rho^j \\ \bar{z}^j/\rho^j \end{bmatrix} + \begin{bmatrix} x_0 + (j-1)\Delta x \\ 0 \\ 0 \end{bmatrix}$$

(1)

where T is a 4x3 transformation matrix calculated as described in [28], ρ^j is a scale factor, Δx is the step taken by the linear slide between each consecutive image acquisitions, and $x_0 = 0$.

If the camera and the root were immersed in the same medium (e.g. air), then these would be the final space coordinates of the illuminated pixel on the root. However, since the root is placed in a different medium, the (u^j, v^j) values observed by the camera are actually distorted due to the refractive indexes of the different media – leading to the calculation of the wrong spacial coordinates from eq(1). The process to undistort these coordinates is explained in the next section.

Undistorting the Cloud of Points: As the laser stripe travels from the laser source, through the gel, off the root and onto the camera sensor, it refracts several times, each refraction depends on the angle of incidence with the specific medium change and their refractive indexes. In order to compensate for the consequent distortions, we must account for each one of the refractions in sequence. Also, to better explain this process, we will separate them into three parts: First, we will account for the refractions as the light coming from the illuminated root travels towards the camera; Then, the refractions as the laser penetrates the glass and gel until it hits the root; and Finally, we will combine these two paths of the light in order to determine the actual position of the desired point on the root.

However, before we can explain the three steps above, we must first calculate the position of the glass cylinder and the camera optical center. These will be required later on in order to calculate the cylinder surface normals and the refracted and incident rays.

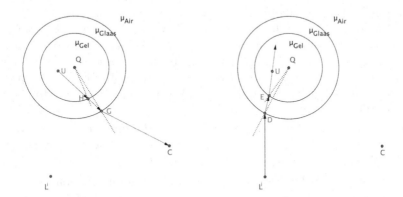

(a) Refraction of the laser coming of the scene. As the point G & H are not on the same plane, we will have center Q_k, where k=1,2.

(b) Refraction of the laser going into the scene. The point D and E are on the same plane, hence the center Q will be the same for these points.

Fig. 5. Refraction on the Cylinder due to Laser and Camera

Calculating the Positions of Cylinder and Camera Center: In order to calculate the position of the vertical axis of the cylinder, we must emphasize that the image acquisition is synchronized with the motion of the linear slide. Hence, we can express the X coordinate of the center of the cylinder as a function of the index of the image j, the velocity of the slide in mm/sec V_{slide}, and the speed of the camera in frames/sec S_{camera}. In summary, the X-coordinate of the center of the cylinder is given by:

$$X^j = \Delta x * (j-1) = \frac{V_{slide}}{S_{camera}} * (j-1)$$

Additionally, since the cylinder moves only in the X direction, $Y^j = 0$ and $Z^j = z^j$, where z^j is obtained from eq(1) for any given pixel (u^j, v^j). So, the center of the cylinder is given by:

$$Q = [X^j, 0, z^j] \qquad (2)$$

Also, the center of the camera C can be evaluated directly from the extrinsic parameters $^C H_P$ and the transformation matrix between the pattern and the world coordinate frames $^P H_W$, both obtained during camera calibration. That is, given:

$$^W H_C = \left(^C H_P * {}^P H_W \right)^{-1}$$

the center of the camera frame is:

$$[X_c, Y_c, Z_c, 1]^T = {}^W H_C * [0, 0, 0, 1]^T \tag{3}$$

Reversed Ray-Tracing from Camera: We are now ready to consider the actual refractions of the light through the glass/gel cylinder. As shown in Figure 5a, the light coming from the root inside the gel suffers two consecutive refractions before reaching the camera. These refractions are due to the thickness of the glass cylinder. So, in order to compensate for this component of the distortion, we follow a reversed ray tracing method similar to the one proposed in [39].

As also shown in the Figure 5a, we let $\overrightarrow{GC}$ be the direction of the ray converging to the image pixel $\left(u^j, v^j \right)$ and passing through the camera center C. This direction can be easily calculated from $\left(u^j, v^j \right)$ and C alone using eq(3) – i.e. without actual knowledge of G – the point at the intersection of $\overrightarrow{GC}$ and the external surface of the glass cylinder. Once this direction $\overrightarrow{GC}$ is found, and using the equation of a cylinder with X-Y coordinates of its center Q_1 given by eq(2) and diameter d_{ext}, finding the coordinate of G becomes a trivial algebraic exercise. The missing Z coordinate of Q_1 is then the same as the Z coordinate of G.

This G point on the surface of the cylinder is the point where the last refraction takes place: i.e. as the light finally leaves a denser medium (glass) into a rarer medium (air). Following Snell's Law of Refraction and its equation, we can calculate the incident ray at that point G. But first, we have to calculate the normal to the cylinder at G, which is defined as:

$$\overrightarrow{Q_1 G} = \frac{G - Q_1}{\|G - Q_1\|}$$

From the normal $\overrightarrow{Q_1 G}$ and the refracted ray $\overrightarrow{GC}$, and given that these are both unity vectors, the angle of refraction is calculated using their cross product:

$$sin(\theta_{air}) = \left\| \overrightarrow{Q_1 G} \times \overrightarrow{GC} \right\| \tag{4}$$

We denote this angle θ_{air} because the refracted ray along $\overrightarrow{GC}$ travels indeed through the *air*. Similarly, the incidence angle will be denoted θ_{glass}, and that angle can be found using Snell's equation: $\mu_{glass} * sin(\theta_{glass}) = \mu_{air} * sin(\theta_{air})$, where μ_{glass} and μ_{air} are the refractive indexes of the glass (incident) and air (refractive) media, respectively. And hence:

$$sin(\theta_{glass}) = \frac{\mu_{air} * sin(\theta_{air})}{\mu_{glass}}$$

From the system setup in Figure 2, one can infer that the direction $\overrightarrow{GC}$ is not necessarily horizontal (i.e. parallel to the world XY plane). So in order to calculate the actual incident ray, we will use the plane containing the incident ray, the refracted ray and the normal of the surface of the glass cylinder at the point G. This plane is known to exist also due to Snell's Law of Refraction and it is given by its surface normal, which can be determined by:

$$\overrightarrow{SN1_C} = \overrightarrow{Q_1G} \times \overrightarrow{GC} \tag{5}$$

Finally, the actual incident ray can be expressed using the vector $\overrightarrow{Q_1G}$ rotated about the vector $\overrightarrow{SN1_C}$ by an angle of θ_{glass} – which can be easily accomplished, for example, through an operation with unity quaternions [15]. This incident ray, $\overrightarrow{HG}$, is the direction of the ray emerging from the internal surface of the cylinder towards the camera, through the glass. This ray intersects the internal surface of the cylinder at point H, which again can be calculated using the direction $\overrightarrow{HG}$ and the equation of a cylinder with center Q_2 and diameter d_{int}. Once again, we must remember that the rays converging into the camera are not necessarily horizontal, thus the center Q_2 differs from Q_1, and it needs to be found. Luckily, Q_2 has the same Z coordinate as H and hence, it can be expressed as $Q_2 = \begin{bmatrix} X^j, 0, H_z \end{bmatrix}^T$.

Next, we need to find the actual ray emerging from the root at point U inside the gel (Figure 5a). Since the normal of the surface of the cylinder at H can be expressed by:

$$\overrightarrow{Q_2H} = \frac{H - Q_2}{\|H - Q_2\|}$$

From here one, the process above for the outside surface of the cylinder can be repeated for its inside surface. In that way, we derive the refracted angle α_{glass} using eq(4) for $\overrightarrow{HG}$ and $\overrightarrow{Q_2H}$. Then, the angle of incidence α_{gel} at H can be determined as a function of the refracted angle α_{glass} using Snell's equation and the refractive indexes μ_{glass} and μ_{gel}. Next, the plane containing the incident ray $\overrightarrow{UH}$, the refracted ray $\overrightarrow{HG}$, and the normal $\overrightarrow{Q_2H}$ of the surface of the glass cylinder at the point G can be represented by its surface normal $\overrightarrow{SN2_C}$ using an equation similar to eq(5). Finally, the emerging ray $\overrightarrow{UH}$ can be evaluated by rotating the vector $\overrightarrow{HG}$ by the angle α_{gel} about the vector $\overrightarrow{SN2_C}$.

Ray-Tracing from Laser: Here, we start by assuming that the laser plane is vertical and so is the axis of the glass cylinder. It is also assumed that the laser is far from the cylinder in comparison to the typical heights of the roots to be scanned, and therefore the laser can be regarded as a diffused line source with parallel rays. These two assumptions lead to the conclusion that the intensities of the refraction are the same for every point in the laser stripe – i.e. independent of the height at which the laser hits the cylinder. In terms of the coordinate frames presented in Figure 3, this means that distortions only occurs on the XY plane, and that the z-value of a point calculated with eq(1) is the same as the height of the illuminating laser ray.

Since the position of the laser is fixed w.r.t the world-frame, the point source of any laser ray can be expressed by $L^j{:}\left[x_l,\,y_l,\,z^j\right]^T$, where x_l is the X-coordinate of the laser during calibration, y_l is chosen arbitrarily large in the world Y-direction, and z^j is obtained from eq(1) – refer to Figures 3 and 5b. It is important to mention also that $\overrightarrow{L^jD}$, representing the unity direction of the laser ray L^j, is always $[0,1,0]^T$ – once again, the laser plane is assumed vertical and the laser is positioned far from the scene in the Y opposite direction.

Similarly to what we did for the reversed ray-tracing approach from the camera, here the calculation of the refractions take the following (summarized) sequence: 1) use the direction $\overrightarrow{L^jD}$ to estimate the coordinate of D; 2) use $\overrightarrow{L^jD}$ and $\overrightarrow{QL^j}$ to determine γ_{air}; 3) use γ_{air} and Snell's law to derive γ_{glass}; 4) use $\overrightarrow{L^jD}$ and $\overrightarrow{QL^j}$ to find the plane with surface normal $\overrightarrow{SN1_L}$; 5) rotate $\overrightarrow{L^jD}$ about $\overrightarrow{SN1_L}$ by γ_{glass} to represent $\overrightarrow{DE}$; 6) use the direction $\overrightarrow{DE}$ to estimate the coordinate of E; 7) use $\overrightarrow{DE}$ and $\overrightarrow{QE}$ to determine ϕ_{glass}; 8) use ϕ_{glass} and Snell's law to derive ϕ_{gell}; 9) use $\overrightarrow{DE}$ and $\overrightarrow{QE}$ to find the plane with surface normal $\overrightarrow{SN2_L}$; and 10) rotate $\overrightarrow{DE}$ about $\overrightarrow{SN2_L}$ by ϕ_{gell} to represent $\overrightarrow{EU}$.

Creating Undistorted Point Cloud: Given $\overrightarrow{UH}$ and $\overrightarrow{EU}$ above, the undistorted point will be the point at intersection of these two vectors. Due to small errors in the calculation of $\overrightarrow{UH}$ and $\overrightarrow{EU}$, these two lines rarely intersect. For this reasons the intersection point is calculated as the midpoint on the line along the shortest distance between $\overrightarrow{UH}$ and $\overrightarrow{EU}$.

This whole process above is repeated for each of the points in the range image, creating the corresponding undistorted points in space.

Final 3D Model: After creating the point clouds for two consecutive scans, the clouds are registered into a single 3D point cloud using the Iterative Closest Points (ICP) algorithm [3]. The next scans are successively registered and appended to that same 3D point cloud to form the final 3D model of the root.

4   Experimental Results

For our experiments, we built a rectangular prism with square cross section. The prism, depicted in Figure 6, was inserted in a glass cylinder with internal and external radius of 41mm and 44mm, respectively. The dimension of the prism's cross section is $38mm\,x\,38mm$. On the surface of the prism, three parallel white stripes were painted so that the coordinates of those stripes could be easily identified in the 3D models. The distance between the top and bottom stripes is 90mm. The refractive index of air, glass and water are assumed to be 1, 1.5 and 1.33 respectively. The proposed SLS scanned the prism from six different viewing angles, creating six point-clouds, with each consecutive view having been rotated by 60 degrees with respect to the previous one.

Because of the camera frame rate of 30 frames/sec and the desired resolution of the 3D model, the speed of the linear slide was set to 10mm/sec. As a result, in each scan 360 images were grabbed and then processed to create each of the six point clouds. At the end, all point clouds were registered and a single 3D model was created. The results for the distorted and undistorted point clouds are shown in Figure 7. It is important to mention here that the system takes 28 seconds to perform phase 1-3, as explained in section 3.2 and 17 seconds for phase 4. Hence, an entire scan using 6 views around the pattern took 270 seconds. For actual root phenotyping this time could be improved by using phase 4 also to scan the object in its return and/or by increasing the camera frame rate. However, a much more important consideration is that our setup was developed in our own lab using off-the-shelf and inexpensive mechanical components. A much faster system could be built to achieve much higher throughput.

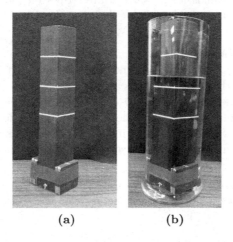

(a)   (b)

Fig. 6. A rectangular prism with square cross section was used for calibration and testing of the proposed system. In a) is a view of the prism outside the cylinder; and in b) the same prism in a glass cylinder half filled with water illustrates the distortions observed by the 3D imaging system.

In order to check the accuracy of the proposed method, two sets of planes were estimated by fitting the points in the 3D clouds. Then, the relationship between those planes were compared against the actual measurements of the rectangular prism and the integrity of the reconstructed rectangular prism was inspected.

The first set of planes utilized the 3D points on each of the four vertical faces of the rectangular prism. The goal of this test was to check the integrity of the square cross section of the prism by computing the angle between these faces. Each face was numbered in sequence and Table 1 presents the dot product between the normals of each possible pair of planes. In Table 2a, we find the dot

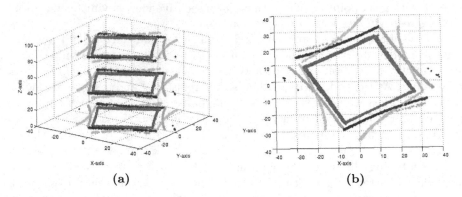

(a)   (b)

Fig. 7. 3D point cloud after registration of all six scans. The distorted points from scans 1 and 4 are plotted in dark blue; distorted points from scans 2 and 5 in green; and distorted scans 3 and 6 in cyan. The undistorted points from all six scans are plotted in red. In a) all point clouds for all three white stripes on the rectangular prims as depicted, while in b) only a single stripe is shown at closer look.

products related to the pairs of adjacent faces, while in Table 2b the dot product of the opposing faces. As expected, the adjacent faces are basically perpendicular to each other, while the opposing faces are parallel.

Next, to check the scale of the 3D cloud, the distances between points on opposing planes were measured. The mean and standard deviation of those distances for each pair of planes is shown in Table 2. Again, as the results indicate, the width of the prism was also preserved during reconstruction process.

Table 1. Relation between the four vertical faces of the reconstructed rectangular prism: a) dot product between the normal vectors of adjacent faces; and b) dot product of opposing faces

Used Planes	Measured Value
1 & 2	0.0204
2 & 3	0.0128
3 & 4	-0.0024
4 & 1	0.0052

(a)

Used Planes	Measured Value
1 & 3	0.9998
2 & 4	1.0000

(b)

Similarly, to check the noise level of the coordinates of the points on each plane, the distance between these points and their own planes was also calculated. Table 4a summarizes these results. Once again, the small mean and standard deviation obtained prove that the rectangular prism was reconstructed with a small error. Table 4b also presents a comparison between our method and the method in [39]. The mean and standard deviation of the error from both methods is summarized as a function of the distance from the laser.

Table 2. Mean and standard deviation of the distances between the points on the first indicated plane and the second indicated plane (e.g. first row shows the distance of the points on plane 1 with respect to entire plane 3)

Used Planes	Mean (mm)	Std (mm)
1 & 3	38.0217	0.2085
2 & 4	38.0017	0.3622
3 & 1	38.0227	0.2056
4 & 2	38.0022	0.4240

Table 3. a) Mean and standard deviation of the distances from points on the indicated plane to that same plane. b) Comparison (mean/std) of the error from our method versus the method in [39] as a function of the distance from the laser.

Used Planes	Mean (mm)	Std (mm)
1	0.1505	0.1095
2	0.1853	0.1452
3	0.1455	0.1265
4	0.1273	0.1053

(a)

Laser Distance	Method in [39]	Our Method
	(mm)	
239.24	0.31/0.14	-
500.37	0.73/0.55	-
300	-	0.1563/0.1243

(b)

Finally, a second set of planes was estimated, this time by fitting the points on the white stripes. In this case, the planes are horizontal and they slice the rectangular prism at three different heights.

Given both this second set of planes and the first set of planes (vertical faces), a set of dot products was again calculated. This time, the goal was to show the perpendicularity of the planes through the white stripes and the vertical faces of the prism. Table 4 presents the dot products between the top most plane and the bottom most plane with each of the face planes. Once again, a value close to zero indicates the almost perpendicularity between these planes.

Table 4. Dot Product between the planes on the top and bottom stripes and the vertical faces of the rectangular prism

Face Plane	Top Plane	Bottom Plane
1	0.0102	0.0112
2	-0.0038	-0.0069
3	0.0112	0.0122
4	0.0047	0.0015

The distances between the points on the top most plane with respect to the bottom most plane were calculated and the result is summarized in the first row of Table 5. The reverse, i.e. the points on the bottom most plane with respect to the top plane is shown on the second row of that same table. As before, the goal here is to show the level of noise of the reconstructed 3D points and that such noise was not affected by the height of the laser rays (which were assumed parallel in Section 3.2:Ray-tracing from Laser). The results are once again very close to the ground truth – in this case, 90mm.

Table 5. Distance from opposing horizontal planes

Used Planes	Mean (mm)	Standard Deviation
Top plane and bottom plane	89.9600	0.1457
Bottom plane and top plane	89.9600	0.0834

The next and final test involved real roots immersed in gel inside the cylinder. This more qualitative test was performed for various roots and four examples were already presented at the beginning of this paper, in Figure 1, but due to page limitations the remaining tests will not be presented here. For this test, the refractive index of the gel was assumed to be 1.42. As Figure 1 shows, the quality of the 3D model from the proposed correction method is quite superior when compared to the 3D model from the distorted points.

5   Conclusion and Future Work

In this work, a new and complete method for undistorting 3D point clouds from a SLS was presented. The source of distortion is in the refraction of the light as it travels through the different media of the commonly used setup of glass/gel cylinder. These distortions have been neglected in many of the recent works in the literature. While in some cases the size of the root system in comparison to the glass/gel cylinder indeed minimizes the error, not all species of plants can benefit from this simplification. Besides, as the results presented here demonstrate, the quality of the 3D model can be very poor if the proposed method is not employed.

In the future, the thickness of the cylinder will be estimated as part of an optimization method to further improved the distortion model. Also, the various refractive indexes should also be estimated in order to further optimize the 3D reconstruction of the RSA. However, despite the already good results achieved here – error in 3D reconstruction smaller than 0.16mm in average – the greatest improvement to be made is with respect to the assumption of parallel laser rays. In practice, it is not convenient to mount the laser far enough from the scene, not to mention the implications in the quality of the image due to its limited power. This fact certainly contributed for the errors obtained in the current work.

Other more obvious and equally certain improvements can be obtained by employing a higher resolution camera, a thinner laser stripe and cameras with faster frame rates.

Acknowledgments. The authors would like to thank Professor Henry T. Nguyen of the National Center for Soybean Biotechnology at the University of Missouri for providing partial financial support for this research. We would also like to thank Silvas Prince, MacKensie Murphy, and Theresa Musket, members of Prof. Nguyen's laboratory, who prepared the roots in the gel medium. Last, but not least, we thank the members of the Student Mechanical Workshop in the College of Engineering at the University of Missouri for allowing us to use their machinery to build calibration patterns.

References

1. Agin, G., Binford, T.: Computer Description of Curved Objects. IEEE Transactions on Computers **C-25**(4), 439–449 (1976)
2. Besl, P.J.: Active optical range imaging sensors. In: Advances in Machine Vision, pp. 1–63. Springer-Verlag New York Inc., New York (1988). http://dl.acm.org/citation.cfm?id=57360.57361
3. Besl, P., McKay, N.D.: A method for registration of 3-D shapes. IEEE Transactions on Pattern Analysis and Machine Intelligence **14**(2), 239–256 (1992)
4. Bidel, L.P.R., Pagès, L., Rivière, L.M., Pelloux, G., Lorendeau, J.Y.: Massflowdyn i: A carbon transport and partitioning model for root system architecture. Annals of Botany **85**(6), 869–886 (2000). http://aob.oxfordjournals.org/content/85/6/869.abstract
5. Bowman, D., Devitt, D., Engelke, M., Rufty Jr., T.: Root architecture affects nitrate leaching from bentgrass turf. Crop Science **38**(6), 1633–1639 (1998). http://www.scopus.com/inward/record.url?eid=2-s2.0-0032447708&partnerID=40&md5=aeea90ddd24b67be28c236f5d178d118, cited By (since 1996)48
6. Chen, C.H., Kak, A.: Modeling and calibration of a structured light scanner for 3-D robot vision. In: Proceedings of the 1987 IEEE International Conference on Robotics and Automation, vol. 4, pp. 807–815 (1987)
7. Chen, Y.L., Dunbabin, V.M., Diggle, A.J., Siddique, K.H.M., Rengel, Z.: Development of a novel semi-hydroponic phenotyping system for studying root architecture. Functional Plant Biology **38**(5), 355–363 (2011)
8. Clark, R.T., MacCurdy, R.B., Jung, J.K., Shaff, J.E., McCouch, S.R., Aneshansley, D.J., Kochian, L.V.: Three-Dimensional Root Phenotyping with a Novel Imaging and Software Platform. Plant Physiology **156**(2), 455–465 (2011). http://dx.doi.org/10.1104/pp.110.169102
9. Doussan, C., Pagès, L., Vercambre, G.: Modelling of the hydraulic architecture of root systems: An integrated approach to water absorption - Model description. Annals of Botany **81**, 213–223 (1998)
10. Fang, S., Yan, X., Liao, H.: 3D reconstruction and dynamic modeling of root architecture in situ and its application to crop phosphorus research. The Plant Journal **60**(6), 1096–1108 (2009). http://dx.doi.org/10.1111/j.1365-313X.2009.04009.x
11. French, A., Ubeda-Tomás, S., Holman, T.J., Bennett, M.J., Pridmore, T.: High-Throughput Quantification of Root Growth Using a Novel Image-Analysis Tool. Plant Physiology **150**(4), 1784–1795 (2009). http://www.plantphysiol.org/content/150/4/1784.abstract
12. Fua, P.: Reconstructing complex surfaces from multiple stereo views. In: Proceedings of the Fifth International Conference on Computer Vision, pp. 1078–1085 (1995)
13. Gregory, P., Hutchison, D., Read, D., Jenneson, P., Gilboy, W., Morton, E.: Non-invasive imaging of roots with high resolution X-ray micro-tomography. Plant and Soil **255**(1), 351–359 (2003). http://dx.doi.org/10.1023/A:1026179919689
14. Heeraman, D., Hopmans, J., Clausnitzer, V.: Three dimensional imaging of plant roots in situ with X-ray Computed Tomography. Plant and Soil **189**(2), 167–179 (1997). http://dx.doi.org/10.1023/B:PLSO.0000009694.64377.6f

15. Horn, B.K.P.: Closed-form solution of absolute orientation using unit quaternions. Journal of the Optical Society of America A **4**(4), 629–642 (1987)
16. Idesawa, M., Yatagai, T., Soma, T.: Scanning moiré method and automatic measurement of 3-D shapes. Appl. Opt. **16**(8), 2152–2162 (1977). http://ao.osa.org/abstract.cfm?URI=ao-16-8-2152
17. Iyer-Pascuzzi, A.S., Symonova, O., Mileyko, Y., Hao, Y., Belcher, H., Harer, J., Weitz, J.S., Benfey, P.N.: Imaging and Analysis Platform for Automatic Phenotyping and Trait Ranking of Plant Root Systems. Plant Physiology **152**(3), 1148–1157 (2010). http://www.plantphysiol.org/content/152/3/1148.abstract
18. Jahnke, S., Menzel, M.I., Van Dusschoten, D., Roeb, G.W., Bühler, J., Minwuyelet, S., Blümler, P., Temperton, V.M., Hombach, T., Streun, M., Beer, S., Khodaverdi, M., Ziemons, K., Coenen, H.H., Schurr, U.: Combined MRI-PET dissects dynamic changes in plant structures and functions. The Plant Journal **59**(4), 634–644 (2009). http://dx.doi.org/10.1111/j.1365-313X.2009.03888.x
19. Kak, A.C., Slaney, M.: Principles of Computerized Tomographic Imaging. IEEE Press, New York (1988)
20. Kazo, C., Hajder, L.: High-quality structured-light scanning of 3D objects using turntable. In: 2012 IEEE 3rd International Conference on Cognitive Infocommunications (CogInfoCom), pp. 553–557 (2012)
21. Lam, D., Hong, R.Z., DeSouza, G.: 3D human modeling using virtual multi-view stereopsis and object-camera motion estimation. In: IEEE/RSJ International Conference on Intelligent Robots and Systems, IROS 2009, pp. 4294–4299 (2009)
22. Lambers, H., Shane, M.W., Cramer, M.D., Pearse, S.J., Veneklaas, E.J.: Root structure and functioning for efficient acquisition of phosphorus: Matching morphological and physiological traits. Annals of Botany **98**(4), 693–713 (2006). http://aob.oxfordjournals.org/content/98/4/693.abstract
23. Lobet, G., Pagès, L., Draye, X.: A Novel Image-Analysis Toolbox Enabling Quantitative Analysis of Root System Architecture. Plant Physiology **157**(1), 29–39 (2011). http://www.plantphysiol.org/content/157/1/29.abstract
24. Lynch, J.: Root Architecture and Plant Productivity. Plant Physiology **109**(1), 7–13 (1995). http://www.plantphysiol.org/content/109/1/7.short
25. Martin, W.N., Aggarwal, J.: Volumetric Descriptions of Objects from Multiple Views. IEEE Transactions on Pattern Analysis and Machine Intelligence **PAMI-5**(2), 150–158 (1983)
26. Nakini, T., DeSouza, G.N., Prince, S.J., Musket, T., Murphy, M.C., T, N.H.: 3d imaging and feature extraction for root phenotyping of soybean. In: PhenoDays Symposium on Imaging & Robotics for the 21st Century. Danforth Plant Science Center, St. Louis (September 2013)
27. Niem, W.: Robust and fast modelling of 3D natural objects from multiple views. In: SPIE Proceedings Image and Video Processing II, vol. 2182 (1994). doi:10.1117/12/12.171088
28. Park, J., DeSouza, G.N.: Photo-realistic modeling of three dimensional objects using range and reflectance data. In: Innovations in Machine Intelligence and Robot Perception. Springer (2005)
29. Pound, M.P., French, A.P., Atkinson, J., Wells, D.M., Bennett, M.J., Pridmore, T.P.: RootNav: Navigating images of complex root architectures. Plant Physiology (2013). http://www.plantphysiol.org/content/early/2013/06/12/pp.113.221531.abstract
30. Ribaut, J.M., Betran, J., Monneveux, P., Setter, T.: Drought tolerance in maize. In: Bennetzen, J., Hake, S. (eds.) Handbook of Maize: Its Biology, pp. 311–344. Springer, New York

31. Scheenen, T., Vergeldt, F., Heemskerk, A., Van As, H.: Intact Plant Magnetic Resonance Imaging to Study Dynamics in Long-Distance Sap Flow and Flow-Conducting Surface Area. Plant Physiology **144**(2), 1157–1165 (2007). http://www.plantphysiol.org/content/144/2/1157.abstract

32. Silverberg, J.L., Noar, R.D., Packer, M.S., Harrison, M.J., Henley, C.L., Cohen, I., Gerbode, S.J.: 3d imaging and mechanical modeling of helical buckling in medicago truncatula plant roots. Proceedings of the National Academy of Sciences (2012). http://www.pnas.org/content/early/2012/09/19/1209287109.abstract

33. Topp, C.N., Iyer-Pascuzzi, A.S., Anderson, J.T., Lee, C.R., Zurek, P.R., Symonova, O., Zheng, Y., Bucksch, A., Mileyko, Y., Galkovskyi, T., Moore, B.T., Harer, J., Edelsbrunner, H., Mitchell-Olds, T., Weitz, J.S., Benfey, P.N.: 3D phenotyping and quantitative trait locus mapping identify core regions of the rice genome controlling root architecture. Proceedings of the National Academy of Sciences **110**(18), E1695–E1704 (2013). http://www.pnas.org/content/110/18/E1695.abstract

34. Trachsel, S., Kaeppler, S., Brown, K., Lynch, J.: Shovelomics: high throughput phenotyping of maize (Zea mays L.) root architecture in the field. Plant and Soil **341**(1–2), 75–87 (2011). http://dx.doi.org/10.1007/s11104-010-0623-8

35. Tracy, S.R., Roberts, J.A., Black, C.R., McNeill, A., Davidson, R., Mooney, S.J.: The X-factor: visualizing undisturbed root architecture in soils using X-ray computed tomography. Journal of Experimental Botany **61**(2), 311–313 (2010). http://jxb.oxfordjournals.org/content/61/2/311.short

36. Van As, H., Scheenen, T., Vergeldt, F.: MRI of intact plants. Photosynthesis Research **102**(2–3), 213–222 (2009). http://dx.doi.org/10.1007/s11120-009-9486-3

37. van der Weerd, L., Claessens, M.M., Ruttink, T., Vergeldt, F.J., Schaafsma, T.J., Van As, H.: Quantitative NMR microscopy of osmotic stress responses in maize and pearl millet. Journal of Experimental Botany **52**(365), 2333–2343 (2001). http://jxb.oxfordjournals.org/content/52/365/2333.abstract

38. Yamashita, A., Higuchi, H., Kaneko, T., Kawata, Y.: Three dimensional measurement of object's surface in water using the light stripe projection method. In: Proceedings of the 2004 IEEE International Conference on Robotics and Automation, ICRA 2004, vol. 3, pp. 2736–2741 (April 2004)

39. Yamashita, A., Hayashimoto, E., Kaneko, T., Kawata, Y.: 3-D measurement of objects in a cylindrical glass water tank with a laser range finder. In: Proceedings of the 2003 IEEE/RSJ International Conference on Intelligent Robots and Systems, pp. 1578–1583 (2003)

40. Yazdanbakhsh, N., Fisahn, J.: High throughput phenotyping of root growth dynamics, lateral root formation, root architecture and root hair development enabled by PlaRoM. Functional Plant Biology **36**(11), 938–946 (2009)

41. Zha, H., Morooka, K., Hasegawa, T., Nagata, T.: Active modeling of 3-D objects: planning on the next best pose (NBP) for acquiring range images. In: Proceedings of the International Conference on Recent Advances in 3-D Digital Imaging and Modeling, pp. 68–75 (1997)

42. Zhu, T., Fang, S., Li, Z., Liu, Y., Liao, H., Yan, X.: Quantitative analysis of 3-dimensional root architecture based on image reconstruction and its application to research on phosphorus uptake in soybean. Chinese Science Bulletin **51**(19), 2351–2361 (2006). http://dx.doi.org/10.1007/s11434-006-2130-0

Surface Reconstruction of Plant Shoots
from Multiple Views

Michael P. Pound[1(✉)], Andrew P. French[1,2], Erik H. Murchie[1],
and Tony P. Pridmore[1,2]

[1] Centre for Plant Integrative Biology, University of Nottingham,
Nottingham, UK
Michael.pound@nottingham.ac.uk
[2] School of Computer Science, University of Nottingham,
Nottingham NG8 1BB, UK

Abstract. Increased adoption of the systems approach to biological research has focused attention on the use of quantitative models of biological objects. This includes a need for realistic 3D representations of plant shoots for quantification and modelling. We present a fully automatic approach to image-based 3D plant reconstruction. The reconstructed plants are represented as a series of small planar sections that together model the more complex architecture of the leaf surfaces. The boundary of each leaf patch is refined using the level set method, optimising the model based on image information, curvature constraints and the position of neighbouring surfaces. The reconstruction process makes few assumptions about the nature of the plant material being reconstructed, and as such is applicable to a wide variety of plant species and topologies, and can be extended to canopy-scale imaging. We demonstrate the effectiveness of our approach on datasets of wheat and rice plants, as well as a novel virtual dataset that allows us to compute distance measures of reconstruction accuracy.

Keywords: Plant phenotyping · Multi-view reconstruction · 3D · Level sets

1 Introduction

In recent years there has been a surge in interest in the construction of geometrically accurate models of plants. Increased adoption of the systems approach to biological research has focussed attention on the use of quantitative models of biological objects and processes to both make and test hypotheses.

Existing plant modelling approaches can be broadly classified as either rule-based, or image-based [1]. Rule-based approaches generate model plants based on rules or grammars with specified structure. These rules, and hence the form and parameters of the models produced, are often derived from measurements of real plants [2,3]. The resulting virtual plants can model different phenotypes, plant response to various growing conditions and stresses, and when based on real-world data will be reasonably accurate. However, the data acquisition process is often extremely time consuming, and is usually tailored to a particular species. In many cases only a small set of varieties can be described, due to the manual measurements required to parameterise the model.

© Springer International Publishing Switzerland 2015
L. Agapito et al. (Eds.): ECCV 2014 Workshops, Part IV, LNCS 8928, pp. 158–173, 2015.
DOI: 10.1007/978-3-319-16220-1_12

Image-based approaches attempt to directly model a given object by extracting the necessary information from one or more images of that object. These approaches are particularly attractive as a means of plant modelling, where in addition to supporting systems biology, they provide a route to plant phenotyping [4,5].

Plants, however, provide a particularly challenging subject, with large amounts of self-occlusion, and depending on plant species, leaves that lack the texture necessary to perform robust feature matching, either to separate leaves from one another, or locate specific leaves across multiple views. To overcome this, where image-based modelling approaches are successful, they have often involved user-interaction to guide the process [1].

Top-down image-based approaches attempt to simplify the model construction problem by instead solving a model refinement problem. An existing model is adjusted to fit the image data, so that the new plant representation is consistent with what is observed. [1,6] take this approach, first obtaining an ideal leaf model from a single leaf, and then fitting it to all other leaves in the scene. By adapting an existing model, topological inconsistency (such as the self-intersection of leaf surfaces) is avoided, but this comes at the expense of generality. [7] guides the segmentation of laser range data using planar or curved-quadratic surface models, however this approach extents only to the refinement of point cloud data, without reconstructing leaf surfaces.

Bottom-up methods begin with one or more images, and reconstruct a plant model based only on the observed pixel data. Two broad approaches exist, both requiring a set of images captured from different, but known, viewpoints. Silhouette-based methods [8,9] segment each image independently to identify the boundary of the object of interest. These regions are combined to determine the maximum possible object size that is consistent with the images presented to the algorithm, the *photo hull* [10]. In many cases, where the number of input images is high, the resulting model will be a good approximation to the true plant structure. However, as the scene becomes increasingly complex, for example with the addition of more leaves in an older plant, the discrepancy between true object and model will increase. This problem becomes more pronounced when extending these techniques to very complex scenes such as plant canopies, where its effectiveness is limited.

Other approaches include correspondence-based methods that identify features of interest independently in each of a set of images, and then match those features between views. If the image features associated with a particular plant feature (e.g. the tip of a leaf) can be identified in multiple images taken from different viewpoints, knowledge of the cameras' positions and orientations allow its 3D location to be computed. The work in [11] extracts the centre lines of wheat plants from two orthogonal viewpoints, improving reliability where single images would fail. This work does not, however, complete the 3D structure of each plant, preserving only the centre-line of each leaf after skeletonisation.

Image-based modelling algorithms are widely applicable and require only easily accessible and affordable cameras. Their generality can, however, become a hindrance, as the challenging nature of plant topology may require additional assumptions to be made as the reconstruction proceeds. The representations they produce may also be unsuitable for direct use in some situations. The volumetric data structures produced by silhouette-based methods, for example, are static: the size and position of the voxels are defined early in the process and are difficult to change. While measurements of e.g. height and volume are easily made from volumetric descriptions, estimating motion e.g. of leaves moving in the breeze is extremely difficult. Similarly, point clouds can be used to calculate density and distributions of plant material, but cannot immediately be used in modelling applications where a surface-based representation is required.

This paper describes a fully automatic, bottom-up approach to image-based 3D plant reconstruction that is applicable to a wide variety of plant species and topologies. The method is accurate, providing a true representation of the original plant, and produces data in a form that can support both trait measurement and modelling techniques such as forward ray tracing [12].

An initial 3D point cloud is first described by a set of planar patches, each representing a small section of plant material, usually a segment of leaf. Where the quality of the input point cloud is high, the initial surface estimate will provide a good model of the plant. Image noise and the complexity of the plant will, however, typically lead to missing areas of leaf material, and poorly defined leaf boundaries. We therefore extend existing approaches by refining the initial surface estimate into a more accurate plant model. Each surface patch is re-sized and re-shaped based on the available image information, and positional information obtained from neighbouring surfaces. The resulting surface patches are then re-triangulated to produce a smooth and geometrically accurate model of the plant.

The reconstruction process makes few assumptions about the nature of the plant material being reconstructed; by representing each leaf as a series of small planar sections, the complete leaf surface itself can take any reasonable shape. The generality of our technique allows it to be scaled to scenes involving multiple plants, and even plant canopies. However, the focus of this paper is on the accurate reconstruction of single plants of varying species.

2   Plant Reconstruction

2.1   Input Point Cloud

The reconstruction algorithm described in this paper uses an initial point cloud estimate as a basis for the growth of plant surfaces in three dimensions. Numerous software- and hardware-based techniques exist to obtain point clouds of objects. We have chosen to make use of a software-based technique, patch-based multi-view stereo (PMVS) [13]. This approach reconstructs dense point clouds from any calibrated image set, and is not restricted to plant data. However, by including robust visibility constraints, it is well suited to plant material that contains large amounts of occlusion. Let $\{X_i\}_{i=1}^n$ be the set of all points in an input cloud of size n. We identify the co-ordinate system used by the point cloud, and the resulting reconstruction, as "world" co-ordinates. An individual point $p \in X$ in world co-ordinates is represented as a 3D vector $\mathbf{w}$.

A requirement of both PMVS and our reconstruction approach is that the intrinsic and extrinsic camera parameters be known. We use the VisualSFM [14] system to perform automatic camera calibration. Any number of arbitrary camera positions may be calibrated using VisualSFM, and calibration is performed quickly. However, as it is based on SIFT features [15], the approach is not suitable for images with insufficient texture and feature information. This is particularly problematic within plant datasets, where leaves may have few suitable feature points. In our datasets, the surrounding scene provides an adequate feature set for correspondence, and in our virtual dataset, we calibrate separately using a highly-textured model.

We capture N_{cam} images of the scene from N_{cam} locations to obtain a set of images $\{I_j\}_{j=1}^{N_{cam}}$. Associated with each camera location is a perspective projection matrix, based on a standard pinhole camera model [16], derived from the calibration information output by VisualSFM. For a given world point, there is a perspective projection function, $\mathcal{V}_j$, that maps onto a point in a specific camera coordinate frame, given by the 2D vector $\mathbf{v}$. This gives a set of functions $\{\mathcal{V}_j(\mathbf{w}): \mathbb{R}^3 \to \mathbb{R}^2\}_{j=1}^{N_{cam}}$. where j is the index of the input image and associated camera geometry. Once in camera coordinates, pixel information for a given location is represented by $I_j(\mathbf{v})$.

PMVS makes no assumptions about the nature of the objects being reconstructed. It is likely that additional points are contained in X that comprise background or other non-plant material. Many such points will be removed by our level set approach, however for computational efficiency many can be removed before reconstruction begins.

The point cloud is pre-filtered to remove obvious errors; those that differ greatly from the expected colour of the plant, or those that appear below the expected location of the plant. Two filters are applied, first a clipping plane positioned at the base of the plant is used to remove the majority of background points on the floor, container etc. Second, colour filtering is achieved by examining the projected pixel values for every point, and removing those that do not appear green in colour. These filters are meant only as a conservative first pass, a more sensitive colour-based metric is used within the speed function during application of the level set method. The final filtered point cloud $X' \subseteq X$ is used for the remainder of the reconstruction process.

2.2   Point Cloud Segmentation

The point cloud representation produced by PMVS contains no explicit surface description. Methods for the reconstruction of a surface mesh from a point cloud exist [17,18] Most, however, construct a single surface describing the entire point cloud. Plants contain complex surface geometry that encourages the separation of leaves. We also wish to approach the more general problem of plant reconstruction, without assuming the connectivity or nature of the plant leaves is known. Instead, we model plant material as a series of small planar patches. Patch size is restricted to avoid fitting surfaces between nearby leaves, and to accurately model the curved nature of each leaf surface. The filtered point cloud is first segmented into small clusters of points using a radially bounded nearest neighbour strategy [19]. Points are grouped with their nearest neighbours, as defined by a pre-set distance, and the method is extended to limit the potential size of each cluster. More formally, from the filtered cloud we obtain a set of clusters $\{C_k\}_{k=1}^{N_{clus}}$ in which each cluster contains at least one point and all clusters are disjoint, so $|C_k| > 0, \forall k$ and $C_k \cap C_l, \forall k \neq l$.

This distance used for the nearest neighbour approach is dependent on the size and resolution of the model being captured. As PMVS and laser scanning devices usually output points with a consistent density, the distance parameter can be set once and then remain unchanged between experiments using the same image capture technique. Reducing this number will increase the number of planar sections fitted to the data, increasing accuracy at the cost of decreased algorithmic efficiency.

Our surface fitting approach begins with an approximation of the surface that will then be refined. A least-squares orthogonal regression plane is fitted to each cluster using singular value decomposition. This best fit plane minimises the orthogonal distance to each point, providing each cluster with a centre point $\mathbf{c}$, a normal vector $\mathbf{n}$, and an orthogonal vector $\mathbf{x}$ indicating the rotation about the normal. The vector $\mathbf{x}$ is aligned along the major-principle axis of the point within the cluster. We then define a set of orthographic projection functions that project individual world points into each cluster plane, $\{\mathcal{C}_k(\mathbf{w}): \mathbb{R}^3 \to \mathbb{R}^2\}_{k=1}^{N_{clus}}$, where $\mathcal{C}_k$ represents the projection into plane k (i.e. the plane associated with cluster C_k). We say that points projected onto any plane now occupy planar co-ordinates. Any such point, denoted by the 2D vector $\mathbf{p}$, can be projected back into world co-ordinates by the set of functions $\{\mathcal{W}_k(\mathbf{p}): \mathbb{R}^2 \to \mathbb{R}^3\}_{k=1}^{N_{clus}}$.

The orthogonal projection in $\mathcal{C}_k$ has the effect of flattening the points in each cluster to lie on their best fit plane, reducing any noise in individual points, and reducing the surface fitting algorithm to a 2D problem. Point and mesh surfaces generated on a cluster plane will have an associated world position that can be output as a final 3D model.

2.3   Surface Estimation

An initial surface estimate is constructed by calculating the α-shape of the set of 2D points in planar co-ordinates. An α-shape is a generalisation of the convex-hull for a set of points, and is closely related to the commonly used Delaunay triangulation. For the incomplete leaf surfaces that exist within the input cloud, the Delaunay triangulation and convex hull represent an over-simplification of the complex boundary topology of the clusters. For a point set S, Edelsbrunner [20] defines the concept of a generalized disk of radius $1/\alpha$, with an edge between two points in S being included in the alpha shape if both points like on the boundary of the generalised disk, and that disk contains the entire point set. The set of α-shapes represent a triangulation of each surface at varying levels of detail. In this work, a negative value of α is used, with larger negative values removing larger edges or faces. The α value can be tuned for a given data set, to preserve the shape of the boundary of each reconstructed point set.

2.4   Boundary Optimisation

The α-shapes computed over each cluster form an initial estimate of the location and shape of the plant surface. The challenging nature of plant datasets in multi-view reconstruction means that in many instances the initial point cloud estimate will be inaccurate or incomplete. The initial surface boundaries based on these points will require further optimisation to adequately reflect the true shape of each leaf surface. Missing leaf surfaces should be reconstructed, and overlapping shapes should be optimised to meet at a single boundary. Many methods, such as active contours [21], parameterise the boundary of shape before attempting this optimisation. However, such approaches are ill-suited to the complex boundary conditions produced by α-shapes. For any value of α < 0, the surface may contain holes or disjoint sections, and as such many surfaces will change topology during any boundary optimisation process.

Tracking of such complex boundaries can be achieved using the level set method [22,23]. The method defines a 3D function φ that intersects the cluster plane. φ is represented as a signed distance function, initialised such that negative values lie within our α-shape boundary, and positive values occur outside. Thus, the boundary itself is defined as the set of all points in φ that intersect the cluster plane, given as:

$$\Gamma = \{(x,y)|\varphi(x,y) = 0\} . \tag{1}$$

A speed function determines the rate of change of φ. It may be based on both global and local parameters, and will act to grow or shrink the boundary Γ as necessary to fit the underlying data. The change in φ, based on a speed function v, is defined as

$$\frac{\delta\varphi}{\delta t} = -v \cdot |\Delta\varphi| , \tag{2}$$

where $\Delta\varphi$ is the gradient of the level set function at a given point, which we calculate through Godunov's upwinding scheme. The speed function is defined as

$$v = v_{curve} + v_{image} + v_{inter} , \tag{3}$$

where v_{curve} is a measure of the local curvature, calculated using a central finite difference approximation

$$v_{curve} = \omega \cdot \frac{\varphi_{xx}\varphi_x^2 - 2\varphi_y\varphi_x\varphi_{xy} + \varphi_{yy}\varphi_x^2}{\left(\varphi_x^2 + \varphi_y^2\right)^{\frac{3}{2}}} . \tag{4}$$

The curvature term encourages the boundary of the level set to remain smooth. The weighting ω is required to prevent curvature from dictating the movement of the front, in cases where the boundary is already sufficiently smooth.

The image term, v_{image}, references colour information in the input images to ascertain whether the projection of the planar surface lies over regions with a high likelihood of containing leaf material. To achieve this, the function φ is discretized and uses the planar co-ordinate system, each planar point **p** maps to a position on φ, and any point on φ will have an associated planar position. By performing consecutive projections, we are able to examine the relevant location in any image of a cluster plane position. Such a projection is given as $(\mathcal{V}_j \circ \mathcal{W}_k)(\mathbf{p}) \colon \mathbb{R}^2 \to \mathbb{R}^2$, where k is the cluster index, and j is the camera index. Not every image will provide a helpful view of every cluster, they may be out of the camera's field of view, or seen at an oblique angle. One reference view is chosen from which to obtain colour information, as follows. We choose a reference image $I_R \in I$ that represents a calculated "best view" of a planar surface. Selection of the reference view begins by projecting each cluster into each camera view. Only the interiors (triangular faces) of each α-shape are projected using a scan-line rasterisation algorithm. Attached to each projected position is a z depth, calculated as the third component output from the function $\mathcal{C}_j(\mathbf{w})$ when using homogenous co-ordinates. This z depth represents the distance that the projected point lies from the camera's image plane, and can be used to sort clusters that project onto the same location. Projections with the lowest z value are seen in front of, so occlude, those with higher z values.

The projection locations and z depths for all clusters are analysed using a series of z-buffer data structures, one z-buffer associated with each input image. We define the z-buffers as a set $\{Z_j\}_{j=0}^{N_{cam}}$, where each buffer contains pixel locations in camera co-ordinates that map directly to the corresponding image. For each image location, any cluster that can be seen in (i.e. projects onto) that point is recorded in the z-buffer. A given position $Z_j(\mathbf{v})$ contains a depth sorted list of all clusters that project into that camera co-ordinate, i.e. $Z_j(\mathbf{v}) = (C_0, \dots, C_n)$.

It is desirable to select camera views that contain as little interference between clusters as possible. For a given z-buffer j, and a given cluster i, we can calculate the following measure:

$$\mathcal{V}_j^{clear}(i) = |\{\mathbf{v} \mid i \in Z_j(\mathbf{v}) \wedge |Z_j(\mathbf{v})| = 1 \}| \; . \tag{5}$$

The clear pixel count represents a measure of the number of pixels each cluster projects into for a given image. This value reflects both the proximity of the cluster to the camera plane, and the angle of incidence between the camera view and the cluster plane. The clear pixel counts for all projections of a given cluster i are normalised to the range [0,1]. This measure does not include pixel positions shared by other clusters, to avoid heavily occluded views affecting the normalised value. The amount of occlusion for each cluster i, in a given z-buffer j are calculated as:

$$\mathcal{V}_j^{occluded}(i) = \frac{|\{\mathbf{v} \mid i \in Z_j(\mathbf{v}) \backslash \{Z_j(\mathbf{v})_{(1)}\} \wedge |Z_j(\mathbf{v})| > 1 \}|}{|\{\mathbf{v} \mid i \in Z_j(\mathbf{v})\}|} \tag{6}$$

$$\mathcal{V}_j^{occluding}(i) = \frac{|\{\mathbf{v} \mid i \in Z_j(\mathbf{v}) \backslash \{Z_j(\mathbf{v})_{(n)}\} \wedge |Z_j(\mathbf{v})| > 1 \}|}{|\{\mathbf{v} \mid i \in Z_j(\mathbf{v})\}|} \; , \tag{7}$$

Where $Z_j(\mathbf{v})_{(k)}$ is the kth ordered element of $Z_j(\mathbf{v})$. Thus, a combination of normalised clear pixel count, occlusion and occluding percentages can be used to sort images in terms of view quality. A reference image, I_R, is chosen where:

$$R = argmax_j(V_j^{clear}(i)(1 - V_j^{occluded}(i))(1 - V_j^{occluding}(i)))$$ (8)

When referencing pixel values using the image I_R, we use a normalised green value to measure the likelihood of leaf material existing at that location,

$$\mathcal{N}_j(\mathbf{v}) = \frac{I_j(\mathbf{v})_{(green)}}{I_j(\mathbf{v})_{(red)} + I_j(\mathbf{v})_{(green)} + I_j(\mathbf{v})_{(blue)}}$$ (9)

We can assume that normalised green values will be higher in pixels containing leaf material, and lower in pixels containing background. Where lighting conditions remain consistent over an image set, we can also assume that distribution of normalised green values are the same over the each image in I. However, between different image sets we cannot assume that the properties of the normalised green values are known. These properties must be ascertained before $\mathcal{N}_j$ can be used to contribute to the v_{image} term in the speed function. We sample from all images those pixels that are projected into by the α-shapes, and use Rosin's unimodal thresholding approach [24] to threshold below the normalised green peak that is observed. Using this threshold, the mean and standard deviation of the peak are calculated, and used to produce an image speed function centred around the calculated threshold t, with a spread based on the standard deviation of the peak:

$$v_{image} = \begin{cases} \max\left(-1, \dfrac{\mathcal{N}_j(\mathbf{v}) - t}{2\sigma}\right), & \mathcal{N}_j(\mathbf{v}) < t \\ \min\left(+1, \dfrac{\mathcal{N}_j(\mathbf{v}) + t}{2\sigma}\right), & \mathcal{N}_j(\mathbf{v}) \geq t \end{cases}$$ (10)

where t is the threshold calculated using Rosin's method, and σ is the standard deviation of the $\mathcal{N}_j$ peak. A width of 2σ was chosen as a value that characterises the spread of the normalised green values.

The final component of the speed function, v_{inter}, works to reshape each surface based on the location and shape of nearby clusters. As each cluster may have different normal orientations, it is challenging to calculate their 3D intersections in terms of 2D positions in planar co-ordinates. Indeed, two nearby clusters that could be considered as overlapping, may not intersect in world co-ordinates. Instead we project each planar position into I_R, and examine the interactions in the 2D camera co-ordinate system.

Any overlapping projections are calculated by maintaining z-buffers that update as each region reshapes. The function v_{inter} is calculated such that each cluster in $Z_j(x)$ is penalised except for the front-most cluster. Thus for a cluster i, the function is calculated as:

$$v_{inter} = \begin{cases} p - v_{image}, & Z_j(\mathbf{v})_1 \neq i \\ 0, & otherwise \end{cases}$$ (11)

where p is a small negative value such that the level set boundary Γ shrinks at this location. Note that the subtraction of v_{image} results in the image component being ignored where clusters are occluded.

The complete speed function is used to update each discrete position on the level set function φ. This process must be repeated until each cluster boundary has re-shaped to adequately fit the underlying image data. The speed function will slow significantly as the boundary approaches an optimal shape. Where a level set boundary no longer moves with respect to the reference image (does not alter the number of projected pixels), we mark this cluster as complete and discontinue level set iterations. Any level sets that do not slow significantly will continue until a maximum time is elapsed, a parameter that can be set by the user. We typically use a value of 100-200 iterations as a compromise between computational efficiency and offering each level set adequate time to optimise.

2.5   Model Output

Once all clusters have been iterated sufficiently, each surface triangulation must be re-computed. The level set function has a known boundary that was not available during the original surface estimation. This can be used to drive a more accurate meshing approach that will preserve the contours of each shape. We use constrained Delaunay triangulation for this task [25]. A constrained triangulation will account for complex boundary shape when producing a mesh from a series of points, however it will not over-simplify the boundary by fitting surfaces across concave sections, and can retain holes in the surface if required. Points are sampled from the boundary of each surface, and a constrained triangulation is fitted. This process will automatically generate additional points, where required, within the shape itself. As each point in the new triangulation exists in planar co-ordinates, they can be easily back-projected into world co-ordinates to be output in mesh format.

3   Experimental Results

In this section we present results obtained when applying our reconstruction approach to multiple views of single plants. Verification of our approach is achieved using a novel artificial dataset, in which a model rice plant is rendered from multiple view-points to generate artificial colour images that are then treated in the same way as a real-world image set. This approach allows the reconstructed plant to be directly compared to the artificial target object, an impossible prospect when working with real-life plants, as no such ground truth can exist.

We have tested our reconstruction methods on datasets obtained from rice and wheat plants. Images were captured using a DSLR camera with a 35mm lens, at 8 megapixel resolution. The number, and nature of the images were left to the user to decide given the subject in question, though we recommend more than 30 images surrounding the subject for a single plant. No special consideration was given to the environment in which the plants were imaged, beyond avoiding large areas of green colour in the background. The rice dataset was captured in an indoor environment, the wheat in a glass house. These environments provide complex backgrounds, which raise additional challenges, but the plants can still be reconstructed using our methods. It is likely that a permanent installation with a more strict protocol for image capture would result in more consistent point cloud reconstruction between datasets, readers are encouraged to explore this option if using our methods over extended periods.

Fig. 1. Reconstruction of rice and wheat images. (*top left*) A sample image from the wheat dataset. (*top right*) A meshed reconstruction of the plant surface using our approach. (*bottom left*) A sample image from the rice dataset. (*bottom right*) A meshed reconstruction of the plant surface using our approach.

Fig. 1 shows the result of applying our reconstruction approach to two image sets containing wheat and rice plants. Quantitative evaluation of the effectiveness of any 3D shoot reconstruction is challenging due to a lack of ground truth models for comparison. Here we offer a qualitative evaluation of the benefits and shortcomings of our approach using live plants, followed by a quantitative evaluation using the virtual rice dataset.

First, live plants were reconstructed. Results showed that the initial surface estimate, obtained by calculating an α-shape over each cluster, will naturally reproduce any flaws present in the PMVS point cloud. Most notable are the lack of point information in areas of poor texture, and noise perpendicular to the leaf surface, where depth has not be adequately resolved. These issues can be caused by the heavy self-occlusion observed in larger plants or canopies, but are often caused in even simple datasets by a lack of image features in the centre of leaves.

Depth noise is significantly reduced by the use of best-fit planes over small clusters, where all points are projected onto a single surface. However, the boundary of each surface is a function of the parameters used to create the α-shape, and the quality of the underlying data. As such, we can expect the α-shape boundaries to be a poor representation of the true leaf shape. With this in mind, we would characterise a successful reconstruction as one that significantly improves upon the initial surface estimate, through the optimisation of the surface boundaries.

Notable characteristics of the α-shape boundaries in both datasets are significant overlap between neighbouring clusters, and frequent missing surface sections (Fig. 2). Fig. 2 also shows the refined boundaries after the level set method has been applied, in which missing sections are filled, and overlapping surfaces have been reduced. The results in Fig. 2 are representative of the results over both datasets.

While the refined surfaces represent an improvement over both the initial point cloud, and the initial α-shape surface, there are still notable areas for improvement. By treating each section of leaf as an individually orientated plane, each plane orientation is susceptible to the error within the input cloud. Since each boundary is refined from one reference view, incorrect orientation of the best-fit plane might cause the surface boundary to be incorrectly aligned with the image, or neighbouring clusters. Consider Fig. 2 (right), in which two patches have been reconstructed in close proximity. When viewed from the reference view in which boundary refinement occurred, the boundaries of neighbouring patches are in good agreement. A rotated view of the same surfaces, however, shows that misaligned normal orientation can lead to gaps between neighbouring surfaces. Conversely, if the right-hand image had been chosen as I_R, the level set equation would increase the size of both boundaries, and overlap would be observed in the left hand view.

In reality, for many clusters with very similar orientations these gaps will be negligible; as the clusters are limited in size, the distance between neighbouring plane orientations will be small, and the resulting gaps between boundaries will also be small. We have quantified the low level of discrepancy between an input model and the reconstruction below. We anticipate that further work on smoothing the normal orientations of neighbouring clusters or merging neighbouring clusters into a

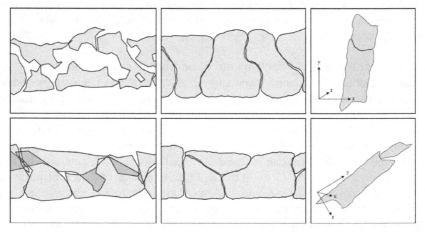

Fig. 2. Boundary refinement using the level set method. (*top left*) An initial surface estimate of a section of the wheat dataset. (*top middle*) A refined version of the wheat model after a level set was applied to each patch. (*bottom left*) An initial surface estimate of a section of the rice dataset. (*bottom middle*) A refined version of the rice model after a level set was applied to each patch. (*top right*) Two example patches, viewed from the same position as the reference image I_R. (*bottom right*) A different orientation of the same two patches.

single curved leaf model will continue to improve results in this regard: this will be a focus of upcoming research.

An additional dataset was created based on the plant used in the rice dataset. The rice plant was first manually captured and modelled using the point cloud created by PMVS, and 3D graphics software [26,27]. This is a time consuming and subjective process, and should not be viewed as a suitable alternative to automatic reconstruction. However, it is possible to produce an easily quantifiable ground truth model that can be used as a target for automated reconstruction. This virtual plant was textured and coloured in order to emulate the original plant leaves. Finally, 40 distinct camera views of the model were rendered, simulating an image capture system moving around a static plant. The resulting dataset can then be reconstructed in the same manner as real-world data, while retaining the ability to compare the reconstruction with the original virtual plant, in particular keeping the same co-ordinate system and scale. The original model, and our reconstruction can be seen in Figure 3.

To quantify the similarity between the original model and the reconstruction, we use the Hausdorff distance, the greatest distance from any point on either mesh, to the nearest point on the other. This concept is extended in [28] to include a measure of the mean distance between two meshes.

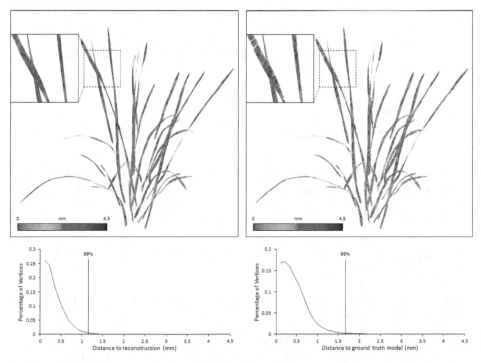

Fig. 3. (top *left*) The original rice plant model, based on the plant reconstructed in Figure 2. Vertices are coloured based on their mm distance to the nearest point on the reconstruction. (*bottom left*) Histogram of smallest distances from each vertex on the model to vertices on the reconstruction. (*top right*) The reconstruction produced by our approach. Vertices are coloured based on their mm distance to the nearest point on the original model. (*bottom right*) Histogram of smallest distances from each vertex on the reconstruction to vertices on the model.

A visual representation of these measures can be seen in Figure 3, in which each vertex is coloured based on the distance to the nearest point on the opposing mesh. This provides a visual clue as to our algorithm performance. The arbitrary world units used within the reconstruction were converted into mm measurements through the use of a calibration target of known size.

The furthest distance between points on both meshes is ~4.5mm, however the average distances between each mesh are significantly lower. The complete model is approximately 48cm tall. These one-sided measurements provide additional information, by distinguishing between the distances in either direction. Increasing distance from the model plant to the reconstruction indicates areas of the model that have not been accurately reconstructed. This is most likely where missing points in the initial cloud and surface estimates are not adequately refined through the level set method. In this case, the low mean and maximum distances show that these regions have been reconstructed successfully. Indeed, 99% of the vertices in the model are within 1.2mm of the reconstructed model.

Table 1. Distance measurements between the model plant and the results of the reconstruction approach. The two-sided Hausdorff distance is the maximum of both single-sided measurements

Vertex Distance (mm)	Model Plant	Reconstruction
Minimum	0	0
Maximum	4.576	4.496
Mean	0.289	0.411
RMS	0.379	0.534
Hausdorff Distance (mm)	4.576	

In the other direction, higher distances from the reconstruction to the original model represent areas that have deviated from the true position of the plant. This could be caused by a number of factors, such as misalignment between the orientation of a surface plane and the original surface, or surface boundaries extending beyond the true boundary of the leaves, possibly due to occlusion. The maximum and mean distances for the reconstruction remain low, and show that the reconstruction is a good reflection of the true model.

Table 2. Details and processing times for the datasets evaluated in this section. Each level set was iterated to a maxmimum of 100 times, or until it halted

Dataset	Cluster Count	Image Count	Time Taken
Rice	785	36	5m34s
Wheat	1486	62	18m28s
Model Rice Plant	517	40	2m11s

The mean distance and RMS error for this single-sided measure is higher than the reverse, which we believe may represent current technical limit of our approach. The distances around the boundaries of many surfaces appear slightly higher than in the centre, where the level sets can over-extend the leaf edge. This is a limitation within the level set speed function, but for the distances observed this usually represents an increase of size, outwards, of less than a pixel on average when projected into the reference image. This sub-pixel accuracy is not resolved by the speed function of the level set method that we use. An immediate improvement could be observed by simply increasing the resolution of the input image set, however this would add significant computational overhead.

The performance of our approach is closely related to the size of the image set, and the number of surface segments being evaluated. For small datasets, reconstruction usually takes a matter of minutes. For complex datasets containing thousands of small surface patches, we can expect performance to decrease. Table 2 shows details and processing times for the datasets evaluated in this section. Tests were run on an Intel Core i7 3820 machine. The algorithms detailed here are suitable for GPU parallelisation in the future if further optimisation is required.

4   Conclusions

The recovery of accurate 3D models of plants from colour images is challenging. A single plant constitutes a crowded scene in the sense of [13] and the construction of accurate 3D models of objects of this level of complexity is an active research topic. Images of plants exhibit high degrees of occlusion, with the occlusion relations between leaves varying from image to image. To complicate matters further, individual leaves are difficult to identify: most of the leaves on a given plant have similar colour and texture properties. Rather than address these issues in a single process that transforms a set of images into a three-dimensional model via feature correspondence or silhouette analysis, the approach presented here develops each leaf segment individually, automatically selecting an image likely to contain the necessary information. The proposed method reduces the effect of occlusion by choosing an image with a clear view of the target surface, and addresses the similarity problem by performing detailed analysis of the colours present in that image.

The mesh representation produced provides a detailed model of the surface of the viewed plant that can be used both in modelling tasks and for shoot phenotyping. At present the surface description output by the proposed technique comprises a large set of distinct planar patches, but it is anticipated to be a simple process to extend this to curved surfaces describing whole leaves if necessary. The level set method re-sizes and re-shapes each patch to maximise its consistency with neighbouring patches and the selected image, and as such the reconstructed patches provide an accurate approximation of the leaf surfaces. By avoiding a model fitting solution, the approach also remains general, and is flexible enough to be applied to a wide variety of plant species with differing leaf shapes.

References

1. Quan, L., Tan, P., Zeng, G., Yuan, L., Wang, J., Kang, S.B.: Image-based plant modeling. ACM Transactions on Graphics **25**(3), 599–604 (2006)
2. Watanabe, T., Hanan, J.S., Room, P.M., Hasegawa, T., Nakagawa, H., Takahashi, W.: Rice morphogenesis and plant architecture: measurement, specification and the reconstruction of structural development by 3D architectural modelling. Annals of Botany **95**(7), 1131–1143 (2005)
3. Alarcon, V.J., Sassenrath, G.F.: Modelling cotton (Gossypium spp.) leaves and canopy using computer aided geometric design (CAGD). Ecological Modelling **222**(12), 1951–1963 (2011)
4. Houle, D., Govindaraju, D.R., Omholt, S.: Phenomics: the next challenge. Nature Reviews Genetics **11**(12), 855–866 (2010)
5. White, J.W., Andrade-Sanchez, P., Gore, M.A., Bronson, K.F., Coffelt, T.A., Conley, M.M., Feldmann, K.A.: Field-based phenomics for plant genetics research. Field Crops Research **133**, 101–112 (2012)
6. Ma, W., Zha, H., Liu, J., Zhang, X., Xiang, B.: Image-based plant modeling by knowing leaves from their apexes. In: 19th International Conference on Pattern Recognition, pp. 1–4 (2008)
7. Alenya, G., Dellen, B., Torras, C.: 3D modelling of leaves from color and ToF data for robotized plant measuring. In: IEEE International Conference on Robotics and Automation (ICRA), pp. 3408–3414 (2011)
8. Clark, R.T., MacCurdy, R.B., Jung, J.K., Shaff, J.E., McCouch, S.R., Aneshansley, D.J., Kochian, L.V.: Three-dimensional root phenotyping with a novel imaging and software platform. Plant Physiology **156**(2), 455–465 (2011)
9. Kumar, P., Cai, J., Miklavcic, S.: High-throughput 3D modelling of plants for phenotypic analysis. In: Proceedings of the 27th Conference on Image and Vision Computing New Zealand, pp. 301–306 (2012)
10. Kutulakos, K.N., Seitz, S.M.: A theory of shape by space carving. International Journal of Computer Vision **38**(3), 199–218 (2000)
11. Cai, J., Miklavcic, S.: Automated extraction of three-dimensional cereal plant structures from two-dimensional orthographic images. Image Processing **6**(6), 687–696 (2012)
12. Qingfeng, S., Guilian, Z., Xin-Guang, Z.: Optimal crop canopy architecture to maximise canopy photosynthetic CO_2 uptake under elevated CO_2 – a theoretical study using a mechanistic model of canopy photosynthesis. Functional Plant Biology **40**, 108–124 (2013)
13. Furukawa, Y., Ponce, J.: Accurate, dense, and robust multiview stereopsis. IEEE Transactions on Pattern Analysis and Machine Intelligence **32**(8), 1362–1376 (2010)
14. Wu, C.: VisualSFM: A visual structure from motion system (2011)
15. Lowe, D.G.: Object recognition from local scale-invariant features. In: The Proceedings of the Seventh IEEE International Conference on Computer Vision, vol. 2, pp. 1150–1157 (1999)
16. Hartley, R., Zisserman, A.: Multiple View Geometry in computer vision. Cambridge University Press (2003)
17. Carr, J.C., Beatson, R.K., Cherrie, J.B., Mitchell, T.J., Fright, W.R., McCallum, B.C., Evans, T.R.: Reconstruction and representation of 3D objects with radial basis functions. In: Proceedings of the 28th Annual Conference on Computer Graphics and Interactive Techniques, pp. 67–76 (2001)
18. Kazhdan, M., Bolitho, M., Hoppe, H.: Poisson surface reconstruction. In: Proceedings of the Fourth Eurographics Symposium on Geometry Processing (2006)

19. Klasing, K., Wollherr, D., Buss, M.: A clustering method for efficient segmentation of 3D laser data. In: International Conference on Robotics and Automation (ICRA), pp. 4043–4048 (2008)
20. Edelsbrunner, H., Kirkpatrick, D.G., Raimund, S.: On the shape of a set of points in the plane. IEEE Transactions on Information Theory 29(4), 551–559 (1983)
21. Kass, M., Witkin, A., Terzopoulos, D.: Snakes: Active contour models. International Journal of Computer Vision 1(4), 321–331 (1988)
22. Osher, S., Sethian, J.A.: Fronts propagating with curvature-dependent speed: algorithms based on Hamilton-Jacobi formulations. Journal of Computational Physics 79(1), 12–49 (1988)
23. Sethian, J.A.: Level set methods and fast marching methods: evolving interfaces in computational geometry, fluid mechanics, computer vision, and materials science. Cambridge University Press 3 (1999)
24. Rosin, P.L.: Unimodal thresholding. Pattern Recognition 34(11), 2083–2096 (2001)
25. Shewchuk, J.R.: Delaunay Refinement Algorithms for Triangular Mesh Generation. Computational Geometry: Theory and Applications 22(1–3), 21–74 (2002)
26. SC Pixelmachine SRL: Topogun, v2.0. www.topogun.com
27. Blender Foundation: Blender, v2.69. www.blender.org
28. Cignoni, P., Rocchini, C., Scopigno, R.: Metro: Measuring error on simplified surfaces. Computer Graphics Forum 17(2), 167–174 (1998)

High-Resolution Plant Shape Measurements from Multi-view Stereo Reconstruction

Maria Klodt[(✉)] and Daniel Cremers

Technische Universität München, Munich, Germany
klodt@in.tum.de

Abstract. Accurate high-resolution 3D models are essential for a non-invasive analysis of phenotypic characteristics of plants. Leaf surface areas, fruit volumes and leaf inclination angles are typically of interest. This work presents a globally optimal 3D geometry reconstruction method that is specialized to high-resolutions and is thus suitable to reconstruct thin structures typically occuring in the geometry of plants. Volumetric 3D models are computed in a convex optimization framework from a set of RGB input images depicting the plant from different view points. The method uses the memory and run-time efficient octree data structure for fast computations of high-resolution 3D models. Results show accurate 3D reconstructions of barley, while an increase in resolution of a factor of up to 2000 is achieved in comparison to the use of a uniform voxel based data structure, making the choice of data structure crucial for feasible resolutions.

Keywords: Stereo Reconstruction · Convex Optimization · Plant Phenotyping · Octrees

1 Introduction

Plant phenotyping increasingly relies on precise 3D models of plants, demanding for automated and accurate reconstruction methods specialized for plant geometry. Applications include the determination of volume and surface dimensions, leaf quantification, and leaf inclination angles [28]. These applications share the benefit from accurate high-resolution 3D plant models. Since manual examination of phenotypic characteristics is usually time consuming and destructive, non-invasive and automated methods are needed for high-throughput applications and monitoring of specimen over time.

Convex optimization methods provide a powerful technique for inferring the 3D structure of an object from a set of images in a globally optimal way [16]. Volumetric methods as used in [11,16] allow for reconstructions of dense surfaces, at limited resolution due to large memory requirements of the underlying data structures. Point cloud reconstructions from images as used in [9] require less memory while neglecting density.

3D reconstruction of plants requires special consideration to the fine scaled features typically occuring in plant geometry. The usual assumption that the

© Springer International Publishing Switzerland 2015
L. Agapito et al. (Eds.): ECCV 2014 Workshops, Part IV, LNCS 8928, pp. 174–184, 2015.
DOI: 10.1007/978-3-319-16220-1_13

object to reconstruct is compact does not apply. Reconstruction of thin structures based on silhouette constraints as proposed in [6] allows to preserve fine structures while the uniform voxel based data structure still limits the resolution. For thin objects volumetric approaches yield large amounts of empty space, implying the need for more efficient non-uniform data structures.

Originally introduced for computer graphics, octrees [23] provide a memory-efficient data structure for large scale 3D objects. Large-scale reconstructions for fusion of RGB-D images into a volumetric model have shown that an octree based data structure avoids memory limitations in 3D reconstructions [31]. A non-hierarchical memory-efficient approach for volumetric representations is the narrow band method. Narrow bands for 3D reconstruction in graph cuts have been presented in [18].

Full 3D shape measurements of plants allow for a variety of phenotypic applications. However, phenotyping is a major bottleneck in crop plant research [14], which strongly benefits of automated approaches especially when dealing with large datasets. A special importance lies on high-resolution reconstruction of plant shapes for a better comprehension of phenotypes [7]. Laser scanners are a capable tool for the aquisition of high-precision 3D point clouds of plants [21], however provide no volumetric and surface area information. Time-of-flight cameras and RGB-D sensors like the *Kinect* capture 3D information at a lower resolution. They are also used in agriculture however are known to be less robust to bright illumination than stereo vision [1,13]. In the last years, image analysis has become a widely used technique for non-invasive methods for plant phenotyping [8]. Applications include the monitoring of growth rates which can be used as a measure for drought tolerance of wheat and barley [25], classification of leaves and stems [26], or computation of leaf inclination angles [3]. In [29] an image based method for 4D reconstruction of plants based on optical flow is introduced. Another application is the determination of the leaf canopy area from images [19], an ecological indicator variable whose estimation usuallly is laborious [17].

This work presents a novel method for volumetric 3D reconstruction of plants from a set of RGB images, specialized on accuracy and high-resolution. The method is implemented in a convex framework allowing for global optimization of the chosen model which makes it independent of initializations. The underlying data structure is based on octrees, which enable a fast and memory-efficient implementation, making high resolutions possible. In this work we show that the choice of data structure is not only beneficial for reducing run-time and memory requirements, but crucial to make high-resolutions possible.

Fig. 1 shows results of the proposed method for a 3D reconstruction of barley. For a plant of 10 cm height a resolution of $1.8 \cdot 10^{-6}$ mm^3 is achieved by the use of an octree data structure. The use of octrees enables a more than 2000 times higher resolution compared to a uniformely spaced voxel grid using the same amount of memory. Especially in the case of thin structures, the data structure is critical to avoid memory limitations.

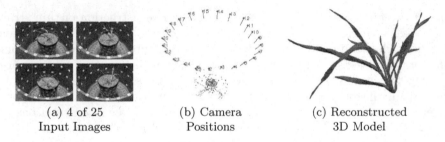

| (a) 4 of 25 | (b) Camera | (c) Reconstructed |
| Input Images | Positions | 3D Model |

Fig. 1. 3D-Reconstruction of a barley, computed from 25 input images. The reconstructed 3D model consists of ~12 million octree nodes.

2   High-Resolution Stereo Reconstruction with Octrees

We consider a continuous image domain $\Omega \subset \mathbb{R}^2$. Given a set of m input images $I_1, \ldots, I_m : \Omega \to \mathbb{R}$ depicting the object from different view points, we compute a surface $\Sigma \subset \mathbb{R}^3$ that gives rise to the images. To reconstruct a full 3D model, each object point must be visible in at least two images. Fig. 1 (b) shows an example for 25 camera positions, computed with software of [22] and [30].

The surface is optimized inside the visual hull [20] $\mathcal{H} \subset \mathbb{R}^3$ which is determined by silhouette images. The silhouette images $S_i : \Omega \to \{0, 1\}, i = 1, \ldots m$ are defined as $S_i(p) = 1$ at points $p \in \Omega$ that depict the plant and $S_i(p) = 0$ otherwise, i.e. at points that depict background. We compute silhouette images using an interactive image segmentation method [33]. The visual hull is the smallest volume whose projections to the input images cover the silhouettes of the object.

We propose the use of volume constraints to ensure a stable substance of the reconstructed object. Volume constraints have been proposed for single view reconstruction [32] and image segmentation [10,15].

2.1   Surface Optimization with Volume Constraints

The surface Σ is represented implicitly by an indicator function $\mathbf{1}_\Sigma : \mathcal{H} \to \{0, 1\}$ that defines a segmentation of the volume enclosed by $\mathcal{H}$ to plant, i.e. $\mathbf{1}_\Sigma(x) = 1$, and background, i.e. $\mathbf{1}_\Sigma(x) = 0$. Relaxing the domain to the continuous domain $[0, 1]$ allows for convex optimization of the corresponding segmentation $u : \mathcal{H} \to [0, 1]$. We consider the following convex optimization problem

$$\min_u \left\{ \int_{\mathcal{H}} g(x) \, |\nabla(u)| + \lambda \int_{\mathcal{H}} f(x) u(x) \, \mathrm{d}x \right\}, \quad \text{s.t.} \quad \mathcal{V}(u) \geq c, \qquad (1)$$

where $\mathcal{V}$ refers to the volume of the object, i.e.

$$\mathcal{V}(u) = \int_{\mathcal{H}} u(x) \, \mathrm{d}x. \qquad (2)$$

and $c \in \mathbb{R}$ is the minimum volume. In the experiments shown in this paper, the volume constraint parameter was set to $c = 0.9 \cdot |\mathcal{H}|$ which implies that the volume of the segmented object should be at least 90% of the volume enclosed by the visual hull. The data term $f : \mathcal{H} \to \mathbb{R}$, weighted with $\lambda \in \mathbb{R}$, implements the assumption that the visual hull is a rough estimator for the object and is based on the distance of a point to the border $\partial\mathcal{H}$ of the domain:

$$f(x) = 1 - \min_{\hat{x} \in \partial\mathcal{H}} \| x - \hat{x} \| . \tag{3}$$

For the m input images $I_1, \ldots, I_m : \Omega \to \mathbb{R}$ the photoconsistency g is computed as the intensity difference of the best matching image pair:

$$g(x) = \min_{i,j \in \{1,\ldots,m\}, i \neq j} (|I_i(\pi_i(x)) - I_j(\pi_j(x))|), \tag{4}$$

where $\pi_i : \mathbb{R}^3 \to \Omega$ is the projection of a 3D point x to image I_i. $g(x)$ is used as a weighting function for the gradient norm $|\nabla(u)|$, directing the surface through points whose projections to the images have similar intensity.

A minimizer of (1) is computed using a primal-dual optimization [5] scheme with gradient descent in the primal variable u and gradient ascent in the dual variable $p : \mathcal{H} \to \mathbb{R}^3$

$$p^{t+1} = \Pi_C \left(p^t + \tau\nabla u^t \right) \tag{5}$$

$$u^{t+1} = \Pi_V \left(u^t + \sigma(\text{div}(p^{t+1}) - \lambda f) \right) \tag{6}$$

and the projections

$$\Pi_C(p) = \frac{p}{\max\left\{1, \frac{|p|}{g}\right\}} \tag{7}$$

$$\Pi_V(u) = u + \max\left\{ \frac{1}{|\mathcal{H}|} \left(c - \int_{\mathcal{H}} u(x)\,dx \right), 0 \right\}. \tag{8}$$

The time steps τ and σ were set to $\tau = \sigma = 0.3$. The projection Π_V projects the current u to the volume constraint $V(u) \geq c$, and is computed analog to the area constraint in [15]. The projection Π_C was presented in [4]. The boundary conditions are Dirichlet conditions for the gradient, i.e. $\nabla u|_{\partial\mathcal{H}} = 0$, and Neumann conditions for the divergence, i.e. $\text{div}(p)|_{\partial\mathcal{H}} = p$.

2.2   A Memory-Efficient Data Structure Using Octrees

An octree is a tree data structure whose nodes have either eight or no sub nodes. Nodes with eight sub nodes are denoted as *inner nodes* and nodes without sub nodes as *leaf nodes*. Octrees provide a memory-efficient data structure for 3D volumes.

Building the Octree. The octree data structure is computed from the silhouette images in a top-down approach starting at a root node enclosing the whole scene depicted in the images. Subsequently, nodes are subdivided depending on

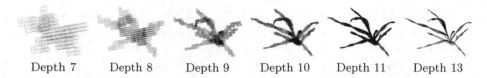

Depth 7   Depth 8   Depth 9   Depth 10   Depth 11   Depth 13

Fig. 2. Octree data structure for increasing resolution, i.e. depth of the tree. The figures show the bounding boxes of all leaf nodes in the deepest level of the octree. The data structure is built in a top-down method where each level is complete in itself but can be refined for higher resolution.

the structure of the visual hull. Fig. 2 shows an example octree at different steps of the iteration.

Each node gets a assigned a bounding cuboid with coordinates $C := (x_{min}, y_{min}, z_{min}, x_{max}, y_{max}, z_{max})$ that define the volume enclosed by the node. The camera positions and viewing angles define a bounding cuboid which define the respective coordinates of the root node. The nodes are subsequently divided into eight sub-nodes of equal size if the visual hull passes the bounding cuboid of the node. The visual hull passes the cuboid if the projection of the cuboid's faces to the images contains both plant and background for at least one of the m input images. The nodes are refined until a predefined maximal depth is reached that corresponds to the desired resolution. In each iteration the octree contains the visual hull in the leaves of the deepest level. Note that it is not necessary that the bounding cuboid is as small as possible since the subsequent subdivision of the data structure will prevent the allocation of too many nodes.

Neighborhood Connectivity of Nodes. To compute the derivatives for the gradient and divergence operators in the optimization update steps (5) and (6) each leaf node in the octree requires access to the function values of its neighboring nodes. Each node stores a reference to its parent node, and the inner nodes also to the eight sub nodes. Storing additional references to the six neighboring nodes respectively saves run-time while needing more memory. We compute the neighboring nodes for each node every time when access to it is needed. We chose not to precompute them, because experiments showed that the run-time improvement is not significant. Due to the bounding cuboid each node has defined, neighboring nodes can be found by its coordinates via traversing one path of the tree from the root to the node. The respective run-time is in $O(\log(n))$, where n is the number of nodes in the octree and $\log(n)$ is the maximal depth.

3   Performance Evaluation

We evaluate the method with respect to accuracy and memory requirements for 3D reconstructions of barley.

Fig. 3. Volumetric 3D Reconstruction of a barley, computed from 25 RGB images. The dense surface is optimized in the leaf nodes of deepest level in an octree of depth 14.

3.1   High-Resolution Volumetric 3D Reconstruction of Barley

Fig. 3 shows reconstruction results for barley for the input images shown in Fig. 1(a). The images were captured with a standard consumer camera at a resolution of 5184 × 3456 pixels. The camera capturing positions were computed using the software of [22] and [30]. The octree that was computed to reconstruct the 3D model has a depth of 14 and its computation took around 30 minutes, making the method suitable for offline reconstructions.

3.2   Accuracy of the Reconstruction

We measure the accuracy of the reconstructed 3D model by projecting its silhouette to the input images and computing the difference to manually segmented ground truth images. Since an objective ground truth in 3D is not available, the projection error is measured in the image domain. Fig. 4 shows that the proposed 3D reconstruction with octrees enables accurate 3D reconstruction of fine-scaled structures of the plant. The figure shows a projection of the reconstructed object to one of the original images. The similarity of the projected silhouette compared to the manually segmented ground truth is 0.96. As similarity measurement the dice coeffient was used, where a value of 1 corresponds

| (a) Silhouette Projection | (b) Close-up View 1 | (c) Close-up View 2 | (d) Close-up View 3 |

Fig. 4. The high-resolution data structure allows for accurate 3D reconstruction. (a): The silhouette of the reconstructed 3D model is projected to one of the input images. (b-d): Close-up views visualize the accuracy of the reconstruction. The similarity of the projected silhouette compared to the ground truth is 0.96.

Table 1. Comparison of memory requirements (approximate values) for 3D reconstruction in a uniformly spaced voxel grid versus octree. Memory limits of a current consumer PC are reached for the regular grid already at a resolution of 1024^3, while an octree of depth 14 fits. This makes the octree a suitable data structure for 3D reconstruction of thin structures occuring in plants.

Octree Depth	Uniform Grid: Number of Voxels	Uniform Grid: Memory Requirement	Octree: Number of Nodes	Octree: Memory Requirement	Comparison Factor
7	64^3	1 MB	10^3	85 KB	12
8	128^3	8 MB	$3 \cdot 10^3$	240 KB	34
9	256^3	64 MB	$9 \cdot 10^3$	650 KB	101
10	512^3	512 MB	$27 \cdot 10^3$	1.9 MB	269
11	1024^3	4 GB	$96 \cdot 10^3$	6.6 MB	621
12	2048^3	32 GB	$413 \cdot 10^3$	29 MB	1129
13	4096^3	256 GB	$2 \cdot 10^6$	172 MB	1524
14	8192^3	2 TB	$15 \cdot 10^6$	1 GB	2048

to a perfect overlap and 0 to no overlap. The close-up view in Fig. 4 (c) shows an example where the reconstructed model is inaccurate: the reconstruction does not contain the whole leaf in the middle of the image. In this case this is due to the fact that the leaf is not visible in some of the images and the region is hence segmented as background in 3D.

3.3   Performance Analysis

The memory requirements and resolution of the proposed method are compared to a standard volumetric approach using regular grids. A regular grid is a subdivision of a 3D volume into uniformly sized cuboids, also denoted as voxels. This yields a data volume with large amounts of empty voxels – in contrast to the octree with nodes of different sizes depending on the structure of the shape.

Tab. 1 shows a comparison of memory requirements for the octree data structure and the alternative representation using a regular grid. The values for the uniform grid were computed for each resolution while the values for the octree were measured experimentally for the example 3D model shown in Fig. 3. In each row of the table the actual size of a voxel is the same as the size of an octree node. Due to the connectivity of nodes the memory requirement for a single octree node is higher than the requirement for a single voxel, however the overall memory consumption is significantly reduced. For the uniform grid a resolution of 1024^3 reaches the limit of a current consumer PC with 4 GB RAM. The octree of depth 14 requires 1 GB, corresponding to a voxel volume of 8192^3. For a plant of 10 cm height, an octree node inside the visual hull covers a volume of $1.8 \cdot 10^{-6}$ mm^3, yielding a 2048 times higher resolution than a voxel of the regular grid fitting in the same memory, which covers a volume of 0.0037 mm^3. The experiment shows that the choice of data structure is crucial to make high-resolutions feasible for volumetric reconstructions.

4   3D Plant Shape Models for Phenotyping

Full 3D models of plants allow for phenoypic analysis including the computation of volumes and surface areas or leaf inclination angles. Further analysis like monitoring of plant growth is possible since the plants are not destroyed during the process of reconstruction.

4.1   Measuring Volume and Surface Area

The volume and surface area of a plant are fundamental indicators for growth analysis [27]. Volumetric models have the advantage that precise information on these features can be directly extracted from the shape.

The volume $\mathcal{V}(u)$ measured in voxels can be computed from the segmented surface u using equation (2). To obtain absolute measurements in cm^3, a reference measurement is necessary, for example the overall height h of the plant in cm, or in case of fixed cameras the baselines between the camera optical centers. The absolute volume $V(u)$ of the plant model can then be computed by a respective scaling of $\mathcal{V}(u)$, i.e. with $h^3/2^{3d}$, where d is the depth of the octree. If no reference measurement is given, the volume can be computed up to a constant scalar factor.

The surface area $A(u)$ corresponds to the boundary size of the reconstructed shape and can be computed from u with

$$A(u) = \int_{\mathcal{H}} |\nabla(u)| \, \mathrm{d}x. \tag{9}$$

For the barley shown in Fig. 3 we measured a volume of $V(u) \approx 3.101$ cm^3 and a surface area of $A(u) \approx 106.1$ cm^2 for a plant height of 10 cm.

4.2   Quantification of Leaves

The total leaf number of a plant is an important trait used to monitor vegetative development. It can be used as an indicator to measure influences of drought [12] or to determine flowering times [24].

The full 3D models of plant shapes allow for automated quantification of leaves as the experiment in Fig. 5 shows for a barley. The reconstructed 3D model (Fig. 5 (a)) is segmented into two regions according to the eigenvalues of the second-moments tensor of the surface (Fig. 5 (b)). The 3D second-moments tensor [2] of a shape u is defined as

$$M(u) = \int_{\mathcal{H}} G_\sigma * \nabla u \nabla u^\top \, \mathrm{d}x \tag{10}$$

where G_σ is a gaussian convolution with standard deviation σ. The eigenvalues of M represent the distribution of gradient directions of the shape, and thus provide a robust classifier for a segmentation based on local geometric structures. Due to the high resolution of the 3D model the eigenvalues can be computed precisely. The connected components (Fig. 5 (c)) of the resulting segmentation allow for an automated quantification of leaves.

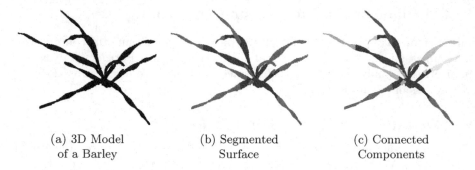

(a) 3D Model	(b) Segmented	(c) Connected
of a Barley	Surface	Components

Fig. 5. Segmentation of the 3D surface, based on the eigenvalues of the second-moments tensor. The connected components of the segmentation yield quantitative information like the number of leaves in the plant.

5   Conclusion

We proposed a method for the reconstruction of high-resolution volumetric 3D models of plants from a set of RGB images. The reconstructed full 3D models allow for accurate phenotypic analysis of the geometric properties of plants including volume and surface areas or quantification of leaves. We showed that the octree data structure is especially suitable for volumetric reconstruction of thin features that typically occur in plant geometry. Moreover, we showed that the choice of a suitable data structure is essential to make high-resolution 3D model reconstruction possible. Compared to standard data structures, like regular grids, up to 2000 times higher resolutions are feasible. Possible future work includes a space-time reconstruction of plant growth. The non-invasiveness of the method allows for a monitoring of specimen over a time period.

Acknowledgments. This work was supported by the AgroClustEr: CROP.SENSe.net (FKZ 0315534D) which is funded by the German Federal Ministry of Education and Research (BMBF). The authors thank Dr. Henrik Schumann from INRES, University of Bonn for providing the image data.

References

1. Abbas, S.M., Muhammad, A.: Outdoor RGB-D slam performance in slow mine detection. In: 7th German Conference on Robotics, Proceedings of ROBOTIK 2012, pp. 1–6. VDE (2012)
2. Bigün, J., Granlund, G.H.: Optimal orientation detection of linear symmetry. In: IEEE First International Conference on Computer Vision (ICCV), London, Great Britain, pp. 433–438 (June 1987)
3. Biskup, B., Scharr, H., Schurr, U., Rascher, U.: A stereo imaging system for measuring structural parameters of plant canopies. Plant Cell Environ. **30**(10), 1299–1308 (2007)

4. Chambolle, A.: Total variation minimization and a class of binary MRF models. In: Rangarajan, A., Vemuri, B.C., Yuille, A.L. (eds.) EMMCVPR 2005. LNCS, vol. 3757, pp. 136–152. Springer, Heidelberg (2005)
5. Chambolle, A., Pock, T.: A first-order primal-dual algorithm for convex problems with applications to imaging. Journal of Mathematical Imaging and Vision **40**(1), 120–145 (2011)
6. Cremers, D., Kolev, K.: Multiview stereo and silhouette consistency via convex functionals over convex domains. IEEE Transactions on Pattern Analysis and Machine Intelligence **33**(6), 1161–1174 (2011)
7. Dhondt, S., Wuyts, N., Inzé, D.: Cell to whole-plant phenotyping: the best is yet to come. Trends in Plant Science **18**(8), 433–444 (2013)
8. Fiorani, F., Schurr, U.: Future scenarios for plant phenotyping. Annual Review of Plant Biology **64**, 267–291 (2013)
9. Furukawa, Y., Ponce, J.: Accurate, dense, and robust multiview stereopsis. IEEE Transactions on Pattern Analysis and Machine Intelligence **32**(8), 1362–1376 (2010)
10. Gorelick, L., Schmidt, F.R., Boykov, Y., Delong, A., Ward, A.: Segmentation with non-linear regional constraints via line-search cuts. In: Fitzgibbon, A., Lazebnik, S., Perona, P., Sato, Y., Schmid, C. (eds.) ECCV 2012, Part I. LNCS, vol. 7572, pp. 583–597. Springer, Heidelberg (2012)
11. Graber, G., Pock, T., Bischof, H.: Online 3D reconstruction using convex optimization. In: 1st Workshop on Live Dense Reconstruction From Moving Cameras, ICCV 2011 (2011)
12. Granier, C., Aguirrezabal, L., Chenu, K., Cookson, S., Dauzat, M., Hamard, P., Thioux, J., Rolland, G., Bouchier-Combaud, S., Lebaudy, A.: Phenopsis, an automated platform for reproducible phenotyping of plant responses to soil water deficit in arabidopsis thaliana permitted the identification of an accession with low sensitivity to soil water deficit. New Phytologist **169**, 623–635 (2006)
13. Kazmi, W., Foix, S., Alenya, G., Andersen, H.J.: Indoor and outdoor depth imaging of leaves with time-of-flight and stereo vision sensors: Analysis and comparison. ISPRS Journal of Photogrammetry and Remote Sensing **88**, 128–146 (2014)
14. Kilian, B., Graner, A.: Ngs technologies for analyzing germplasm diversity in genebanks. Brief Funct Genomics **11**(1), 38–50 (2012)
15. Klodt, M., Cremers, D.: A convex framework for image segmentation with moment constraints. In: IEEE International Conference on Computer Vision (ICCV) (2011)
16. Kolev, K., Klodt, M., Brox, T., Cremers, D.: Continuous Global Optimization in Multiview 3D Reconstruction. International Journal of Computer Vision (IJCV) **84**(1), 80–96 (2009)
17. Korhonen, L., Heikkinen, J.: Automated Analysis of in Situ Canopy Images for the Estimation of Forest Canopy Cover. Forest Science **55**(4), 323–334 (2009)
18. Ladikos, A., Benhimane, S., Navab, N.: Multi-view reconstruction using narrow-band graph-cuts and surface normal optimization. In: BMVC, pp. 1–10 (2008)
19. Lati, R.N., Filin, S., Eizenberg, H.: Robust methods for measurement of leaf-cover area and biomass from image data. Weed Science **59**(2), 276–284 (2011)
20. Laurentini, A.: The visual hull concept for silhouette-based imageunderstanding. IEEE Trans. Pattern Anal. Mach. Intell. **16**(2), 150–162(1994)
21. Louarn, G., Carré, S., Boudon, F., Eprinchard, A., Combes, D.: Characterization of whole plant leaf area properties using laser scanner point clouds. In: Fourth International Symposium on Plant Growth Modeling, Simulation, Visualization and Applications, Shanghai, Chine (2012)

22. Lowe, D.G.: Distinctive image features from scale-invariant keypoints. International Journal of Computer Vision **60**(2), 91–110 (2004)
23. Meagher, D.: Octree Encoding: a New Technique for the Representation, Manipulation and Display of Arbitrary 3-D Objects by Computer. Electrical and Systems Engineering Department Rensseiaer Polytechnic Institute Image Processing Laboratory (1980)
24. Mendez-Vigo, B., de Andres, M., Ramiro, M., Martinez-Zapater, J., Alonso-Blanco, C.: Temporal analysis of natural variation for the rate of leaf production and its relationship with flowering initiation in arabidopsis thaliana. Journal of Experimental Botany **61**(6), 1611–1623 (2010)
25. Munns, R., James, R.A., Sirault, X.R.R., Furbank, R.T., Jones, H.G.: New phenotyping methods for screening wheat and barley for beneficial responses to water deficit. Journal of Experimental Botany **61**(13), 3499–3507 (2010)
26. Paproki, A., Sirault, X., Berry, S., Furbank, R., Fripp, J.: A novel mesh processing based technique for 3D plant analysis. BMC Plant Biology **12**(1), 63 (2012)
27. Paulus, S., Schumann, H., Kuhlmann, H., Leon, J.: High-precision laser scanning system for capturing 3D plant architecture and analysing growth of cereal plants. Biosystems Engineering **121**, 1–11 (2014)
28. Pisek, J., Sonnentag, O., Richardson, A.D., Mottus, M.: Is the spherical leaf inclination angle distribution a valid assumption for temperate and boreal broadleaf tree species? Agricultural and Forest Meteorology **169**, 186–194 (2013)
29. Schuchert, T., Scharr, H.: Estimation of 3D object structure, motion and rotation based on 4D affine optical flow using a multi-camera array. In: Daniilidis, K., Maragos, P., Paragios, N. (eds.) ECCV 2010, Part IV. LNCS, vol. 6314, pp. 596–609. Springer, Heidelberg (2010)
30. Snavely, N., Seitz, S.M., Szeliski, R.: Photo tourism: Exploring photo collections in 3D. In: SIGGRAPH Conference Proceedings, pp. 835–846. ACM Press, New York (2006)
31. Steinbruecker, F., Kerl, C., Sturm, J., Cremers, D.: Large-scale multi-resolution surface reconstruction from rgb-d sequences. In: IEEE International Conference on Computer Vision (ICCV), Sydney, Australia (2013)
32. Toeppe, E., Nieuwenhuis, C., Cremers, D.: Volume constraints for single view reconstruction. In: IEEE Conference on Computer Vision and Pattern Recognition (CVPR), Portland, USA (2013)
33. Unger, M., Pock, T., Bischof, H.: Continuous globally optimal image segmentation with local constraints. In: Computer Vision Winter Workshop 2008, Moravske Toplice, Slovenija (February 2008)

Texture-Based Leaf Identification

Milan Sulc[✉] and Jiri Matas

Center for Machine Perception, Department of Cybernetics,
Faculty of Electrical Engineering, Czech Technical University in Prague,
Prague, Czech Republic
sulcmila@cmp.felk.cvut.cz

Abstract. A novel approach to visual leaf identification is proposed. A leaf is represented by a pair of local feature histograms, one computed from the leaf interior, the other from the border. The histogrammed local features are an improved version of a recently proposed rotation and scale invariant descriptor based on local binary patterns (LBPs).

Describing the leaf with multi-scale histograms of rotationally invariant features derived from sign- and magnitude-LBP provides a desirable level of invariance. The representation does not use colour.

Using the same parameter settings in all experiments and standard evaluation protocols, the method outperforms the state-of-the-art on all tested leaf sets - the Austrian Federal Forests dataset, the Flavia dataset, the Foliage dataset, the Swedish dataset and the Middle European Woods dataset - achieving excellent recognition rates above 99%.

Preliminary results on images from the north and south regions of France obtained from the LifeCLEF'14 Plant task dataset indicate that the proposed method is also applicable to recognizing the environmental conditions the plant has been exposed to.

1 Introduction

Recognition of plants is a challenging computer vision problem that requires dealing with irregular shapes and textures with high intraclass variability. Interest in methods for visual classification of plants has grown recently [4,5,13,18] as devices equipped with cameras became ubiquitous, making intelligent field guides, education tools and automation in forestry and agriculture practical. Belhumeur et al. [4] discuss, how using such a system in the field a botanist can quickly search entire collections of plant species - a process that previously took hours can now be done in seconds.

Plant recognition has been posed, almost without exceptions [3], as recognition of specific organs such as flowers, bark, fruits or leaves or their combination [1,4,5,7–15,18,19,26,28,32,33]. Leaf recognition has been by far the most popular and a wide range of methods has been reported in the literature [1,4,5,7–15,19,26,28,32,33].

We propose a novel approach to leaf recognition. It achieves excellent recognition rates above 99% on a number of public datasets, outperforming the state-of-the-art. The method uses neither color nor an explicit shape model, focusing

© Springer International Publishing Switzerland 2015
L. Agapito et al. (Eds.): ECCV 2014 Workshops, Part IV, LNCS 8928, pp. 185–200, 2015.
DOI: 10.1007/978-3-319-16220-1_14

on leaf texture, which is represented by a pair of local feature histograms, one computed from the leaf interior, the other from the border. Experimental evaluation of the proposed method shows the importance of both the border and interior textures and that global point-to-point registration to reference models is not needed for precise leaf recognition.

The histogrammed local features are an improved version of the recently proposed rotation and scale invariant descriptor [29] which is based on local binary patterns (LBPs). Describing the leaf with multi-scale histograms of powerful rotationally invariant features derived from sign and magnitude LBPs provides a desirable level of invariance. It avoids the need for registration of the leaf stem, axis and boundary. Compound leaves are handled naturally.

The leaf recognition task is commonly understood as the identification of plant species and several leaf datasets have been collected [5,7,9,19,28,33] containing images of leaves labeled by plant species. While the leaf species is determined by its genotype, its appearnace is influenced by environmental conditions. We provide preliminary results on binary classification of leaves from different locations (south and north regions of France), assuming that the plants are exposed to different environmental conditions while having similar genotypes and show the Ffirst representation is capable of fairly accurate prediction of the collection site location.

The rest of this paper is organized as follows: Section 2 reviews the art in automatic plant identification from images of leaves or combinations of leaves with other images. Section 3 describes the texture recognition method called Ffirst (Fast Features Invariant to Rotation and Scale of Texture). Section 4 explains how the Ffirst descriptor is used for the leaf region. Experiments and results are presented in Section 5. Section 6 concludes the paper.

2   State of the Art

Recognition of leaves usually refers only to recognition of broad leaves, needles are treated separately. Several techniques have been proposed for leaf description, often based on combining features of different character (shape features, colour features, etc.).

The leaf recognition method by Fiel and Sablatnig [5] is based on a Bag of Words model with SIFT descriptors and achieves 93.6% accuracy on a leaf dataset of 5 Austrian tree species. This dataset denoted as AFF is also used in our experiments in Sections 5.3.

Kadir et al. compare several shape methods on plant recognition [8]. Of the compared methods - geometric features, moment invariants, Zernike moments and Polar Fourier Transform - Polar Fourier Transform performed best achieving 64% accuracy on a database of 52 plant species. The dataset has not been published.

Kumar et al. [13] describe Leafsnap, a computer vision system for automatic plant species identification, which has evolved from the earlier plant identification systems by Agarwal et al. [1] and Belhumeur et al. [4]. Compared to the earlier versions, they introduced a pre-filter on input images, numerous speed-ups and additional post-processing within the segmentation algorithm, the use of a simpler and more efficient curvature-based recognition algorithm instead of Inner Distance Shape Context (IDSC); a larger dataset of images, and a new interactive system for use by non-expert users. Kumar et al. [13] introduce the Leafsnap database of 184 tree species, however at the time of writing this paper it was not publicly available. On this database, 96.8% of queries have a species match within the top 5 results shown to the user with the used method. The resulting electronic field guide, developed at Columbia University, the University of Maryland, and the Smithsonian Institution, is available as a free mobile app for iOS devices. Although the app runs on iPhone and iPad devices, the leaf images are processed on a server, internet connection is thus required for recognition, which might cause problems in natural areas with slow or no data connection. Another limit is the need to take the photos of the leaves on a white background.

Wu et al. [33] proposed a Probabilistic Neural Network for leaf recognition using 12 commonly used Digital Morphological Features (DMFs), derived from 5 basic features (diameter, physiological length, physiological width, leaf area, leaf perimeter). The authors collected a publicly available database of plant leaves called Flavia, containing 1907 images of leaves from 32 species. The average accuracy on the current version of the dataset is 93%[1]. The Flavia dataset is discussed in Section 5.1. In Section 5.3 our results are compared to the best reported by Kadir et al. [7,10] and Lee et al. [14,15], as well as to the results in Novotný and Suk [19], and Karuna et al. [11], who used a different evaluation protocol.

Kadir et al. [9] prepared the Foliage dataset, consisting of 60 classes of leaves, each containing 120 images. Results on the Foliage dataset are compared in Section 5.3. The best reported result by Kadir et al. [10] was achieved by a combination of shape, vein, texture and colour features processed by Principal Component Analysis before classification by a Probabilistic Neural Network.

Söderkvist [28] proposed a visual classification system of leaves and collected the so called Swedish dataset containing scanned images of 15 classes of Swedish trees. Wu et al. [32] introduced a visual descriptor for scene categorization called the spatial Principal component Analysis of Census Transform (spatial PACT), achieving a 97.9% recognition rate on the Swedish dataset. Qi et al. achieve[2] 99.38% accuracy on the Swedish dataset using a texture descriptor called Pairwise Rotation Invariant Co-occurrence Local Binary Patterns (PRI-CoLBP) [26] with SVM classification. In Section 5.3 we provide experimental results on the Swedish dataset.

Novotný and Suk [19] proposed a leaf recognition system, using Fourier descriptors of the leaf contour normalised to translation, rotation, scaling and starting point of the boundary. The authors also collected a new large leaf dataset called Middle European Woods (MEW) containing 153 classes of native or

---

[1] http://flavia.sourceforge.net
[2] http://qixianbiao.github.io

frequently cultivated trees and shrubs in Central Europe. Their method achieves 84.92% accuracy when the dataset is split into equally sized training and test set. Section 5.3 contains the comparison to our results.

One possible application of leaf description is the identification of a disease. Pydipati et al. [25] proposed a system for citrus disease identification using Color Co-occurrence Method (CCM), achieving accuracies of over 95% for 4 classes (normal leaf samples and samples with a greasy spot, melanose, and scab).

Kim et al. [12] proposed a tree classification method using a combination of leaf, flower and bark photos of the same tree. The description consists of 20 features of wavelet decomposition with 3 levels for a grey and a binary image for description of bark, 32 features of Fourier descriptor for leaves and 72 features in the HS colour space for flowers. The results were obtained on an unpublished dataset consisting of 16 classes. Recognition accuracy of 31%, 75% and 75% is reported for individual leaf, flower and bark classification and 84%, 75% and 100% accuracy for combinations of leaf+flower, leaf+bark and bark+flower. However, in all cases only a single image per class was tested. The statistical significance of such result is questionable and may be prone to overfitting and unreliable.

Pl@ntNet[3] [3] is an interactive plant identification and collaborative information system providing an image sharing and retrieval application for plant identification. It has been developed by scientists from four French research organizations (Cirad, INRA, INRIA and IRD) and the Tela Botanica network. The Pl@ntNet-identify Tree Database provides identification by combining information from images of the habitat, flower, fruit, leaf and bark. The exact algorithms used in the Pl@ntNet-identify web service[4] and their accuracies are not publicly documented.

3   The Ffirst Method

In order to describe the leaf texture independently of the leaf size and orientation in the image, a description invariant to rotation and scale is needed. For applications like intelligent field guides, the recognition method also has to be reasonably fast.

In this section we describe a novel texture description called Ffirst (Fast Features Invariant to Rotation and Scale of Texture), which combines several state-of-the-art approaches to satisfy the given requirements. This method builds on and improves a texture descriptor for bark recognition introduced in [29].

3.1   Completed Local Binary Pattern and Histogram Fourier Features

The Ffirst description is based on the Local Binary Patterns (LBP) [20,22]. The common LBP operator (further denoted as sign-LBP) computes the signs of

---

[3] http://www.plantnet-project.org/
[4] http://identify.plantnet-project.org/en/

differences between pixels in the 3×3 neighbourhood and the center pixel. LBP have been generalized [21] to arbitrary number of neighbours P on a circle of radius R, using an image function $f(x, y)$ and neighbourhood point coordinates (x_p, y_p):

$$\text{LBP}_{P,R}(x, y) = \sum_{p=0}^{P-1} s(f(x, y) - f(x_p, y_p))2^p, \quad s(z) = \begin{cases} 1 : z \leq 0 \\ 0 : \quad \text{else} \end{cases}. \quad (1)$$

To achieve rotation invariance[5], Ffirst uses the so called LBP Histogram Fourier Features (LBP-HF) introduced by Ahonen et al. [2], which describe the histogram of uniform patterns using coefficients of the discrete Fourier transform. Uniform LBP are patterns with at most 2 spatial transitions (bitwise 0-1 changes). Unlike the simple rotation invariants using LBP^{ri} [21,23], which assign all uniform patterns with the same number of 1s into one bin,

$$\text{LBP}_{P,R}^{ri} = \min \left\{ \text{ROR} \left(\text{LBP}_{P,R}, i \right) \mid i = 0, 1, .., P - 1 \right\}, \quad (2)$$

the LBP-HF features preserve the information about relative rotation of the patterns.

Denoting a uniform pattern $U_p^{n,r}$, where n is the number of "1" bits and r denotes the rotation of the pattern, the DFT for given n is expressed as:

$$H(n, u) = \sum_{r=0}^{P-1} h_I(U_p^{n,r})e^{-i2\pi ur/P}, \quad (3)$$

where the histogram value $h_I(U_p^{n,r})$ denotes the number of occurrences of a given uniform pattern in the image.

The LBP-HF features are equal to the absolute value of the DFT magnitudes (which are not influenced by the phase shift caused by rotation):

$$\text{LBP-HF}(n, u) = |H(n, u)| = \sqrt{H(n, u)\overline{H(n, u)}}. \quad (4)$$

Since h_I are real, $H(n, u) = H(n, P - u)$ for $u = (1, .., P - 1)$, and therefore only $\lfloor \frac{P}{2} \rfloor + 1$ of the DFT magnitudes are used for each set of uniform patterns with n "1" bits for $0 < n < P$. Three other bins are added to the resulting representation, namely two for the "1-uniform" patterns (with all bins of the same value) and one for all non-uniform patterns.

The LBP histogram Fourier features can be generalized to any set of uniform patterns. In Ffirst, the LBP-HF-S-M description introduced by Zhao et al. [34] is used, where the histogram Fourier features of both sign- and magnitude-LBP are calculated to build the descriptor. The combination of both sign- and magnitude-LBP called Completed Local Binary Patterns (CLBP) was introduced by Guo and Zhang [6]. The magnitude-LBP checks if the magnitude of the difference of

---

[5] LBP-HF (as well as LBP^{ri}) are rotation invariant only in the sense of a circular bit-wise shift, e.g. rotation by multiples 22.5° for $\text{LBP}_{16,R}$.

the neighbouring pixel (x_p, y_p) against the central pixel (x, y) exceeds a threshold t_p:

$$\text{LBP-M}_{P,R}(x,y) = \sum_{p=0}^{P-1} s(|f(x,y) - f(x_p, y_p)| - t_p)2^p. \tag{5}$$

We adopted the common practice of choosing the threshold value (for neighbours at p-th bit) as the mean value of all m absolute differences in the whole image:

$$t_p = \sum_{i=1}^{m} \frac{|f(x_i, y_i) - f(x_{ip}, y_{ip})|}{m}. \tag{6}$$

The LBP-HF-S-M histogram is created by concatenating histograms of LBP-HF-S and LBP-HF-M (computed from uniform sign-LBP and magnitude-LBP).

3.2   Multi-Scale Description and Scale Invariance

A scale space is built by computing LBP-HF-S-M from circular neighbourhoods with exponentially growing radius R. Gaussian filtering is used[6] to overcome noise.

Unlike the MS-LBP approach of Mäenpää and Pietikäinen [17], where the radii of the LBP operators are chosen so that the effective areas of different scales touch each other, Ffirst uses a finer scaling with a $\sqrt{2}$ step between scales radii R_i, i.e. $R_i = R_{i-1}\sqrt{2}$.

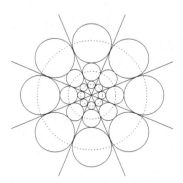

(a) Scale space of Mäenpää and Pietikäinen [17]

(b) Scale space from [29] used in Ffirst

Fig. 1: The effective areas of filtered pixel samples in a multi-resolution $\text{LBP}_{8,R}$ operator

---

[6] The Gaussian filtering is used for a scale i only if $\sigma_i > 0.6$, as filtering with lower σ_i leads to significant loss of information.

This radius change is equivalent to decreasing the image area to one half. The finer sampling uses more evenly spaced information compared to [17], as illustrated in Figures 1a, 1b. The first LBP radius used is $R_1 = 1$, as the LBP with low radii capture important high frequency texture characteristics.

Similarly to [17], the filters are designed so that most of their mass lies within an effective area of radius r_i. We select the effective area diameter, such that the effective areas at the same scale touch each other: $r_i = R_i \sin \frac{\pi}{P}$.

LBP-HF-S-M histograms from c adjacent scales are concatenated into a single descriptor. Invariance to scale changes is increased by creating n_{conc} multi-scale descriptors for one image. See Algorithm 1 for the overview of the texture description method.

Algorithm 1. The Ffirst description method overview

$R_1 := 1$
for all scales $i = 1...(n_{conc} + c - 1)$ **do**
    $\sigma_i := R_i \sin \frac{\pi}{P} / 1.96$
    if $\sigma_i > 0.6$ **then**
        apply Gaussian filter (with std. dev. σ_i) on the original image
    end if
    extract $\text{LBP}_{P,R_i}\text{-S}$ and $\text{LBP}_{P,R_i}\text{-M}$ and build the LBP-HF-S-M descriptor
    for $j = 1...n_{conc}$ **do**
        if $i \geq j$ and $i < j + c$ **then**
            attach the LBP-HF-S-M to the j-th multi-scale descriptor
        end if
    end for
    $R_{i+1} := R_i \sqrt{2}$
end for

3.3   Support Vector Machine and Feature Maps

In most applications, a Support Vector Machine (SVM) classifier with a suitable non-linear kernel provides higher recognition accuracy at the price of significantly higher time complexity and higher storage demands (dependent on the number of support vectors). An approach for efficient use of additive kernels via explicit feature maps is described by Vedaldi and Zisserman [31] and can be combined with a linear SVM classifier. Using linear SVMs on feature-mapped data improves the recognition accuracy, while preserving linear SVM advantages like fast evaluation and low storage (independent on the number of support vectors), which are both very practical in real time applications. In Ffirst we use the explicit feature map approximation of the χ^2 kernel.

The "One versus All" classification scheme is used for multi-class classification, implementing the Platt's probabilistic output [16,24] to ensure SVM results comparability among classes. The maximal posterior probability estimate over all scales is used to determine the resulting class.

In our experiments we use a Stochastic Dual Coordinate Ascent [27] linear SVM solver implemented in the VLFeat library [30].

4   Describing the Leaf Region

Before a description of a leaf is calculated, it has to be segmented. All datasets used in our experiments contain images of leaves on a white background, thus simple segmentation by thresholding is applicable. The threshold value is set automatically using the Otsu's method. Hole-filling is applied after the thresholding in order to ensure that even lighter spots in the leaf are labeled as foreground. This paper does not address the problem of leaf segmentation on a complicated background.

The Ffirst description is computed on the segmented region $\mathbb{A}$. One option is to describe only such points that have all neighbours at given scale inside $\mathbb{A}$. This description is less dependent on segmentation quality. However describing a correctly segmented border, i.e. points in $\mathbb{A}$ with one or more neighbours outside $\mathbb{A}$, can add additional discriminative information.

In total there will be 5 variations of the leaf recognition method used in our experiments in Section 5, differing in the processing of the border region:

1. Ffirst^a describes all pixels in $\mathbb{A}$. Classification maximizes the posterior probability estimate (i.e. SVM Platt's probabilistic output) over all n_{conc} scales.
2. Ffirst^i describes the leaf interior, i.e. pixels in $\mathbb{A}$ with all neighbours in $\mathbb{A}$. Classification maximizes the posterior probability estimate over all n_{conc} scales.
3. Ffirst^b describes the leaf border, i.e. pixels in $\mathbb{A}$ with at least one neighbour outside $\mathbb{A}$. Classification maximizes the posterior probability estimate over all n_{conc} scales
4. Ffirst$^{ib}_{\Sigma}$ combines the description from Ffirst^i and Ffirst^b. Classification maximizes the sum of posterior probability estimates over all n_{conc} scales.
5. Ffirst$^{ib}_{\Pi}$ combines the description from Ffirst^i and Ffirst^b. Classification maximizes the product of posterior probability estimates over all n_{conc} scales.

5   Experiments

5.1   Datasets

The following leaf databases are used for results evaluation in Section 5.3, all of them being public with the exception of the Austrian Federal Forest dataset.

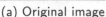

(a) Original image   (b) Segmentation for R=2.8 (c) Segmentation for R=11.3

Fig. 2: Examples of leaf interior (blue) and border region (red) at different scales

The Austrian Federal Forest (AFF) Datasets were used by Fiel and Sablatnig [5] for recognition of trees based on images of leaves, bark and needles. The datasets are not publicly available, the Computer Vision Lab, TU Vienna, kindly made them available to us for academic purposes, with courtesy by Österreichische Bundesforste/Archiv. In this paper we use the AFF dataset of leaves, which contains 134 photos of leaves (on white background) of the 5 most common Austrian broad leaf trees. The results are compared using the protocol of Fiel and Sablatnig, i.e. using 8 training images per leaf class.

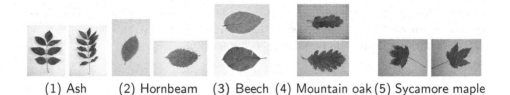

(1) Ash   (2) Hornbeam   (3) Beech (4) Mountain oak (5) Sycamore maple

Fig. 3: Examples from the AFF leaf dataset

The Flavia Leaf Dataset contains 1907 images (1600x1200 px) of leaves from 32 plant species on white background, 50 to 77 images per class.

Even though in the original paper by Wu et al. [33] 10 images per class are used for testing and the rest of the images for training, most recent publications use 10 randomly selected test images and 40 randomly selected training images per class, achieving better recognition accuracy even with the lower number of training samples. In the case of the two best result reported by Lee et al. [14,15], the number of training samples is not clearly stated[7]. Some papers divide the set of images for each class into two halves, one being used for training and the other for testing.

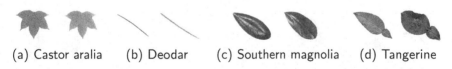

(a) Castor aralia   (b) Deodar   (c) Southern magnolia   (d) Tangerine

Fig. 4: Examples of 4 classes from the Flavia leaf dataset

The Foliage Leaf Dataset [7,9] contains 60 classes of leaves from 58 species. The dataset is divided into a training set with 100 images per class and a test set with 20 images per class.

---

[7] In [15], the result presented as "95.44% (1820 / 1907)" seems to be tested on all images

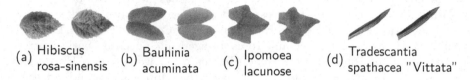

(a) Hibiscus rosa-sinensis   (b) Bauhinia acuminata   (c) Ipomoea lacunose   (d) Tradescantia spathacea "Vittata"

Fig. 5: Examples of 4 classes from the Foliage dataset

The Swedish Leaf Dataset was introduced in Söderkvist's diploma thesis [28] and contains images of leaves scanned using 300 dpi colour scanner. There are 75 images for each of 15 tree classes. The standard evaluation scheme uses 25 images for training and the remaining 50 for testing.

(a) Ulmus carpinifolia   (b) Acer   (c) Salix aurita   (d) Quercus

Fig. 6: Examples of 4 classes from the Swedish dataset

The Middle European Woods (MEW) Dataset was recently introduced by Novotný and Suk [19]. It contains 300 dpi scans of leaves belonging to 153 classes (from 151 botanical species) of Central European trees and shrubs. There are 9745 samples in total, at least 50 per class. The experiments are performed using half of the images in each class for training and the other half for testing.

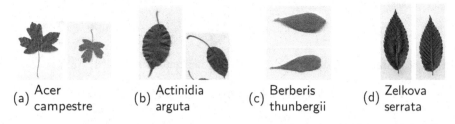

(a) Acer campestre   (b) Actinidia arguta   (c) Berberis thunbergii   (d) Zelkova serrata

Fig. 7: Examples of 4 classes from the MEW dataset

5.2 Parameters

In all following experiments, we use the same setting of our method: $n_{\mathrm{conc}} = 3$ multi-scale descriptors per image are used, each of them consisting of $c = 6$

scales described using LBP-HF-S-M. The final histogram is kernelized using the approximate χ^2 feature map. In the application, the data are only trained once and the training precision is more important than the training time. Thus we demand high accuracy, setting SVM parameters to: regularization parameter $\lambda = 10^{-7}$, tolerance for the stopping criterion $\epsilon = 10^{-7}$, maximum number of iterations: 10^8. We use the unified setting in order to show the generality of the Ffirst description, although setting the parameters individually for a given dataset might further increase the accuracy.

5.3   Experimental Results

Table 1 shows our classification results on all available datasets, using the standard evaluation schemes. To reduce the effect of random training and test data choice, the presented results are averaged from 10 experiments.

Table 1: Evaluation of Ffirst on available leaf datasets: Austrian Federal Forests, Flavia, Foliage, Swedish, Middle European Woods

	AFF	Flavia 10×40	Flavia $\frac{1}{2} \times \frac{1}{2}$	Foliage	Swedish	MEW
Num. of classes	5	32	32	60	15	153
Ffirst[a]	97.8±1.0	98.9±0.6	98.4±0.3	98.6	99.7±0.2	97.7±0.3
Ffirst[i]	97.6±1.4	98.1±0.8	97.9±0.4	96.7	99.6±0.4	96.9±0.3
Ffirst[b]	98.9±1.6	98.9±0.4	98.4±0.3	96.1	98.8±0.5	96.0±0.4
Ffirst$_{\Sigma}^{ib}$	99.8±0.5	99.6±0.3	**99.5±0.2**	98.8	99.8±0.3	98.7±0.1
Ffirst$_{\prod}^{ib}$	**100.0±0.0**	**99.7±0.3**	99.4±0.2	**99.0**	**99.8±0.3**	**99.2±0.1**
Fiel, Sablatnig [5]	93.6	–	–	–	–	–
Novotný, Suk [19]	–	–	91.5	–	–	84.9
Karuna et al. [11]	–	–	96.5	–	–	–
Kadir et al. [10]	–	95.0	–	95.8	–	–
Kadir et al. [7]	–	94.7	–	93.3	–	–
Lee et al. [8] [15]	–	95.4	–	–	–	–
Lee et al. [8] [14]	–	97.2	–	–	–	–
Wu et al. [32]	–	–	–	–	97.9	–
Qi et al. [9] [26]	–	–	–	–	99.4	–

---

[8] the evaluation schemes in [14,15] are not clearly described, as discussed in Section 5.1

[9] according to the project homepage http://qixianbiao.github.io

5.4   Species Retrieval

In some applications, even results which are not correctly classified may be useful if the correct species is retrieved among the top results. For example, in an intelligent field guide it is enough to show the correct result in a shortlist of possible results, allowing the user to make the final decision.

We conducted a species retrieval experiment, performed using the Ffirst$_{\Pi}^{ib}$ method on the MEW dataset, the largest available, containing 153 classes. Half of the images were used for training and half for testing. The results are presented in Figure 8.

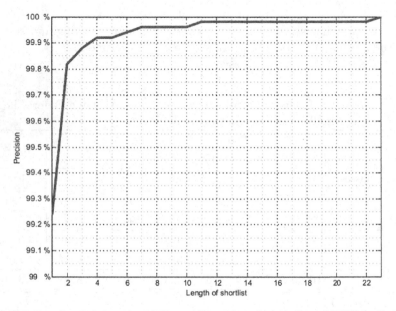

Fig. 8: Retrieval precision for different lengths of shortlist, MEW leaf dataset (153 classes)

5.5   Classifying Leaf Collection Sites

Leaf phenotype, and thus its appearance, is not only determined by the plant species, but also by the influence of the environment. In the experiment, we test whether the Ffirst representation is sufficiently rich to allow determining, besides the leaf species, the location where the leaf was collected.

The experiment was conducted on the publicly available training images from the LifeCLEF'14 Plant identification task[10]. We selected species that have at least 10 specimen collected *from different trees* in the north of France and 10 specimen in the south of France, as illustrated in Figure 9.

---

[10] http://www.imageclef.org/2014/lifeclef/plant

Fig. 9: Two classes of leaf collection sites

Table 2: Enviromental conditions recognition, 10-fold cross validation.

	Betula pendula Roth	Corylus avellana L.	Castanea sativa Mill.	Acer campestre L.
Ffirst[a]	90.0±21.1	90.0±21.1	90.0±21.1	70.0±42.2
Ffirst[i]	85.0±33.8	95.0±15.8	85.0±24.2	70.0±35.0
Ffirst[b]	90.0±31.6	80.0±25.8	80.0±25.8	75.0±35.4
Ffirst$_\Sigma^{ib}$	90.0±31.6	85.0±24.2	90.0±21.1	85.0±33.8
Ffirst$_\Pi^{ib}$	90.0±31.6	85.0±24.2	90.0±21.1	85.0±33.8

The resulting material contained 80 leaf images of 4 species - Betula pendula Roth, Corylus avellana L., Castanea sativa Mill. and Acer campestre L. For each species, a kernelized SVM was trained on the binary North-South classification task. The parameters and the SVM training used the Ffirst method with 10-fold cross validation, exactly as in the species classification. The results presented in Table 2 show that the recognition rate is well above chance, ranging from 85%-90% for the Ffirst$_\Pi^{i,b}$. It is important to note that factors beyond phenotype changes due to the environment might facilitate the classification task, e.g. systematic differences in the cameras, dates of acquisition and lighting conditions.

Fig. 10: Examples of misclassified leaves from the Foliage dataset with wrong segmentation (Original image, Segmentation for R=2.8, Segmentation for R=11.3)

6   Conclusions

A new method for leaf classification has been proposed. Its novelties include the use of a pair of histograms representing the texture on the border and in the interior of the leave, the application of Ffirst, the Fast Features Invariant to Rotation and Scale of Texture, and the χ^2 kernel to leaf recognition.

Best results were obtained by the new $\text{Ffirst}_{\Pi}^{i,b}$ method, which combines the classifiers for the leaf border and leaf interior, achieving more than 99% recognition accuracy on all used leaf datasets using the same setting and describing only the gray-scale image texture information. The species retrieval experiment on the largest dataset containing 153 classes shows that the correct result will be displayed among the top 4 results in more than 99.9% of cases.

Even Ffirst^a, the simple, less accurate variant not distinguishing the leaf border and interior that is more robust to small errors in leaf segmentation and to leaf border damage, outperforms the state-of-the-art on all tested datasets.

A robust segmentation method might further improve the results. It will also broaden the applicability to leaf picture taken on unconstrained backgrounds. Examples of misclassified leaves with wrong segmentation are shown in Figure 10. Further improvements might be achieved by combining the proposed method with complementary features, such as color or the global leaf shape.

An experiment in plant location classification based on leaf appearance indicates that the Ffirst methods can be used for classification of environmental conditions and, more generally, for the study of phenotype plasticity.

Acknowledgments. Jiri Matas was supported by Czech Science Foundation Project GACR P103/12/G084, Milan Sulc by Czech Technical University project SGS13/142/OHK3/2T/13.

References

1. Agarwal, G., Belhumeur, P., Feiner, S., Jacobs, D., Kress, W.J., Ramamoorthi, R., Bourg, N.A., Dixit, N., Ling, H., Mahajan, D., et al.: First steps toward an electronic field guide for plants. Taxon **55**(3), 597–610 (2006)
2. Ahonen, T., Matas, J., He, C., Pietikäinen, M.: Rotation invariant image description with local binary pattern histogram fourier features. In: Salberg, A.-B., Hardeberg, J.Y., Jenssen, R. (eds.) SCIA 2009. LNCS, vol. 5575, pp. 61–70. Springer, Heidelberg (2009)
3. Barthélémy, D., Boujemaa, N., Mathieu, D., Molino, J.F., Bonnet, P., Enficiaud, R., Mouysset, E., Couteron, P.: The pl@ntnet project: A computational plant identification and collaborative information system. Tech. Rep., XIII World Forestry Congress (2009)
4. Belhumeur, P.N., Chen, D., Feiner, S.K., Jacobs, D.W., Kress, W.J., Ling, H., Lopez, I., Ramamoorthi, R., Sheorey, S., White, S., Zhang, L.: Searching the world's herbaria: a system for visual identification of plant species. In: Forsyth, D., Torr, P., Zisserman, A. (eds.) ECCV 2008, Part IV. LNCS, vol. 5305, pp. 116–129. Springer, Heidelberg (2008)

5. Fiel, S., Sablatnig, R.: Automated identification of tree species from images of the bark, leaves and needles. In: Proc. of 16th Computer Vision Winter Workshop, Mitterberg, Austria, pp. 1–6 (2011)
6. Guo, Z., Zhang, D.: A completed modeling of local binary pattern operator for texture classification. IEEE Transactions on Image Processing 19(6), 1657–1663 (2010)
7. Kadir, A., Nugroho, L.E., Santosa, P.I.: Experiments of zernike moments for leaf identification 1 (2012)
8. Kadir, A., Nugroho, L.E., Susanto, A., Santosa, P.I.: A comparative experiment of several shape methods in recognizing plants. International Journal of Computer Science & Information Technology 3(3) (2011)
9. Kadir, A., Nugroho, L.E., Susanto, A., Santosa, P.I.: Neural network application on foliage plant identification. International Journal of Computer Applications 29 (2011)
10. Kadir, A., Nugroho, L.E., Susanto, A., Santosa, P.I.: Performance improvement of leaf identification system using principal component analysis. International Journal of Advanced Science & Technology 44 (2012)
11. Karuna, G., Sujatha, B., Giet, R., Reddy, P.C.: An efficient representation of shape for object recognition and classification using circular shift method
12. Kim, S.J., Kim, B.W., Kim, D.P.: Tree recognition for landscape using by combination of features of its leaf, flower and bark. In: 2011 Proceedings of SICE Annual Conference (SICE) (2011)
13. Kumar, N., Belhumeur, P.N., Biswas, A., Jacobs, D.W., Kress, W.J., Lopez, I.C., Soares, J.V.B.: Leafsnap: a computer vision system for automatic plant species identification. In: Fitzgibbon, A., Lazebnik, S., Perona, P., Sato, Y., Schmid, C. (eds.) ECCV 2012, Part II. LNCS, vol. 7573, pp. 502–516. Springer, Heidelberg (2012)
14. Lee, K.B., Chung, K.W., Hong, K.S.: An implementation of leaf recognition system (2013)
15. Lee, K.B., Hong, K.S.: Advanced leaf recognition based on leaf contour and centroid for plant classification. In: The 2012 International Conference on Information Science and Technology, pp. 133–135 (2012)
16. Lin, H.T., Lin, C.J., Weng, R.C.: A note on platts probabilistic outputs for support vector machines. Machine Learning 68(3) (2007)
17. Mäenpää, T., Pietikäinen, M.: Multi-scale binary patterns for texture analysis. In: Bigun, J., Gustavsson, T. (eds.) SCIA 2003. LNCS, vol. 2749, pp. 885–892. Springer, Heidelberg (2003)
18. Nilsback, M.E., Zisserman, A.: An Automatic Visual Flora: Segmentation and Classification of Flower Images. Ph.D. thesis, Oxford University (2009)
19. Novotný, P., Suk, T.: Leaf recognition of woody species in central europe. Biosystems Engineering 115(4), 444–452 (2013)
20. Ojala, T., Pietikainen, M., Harwood, D.: Performance evaluation of texture measures with classification based on kullback discrimination of distributions. In: Proc. IAPR 1994, vol. 1, pp. 582–585 (1994)
21. Ojala, T., Pietikainen, M., Maenpaa, T.: Multiresolution gray-scale and rotation invariant texture classification with local binary patterns. PAMI 24(7), 971–987 (2002)
22. Ojala, T., Pietikäinen, M., Harwood, D.: A comparative study of texture measures with classification based on featured distributions. Pattern Recognition 29(1), 51–59 (1996)

23. Pietikäinen, M., Ojala, T., Xu, Z.: Rotation-invariant texture classification using feature distributions. Pattern Recognition **33**(1), 43–52 (2000)
24. Platt, J.: Probabilistic outputs for support vector machines and comparisons to regularized likelihood methods. Advances in Large Margin Classifiers 10(3) (1999)
25. Pydipati, R., Burks, T., Lee, W.: Identification of citrus disease using color texture features and discriminant analysis. Computers and Electronics In Agriculture **52**(1), 49–59 (2006)
26. Qi, X., Xiao, R., Guo, J., Zhang, L.: Pairwise rotation invariant co-occurrence local binary pattern. In: Fitzgibbon, A., Lazebnik, S., Perona, P., Sato, Y., Schmid, C. (eds.) ECCV 2012, Part VI. LNCS, vol. 7577, pp. 158–171. Springer, Heidelberg (2012)
27. Shalev-Shwartz, S., Zhang, T.: Stochastic dual coordinate ascent methods for regularized loss minimization. arXiv preprint arXiv:1209.1873 (2012)
28. Söderkvist, O.: Computer vision classification of leaves from swedish trees (2001)
29. Sulc, M., Matas, J.: Kernel-mapped histograms of multi-scale lbps for tree bark recognition. In: 2013 28th International Conference on Image and Vision Computing New Zealand (IVCNZ), pp. 82–87 (November 2013)
30. Vedaldi, A., Fulkerson, B.: VLFeat: An open and portable library of computer vision algorithms (2008). http://www.vlfeat.org/
31. Vedaldi, A., Zisserman, A.: Efficient additive kernels via explicit feature maps. PAMI 34(3) (2011)
32. Wu, J., Rehg, J.M.: Centrist: A visual descriptor for scene categorization. IEEE Transactions on Pattern Analysis and Machine Intelligence **33**(8), 1489–1501 (2011)
33. Wu, S.G., Bao, F.S., Xu, E.Y., Wang, Y.X., Chang, Y.F., Xiang, Q.L.: A leaf recognition algorithm for plant classification using probabilistic neural network. In: 2007 IEEE International Symposium on Signal Processing and Information Technology, pp. 11–16. IEEE (2007)
34. Zhao, G., Ahonen, T., Matas, J., Pietikainen, M.: Rotation-invariant image and video description with local binary pattern features. IEEE Transactions on Image Processing **21**(4), 1465–1477 (2012)

Hybrid Consensus Learning for Legume Species and Cultivars Classification

Mónica G. Larese[✉] and Pablo M. Granitto

CIFASIS, French Argentine International Center for Information and Systems
Sciences, UAM (France) / UNR-CONICET (Argentina), Bv. 27 de Febrero 210 Bis,
2000 Rosario, Argentina
{larese,granitto}@cifasis-conicet.gov.ar

Abstract. In this work we propose an automatic method aimed at classifying five legume species and varieties using leaf venation features. Firstly, we segment the leaf veins and measure several multiscale morphological features on the vein segments and the areoles. Next, we build a hybrid consensus of experts formed by five different automatic classifiers to perform the classification using the extracted features. We propose to use two strategies in order to assign the importance to the votes of the algorithms in the consensus. The first one is considering all the algorithms equally important. The second one is based on the accuracy of the standalone classifiers. The performance of both consensus classifiers show to outperform the standalone classification algorithms in the five class recognition task.

Keywords: Legume and variety classification · Venation images · Consensus learning

1 Introduction

In the current literature, many approaches have been proposed aimed at performing automatic plant classification via leaf image analysis. The shape of the leaves [1,5–7,13], the color and the texture [20] or the combination of the three former traits [2,10] are the most common analyzed features.

Recently, when attempting to classify plant species by means of their leaves, several works have pointed out the importance of incorporating vein information among other features [8,18], or using them solely [16,17]. This last case is specially useful when the leaves share a similar appearance in shape, size, color and texture, as it happens when dealing with several varieties within the same species [15].

Previous related works in the literature which investigated the classification of leaves using exclusively the venation features focused on identifying only different species [16,17], but did not deal with the varieties recognition problem. Varieties identification is challenging since the differences in venation between

---

Author to whom all correspondence should be addressed.

© Springer International Publishing Switzerland 2015
L. Agapito et al. (Eds.): ECCV 2014 Workshops, Part IV, LNCS 8928, pp. 201–214, 2015.
DOI: 10.1007/978-3-319-16220-1_15

the classes are not identifiable by humans. However, it is reasonable to expect some venation differences caused by variety adaptation (e.g., draught tolerance). In a recent work, Larese et al. [15] proposed a method based on the classification of multiscale vein features in order to also evaluate the automatic recognition of soybean varieties. However, the species identification and the varieties identification were treated as two separated problems. In addition, only single classifiers were proposed to perform the classification task.

In contrast, in this paper we focus on the problem of classifying leaves which can belong to different species, or come from different varieties from one common species. Specifically, we experimented with 3 different legumes, namely red and white beans (*Phaseolus Vulgaris*), and soybean (*Glycine max (L) Merr*). For the latter case we have available specimens from 3 possible varieties. In consequence, we are dealing with a five-class multiclass problem. This problem is more difficult than the two 3-class problems considered in previous work [15], since species and varieties are now mixed up. We pursue a single procedure able to perform the leaf identification both for very different leaves, such as from different species, as well as leaves with similar appearance (leaf shape, size, color, texture), such as from different varieties from the same species.

Following the approach in Larese et al. [15], we characterize the leaves by means of multiscale morphological vein and areole features. Firstly, we process the leaf images by means of computing the Unconstrained Hit-or-Miss Transform (UHMT) [22] at different scales in order to highlight the veins. Next, we apply contrast enhancement and adaptive thresholding in order to segment the venation. After that, we measure different vein and areole multiscale morphological features in order to describe the venation morphology.

Our method is focused on developing automatic classification based exclusively on the characterization of the leaf venation system. For species recognition, these differences are recognizable in plain sight and can be approximately described by the human experts (e.g. differences in veins orientation). However, for the varieties recognition, the experts cannot establish the differences between the veins of each cultivar. Our method provides with an exploratory procedure or knowledge discovery tool which allows to determine if there exist different venation patterns for the different species and varieties, even though humans cannot identify them in plain sight.

Larese et al. [15] showed that it is possible to find some differences between the varieties, as well as how to analyze the relevance of the traits for the classes characterization. However, the accuracies reported using single classifiers in the recognition were not very high. This may be due to the existence of subtle differences between the cultivars, showing the need to improve the automatic classifiers. In this paper we investigate how to perform species and varieties classification of the features by means of consensus theory and multiple classifiers fusion, which have shown to improve accuracies in the literature [3,14,24]. Better classification methods could lead to an improved identification of the most informative distinctive features, which could be related to genotype differences. Within this context, we build a heterogeneous committee formed by five different automatic classifiers. The classifiers are aggregated through a majority vote rule in order to obtain a single prediction for the class. The five individual classifiers that we employ are of very diverse nature, consisting of Support Vector Machines [23], Penalized Discriminant Analysis [11], Näive Bayes [12] and two ensemble algorithms, namely Random Forests [4] and AdaBoost [9].

In this work, we consider two different strategies in order to weight the vote of each classifier in the committee. First of all, we consider all the algorithms equally important, *i.e.*, the vote of each algorithm is $1/5$. The other strategy consists on weighting each classifier according to its accuracy obtained in a validation step. We show that we obtain better classification results by the aggregation of the algorithms into a committee of experts, compared to the ones achieved by the standalone classifiers. This is possible since our algorithm can take advantage of the contribution that each standalone algorithm provides to the consensus. When compared to manual classification, the hybrid automatic consensus is the only algorithm which outperforms the human experts for all the classes under consideration simultaneously.

The rest of the paper is organized as follows. In Section 2 we describe the dataset used in this work. We explain the segmentation and feature extraction steps in Section 3. We detail the individual classification algorithms, as well as the hybrid consensus strategy, in Section 4. We present and discuss the experimental results as long as the comparison of the performances for the different algorithms in Section 5. Finally, we draw some conclusions in Section 6.

2   Species and Varieties Dataset

The image dataset is composed by 866 color leaf images provided by Instituto Nacional de Tecnología Agropecuaria (INTA, Oliveros, Argentina). It consists of 272 images of red bean leaves, 172 images of white bean leaves (*Phaseolus Vulgaris*) and 422 images of soybean leaves (*Glycine max (L) Merr*). The soybean images are divided into three cultivars: 198 from cultivar #1, 176 from cultivar #2 and 48 from cultivar #3. They correspond to the images of the two first foliage leaves (pre-formed in the seed) of each specimen after 12 days of seedling grow. First foliage leaves were selected since their characteristics are less influenced by the environment. The leaves were acquired using a standard flatbed scanner (Hewlett Packard Scanjet-G 3110) at a resolution of 200 pixels per inch, and the images were stored as 24-bit uncompressed TIFF images. The abaxial surfaces of the leaves were scanned since veins appear stronger on this side. All the leaves lay in the same vertical position, thus avoiding significant rotation influences.

Figure 1 shows some exemplars from each one of the species and varieties which compose the dataset. The reader should notice that the differences between individuals from some of the classes do not compensate for the high variability also present between individuals within the same class. Thus, this application problem is characterized by relatively low inter-class and high intra-class variabilities.

3 Segmentation and Feature Extraction

In this paper we followed the segmentation and multiscale feature extraction procedures described by Larese *et al.* [15]. We worked with the gray scale image for each leaf. The leaf segmentation is based on the computation of the Unconstrained Hit-or-Miss Transform (UHMT)[22] on five leaf scale images (at 60%, 70%, 80%, 90% and 100% of the original image size). Each UHMT image highlights a different level of vein detail. Next, we added the five UHMTs (resized to the original size) to form the combined UHMT. This combined image highlights both small and large veins. In addition, we also picked up the UHMTs at scales 100% (the original image size), 80% and 60% for further processing.

On the four resulting UHMT images we applied contrast enhancement techniques (adaptive histogram equalization) and umbralization (adaptive thresholding) in order to obtain the segmented veins.

In order to discard the leaf shape contour, we cropped a centered patch of 100×100 pixels from each one of the four previously described segmented images. On these four patches, we measured the 208 vein and areole multiscale morphological features per leaf image (52 features $\times 4$ patches) described in the work by Larese *et al.* [15]. The 52 features are described in Appendix A for completeness.

4 Classification Algorithms

We considered 5 different classifiers, namely Support Vector Machines with Gaussian kernel, Penalized Discriminant Analysis, Naïve Bayes, Random Forests and AdaBoost. We briefly describe them in the following. In the last subsection we present the consensus learning proposed approach, formed by the aggregation of the previously mentioned standalone classifiers.

We used inner 5-fold cross validation to optimize the parameters of the classifiers where necessary.

4.1 Support Vector Machines

Support Vector Machines (SVM) [23] is a state-of-the-art classifier which assumes that applying an appropriate nonlinear mapping of the data into a sufficiently high dimensional space, two classes can be separated by an optimum hyperplane. This decision hyperplane is chosen in such a way that the distance between the nearest patterns of different classes (i.e., the margin) is maximized. SVM depends on a regularization parameter, C, which controls the trade-off between the complexity of the classifier and the number of allowed misclassifications. In this work we used inner validation during the training phase in order to set this parameter.

The decision surface may be linear or nonlinear. In the latter case, a kernel function can be used to map the patterns into a high dimensional space. In this work, we considered SVMs with a Gaussian kernel (SVMG). We optimized the Gaussian standard deviation in a validation step during the training.

SVM is a binary classifier in nature. In order to extend its use to the present multiclass problem, we used the one-vs-one strategy.

4.2   Penalized Discriminant Analysis

Fisher's Linear Discriminant Analysis (LDA) [12] is a classical classifier and dimension reduction tool which searches for linear combinations of the features in such a way that the class means of the linear combinations are maximally separated relative to the intra-class variance. The classification of new observations is then performed by assigning them to the closest centroid according to a distance metric (typically the Mahalanobis distance) in the transformed space.

In order to improve LDA, Hastie *et al.* [11] proposed Penalized Discriminant Analysis (PDA). PDA is a regularized version of LDA, which adds a penalty term to the intra-class covariance matrix. PDA is useful for image classification problems with large number of highly correlated features.

In this work, we used standard Ridge Regression (GenRidge) [12], which has the ridge constant λ as the only free parameter. This constant penalizes high values of the fitted variables, and is similar to the C parameter in SVM. We automatically selected this parameter using a validation set in the training phase.

4.3   Näive Bayes

Näive Bayes (NB) [12] is a simple probabilistic classifier which assumes independence among the features, specially useful when dealing with a high-dimensional feature space. In spite of this unrealistic assumption, NB has shown to perform very well in real world applications.

The method applies the Bayes' Theorem in order to compute the *a posteriori* probabilities (class conditional probabilities) for a test observation. These probabilities are calculated as the product of the individual distributions for each feature (since they are assumed to be independent). In this work we assumed Gaussian distributions.

Once the probabilistic model is constructed, the classification is performed according to the Maximum a Posteriori decision rule (the most probable class is chosen).

4.4   Random Forests

Random Forests (RF) [4] is a state-of-the-art ensemble algorithm where the individual classifiers are a set of de-correlated trees. They perform comparably well to other state-of-the-art classifiers and are also very fast.

The algorithm constructs a set of unpruned trees from B random samples with replacement (bootstrap versions) of the original training dataset. For each random forest tree, a random sample of m variables from the full set of p variables ($m \le p$) is selected to split the data at each node and grow the decision tree. The final classification result is the class corresponding to the majority vote of the ensemble of trees. In this work, we used 500 trees and a standard value of $m = \sqrt{p}$.

4.5   AdaBoost

Boosting classifiers are based on the idea that if many "weak" classifiers (slightly better than chance) are combined into a "strong" classifier, the overall performance will be highly improved [21]. AdaBoost [9] creates a sequence of weak classifiers aimed at discriminating the training observations. Initially, all the observations are assigned a unique weight. This distribution of weights is modified along with the number of iterations (rounds), *i.e.*, observations which are badly classified (more difficult to learn) are given higher weights. The algorithm attempts to find an optimum classifier at each round. Each weak classifier is weighted according to its performance on the current distribution of weights on the observations. At the end, the final strong classifier is the weighted linear combination of the weak classifiers. The algorithm minimizes the expectation of the exponential loss. In this work, we used 500 rounds and stumps as weak learners.

4.6   Hybrid Consensus of Experts

Consensus theory [3] combines multiple single probability distributions in order to build a unique predictive model from the opinion of several experts, assuming that the individual judgments are based on Bayesian decision theory.

Let $D = \{(\mathbf{x}_i, y_i)\}$, with $i = \{1, ..., n\}$, be a training dataset of n pairs of feature vectors $\mathbf{x}_i \in \mathbb{R}^p$ and class labels $y_i \in \{1, 2, ..., k\}$. The M probability distributions from each one of the M experts are combined using a so-called *consensus rule*. The consensus rule P_k for each pattern $\mathbf{x}_i$ is calculated for each one of the K classes. The simplest and most common consensus rule is the *Linear Opinion rule* (LOP), which is computed as a weighted linear combination of the posterior probabilities P_j from each expert (Eq. 1), with $j = \{1, ..., M\}$, and α_j denoting the weights associated to each expert. The coefficients α_j are nonnegative and $\sum_{j=1}^{M} \alpha_j = 1$. The simplest approach of the weighting scheme consists in assigning the same weights to all the experts.

$$P_k(\mathbf{x}_i) = \sum_{j=1}^{M} \alpha_j P_j(\mathbf{x}_i) \tag{1}$$

Pattern $\mathbf{x}_i$ is then classified to belong to class $\hat{y}_i$, which is the class with the highest probability, as below.

$$\hat{y}_i = \max_{k=1}^{K} P_k(\mathbf{x}_i) \tag{2}$$

In this work, we propose to constitute a *Hybrid Consensus of Experts (HCE)* formed by one instance of each one of the five classifiers described in the previous subsections. This approach is also known in the literature as multiple classifiers fusion or combination of multiple classifiers [14,24].

In this context, we set P_j to be the probability predicted by each one of the $M = 5$ classifiers. We propose to use two different strategies in order to assign the importance to the opinion of each classifier. The first strategy considers them equally important, and therefore $\alpha_j = 1/5$. The second strategy takes into account the accuracy obtained by each classifier in a validation step. In this case we set α_j to be this accuracy value (a real value between 0 and 1 normalized by the sum of the α's). We call this second strategy *Weighted Hybrid Consensus of Experts (WHCE)*.

5 Experimental Results

In Fig. 2 we show one example leaf for each class, *i.e.*, 3 varieties of soybean, white and red beans. Below each leaf we show the corresponding segmented vein images. From this figure it can be noticed that there are many morphological differences between the veins of soybean and white or red beans. White and red beans present some visual differences, even though they are less strong than with respect to soybean. On the contrary, the three varieties of soybean look like very much the same. Moreover, we have encountered that in this case there is a high intra-class variability within each variety.

We filtered out the features having near zero variance. We scaled the remaining features in order to have zero mean and variance 1. For all the classification experiments, we computed the average classification accuracy after performing 10 runs of 5-fold cross validation. We also used 5-fold cross validation for inner validation to automatically optimize the parameters of the classifiers where necessary.

In Table 1 we show the average total accuracy computed for each one of the standalone algorithms as well as for the two hybrid consensus strategies. According to this table, it can be noticed that the most accurate results can be achieved by PDA, HCE and WHCE, with over 72%. The lowest value is obtained by NB (59%), whereas SVM, RF and AB show a similar performance around 71%.

In order to analyze the results with more detail, we present in Table 2 the average per class accuracies. These results are important since the five classes are not balanced, and we want to ensure that none of the implemented algorithms tends to favour majority classes. From this table it is noticeable that the easiest leaves to be recognized for all the algorithms are red and white beans. The distinction among the three soybean cultivars is the most difficult problem, as revealed by the general low accuracies obtained by all the methods. In the case of NB, the third cultivar of soybean is also well predicted. However, in this case it is to the detriment of cultivars #1 and #2 recognition, leading to a low overall accuracy as previously described in Table 1. With this respect, NB has a tendency to prefer soybean cultivar #3 over the other two soybean cultivars.

Table 1. Total accuracy (mean±S_E) for the five-class species and varieties classification problem

Classification Algorithm	Total accuracy (mean±S_E%)
SVM	71.05 ± 0.41
PDA	73.64 ± 0.39
NB	58.65 ± 0.42
RF	71.03 ± 0.40
AB	71.30 ± 0.39
HCE	72.45 ± 0.42
WHCE	72.97 ± 0.44

Table 2. Accuracy (mean±S_E) for the five-class species and varieties classification problem

Classification Algorithm	Per class Accuracy (mean±S_E%)				
	RBean (272 images)	WBean (172 images)	SBean#1 (198 images)	SBean#2 (176 images)	SBean#3 (48 images)
SVM	89.86 ± 0.60	82.96 ± 0.91	67.31 ± 1.16	51.41 ± 1.32	9.16 ± 1.37
PDA	91.54 ± 0.45	89.53 ± 0.72	62.73 ± 1.06	52.66 ± 1.12	37.00 ± 1.86
NB	84.60 ± 0.64	76.85 ± 1.11	22.21 ± 1.00	36.70 ± 1.25	77.13 ± 2.06
RF	89.27 ± 0.63	81.79 ± 0.93	66.60 ± 1.04	53.01 ± 0.93	13.38 ± 1.34
AB	89.75 ± 0.65	83.07 ± 0.85	64.29 ± 1.04	53.37 ± 1.26	19.40 ± 1.57
HCE	89.89 ± 0.55	86.97 ± 0.90	59.79 ± 1.05	53.13 ± 1.15	44.56 ± 2.33
WHCE	90.26 ± 0.54	87.26 ± 0.85	61.86 ± 1.07	53.58 ± 1.16	40.60 ± 2.08
Manual classification	83.28 ± 3.71	70.82 ± 13.15	44.95 ± 2.00	42.78 ± 5.37	43.98 ± 6.97

However, the poor performance of NB for cultivars #1 and #2 is compensated by the other 4 classification algorithms in the HCE and WHCE. Moreover, NB contribution helps the consensus to reinforce soybean cultivar #3 recognition, since this class is badly detected by all the standalone classifiers except for NB.

In our experiments, the best results for red and white beans are provided by PDA (92% and 90%, respectively), followed by WHCE and HCE, which are slightly lower. In the case of soybean cultivar #1 all the standalone algorithms (except for NB, as explained before) obtain better performance, being SVM and RF the best accuracies (67% for both of them). On the other hand, WHCE gets 62% and HCE 60%. Regarding the second cultivar, WHCE reaches an accuracy of 54%, closely followed by AB, HCE, RF and PDA. In the case of the third cultivar, WHCE and HCE obtain the highest accuracies. As previously explained, this value is only beaten by NB. The closest accuracy value is 37% obtained by PDA, whereas the rest of the classifiers obtain less than 20% of accuracy.

When comparing HCE and WHCE to each other, we find that, as previously shown in Table 1, the average accuracy of WHCE is slightly higher. From Table 2 we can notice that the usage of the validation accuracies as weights in the consensus reduces the impact of the NB vote, slightly augmenting the accuracy of 4 classes, but resulting in a lower recognition of soybean cultivar #3.

For reference purposes only, we show the average classification results obtained by five human experts who manually classified the leaves. It is worth noticing that the experts solved two easier problems. Instead of classifying the leaves into 5 classes, they performed the classification into 3 classes, namely red bean, white bean and soybean. In a second independent experiment, they classified only soybean leaves into the three possible cultivars. From Table 2 it is evident that HCE obtained a better performance than the manual classification for all the five classes under consideration in the context of a more difficult problem. None of the five standalone classification algorithms could achieve this goal. WHCE obtains a lower performance only for cultivar #3.

The implementation of the consensus allows to improve the classification of the more difficult classes, while obtaining a good performance for the rest of them. Additionally, there is not need to choose between several different classifiers, since the consensus provides accuracies which are, at least, as good as the best standalone classifier in the committee, taking advantage of the goodness of each algorithm.

6   Concluding Remarks

In this work we propose to use a hybrid consensus approach in order to classify five different species and varieties leaves. We use multiscale morphological features extracted from the segmented leaf veins. The hybrid consensus is formed by five standalone classifiers, namely Support Vector Machines, Penalized Discriminant Analysis, Näive Bayes, Random Forests and AdaBoost. These classifiers are very different in nature, allowing to introduce diversity in the committee. This diversity helps to compensate the classification difficulties found by the algorithms in the complex task of plant recognition.

We implemented two different strategies to weight the vote of the classifiers in the consensus. The first one assigns the same importance to all the standalone classifiers. The other one assigns a different weight to the classification algorithms, which is based on the accuracy that they obtained during a validation step. Both strategies help to improve the recognition of the more difficult classes, and the second one provides with a slightly higher overall result.

The problem under analysis is difficult in the sense that within each class the leaf differences are high, and specially for the cultivars classification, even humans find it difficult to perform recognition since in this case the characteristics for each cultivar are not clear. The hybrid consensus is the only algorithm able to overcome human recognition for all the classes under analysis simultaneously. The usage of an automatic algorithm aimed at performing the classification provides with a reliable and repetible process, removing the tediousness of the task. Moreover, the classification procedure can help to highlight distinctive vein features which could be related to differences in the genotype of the species and cultivars under analysis.

We are currently working on the research of new features which can better characterize the veins. These features may include semantic information and relations between the vein branches. Additionally, we are considering adding patches from other locations of the leaf apart from the central patch used in this work.

Acknowledgments. MGL and PMG acknowledge grant support from ANPCyT PICT 2012-0181. We also acknowledge technical support from R. Craviotto, M. Arango and C. Gallo at Instituto Nacional de Tecnología Agropecuaria (INTA Oliveros, Argentina).

Appendix A

Following, the 52 morphological features computed on the veins and areoles are described. These features are an adaptation for classification purposes of the individual features proposed by Price et al. [19].

Feature #1: Total number of edges, i.e., estimated veins.
Feature #2: Total number of nodes. The number of connecting nodes between edges.
Feature #3: Total network length. Total distance (in mm) along the skeleton of the vein image patch.
Features #4, #5, #6: Median/min/max edge length. The edge length (in mm) is the distance along the skeleton of a vein.
Features #7, #8, #9: Median/min/max edge width. The edge width (in mm) is the mean of the doubled distances between each skeleton pixel of the current edge and the nearest non-vein pixel, i.e., areole pixel.
Features #10, #11, #12: Median/min/max edge 2D area. The edge 2D area (in mm^2) is the sum of the widths at every skeleton pixel of the current edge times the length of one pixel.
Features #13, #14, #15:. Median/min/max edge surface area. The surface area (in mm^2) of the cylinder centered at the edge skeleton is computed as the sum of the individual surface areas for each skeleton pixel of the current edge, as $\sum_i SA_i = 2\pi(d_i/2)l_i$, where d_i is the diameter (width) and l_i is the length for a skeleton pixel i.
Features #16, #17, #18:. Median/min/max edge volume. The edge volume (in mm^3) corresponds to the volume of the same cylinder as in surface area, and is computed as $\sum_i V_i = \pi(d_i/2)^2 l_i$.
Features #19, #20, #21: Median/min/max edge orientation. The orientation is the angle in degrees between the x-axis and the major axis of the ellipse with the same second moments as the vein.
Feature #22: Total number of areoles in the image patch.
Features #23, #24, #25: Median/min/max areole perimeter. The perimeter (in mm) is the distance along the pixels of the border of the areole.
Features #26, #27, #28: Median/min/max areole area. The areole area (in mm^2) is the number of pixels in each areole times the area of one pixel.

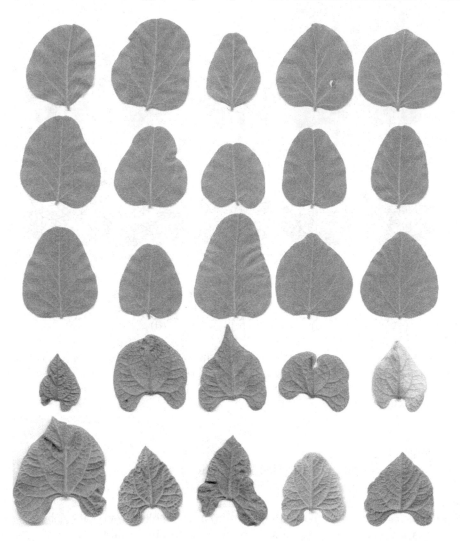

Fig. 1. Sample leaves from each class. First row: Soybean (cultivar #1). Second row: Soybean (cultivar #2). Third row: Soybean (cultivar #3). Fourth row: Red bean. Fifth row: White bean.

Features #29, #30, #31: Median/min/max areole convex area. The convex area (in mm^2) is the area of the convex hull for the areole.

Features #32, #33, #34: Median/min/max areole solidity. The solidity is a dimensionless parameter between 0 and 1 which measures the proportion of the pixels in the convex hull that are also in the area (ratio between the areole area and the convex area).

Features #35, #36, #37: Median/min/max areole major axis. The major axis (in mm) corresponds to the ellipse with the same normalized second

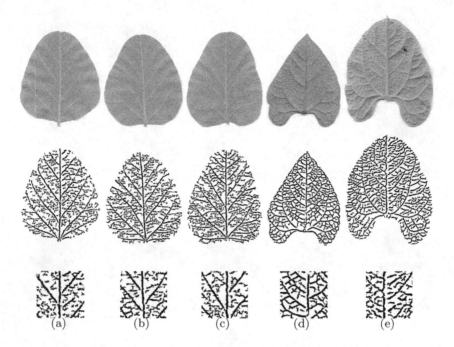

Fig. 2. Example leaves with their corresponding segmented veins and (amplified) cropped centered patches (only segmentation for the combined UHMT is shown). (a) Soybean (cultivar #1). (b) Soybean (cultivar #2). (b) Soybean (cultivar #3). (d) Red bean. (e) White bean.

moments as the areole.

Features #38, #39, #40: Median/min/max areole minor axis. The minor axis (in mm) corresponds to the ellipse with the same normalized second moments as the areole.

Features #41, #42, #43: Median/min/max areole eccentricity. The eccentricity is a dimensionless parameter between 0 (a circle) and 1 (a line), which measures the ratio of the distance between the foci of the ellipse having the same normalized second moments as the areole and its major axis.

Features #44, #45, #46: Median/min/max areole equivalent diameter. The equivalent diameter (in mm) is the diameter of a circle having the same area as the areole.

Features #47, #48, #49: Median/min/max areole mean distance. The mean distance (in mm) is the mean value of the Euclidean distances between each areole pixel and the nearest vein pixel.

Features #50, #51, #52: Median/min/max areole variance distance. The variance distance (in mm) is the variance of the Euclidean distances between each areole pixel and the nearest vein pixel.

References

1. Agarwal, G., Ling, H., Jacobs, D., Shirdhonkar, S., Kress, W., Russell, R., Belhumeur, P., Dixit, N., Feiner, S., Mahajan, D., Sunkavalli, K., White, S.: First Steps Toward an Electronic Field Guide for Plants. Taxon, Journal of the International Association for Plant Taxonomy **55**, 597–610 (2006)
2. Bama, B.S., Valli, S.M., Raju, S., Kumar, V.A.: Content based leaf image retrieval (CBLIR) using shape, color and texture features. Indian Journal of Computer Science and Engineering **2**(2), 202–211 (2011)
3. Benediktsson, J.A., Swain, P.H.: Consensus theoretic classification methods. IEEE Trans. Systems, Man Cybernet. **22**, 688–704 (1992)
4. Breiman, L.: Random Forests. Machine Learning **45**, 5–32 (2001)
5. Neto Camargo, J., Meyer, G.E., Jones, D.D., Samal, A.K.: Plant species identification using Elliptic Fourier leaf shape analysis. Computers and Electronics in Agriculture **50**, 121–134 (2006)
6. Chaki, J., Parekh, R.: Designing an automated system for plant leaf recognition. International Journal of Advances in Engineering & Technology **2**(1), 149–158 (2012)
7. Du, J.X., Wang, X.F., Zhang, G.J.: Leaf shape based plant species recognition. Applied Mathematics and Computation 185(2), 883–893 (2007), special Issue on Intelligent Computing Theory and Methodology
8. Du, J.X., Zhai, C.M., Wang, Q.P.: Recognition of plant leaf image based on fractal dimension features. Neurocomputing **116**, 150–156 (2013)
9. Freund, Y., Schapire, R.E.: A decision-theoretic generalization of on-line learning and an application to boosting. J. Comput. Syst. Sci. **55**(1), 119–139 (1997)
10. Golzarian, M.R., Frick, R.A.: Classification of images of wheat, ryegrass and brome grass species at early growth stages using principal component analysis. Plant Methods **7**, 28 (2011)
11. Hastie, T., Buja, A., Tibshirani, R.: Penalized discriminant analysis. Ann. Statist. **23**(1), 73–102 (1995)
12. Hastie, T., Tibshirani, R., Friedman, J.: The Elements of Statistical Learning, 2nd edn. Springer (2009)
13. Im, C., Nishida, H., Kunii, T.L.: Recognizing Plant Species by Leaf Shapes-A Case Study of the Acer Family. In: International Conference on Pattern Recognition, vol. 2, p. 1171 (1998)
14. Kuncheva, L.I., Bezdek, J.C., Duin, R.P.: Decision templates for multiple classifier fusion: an experimental comparison. Pattern Recognition 34(2), 299–314 (2001). http://www.sciencedirect.com/science/article/pii/S003132039900223X
15. Larese, M.G., Bayá, A.E., Craviotto, R.M., Arango, M.R., Gallo, C., Granitto, P.M.: Multiscale recognition of legume varieties based on leaf venation images. Expert Systems with Applications 41(10), 4638–4647 (2014), http://www.sciencedirect.com/science/article/pii/S0957417414000529
16. Larese, M.G., Craviotto, R.M., Arango, M.R., Gallo, C., Granitto, P.M.: Legume identification by leaf vein images classification. In: Alvarez, L., Mejail, M., Gomez, L., Jacobo, J. (eds.) CIARP 2012. LNCS, vol. 7441, pp. 447–454. Springer, Heidelberg (2012)
17. Larese, M.G., Namías, R., Craviotto, R.M., Arango, M.R., Gallo, C., Granitto, P.M.: Automatic classification of legumes using leaf vein image features. Pattern Recognition **47**(1), 158–168 (2014)

18. Park, J., Hwang, E., Nam, Y.: Utilizing venation features for efficient leaf image retrieval. J. Syst. Softw. **81**(1), 71–82 (2008)
19. Price, C.A., Symonova, O., Mileyko, Y., Hilley, T., Weitz, J.S.: Leaf Extraction and Analysis Framework Graphical User Interface: Segmenting and Analyzing the Structure of Leaf Veins and Areoles. Plant Physiology **155**, 236–245 (2011)
20. Pydipati, R., Burks, T.F., Lee, W.S.: Identification of citrus disease using color texture features and discriminant analysis. Computers and Electronics in Agriculture **52**, 49–59 (2006)
21. Schapire, R.E.: The Strength of Weak Learnability. Mach. Learn. **5**(2), 197–227 (1990)
22. Soille, P.: Morphological Image Analysis: Principles and Applications. Springer-Verlag (1999)
23. Vapnik, V.: The nature of statistical learning theory. Springer-Verlag (1995)
24. Xu, L., Krzyzak, A., Suen, C.: Methods of combining multiple classifiers and their applications to handwriting recognition. IEEE Transactions on Systems, Man and Cybernetics **22**(3), 418–435 (1992)

A Model-Based Approach to Recovering the Structure of a Plant from Images

Ben Ward[1]($\boxtimes$), John Bastian[1], Anton van den Hengel[1], Daniel Pooley[1],
Rajendra Bari[2], Bettina Berger[3], and Mark Tester[4]

[1] School of Computer Science, The University of Adelaide, Adelaide, Australia
{ben.ward,john.bastian,anton.vandenhengel,daniel.pooley}@adelaide.edu.au
[2] Bayer CropScience, Ghent, Belgium
rajendra.bari@bayer.com
[3] The Plant Accelerator, The University of Adelaide, Adelaide, Australia
bettina.berger@adelaide.edu.au
[4] Center for Desert Agriculture, King Abdullah University of Science
and Technology, Thuwal, Saudi Arabia
mark.tester@kaust.edu.sa

Abstract. We present a method for recovering the structure of a plant directly from a small set of widely-spaced images for automated analysis of phenotype. Structure recovery is more complex than shape estimation, but the resulting structure estimate is more closely related to phenotype than is a 3D geometric model. The method we propose is applicable to a wide variety of plants, but is demonstrated on wheat. Wheat is composed of thin elements with few identifiable features, making it difficult to analyse using standard feature matching techniques. Our method instead analyses the structure of plants using only their silhouettes. We employ a generate-and-test method, using a database of manually modelled leaves and a model for their composition to synthesise plausible plant structures which are evaluated against the images. The method is capable of efficiently recovering accurate estimates of plant structure in a wide variety of imaging scenarios, without manual intervention.

Keywords: Plant phenotyping · Image processing · Plant architecture

1 Introduction

Computer vision techniques can provide fast, accurate, automated, and noninvasive measurements of phenotypic properties of plants. Measurements of properties such as leaf length and leaf angle can be used to evaluate the effect on plants of variation in environmental conditions or genetic properties [1]. Obtaining these measurements from image data can be difficult. Plants typically have

Electronic supplementary material The online version of this chapter (doi:10.
1007/978-3-319-16220-1_16) contains supplementary material, which is available to
authorized users.

L. Agapito et al. (Eds.): ECCV 2014 Workshops, Part IV, LNCS 8928, pp. 215–230, 2015.
DOI: 10.1007/978-3-319-16220-1_16

properties such as uniform colour, specular surfaces, and thin regions which present challenges for typical reconstruction techniques.

Existing methods have focused largely on the problem of recovering the shape of the plant independent of its structure. Structure, here, is intended to encompass various parts of the plant and the relationship between them, as opposed to purely a geometric shape representation, such as a 3D volume or point cloud, of the whole plant without any semantic information. The structure may be represented in terms of anatomical aspects of the plant, but may equally be described in terms of more basic elements. Importantly, structure allows the application of prior knowledge about the grammar of particular types of plants.

There are two primary advantages of considering structure rather than shape. The first is that structure is much more closely related to plant anatomy, and therefore a much better indication of phenotype and function. The second advantage is that the structural properties of a plant provide a strong indication of the likelihood of a particular shape, which is a valuable cue when trying to select from among multiple feasible shapes. For plants with potentially complex structures, such as wheat, there may be many possible plant shape hypotheses which are supported by an image set, whereas prior knowledge of plant anatomy may indicate that only one structure is feasible. This means that structure recovery is possible when shape estimation alone would be ambiguous, or equivalently, that fewer cameras are required to estimate structure than shape. A related advantage is that even if more than one shape is supported by the image set, these shapes often have closely related structures, so although the images are ambiguous (in terms of shape) they may still support an estimate of structure, and thus a phenotypic interpretation.

Structure, for the purposes of the method we propose here, includes information about the identity, length, and curvature of each leaf in the plant, and the relationships between leaves. In this method each leaf is represented by a 3D curve tracing the central axis of the leaf from its tip to the base of the plant. The combination of multiple leaf models gives a model of a complete plant. This estimate of structure implies a particular 3D shape of the plant, which may be used to estimate which pixels belong to each plant element. Estimating structure thus enables the length of leaf 4 on day 10 to be measured, for example, and post-processing would allow an estimate of the width of the leaf or the area of senescence.

The method we describe is capable of estimating the structure of a plant made up of thin elements from a small set of images taken from widely-spaced viewpoints. Because the properties of these plants make reconstruction difficult using standard feature matching techniques, we reconstruct the plants using only their silhouettes. We employ a generate-and-test method, generating possible plant structures which are evaluated against the images. The generation process makes use of a database of leaf models, providing prior information on plausible leaf curves, which we use to restrict the generated models to plausible plant structures. The space of possible generated models is therefore significantly smaller than if we were to generate models by naively sampling 3D curves,

Fig. 1. A reconstructed plant model projected into the original images, and another view of the 3D model

allowing for a more efficient reconstruction process. Likely leaf tip locations are also detected, and used to further constrain the space of possible models. Figure 1 shows a 3D plant model estimated with this method projected into the original image set.

2   Related Work

A range of techniques currently exist for automated extraction of phenotypic properties from image or depth data. Highly detailed and accurate point-cloud reconstructions can be obtained with the use of technology such as laser scanners [2] or structured light [3,4]. However, this technology can be prohibitively expensive or infeasible to incorporate into existing systems, may not provide sufficient resolution for recovering thin structures, and can be difficult to apply when plant size varies greatly. Reconstruction from images can provide a lower cost and a more easily implemented solution. Methods based on identifying plant pixels can be used to estimate volume without recovering 3D structure [5,6]. Image based approaches for recovering 3D reconstructions employ techniques such as dynamic programming [7] and simulated annealing [8] to overcome the difficulty of identifying corresponding points between frames.

Reconstruction based on matching line features can provide robustness to appearance variation in different views [9–11]. Complex plant structures with overlapping leaves mean a large number of views of the plant are usually required for a complete reconstruction. Techniques for obtaining a dense set of views of a plant include the use of mirrors [12] or cameras mounted on robotic arms [13]. Mechanisms for turning the plants [5] can be used to generate a range of views, but can cause leaf movement which leads to additional difficulties for reconstruction. For methods which recover a point cloud or volumetric description of a plant, additional processing such as applying skeletonisation operations to a point cloud is required to recover a structural description [14]. Interactive methods avoid some of the difficulty of fully automated techniques [15,16] but significantly increase the time and manual effort required for reconstruction.

3   Method

We aim to recover an estimate of the length, curvature, and identity of each leaf of a grass plant, in this case wheat, from a set of images. The image set may be

Fig. 2. A visual hull reconstruction illustrating the spurious shapes beyond the true plant reconstruction which are inherent to the visual hull

small (the results in this paper were obtained from four images), and captured with widely-spaced cameras. Widely-spaced views, and the thin components and relatively uniform colour of these plants, make accurate reconstruction infeasible using standard feature matching techniques. Such techniques would also not provide data on the structure of the plant in occluded regions.

Given that attempting to match the appearance of individual points on leaves is infeasible, we instead analyse the silhouette of the plant in each view. Using standard silhouette-based reconstruction methods [17] could leave the 3D structure ambiguous when only a small number of views is available. Figure 2 shows three views of the visual hull generated from the four silhouettes for the plant on the left. Due to self occlusion and the limited set of views, this visual hull reconstruction includes leaf-like regions which do not correspond to actual leaves of the plant.

Instead of directly recovering the 3D shape of the plant from the silhouettes, we use a generate-and-test method to recover the 3D structure, generating plausible 3D plant models and evaluating them against the image set. A process of using prior knowledge to generate plausible structures which are evaluated against the data is employed for tree and plant reconstruction by methods such as [18–20].

This method allows us to use prior information about the plants being reconstructed to aid in determining the structure in regions where that structure would be ambiguous given only the image data. We make use of a database of manually modelled leaves. The reconstruction process generates 3D plant models by finding leaf models in the database which closely match the current image set, then refining these individual leaf models, and selecting an optimal combination of leaf models to model the complete plant.

3.1   Input Data

The input to our process is a set of images of a plant. The method is suitable for use with any number and placement of cameras, provided each leaf is visible in at least two views with a sufficiently wide baseline. For results in this paper, we used four images captured by cameras covering 360° around the plant. These images were captured with a set of consumer-grade DSLR cameras. The method requires calibrated cameras with known scale. We also require the approximate

Fig. 3. The calibration object   **Fig. 4.** A plant model manually constructed from two views

location of the centre of the pot, and a vector giving the vertical orientation of the pot. To obtain the necessary calibration information with minimal manual intervention, we make use of a calibration object providing features on multiple planes in each view. A 3D model giving the approximate structure of the pot and pot holder is also used to estimate occlusion. We require that the leaves are static while images are being captured, and that the leaves do not move between images being captured.

The structure recovery process estimates a silhouette of the plant for each frame. Depending on the background of the scene, a colour histogram thresholding method (as applied, for example, in [5]) may be sufficient. Due to the variation in colour and texture of the plants and background in the image sets we are using, a pixel classifier using a Support Vector Machine trained on manually labelled images was applied for the mask generation.

3.2 Calibration

Camera calibration is achieved using a calibration object that displays known patterns to a variety of viewpoints. Rather than using independent planes as proposed in [21] and [22], a single rigid object is favourable here as it does not require that fixed cameras view planes in common. Such an object can also be placed within an automated greenhouse system so that calibration can be periodically performed or verified. The shape of the object is recorded in a file such as may be sent to one of the many acrylic laser cutting services so it can be rapidly constructed anywhere in the world.

QR codes are used as calibration patterns as they are rich in features and can be uniquely identified. The patterns are printed onto durable adhesive labels for robustness against humidity and temperature. The adhesive labels are placed onto the object manually, resulting in some ambiguity in their true locations. Rather than rely on a large number of manual measurements, adhesive label placements are described by calibration object parameters which are estimated as part of the calibration process.

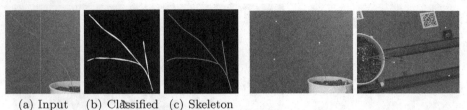

(a) Input   (b) Classified   (c) Skeleton

Fig. 5. Extracting a skeleton for a frame

Fig. 6. 2 views of the 3D tip and base points

Initial camera poses and intrinsic parameters are estimated assuming ideal (known) placements of calibration patterns. Subsequently, both camera parameters and calibration object parameters are refined so as to minimise the sum of squared reprojection distances and error terms based on prior estimates of the calibration object parameters. Figure 3 shows the calibration object.

3.3 Database Building

The goal of the method is to generate a plausible plant model given the silhouette in each view. To generate candidate models representing plausible plant structures, we use a database of pre-defined leaf models. These models are manually constructed using an interactive tool. Plants are modelled by specifying a series of 3D point locations tracing the axis of each leaf. To specify a point location, the user first selects a point on a leaf in one view of the plant, then selects the corresponding point in a second view. The selected point in the second view is constrained to lie on the corresponding epipolar line. The database currently contains models for 480 leaves, modelled from 230 plants. Each leaf is modelled with an average of 8 points. Figure 4 shows two views of a manually modelled plant. To increase the density of the database, additional leaf models are generated by transforming modelled leaves to stretch their shape in multiple directions within a small distance range. This generates 100 models for each modelled leaf.

3.4 Skeleton Extraction

A set of 2D skeletons extracted from the silhouette for each view are used as estimates of the projection of the set of 3D leaf axes. An example of such skeletons being used for plant reconstruction is given in the reconstruction method of [23], where matching between skeleton points in orthographic images is used to recover 3D leaf paths. To generate the skeletons, we use the thinning algorithm of [24]. An example of a skeleton extracted from a silhouette is shown in Figure 5.

3.5 Leaf Tip Detection

To limit the number of candidate models which need to be evaluated to find a model which corresponds to the current image set, information extracted from the 2D skeletons is used to guide the generation process. To identify possible tip points, we first construct a graph from each skeleton image. As some plant regions in the silhouettes may be disconnected due to sections of the plant which are too thin to be detected, edges are added between nearby points to connect these isolated regions in the graph.

From the graphs, we extract a set of possible 3D leaf tip points and a base point. We significantly reduce the space of possible models by considering only candidate leaf models with ends corresponding to these tip and base points. For each graph, we first detect a set of 2D points possibly corresponding to leaf tips by measuring the distance to the graph centre for each node and finding local maxima for this distance. These 2D points are matched between images to give possible 3D leaf tip locations. Matches for a point are found by locating points close to the corresponding epipolar line in a second view. 3D tip points are then determined by triangulation. Matches in further views are located by finding points close to the projection of the 3D points. The final position for each point is determined as the 3D point minimizing the sum of squared distances to the corresponding 2D points in all views. We select the 3D point closest to the input pot centre position as the base point. The selected base point and set of possible tip points for a plant are shown in Figure 6.

The boundary of the extracted silhouette may not be smooth due to mis-classified background pixels. This results in extreme points in the graph which do not correspond to leaf tips, and 3D tip points being generated corresponding to points part way along the leaves. While such points could be removed using morphological filtering operations, doing so also eliminates important structural information.

Instead, we use the set of graphs to detect 3D tip points which are likely to be part way along the path to a true leaf tip. We find the shortest path in the graph from each 3D tip point to the base point in each view where that point is visible, and remove any point for which these paths do not include at least 150 pixels not included in the paths to a tip point farther from the base. Points with 2D projections which are not close to the silhouettes are also rejected.

3.6   Leaf Generation

For each possible tip point, we build a set of candidate leaf models. Leaves from the database of manually modelled plants are linearly transformed to fit the tip and base points for each leaf to the selected tip point and base point positions. The transformed leaves are then evaluated against the images. The leaf models which best match the images are determined by measuring the distance in each image between sampled points on the models and the nearest point on the 2D skeleton for that image.

The tip point, base point, and the orientation vector determined in the calibration process are used to define a linear transform mapping the base and tip of each leaf chosen from the database to the corresponding points in the current scene. This transform can then be used to map all points of the leaf into the scene. To efficiently evaluate distances from model points to skeleton points, a

(a) with penalty   (b) without penalty

Fig. 7. The effect of the curvature penalty

distance transform is applied to the 2D skeleton in each view, assigning each pixel in the image the distance to the nearest skeleton point. As leaves can hang over the edge of the pot, where they cannot be seen by some cameras, we also make use of a 3D model giving the approximate structure of the pot and pot holder. This allows occlusion to be estimated and incorporated into the reconstruction. After evaluating the full set of transformed leaf models against the images, parameters for the best models are refined to improve their fit to the image set, as we do not expect the database to contain an exact match for each leaf.

To refine the leaf while preserving its shape, we model each leaf using cubic B-splines $b_{\mathbf{C}}(t) \rightarrow \Re^3$, $t \in (0,1)$ parameterised by a set of control points $\mathbf{C}$. The control points are optimised with respect to $\mathcal{S} = \{\mathbf{S}^v\}_{\forall v}$, where $\mathbf{S}^v = [s_1^v, \ldots, s_n^v]$ is the set of skeleton points in view v, by minimising

$$d(\mathcal{S}, \mathbf{C}) = \sum_{i=0}^{N} \left(\frac{\sum_v r_v(b_{\mathbf{C}}(iN^{-1}))}{\sum_v o_v(b_{\mathbf{C}}(iN^{-1}))} + c_{\mathbf{C}}(iN^{-1}) \right) \tag{1}$$

where the residual

$$r_v(\boldsymbol{x}) = o_v(\boldsymbol{x}) \left(\min_j \| s_j^v - \mathbf{A}_v \boldsymbol{x} \|_2 \right) \tag{2}$$

measures the distance between the projection of a point on the leaf against the closest skeleton point in view v for an experimentally chosen set of (N+1) measurement points. Here, $\mathbf{A}_v$ is the projection matrix for view v and $o_v(\boldsymbol{x})$ is a delta function that is 0 if $\boldsymbol{x}$ is occluded in view v and 1 otherwise. Residuals are inversely weighted by the number of views where a point is visible to avoid biasing the optimisation towards a better fit for points which are visible in more views. To prevent significant changes in the leaf shape, the term

$$c_{\mathbf{C}}(t) = \alpha(\kappa_{\mathbf{C}}(t) - \kappa_{\mathbf{C}_0}(t))^2 \tag{3}$$

Fig. 8. Refining parameters for a leaf model

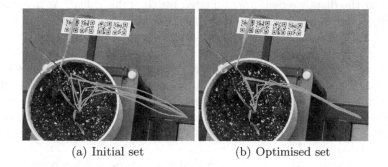

(a) Initial set   (b) Optimised set

Fig. 9. Initial and optimised set of leaf candidates

is added to the residuals to penalise changes in curvature with respect to the control points $\mathbf{C}_0$ of the original curve. The term

$$\kappa_{\mathbf{C}}(t) = \frac{\|b'_{\mathbf{C}}(t) \times b''_{\mathbf{C}}(t)\|}{\|b'_{\mathbf{C}}(t)\|^3} \tag{4}$$

measures curvature of the B-spline $b_{\mathbf{C}}$ evaluated at t. The effect of the curve penalty on the reconstruction is illustrated in Figure 7. In both cases the optimisation began from the curve illustrated in Figure 7(a). Without the penalty, the different parts of the hypothesised curve latch onto different, disjoint leaves in the image (Figure 7(b)).

The curvature of a leaf may not be continuous, particularly where the leaf meets the stem. We therefore find any points in the 3D path of the original leaf model where a sharp change of angle ($> 45°$) occurs, and model the path as a set of one or more connected splines, with discontinuous curvature at these points. The number of control points for each segment is determined from the segment length.

To fit a leaf to the image set, the positions of the 3D control points are refined by applying Levenberg-Marquardt optimisation to the set of measurement points along the leaf. We select points that are separated by approximately 7.5mm along the original curve and define the distance residual in (2) by the distance transform over the skeletonised observation. The change in the shape of a leaf during refinement is illustrated in Figure 8.

The distance measure is used to rank the full set of leaf models generated from the database. The best 200 leaf models are then selected and refined. Figure 9 shows a set of initial candidate models obtained for a point, and the same set of models after refinement.

3.7   Structure Estimation

The above process generates a set of possible leaf models which may be combined into a full plant model. In generating the complete plant model, multiple candidates for each tip are tested, because overlapping leaves may result in several plausible paths from a tip to the base. For each tip point, we select 5 candidate leaves using the distance measure evaluated for the refined leaf. As multiple leaf models may converge to the same shape in refinement, additional leaf models are not selected if there is only minimal deviation from an already selected model.

On the basis of the leaf hypothesis set, and the anatomy-based prior which describes the ways in which such leaves may be combined, it is possible to construct a set of full-plant hypotheses. This process may be seen as a data-driven means of exploiting a generative model in a situation where sampling from a full generative model directly would be too computationally expensive. The generative model for a plant such as wheat is relatively simple, but nonetheless far too complex to be sampled from directly.

Each hypothesised structure is evaluated against the number of skeleton pixels covered by the model, the number of pixels outside the plant which are covered, and the number of leaves used. Let $\mathcal{I}_v$ be the set of skeleton pixels in view v. The set of *'interior'* pixels which are supported by the set of leaves $\mathcal{L}$ is given by

$$i_v(\mathcal{L}) = \{i \mid (i \in \mathcal{I}_v) \wedge (a_v(i, \mathcal{L}) > 0)\} \tag{5}$$

where

$$a_v(i, \mathcal{L}) = \sum_{\mathbf{L} \in \mathcal{L}} m_v(i, \mathbf{L}) \tag{6}$$

and

$$m_v(i, \mathbf{L}) = \begin{cases} 1 \text{ if } \min_t \|i - \mathbf{A}_v b_{\mathbf{L}}(t)\| < \tau \\ 0 \text{ otherwise.} \end{cases} \tag{7}$$

counts the number of leaves which project to the pixel $i \in \mathcal{I}_v$ within a tolerance $\tau = 10$ pixels. This threshold helps to account for divergence between the skeleton extracted for each frame and the projection of the true axis of each leaf. The set of *'exterior'* pixels

$$e_v(\mathcal{L}) = \{j \mid (j \in \mathcal{R}) \wedge (\min_{i \in \mathcal{I}_v} \|i - j\| > \tau)\} \tag{8}$$

are in the image $\mathcal{R}$ generated by rendering $\mathcal{L}$ with projection matrix $\mathbf{A}_v$ but are not within the threshold distance of any skeleton pixels. The quality of the leaf set is

$$q(\mathcal{L}) = \sum_{v \in \mathcal{V}} (|i_v(\mathcal{L})| - \beta|e_v(\mathcal{L})| - \gamma o_v(\mathcal{L})) \tag{9}$$

where β controls the penalty for covering exterior pixels and γ with

$$o_v(\mathcal{L}) = \sum_{i \in i_v(\mathcal{L})} (a_v(i, \mathcal{L}) - 1) \tag{10}$$

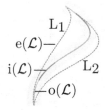

Fig. 10. The interior, exterior and overlapping areas of the set metric

Fig. 11. Partially reconstructed leaves

penalises solutions where multiple leaves overlap the same set of pixels. Consequently, (9) favours models that closely match the skeletons in each view while using the smallest number of leaves. Figure 10 illustrates the segmentation of the observed image into interior, exterior and overlapping pixels given a hypothesised leaf set $\mathcal{L}$.

A set of leaves $\mathcal{L}$ is chosen from a larger set of candidate leaves by a random, greedy search. Let $\mathcal{C}^l = \{\mathbf{C}^l_1, \ldots, \mathbf{C}^l_n\}$ be the set of n candidate control point sets for leaf tip l. A leaf model $\mathbf{C}'$ is randomly chosen and removed from the set $\mathcal{P} = \{\mathcal{C}^l\}_{\forall l}$. If $q(\mathcal{L} \cup \{\mathbf{C}'\}) > q(\mathcal{L})$, then $\mathbf{C}'$ is added to the initially empty set of hypothesised leaves $\mathcal{L}$ and $\mathcal{C}^l \to \varnothing$ where $\mathcal{C}^l$ is the set of candidate leaves that contained $\mathbf{C}'$. The process of sampling leaves from $\mathcal{P}$ and adding them to the model set continues until $\mathcal{P}$ is empty.

4   Results

This method has been tested on a set of plants with up to 8 leaves each, with manual measurements taken for the first 4 leaves of each plant. Figure 12 shows the original images from two cameras, and the reconstructed plant model projected into those images, for 6 plants. These results show the structure of the plant being accurately recovered despite overlap between multiple leaves. These results were generated with 50000 runs of the model generation process, and with weights set to $\alpha = 2 \times 10^{-7}$, $\beta = 1.4$ and $\gamma = 0.3$. Result images for more plants are included in Online Resource 1.

In most cases, the reconstruction process determined the correct number of leaves and generated a model close to the true shape of the plant. Figure 11 shows some cases where a leaf was not reconstructed, or was only partially reconstructed. In Figure 11(a), a leaf was not reconstructed due to the leaf tip and most of the length of the leaf being occluded in all views by the leaf labelled in red. In Figure 11(b), only part of the shape of the leaf labelled in yellow was recovered, as a close match for the leaf was not found in the database. This limitation would be improved with a more comprehensive model database. A leaf model was not fitted to the full extent of the leaf labelled in green in Figure 11(c), due to the pixels of a dead leaf tip being classified as background during silhouette generation.

Table 1. Measurement results for the first 4 leaves

	Plant 1				Plant 2			
Manual (mm)	150.64	220.68	299.53	245.26	138.74	243.89	332	351
Estimated (mm)	147.0	216.79	299.89	241.99	145.99	214.75	292.73	337.99
Absolute (mm)	3.64	3.89	0.36	3.27	7.25	29.14	39.27	13.01
Relative (%)	2.42	1.76	0.12	1.33	5.23	11.95	11.83	3.7
	Plant 3				Plant 4			
Manual (mm)	144.97	263.75	378	224.13	115.73	203.23	279.82	320.0
Estimated (mm)	145.91	259.87	376.73	242.94	137.0	200.99	279.0	287.92
Absolute (mm)	0.94	3.88	1.27	18.81	21.27	2.24	0.82	32.08
Relative (%)	0.65	1.47	0.34	8.39	18.38	1.1	0.29	10.03
	Plant 5				Plant 6			
Manual (mm)	101.4	185.82	259.16	299.87	119.22	211.86	273.85	304.55
Estimated (mm)	117.0	162.0	255.81	251.98	130.99	184.51	272.54	265.98
Absolute (mm)	15.60	23.82	3.35	47.89	11.77	27.35	1.31	38.57
Relative (%)	15.38	12.82	1.29	15.97	9.87	12.91	0.48	12.66

For this set of plants, we have compared leaf length measurements automatically extracted from the models with manual measurements of the first 4 leaves of each plant. Manual measurements were taken from the leaf tip to the point at which the leaf meets the stem. To measure this distance from the reconstructed leaf models, we estimate this point by finding the point at which overlapping leaf models diverge. Table 1 shows automatically and manually measured leaf lengths in millimetres and relative percentage error for the set of plants seen in Figure 12. For tests on a set of 40 plants, the average difference between the manual measurements and our estimated leaf lengths was $19.06mm$. The average relative error was 8.64%.

This testing has highlighted an unforeseen ambiguity in the (stem-side) end point of such leaf measurements which leads to differences between the manually measured quantity and that estimated from the recovered structure. It also indicates a need to conduct repeated manual measurements so as to estimate the error in that process. Despite these limitations, the results show that the method is capable of automatically recovering meaningful plant structure estimates from image sets.

Figure 13 shows results of applying this method to more mature plants with a greater density of leaves. In these cases, the structure of the majority of leaves was still recovered. However, some leaves with tips in regions where structure is dense were not identified, and the accuracy of the curves for the reconstructed leaves was also lower in these regions. Improving reconstruction accuracy for more mature plants will be a focus of further development of this method.

5   Conclusions and Future Work

We have presented a method suitable for recovering the structure of thin plants from a small set of images captured by widely spaced cameras. There are a range of potential future developments for this method. Although the present method operates only on RGB images, it would be straightforward to incorporate depth

Fig. 12. Original images and reconstruction results

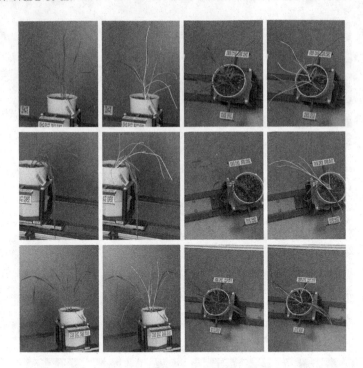

Fig. 13. Reconstruction results for more mature plants

map information into the fitting process, allowing for reconstruction using depth camera or laser data from a limited range of views.

The method could potentially be applied to single images, using the variation in plausible reconstructions of the image to determine the range of possible values for various plant properties. The method could also provide a means of estimating further physical properties of leaves from measured properties of leaves represented in the database. The structure estimates can be used for leaf angle and length measurements, and we plan to use these paths as a basis for also measuring leaf width and senescence.

We plan to use the estimated structures of plants over time to track plant growth, with a database of models of developing plants used to determine plausible matches between the estimated leaves at different time steps. The method will also be refined to improve the reconstruction accuracy for more mature plants, where the structure of individual leaves is more difficult to distinguish using only skeletons extracted from silhouettes.

Acknowledgements. This work was supported by Australian Research Council (ARC) Linkage Project grant LP130100156, and the ARC Centre of Excellence on Robotic Vision.

References

1. Vos, J., Evers, J.B., et al.: Functional structural plant modelling: a new versatile tool in crop science. Journal of Experimental Botany **61**(8), 2101–2115 (2010)
2. Paulus, S., Dupuis, J., Mahlein, A.K., Kuhlmann, H.: Surface feature based classification of plant organs from 3d laserscanned point clouds for plant phenotyping. BMC Bioinformatics **14**, 238 (2013)
3. Li, Y., Fan, X., et al.: Analyzing growing plants from 4d point cloud data. ACM Transactions on Graphics (Proceedings of SIGGRAPH Asia 2013) 32 (2013)
4. Bellasio, C., Olejníčková, J., et al.: Computer reconstruction of plant growth and chlorophyll fluorescence emission in three spatial dimensions. Sensors **12**(1), 1052–1071 (2012)
5. Hartmann, A., Czauderna, T., et al.: HTPheno: An image analysis pipeline for high-throughput plant phenotyping. BMC Bioinformatics **12**, 148 (2011)
6. Golzarian, M.R., Frick, R.A., et al.: Accurate inference of shoot biomass from high-throughput images of cereal plants. Plant Methods 1 (2011)
7. Lati, R.N., Filin, S., Eizenberg, H.: Estimating plant growth parameters using an energy minimization-based stereovision model. Computers and Electronics in Agriculture **98**, 260–271 (2013)
8. Andersen, H.J., Reng, L., Kirk, K.: Geometric plant properties by relaxed stereo vision using simulated annealing. Computers and Electronics in Agriculture **49**(2), 219–232 (2005)
9. Lati, R.N., Manevich, A., Filin, S.: Three-dimensional image-based modelling of linear features for plant biomass estimation. International Journal of Remote Sensing **34**(17), 6135–6151 (2013)
10. Wang, H., Zhang, W., et al.: Image-based 3d corn reconstruction for retrieval of geometrical structural parameters. International Journal of Remote Sensing **30**(20), 5505–5513 (2009)
11. Laga, H., Miklavcic, S.: Curve-based stereo matching for 3d modeling of plants. In: 20th International Congress on Modelling and Simulation (2013)
12. Kumar, P., Cai, J., Miklavcic, S.: High-throughput 3d modelling of plants for phenotypic analysis. In: Image and Vision Computing New Zealand, pp. 301–306. ACM (2012)
13. Alenyà, G., Dellen, B., Torras, C.: 3d modelling of leaves from color and ToF data for robotized plant measuring. In: IEEE International Conference on Robotics and Automation, pp. 3408–3414 (2011)
14. Preuksakarn, C., Boudon, F., et al.: Reconstructing plant architecture from 3d laser scanner data. In: 6th International Workshop on Functional-Structural Plant Models, pp. 16–18 (2010)
15. Quan, L., Tan, P., et al.: Image-based plant modeling. ACM Transactions on Graphics **25**(3), 599–604 (2006)
16. Dornbusch, T., Wernecke, P., Diepenbrock, W.: A method to extract morphological traits of plant organs from 3d point clouds as a database for an architectural plant model. Ecological Modelling 200(12), 119–129 (2007)
17. Laurentini, A.: The visual hull concept for silhouette-based image understanding. IEEE Transactions on Pattern Analysis and Machine Intelligence **16**(2), 150–162 (1994)
18. Guénard, J., Morin, G., Boudon, F., Charvillat, V.: Realistic plant modeling from images based on analysis-by-synthesis. In: Floater, M., Lyche, T., Mazure, M.-L., Mørken, K., Schumaker, L.L. (eds.) MMCS 2012. LNCS, vol. 8177, pp. 213–229. Springer, Heidelberg (2014)

19. Lopez, L.D., Ding, Y., Yu, J.: Modeling complex unfoliaged trees from a sparse set of images. Computer Graphics Forum **29**(7), 2075–2082 (2010)
20. Huang, H., Mayer, H.: Generative statistical 3d reconstruction of unfoliaged trees from terrestrial images. Annals of GIS **15**(2), 97–105 (2009)
21. Sturm, P.F., Maybank, S.J.: On plane-based camera calibration: A general algorithm, singularities, applications. In: IEEE Computer Society Conference on Computer Vision and Pattern Recognition, vol. 1, pp. 432–437 (1999)
22. Zhang, Z.: A flexible new technique for camera calibration. IEEE Transactions on Pattern Analysis and Machine Intelligence **22**(11), 1330–1334 (2000)
23. Cai, J., Miklavcic, S.: Automated extraction of three-dimensional cereal plant structures from two-dimensional orthographic images. IET Image Processing **6**, 687–696 (2012)
24. Zhang, T.Y., Suen, C.Y.: A fast parallel algorithm for thinning digital patterns. Communications of the ACM **27**(3), 236–239 (1984)

Image-Based Phenotyping of the Mature Arabidopsis Shoot System

Marco Augustin[1], Yll Haxhimusa[1(✉)], Wolfgang Busch[2],
and Walter G. Kropatsch[1]

[1] Pattern Recognition and Image Processing Group,
Vienna University of Technology, Vienna, Austria
{marco,yll}@prip.tuwien.ac.at
[2] Gregor Mendel Institute of Molecular Plant Biology,
Austrian Academy of Sciences, Vienna, Austria

Abstract. The image-based phenotyping of mature plants faces several challenges from the image acquisition to the determination of quantitative characteristics describing their appearance. In this work a framework to extract geometrical and topological traits of 2D images of mature *Arabidopsis thaliana* is proposed. The phenotyping pipeline recovers the realistic branching architecture of dried and flattened plants in two steps. In the first step, a tracing approach is used for the extraction of centerline segments of the plant. In the second step, a hierarchical reconstruction is done to group the segments according to continuity principles. This paper covers an overview of the relevant processing steps along the proposed pipeline and provides an insight into the image acquisition as well as into the most relevant results from the evaluation process.

Keywords: Image-based phenotyping · Geometrical/topological traits · Tracing · Hierarchical reconstruction · Network of curvilinear structures

1 Introduction

The functional analysis of genes became a popular and interesting challenge in life science in the last 30 years [31]. The correlation between genetic data and the likelihood for certain pathologies in humans or genes causing an increasing crop yield are only two important and relevant examples [9]. While sequencing the genome of model organisms can be solved effectively nowadays, the automatic extraction of quantitative characteristics describing the phenotype, so called *traits*, became the bottleneck for many large-scale functional genomic studies [11]. Modern image acquisition tools and the progress in computer vision offer new possibilities for high-throughput phenotyping studies. The development of image-based phenotyping pipelines can help to overcome the current drawbacks of large-scale genetic studies, which are the manipulation of thousands of samples and the subsequent manual determination of relevant traits [27]. *Arabidopsis thaliana* is a small flowering plant and a popular model organism. The determination of quantitative traits, e.g. the plant's root length, became

© Springer International Publishing Switzerland 2015
L. Agapito et al. (Eds.): ECCV 2014 Workshops, Part IV, LNCS 8928, pp. 231–246, 2015.
DOI: 10.1007/978-3-319-16220-1_17

an important challenge during large-scale genetic studies [15]. In this work 2D images of mature *Arabidopsis thaliana* are analyzed and traits concerning the *final* appearance of the plant are extracted. During the last stages of growing, the plant mostly consists out of stems and siliques (see sample image in Fig. 1). The analysis of the rosette and the roots of the plant are not of interest for this work. The plants used in this work grew in a natural environment where the environmental conditions were well known. Due to storage and shipping reasons the plants are dried and pressed before the images are taken. Thus some stems overlap and appear as possible branching points in a segmented image. Hence a correct reconstruction of the plant's "realistic" architecture has to be done before the relevant traits can be extracted. The complexity of the reconstruction increases with the number of critical points: branching-, crossing- and termination- points. Branching points are defined as points where one branch splits in multiple branches. Due to the projection into the 2D image space as well as the flattening of the plants, overlapping stems appear as branching points in the images without having a correlating physical connection in nature. A distinction between branching and overlapping regions has to be done and is crucial for the correct reconstruction of the branching topology. Termination points are defined as end points of the plant (e.g. siliques' tips) and start points are located nearby the rosette.

The study of plants using computer vision approaches is a rather *new* field compared to the study of other biological objects, e.g. blood vessels. The latest works focus on the extraction of quantitative traits describing the root system of different plants like *A. thaliana*, maize or rice [27]. While the early root

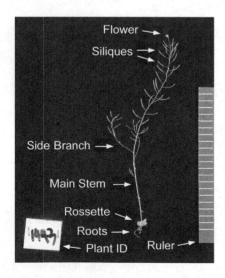

Fig. 1. Image of mature *A. thaliana*. The plant mainly consists out of stems/branches and siliques.

Fig. 2. Intensity profile of a branching region

Fig. 3. Intensity profile of a crossing region

development (growth rate) is in focus of the works [4,14,23] other approaches investigate the ability of a root to respond to gravity changes in high-temporal analysis [28]. Systems, like in [1,32] analyze the root architecture only at a certain moment using a single image and traits like the root length or root angles are extracted. A number of high-throughput approaches exist to analyze details of plants' shoot systems (parts which are growing above ground). The authors in [2] developed a phenotyping pipeline for high-throughput studies which focuses on the analysis of the leaf growth behaviour. The interested reader is referred to [11] for an extended list of frameworks for *next-generation phenotyping*. It can be noticed that there is a lack of approaches for the analysis of the shoot system of *Arabidopsis*. Furthermore, most techniques focus on geometrical traits like curvature characteristics or lengths of certain plant parts. More complex traits describing the branching topology network of roots or stems, like branching patterns or branching orders are barely noted.

The detailed analysis of curvilinear structures like roots or stems is limited in the field of image-based plant phenotyping. Computer vision approaches are successfully developed in other fields dealing with similar structures like blood vessels or biological neural networks [13,22]. Generally, the approach of analyzing such networks is executed as a two-step approach in which the object is segmented in a first step and labeled in a second step. It already exists a great amount of different approaches [12,20,24,33–35] for the automated segmentation or skeleton extraction, the amount of approaches for labeling and grouping of trees or sub-trees inside these networks is rather limited [5,17,18,21,30].

In this work we propose the use of a tracing algorithm with a semi-circular search window to extract centerline segments of the plant's shoot system. Geometrical and topological properties, which are determined during tracing, are further used to group and label these segments based on continuity principles. We show that geometrical traits can be extracted accurately, whereas, a detailed topological analysis is still limited by the morphological complexity of the network as well as by noise.

The paper is structured as follows. In Sec. 2 a short overview of the image acquisition setup is described. In Sec. 3 we introduce the methodology used to extract the traits of the plant. The paper is concluded with experiments (Sec. 4) and conclusion (Sec. 5).

2   Image Acquisition of the *Arabdiopsis* Shoot System

The images which are analyzed in this work were taken as part of a project entitled *"The molecular basis of local adaption in A. thaliana"* led by Benjamin Brachi (Bergelson Lab, University of Chicago, US). Originally the images were acquired for the use of a manual phenotyping study and the use of computer vision methods for a computer guided analysis was originally not planned. The images were acquired in a darkened room using a digital single lens reflex camera. Two additional flashlights were used to ensure equal light conditions during the whole image acquisition process. The plants were put on a black velvet board to guarantee a high contrast between object and background. A wipeable plant ID sign and a ruler were added to the velvet for later analysis (see Fig. 1). While the sign can be used for an automated data handling during phenotyping, the ruler is used for an automated spatial calibration. The images are taken with 12.1 megapixels (4284 × 2844 pixels) and are stored as TIFF (tagged image file format) in RGB color mode with 8 bit color depth.

To simplify the task of analyzing the architecture of a plant a few assumptions are made based on the image acquisition setup and preliminary experiments. In this work, the plants' stems and branches are defined as piecewise linear and their medial axis is represented by connected line segments. The stems' and branches' crosswise intensity profile approximates a Gaussian profile and the gray level changes along the stems and branches are smooth. The region of the rosette is defined as the origin of all main stems and the plant forms a tree-like structure. The stems' and branches' diameter decreases coming closer to the plant's end points and does not change abruptly. Further, the siliques' diameter increases before it decreases until a termination point is reached. Figure 2 and 3 show 3D intensity profile plots of specific parts (branching and crossing region) of a plant to illustrate some of the characteristics defined above. The term *"architecture"* of a plant is used to describe the different components of a plant regarding to space and time. Describing the plant's architecture is done by topological as well as geometrical information. Topological information describes the physical connection between different parts (e.g. siliques, leaves, flowers, branches) of the plant [16]. Concerning the topological characteristics, this architecture can range from simple plants (low number of critical points) to complex plants (high number of critical points). Geometrical information is used for a detailed description of the plant's components like size, shape, orientation or the spatial location of the components [16]. The quantitative traits extracted in this work comprise topological and geometrical information and are denoted in the following either as geometrical or topological traits. While the number of siliques (on different stems) is considered as a topological trait, the individual silique's length is considered as a geometrical trait.

3   Analysis and Reconstruction of the Plant's Architecture

To analyze 2D images of mature *Arabidopsis* a pipeline based on several computer vision methods is proposed as shown in Fig. 4. This section is divided according to the steps of this pipeline.

3.1   Pre-Processing

Due to logistical reasons the plants dried and the RGB color information of different plant components is distributed uneven in one image and over the whole dataset. Hence the images are transformed into grayscale images using the R-channel of the RGB color space. The images contain three different regions-of-interest (ROI) which are the *plant ID sign*, the *ruler* and the *plant* itself. These

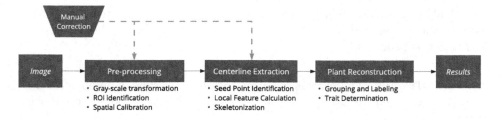

Fig. 4. Analysis and reconstruction framework

regions are extracted using image processing methods such as image pyramids, bit-plane slicing and mathematical morphology operators. These principles combined with constraints concerning the approximative location of the ROIs (e.g. the plant is always the most central object) are used to crop each image to the borders of the objects' bounding boxes. To make quantitative traits comparable to results of other studies the pixel units are transformed to *real-world metric units*, e.g. *mm*. The spatial calibration is achieved by use of the ruler. A routine based on gray-level thresholding and mathematical morphology operators is used to extract the conversion factor automatically in each image. A more detailed description regarding the sequence of steps during pre-processing is given in [3].

3.2   Centerline Extraction

The medial axis of curvilinear structures is an efficient representation to analyze characteristics concerning the geometry as well as topology. In this work a tracing approach is used to extract the centerline of the plant iteratively. Different variation of tracing algorithms are already successfully used for blood vessel analysis [7,12,29] as well as biological neural network analysis [22,35]. Tracing is a direct exploratory centerline extraction approach where a structure (often curvilinear/tubular) is followed from a starting point to an end point. Tracing provides a sequence of extracted centerline points, which represent samples on the medial axis of an object. Local features like tracing direction or radius at these points are determined and used for travelling along the object.

Seed Point Identification. Tracing algorithms are initialized at certain (starting) positions, so called *seed points*. A set of seed points is chosen either manually or by an automated procedure. Automated seed point identification procedures focus either on the detection of ridges/edges along scan lines [8,12] or on detection of these points in a certain ROI's neighborhood [17]. The automated seed point identification method in this work, is based on the assumption that one seed point per main stem is sufficient for a complete centerline extraction. This assumption should hold under regular conditions: low gray-value discontinuities and little noise in the images. As all main stems originate from the rosette, the rosette is roughly segmented and possible seed point candidates (ridge points) in its neighborhood are estimated before the seed points are validated. The interested reader is referred to [3] for a detailed description about the seed point identification procedure.

Iterative Tracing. The process of extracting the centerline of an object using tracing is executed iteratively until at least one of certain stopping criteria is fulfilled.

Initialization. Each iteration is initialized at a start point p^k. While at the very beginning of the tracing procedure the seed point is chosen from the set of points from the seed point identification routine, subsequent start points are for example neighbouring centerline points or branching points which are determined during tracing.

Estimation. The location of the next centerline point along the structure is estimated by a dynamic semi-circular search window (Fig. 5). This window guarantees a constant look-ahead distance in all directions and the next centerline point is expected to be located along its circumference. The gray-value profile $S_r^k(p^k)$ along the circumference of a semi-circle with radius r^k at p^k is defined as a sequence of equally spaced samples n [7]:

$$S_r^k(p^k) = \{c_i, \ i = 0, 1, \cdots, n-1\} \ . \tag{1}$$

$$c_i = V\left(p_x^k + r^k \cdot \cos(i \cdot \delta\theta), p_y^k + r^k \cdot \sin(i \cdot \delta\theta)\right), \qquad \delta\theta = \frac{\pi}{n-1} \ . \tag{2}$$

Since V (normalized intensity values of the image I) is defined in the discrete space the values of c_i are determined using the nearest pixel values. The gray-values along the circumference are smoothed using a Gaussian filter. The radius r^k of the semi-circle must be defined "big" enough to cover all different stem widths and must be "small" enough to not detect points along neighbouring structures. For this reason, the radius r^k is adapted dynamically to the current structure at each iteration of the algorithm by [7]:

$$r^k = \rho \cdot \left[\max\{R^k, R^{k+1}\}\right] \ . \tag{3}$$

R^k and R^{k+1} are the radius of the stem at the current and the next centerline point position. The constant factor ρ should be defined bigger than 1 to guarantee the coverage of the whole width of a stem.

Identification. The stems in this work appear as bright structures on a dark background and thus the intensity profile across the stems appears as a Gaussian-like shape (Fig. 2 and 3). To identify relevant centerline candidate points q_i, the intensity profile along the circumference is searched for local maxima (as indicated in Fig. 6 with triangles). If two or more stems run very close to each other, it can occur that local maxima are identified which belong to a neighboring stem. This can normally be avoided by choosing a small value for r^k in (2). Additionally,

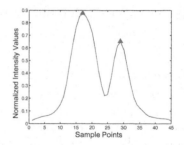

Fig. 5. A semi-circular template is propagating along a stem until a branching point is detected

Fig. 6. The intensity profile along the semi-circular circumference of the search window is shown for the detection of the branching point. The triangles indicate the identified candidate points.

the intensity profile along the connection between p^k and the candidate points q_i is checked for values below 20% of the normalized intensity values [17]. If any point undercuts this threshold the candidate point is flagged as outlier-stem point. These points are stored in an additional list which is used for initialization at the very end of the tracing procedure. Figure 7 shows an overview of different points along the circumference of the search window.

Validation. At the end of an iteration each candidate point is validated by determining its local features. The accuracy of the features depends on the tracing direction as well as on small intensity variations across the stems. To gain a higher accuracy regarding the location, the first estimate q_0 (position of the local maxima) is refined by taking into account the stem's edge points. The refinement involves the following steps (see Fig. 8 for illustration) [7,17,29]:

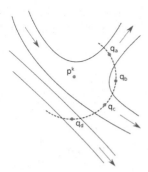

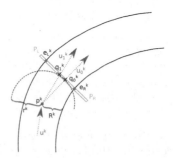

Fig. 7. Different types of candidate points can be identified: Stem points (q_a, q_c), outlier points (q_d) and non-stem points (q_b)

Fig. 8. The geometric determination and extraction of the local features at a centerline point

1. Calculate tracing direction for q_0^k

$$\vec{u_0^k} = \frac{p^k - q_0^k}{\|p^k - q_0^k\|} \ . \tag{4}$$

2. Detect edge points along two linear intensity profiles P_L and P_R perpendicular to the direction $\vec{u_0^k}$ by finding the gradient's maxima. The width of the intensity profiles is chosen to be the same value as r^k.
3. The location of the final stem point q_1^k is calculated as the medial point between the edge points. The radius R^{k+1} is determined.
4. Update tracing direction

$$\vec{u_1^k} = \frac{p^k - q_1^k}{\|p^k - q_1^k\|} \ . \tag{5}$$

The final position of the validated points can be influenced by a parameter α (set to 0.9 in this work) which regulates the step size according to:

$$p^{k+1} = p^k + \alpha \vec{u_1^k} \ . \tag{6}$$

A centerline point, denoted as *STEL (STem-ELement)*, is defined as a set of geometrical and topological properties in this work:

- p^k: Location of current $STEL_k$ in pixel units
- $\vec{u}^k$: Tracing direction (unit vector) at p^k
- R^k: Radius of the stem at position p^k
- e_L^k, e_R^k: Edge point positions
- s^k: Normalized intensity level at p^k
- γ^k: Percent dynamic range from perpendicular intensity profile at p^k
- ID: A unique ID for each STEL
- *Parent*: ID of the previous STEL
- *Type*: Regular (one child), branching/crossing (two or more children), root (no parent/seed point), termination (no child), outlier (no parent)

Stopping Criteria. The skeleton of the plant structure is extracted by executing the previously described steps iteratively until certain criteria are fulfilled:

- Any of the pixels of the search window is outside the image range.
- No *valid* candidate points are identified.
- More than one valid candidate point is identified (branching/crossing).
- Connection between the current point p^k and one of the current candidate points q_i^k intersects the actual skeleton.
- Percent-dynamic-range falls below a threshold (e.g. 10 %).

To prevent tracing of already traced stem parts a centerline image is created and updated during the tracing procedure. The centerline image is a binary image with the size of the plant's image I (initialized with pixel values equal zero). During tracing the pixel values of the current stem-segments are set to one. Two STELs are connected using the Bresenham line drawing algorithm [10]. To validate for example a seed point, its neighborhood (e.g. 5 × 5) in the centerline image is checked for non-zero elements.

3.3   Plant Reconstruction

The tracing procedure results in a set of *unconnected* centerline stem segments (set of STELs). Due to the fact that the branching pattern of the plants do not follow an a-priori known principle and the *local* knowledge at branching and crossing points is not sufficient, the plant's realistic architecture cannot be reconstructed during tracing. A hierarchical reconstruction is proposed in this work to rebuilt the realistic architecture of the plants (see Fig. 9 for illustration).

Filtering. The structure of centerline segments is represented as an undirected graph $G = (V, E)$ where the segments are the nodes V and possible connections between two segments are represented as edges E. Segments shorter than 5 pixel are removed.

Clustering. Assuming that each centerline segment V_i can be connected to any other centerline segment V_j we obtain a complete graph. We know that a segment at the very top of the image is unlikely to be connected to a segment at the very bottom. Thus we are looking for a representation (i.e. a layer on top of the G) with a reduced set of possible connections. At this level each centerline segment is represented by an edge (S) and a set of possible connections between adjacent centerline segments as a (cluster) node (CN). Since we have topological information (STEL relations) that we found during tracing, we can reduce the set of possible connections. The tracing procedure can not distinguish between

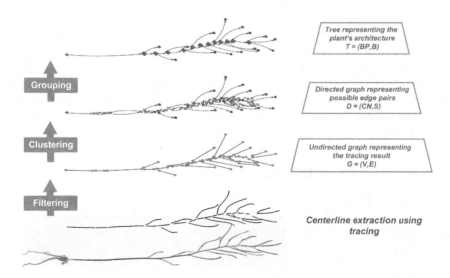

Fig. 9. Hierarchical reconstruction of the plants' architecture. The base layer consists of the centerline segments from the tracing procedure. The top layer represents the plant with use of branches and branching points. The root node is shown by a triangle, end nodes are represented by circles and branching points are represented by "+"-signs.

crossing and branching points. Thus intersection and unrelated stems can occur. Therefore we defined heuristic rules and an Euclidean distance to merge nearby critical points.

Grouping. Determining the costs for grouping possible edge pairs is based on continuity principles in this work. A cost term $c(S_i, S_j)$ for traveling from one segment S_i to another segment S_j is proposed as

$$c(S_1, S_2) = \theta(S_1, S_2) + d_1 \cdot \exp^{tor(S_1, S_2)} \quad . \tag{7}$$

Where $\theta(S_1, S_2)$ is defined as the edge direction similarity between two segments S_1, S_2 with directions $\vec{u}_1$, $\vec{u}_2$ [30]:

$$\theta(S_1, S_2) = acos\left(\frac{\vec{u}_1 \bullet \vec{u}_2}{|\vec{u}_1| \cdot |\vec{u}_2|}\right) \quad . \tag{8}$$

The "$\bullet$" operator is denoting the dot product. Experiments during the empirical modeling of the cost function showed that the edge direction similarity is a good feature to group segments if the lengths of involved edge candidates are similar. To include information regarding the curvature of the resulting path B_{12} into the cost function an additional term in (7) was added. This curvature term is modeled using the tortuosity, which is calculated as the ratio between the path length l_{12} and the Euclidean distance between the endpoints d_{12} [30]:

$$tor(S_1, S_2) = \frac{l_{12}}{d_{12}} \quad . \tag{9}$$

The Euclidean distance d_1 between segments' end points is used to weight the curvature term of the cost function. The grouping process follows a trace-back principle which means that the tree is constructed from the exterior regions to the interior regions. Further, the cluster nodes are visited from less complex to more complex nodes. The number of possible edge-pairs in a cluster is defined as the grade of complexity. A tree is iteratively build by minimizing the cost function in (7).

3.4   Geometrical and Topological Traits

After constructing the realistic architecture of the plant, the quantitative traits for each plant are determined. *Topological traits* are used to quantify the "network topology" of the plant. Different branch types are identified in the reconstructed tree and their occurrence is determined:

- *Main Stem (MS):* Stems which originate from the rosette area.
- *Silique:* Terminating branch containing the seeds and having a characteristic width variation.
- *Leaf:* Terminating branch which is not classified as a silique.
- *Side Branch (SB):* Branch originating from a main stem/side branch.

The *geometrical traits* are calculated for each branch B:

- *Path Length* l_B: The length of the branch centerline calculated by the number of odd N_o and even N_e Freeman (8-directional) chain codes along the centerline:

$$l_B = N_e + N_o \cdot \sqrt{2} \ . \tag{10}$$

- *Euclidean Length* d_B: The Euclidean distance between the branches' end points [21].

Silique Detection. The classification into siliques and *leaves* is based on the assumption that the majority of the exterior parts of a mature plant are siliques. Furthermore, siliques generally tend to have a higher variation in width and the lengths of siliques on one plant is more evenly distributed than the length of other leave parts. For this reason, the path length, the average width and the standard deviation of the width of the exterior branches are used to differentiate between siliques and other leaves. If the number of leaves on a plant is greater or equal 20, the robust *Minimum Covariance Determinant* estimator is used (outlier detection based on all three features) [25]. Otherwise the *Median Absolute Deviation* is used based on the branches' path lengths [26].

4 Experiments and Evaluation

The evaluation in this work was done with a set of 106 images (see Sec. 2). The traits extracted with the proposed framework (*PPFW*) are compared with traits from a semi-automatic analysis using *Fiji Simple Neurite Tracer* [19] (*GT Fiji*).

4.1 Measurement of the Plant Size

The accuracy of the final traits is evaluated using only images where the grouping process resulted in one connected object. This was the case in 89 out of 106 images. In the remaining approximately 15% the grouping process yield to multiple separated (sub)trees instead of one tree per main stem. This is caused by wrong local decisions in certain cluster nodes and an error propagation during the systematic grouping of edge candidates. Wrong local decisions were frequently observed in big cluster nodes with multiple smaller segments (multiple overlapping regions). These limitations originating from the grouping process should be reconsidered in future works. The lengths of certain branch types (MS, SB and Siliques) are averaged per plant and compared to GT Fiji. The evaluation concerning the stems' lengths is summarized in Tab. 1. The average relative error concerning the MS length between the two measurements is $(3.64 \pm 3.19)\,\%$. The average relative error concerning the siliques length is $(6.73 \pm 4.77)\,\%$. Scatter plots showing the individual measurements as well as the linear regression line (solid black) and the identity function (dashed line) for both measurements are shown in Fig. 10 and 11. The evaluation concerning the side branches shows a much higher deviation between GT Fiji and PPFW (see Tab. 1). This can be

Table 1. Comparison regarding the branches' lengths (path length l_B in pixels (Px)) and number of branches (N_B)

Branch Type	Ground Truth Fiji		Proposed Framework	
	l_B [Px]	N_B	l_B [Px]	N_B
MS	1983 ($\pm$731)	99	2030 ($\pm$756)	97
SB	667 ($\pm$441)	143	253 ($\pm$367)	540
Siliques	179 ($\pm$24)	2953	168 ($\pm$21)	2680

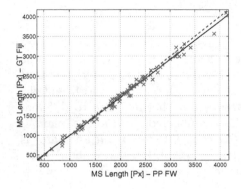

Fig. 10. Scatter plot comparing the GT Fjiji and the PPFW MS lengths (Pearson's r = 0.99 ($p < 0.01$))

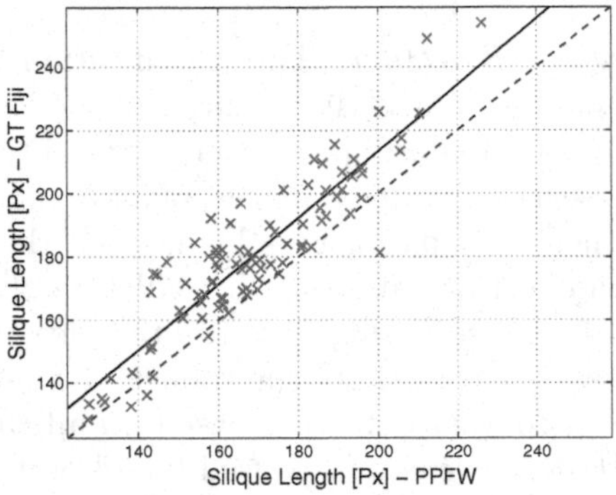

Fig. 11. Scatter plot comparing the GT Fjiji and the PPFW Siliques lengths (Pearson's r = 0.90 ($p < 0.01$))

explained by extensive overlappings in the exterior parts of the plant. Thereby a crossing is wrongly resolved as a new (mostly very short) side branch and terminating branches instead of only terminating branches. During the trait extraction this results in an overestimation of number of side-branches and an underestimation of number of siliques (compare deviation of number of siliques and SB in Tab. 1). Furthermore, this is also an explanation of the underestimation of the siliques' lengths which is noticeable in the scatter plot (Fig. 11) and the underestimation of the averaged side-branches lengths in Tab. 1.

4.2   Number of Siliques

The identification of the siliques is one of the major interests for biologists. The relative error is calculated by the difference between the number of siliques of GT Fiji and the number of siliques determined by the proposed framework. The mean relative error between GT Fiji and PPFW is (11.66 ± 9.09) %. To compare the deviation between GT Fiji and the PPFW more in detail a Bland-Altman plot [6] is shown in Fig. 12. While the mean number of siliques per plant is shown on the x axis, the absolute differences between the number of siliques determined for both measuring methods are shown on the y-axis. It can be noticed that more samples are spread below the zero line and the deviation increases by a rising number of siliques. An example of a labeled plant image

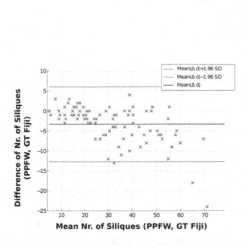

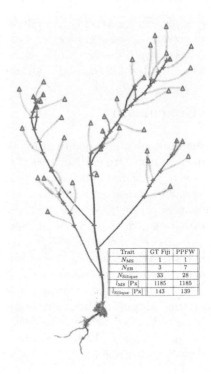

Trait	GT Fiji	PPFW
N_{MS}	1	1
N_{SB}	3	7
$N_{Silique}$	33	28
l_{MS} [Px]	1185	1185
$l_{Silique}$ [Px]	143	139

Fig. 12. Bland-Altman plot for number of siliques evaluation. An underestimation of number of siliques and can be observed. This underestimation increases with the number of siliques on a plant. The underestimation yields mainly from an error-prone classification of siliques in regions where many siliques tend to overlap with each other. This occurs in complex plants at the very upper parts.

Fig. 13. Exemplary output of PPFW. The table summarizes the plant's traits determined by GT Fiji and PPFW. (N_B Number of branches type B; l_B Avg. length of branches type B.).

as well as its corresponding table of traits is shown in Fig. 13. For illustration reasons the plant image is inverted and the (overlaid) centerline is thickened. The different branches are marked in different colors while the siliques and leafs are shown in turquoise respectively blue. The green triangle denotes the start of the MS, red triangles denote the termination points and the purple "+" signs denote branching points. The table of traits contains the number of different branches (MS, SB, Siliques) as well as the lengths of the MS and the siliques.

4.3 Performance

Besides the accuracy of the measurements the performance of image-based phenotype systems is crucial when it comes to a laboratory use. Thus the performance of the framework was evaluated concerning the need of manual corrections (clicks). A manual correction of preliminary results is provided for the steps of the automated seed point identification and the tracing algorithm. While during the seed point identification 7 clicks were needed to overcome false positives and false negatives, the tracing procedure required 112 additional clicks to complete the centerline extraction process (due to missed branchings or crossings). In total 119 clicks were necessary while processing all 106 images. The user decides if a mistakes has been made and if an interaction with the framework is needed.

5   Conclusion

In this work a semi-automatic framework is presented to extract geometrical and topological traits from 2D images of mature *Arabidopsis* plants. We showed that the use of a tracing approach to gain geometrical and topological information already during the segmentation of curvilinear objects can be valuable when topological characteristics are in focus of analysis. The accuracy and the grade of automation during the plant reconstruction depends on the quality of the pictures and on the morphological complexity of the plant structure. Unsupervised trait extraction using the proposed framework is reserved to plants with a limited morphological complexity and images with a uniformly high contrast.

The biggest source of error could be identified with overlapping branches and stems originating from the image acquisition. If bushy parts of the plants could be untangled before taking the images, the quality of the trait extraction would be improved. We have encountered problems finding reliable topological properties if multiple overlaps occur close to each other. In this case our tracing method produces a lot of small segments and the *"local"* systematic classification between branching and crossing regions gets error-prone. The problem lays in the way of how we set the rules for clustering and grouping. Especially when grouping small segments in large clusters (i.e. more than four candidate edges), there are many plausible way to connect them. Another drawback of is the side-effect of the error propagation as a wrong, local decision in a cluster node can lead to a propagation of this error to other nodes. An alternative to overcome this drawback would be the use of a global optimization approach, such as finding a minimum spanning tree. This could raise the quality of the results and should be part of future investigations.

From the phenotypic point of view an accurate topological reconstruction would rise the number of extractable traits in future works. Such traits can be the bifurcation ratio or the internodal distance between types of branches. Furthermore, with use of reliable topological and geometrical traits a context between these properties could be established. Image-based phenotyping of mature plants can be a valuable approach for the understanding of the correlation between the genotype, the phenotype and the environmental conditions of a plant. Combined with approaches to phenotype plants in earlier stages of growing, these approaches would open the way to (high-throughput) longitudinal studies covering the whole life-cycle of a plant.

Acknowledgments. We want to thank Svante Holm (Mid Sweden University, SE) and Alison Anastasio (University of Chicago, US) for planting and harvesting the plants, Man Yu and Andrew Davis for taking the photos and Benjamin Brachi

(Bergelson Lab, University of Chicago, US) for his valuable inputs and support along the stages of development.

References

1. Armengaud, P., Zambaux, K., Hills, A., Sulpice, R., Pattison, R.J., Blatt, M.R., Amtmann, A.: EZ-Rhizo: integrated software for the fast and accurate measurement of root system architecture. The Plant Journal **57**(5), 945–956 (2009)
2. Arvidsson, S., Perez-Rodriguez, P., Mueller-Roeber, B.: A growth phenotyping pipeline for Arabidopsis thaliana integrating image analysis and rosette area modeling for robust quantification of genotype effects. New Phytologist **191**(3), 895–907 (2011)
3. Augustin, M.: Extraction of quantitative traits from 2D images of mature arabidopsis plants. Vienna University of Technology, Master's Thesis (2014)
4. Basu, P., Pal, A., Lynch, J.P., Brown, K.M.: A novel image-analysis technique for kinematic study of growth and curvature. Plant Physiology **145**(2), 305–316 (2007)
5. Benmansour, F., Fua, P., Turetken, E.: Automated reconstruction of tree structures using path classifiers and mixed integer programming. In: 2012 IEEE Conference on Computer Vision and Pattern Recognition, pp. 566–573 (2012)
6. Bland, J.M., Altman, D.G.: Measuring agreement in method comparison studies. Statistical Methods in Laboratory Medicine **8**(2), 135–160 (1999)
7. Boroujeni, F.Z., Rahmat, O., Wirza, R., Mustapha, N., Affendey, L.S., Maskon, O.: Coronary artery center-line extraction using second order local features. Computational and Mathematical Methods in Medicine (2012)
8. Boroujeni, F.Z., Wirza, R., Rahmat, O., Mustapha, N., Affendey, L.S., Maskon, O.: Automatic selection of initial points for exploratory vessel tracing in fluoroscopic images. Defence Science Journal **61**, 443–451 (2011)
9. Brachi, B., Morris, G., Borevitz, J.: Genome-wide association studies in plants: the missing heritability is in the field. Genome Biology **12**(10), 232–240 (2011)
10. Bresenham, J.E.: Algorithm for computer control of a digital plotter. IBM Systems Journal **4**(1), 25–30 (1965)
11. Cobb, J.N., DeClerck, G., Greenberg, A., Clark, R., McCouch, S.: Next-generation phenotyping: requirements and strategies for enhancing our understanding of genotypephenotype relationships and its relevance to crop improvement. Theoretical and Applied Genetics **126**(4), 867–887 (2013)
12. Delibasis, K.K., Kechriniotis, A.I., Tsonos, C., Assimakis, N.: Automatic model-based tracing algorithm for vessel segmentation and diameter estimation. Computer Methods and Programs in Biomedicine **100**(2), 108–122 (2010)
13. Fraz, M.M., Remagnino, P., Hoppe, A., Uyyanonvara, B., Rudnicka, A.R., Owen, C.G., Barman, S.A.: Blood vessel segmentation methodologies in retinal images - a survey. Computer Methods and Programs in Biomedicine **108**(1), 407–433 (2012)
14. French, A.P., Ubeda-Tomas, S., Holman, T., Bennett, M., Pridmore, T.: High-throughput quantification of root growth using a novel image-analysis tool. Plant Physiology **150**(4), 1784–1795 (2009)
15. Furbank, R.T., Tester, M.: Phenomics technologies to relieve the phenotyping bottleneck. Trends in Plant Science **16**(12), 635–644 (2011)
16. Godin, C., Costes, E., Sinoquet, H.: A method for describing plant architecture which integrates topology and geometry. Annals of Botany **84**(3), 343–357 (1999)

17. Huang, Y., Zhang, J., Huang, Y.: An automated computational framework for retinal vascular network labeling and branching order analysis. Microvascular Research **84**(2), 169–177 (2012)
18. Lin, K.S., Tsai, C.L., Tsai, C.H., Sofka, M., Chen, S.J., Lin, W.Y.: Retinal vascular tree reconstruction with anatomical realism. IEEE Transactions on Biomedical Engineering **59**(12), 3337–3347 (2012)
19. Longair, M.H., Baker, D.A., Armstrong, J.D.: Simple neurite tracer: Open source software for reconstruction, visualization and analysis of neuronal processes. Bioinformatics (2011)
20. Martínez-Pérez, MElena, Hughes, Alun D., Stanton, Alice V., Thom, Simon A., Bharath, Anil A., Parker, Kim H.: Retinal blood vessel segmentation by means of scale-space analysis and region growing. In: Taylor, Chris, Colchester, Alain (eds.) MICCAI 1999. LNCS, vol. 1679, pp. 90–97. Springer, Heidelberg (1999)
21. Martinez-Perez, M.E., Hughes, A.D., Stanton, A.V., Thom, S.A., Chapman, N., Bharath, A.A., Parker, K.H.: Retinal vascular tree morphology: a semi-automatic quantification. IEEE Trans. Biomed. Engineering **49**(8), 912–917 (2002)
22. Meijering, E.: Neuron tracing in perspective. Cytometry Part A **77A**(7), 693–704 (2010)
23. Naeem, A., French, A.P., Wells, D.M., Pridmore, T.: High-throughput feature counting and measurement of roots. Bioinformatics **27**(9), 1337–1338 (2011)
24. Nguyen, U.T.V., Bhuiyan, A., Park, L.A.F., Ramamohanarao, K.: An effective retinal blood vessel segmentation method using multi-scale line detection. Pattern Recognition **46**(3), 703–715 (2013)
25. Rousseeuw, P.J., Driessen, K.V.: A fast algorithm for the minimum covariance determinant estimator. Technometrics **41**(3), 212–223 (1999)
26. Rousseeuw, P.J., Leroy, A.M.: Robust regression and outlier detection. John Wiley & Sons Inc., New York (1987)
27. Sozzani, R., Benfey, P.: High-throughput phenotyping of multicellular organisms: finding the link between genotype and phenotype. Genome Biology **12**(3), 219–225 (2011)
28. Subramanian, R., Spalding, E.P., Ferrier, N.J.: A high throughput robot system for machine vision based plant phenotype studies. Machine Vision and Applications **24**(3), 619–636 (2013)
29. Sun, Y.: Automated identification of vessel contours in coronary arteriograms by an adaptive tracking algorithm. IEEE Trans. Med. Imaging **8**(1), 78–88 (1989)
30. Tueretken, E., Gonzalez, G., Blum, C., Fua, P.: Automated reconstruction of dendritic and axonal trees by global optimization with geometric priors. Neuroinformatics **9**(2–3), 279–302 (2011)
31. Weigel, D.: Natural variation in arabidopsis: From molecular genetics to ecological genomics. Plant Physiology **158**(1), 2–22 (2012)
32. WinRHIZO: Winrhizo pro 2004a software: Root analysis. Regent Instruments Inc., Quebec, Canada (2004)
33. Yin, Y., Adel, M., Bourennane, S.: Retinal vessel segmentation using a probabilistic tracking method. Pattern Recognition **45**(4), 1235–1244 (2012)
34. Zana, F., Klein, J.C.: Segmentation of vessel-like patterns using mathematical morphology and curvature evaluation. Trans. Img. Proc. **10**(7), 1010–1019 (2001)
35. Zhang, Y., Zhou, X., Degterev, A., Lipinski, M., Adjeroh, D., Yuan, J., Wong, S.: A novel tracing algorithm for high throughput imaging screening of neuron-based assays. Journal of Neuroscience Methods **160**(1), 149–162 (2007)

3D Plant Modeling: Localization, Mapping and Segmentation for Plant Phenotyping Using a Single Hand-held Camera

Thiago Teixeira Santos[(⊠)], Luciano Vieira Koenigkan,
Jayme Garcia Arnal Barbedo, and Gustavo Costa Rodrigues

Embrapa Agricultural Informatics Campinas, Campinas, SP 13083-886, Brazil
{thiago.santos,luciano.vieira,jayme.barbedo,gustavo.rodrigues}@embrapa.br

Abstract. Functional-structural modeling and high-throughput phenomics demand tools for 3D measurements of plants. In this work, structure from motion is employed to estimate the position of a hand-held camera, moving around plants, and to recover a sparse 3D point cloud sampling the plants' surfaces. Multiple-view stereo is employed to extend the sparse model to a dense 3D point cloud. The model is automatically segmented by spectral clustering, properly separating the plant's leaves whose surfaces are estimated by fitting trimmed B-splines to their 3D points. These models are accurate snapshots for the aerial part of the plants at the image acquisition moment and allow the measurement of different features of the specimen phenotype. Such state-of-the-art computer vision techniques are able to produce accurate 3D models for plants using data from a single free moving camera, properly handling occlusions and diversity in size and structure for specimens presenting sparse canopies. A data set formed by the input images and the resulting camera poses and 3D points clouds is available, including data for sunflower and soybean specimens.

Keywords: Plant phenotyping · SLAM, Structure from motion · Segmentation

1 Introduction

In recent years, high-throughput plant phenotyping earned momentum, focusing mainly on non-invasive image-based techniques [17,21,39,40]. Several of these phenotyping efforts rely on some sort of 3D digitizing for the characterization of shoots or roots [12], a useful snapshot of the plant macroscopic state at a precise moment. If the 3D model presents an appropriate sampling of the plant surface at a convenient resolution, different measurements can be performed, such as leaf area, leaf angle and plant topology. Even biomass could be estimated

Electronic supplementary material The online version of this chapter (doi:10.1007/978-3-319-16220-1_18) contains supplementary material, which is available to authorized users.

© Springer International Publishing Switzerland 2015
L. Agapito et al. (Eds.): ECCV 2014 Workshops, Part IV, LNCS 8928, pp. 247–263, 2015.
DOI: 10.1007/978-3-319-16220-1_18

using regression methods. Although phenotypes cannot be fully characterized, 3D models are a multipurpose representation: a batch of models produced for leaf area measurements, for example, could be reused in a further study interested in leaf orientation or plant morphology, considering that germplasm and experimental setting data is also available.

A 3D model is also useful for automation. If a robotic device has to interact with a plant, for sensing, pruning or tissue sampling, knowledge about the 3D structure of the plant and the relative pose of the device is essential [2]. For the automation of sensing methodologies such as thermal imaging or chlorophyll fluorescence, pose information can meet requirements regarding sensor orientation relative to the leaf surface.

A system employing 3D modeling for plant phenotyping has to address at least two steps. In the *localization and mapping* step, the sensors' poses must be defined or recovered and the scene 3D model has to be computed. Further, in the *understanding* step, the plant must be detected, its parts segmented and classified, and measurements must be performed.

The present work approaches the first step employing a hand-held, free moving camera. Plant phenotyping systems described in literature use a set of few fixed cameras and a motorized turning table under the specimen to capture images from different poses [34,48]. Those *fixed-camera-moving-plants* approaches are suitable for automation, but present issues regarding occlusion. Alternatively, a *fixed-plant-moving-camera* approach can address occlusions for plants of different species, sizes and development stages. It is also convenient for low-cost phenotyping solutions, since digital cameras are affordable and ubiquitous. A structure from motion (SfM) framework is employed: visual local features in video frames are detected in the plant surface and in surrounding objects, matched across frames and used to recover the camera pose and the 3D location using projective geometry and robust estimation techniques [20]. Once the camera's poses are defined, multiple-view stereo can be used to get a sampling for the plant's surface with greater resolution.

This work also presents alternatives for two parts of the understanding step: segmentation of plants' parts and surface estimation. After segmentation, the surface of each part is estimated by fitting trimmed B-splines to the segment's 3D points. For measurements such as leaf area, a proper surface representation is more adequate than a set of irregularly-spaced points.

2   Related Work

The first attempts to perform 3D digitizing for plants employed mechanical devices [25], sonic digitizers [47] or magnetic trackers [38]. These contact methods were important on the development of functional-structural models for plant development [19], but are unable to scale for high-throughput phenotyping. Current phenotyping initiatives generally rely on contactless methods such as laser scanning using LiDAR devices [9,10], Time-of-Flight (ToF) cameras [1,50] or stereo vision [6,34,44,48].

Kaminuma *et al.* [24] employed a laser range finder for building three-dimentional models for *Arabidopsis thaliana*. Leaves and petioles were represented as polygonal meshes. The meshes were used to quantitatively determine two morphological attributes: the direction of the leaf blade and leaf epinasty, in order to characterize two different ecotypes. The setting was able to produce a good sampling for surfaces: the distance and the sample size allowed a resolution of 0.045 mm per pixel, producing a dense 3D points cloud. However, different plants presenting larger dimensions, or even *Arabidopsis* specimens in more advanced stages of development, could produce a sparse set of points.

The work of Ivanov *et al.* [23] is possibly the first work in the literature using stereo vision to reconstruct the 3D surface of a plant for measurement and analysis. The authors estimated the position, orientation and area of maize leaves (*Zea mays L.*). Unfortunately, the difficulties imposed by the equipment available at the time (digital photography was not yet widespread) undermined the experiments. The segmentation of the leaves and determination of correspondences between images were performed manually, using photographic enlargements. Despite the limitations, this work was the forerunner of more recent systems, which employ more up-to-date advances in computing performance, digital imaging and computer vision. Biskup *et al.* [6] developed a stereo vision system based on two digital cameras to create three-dimensional models of soybean plants foliage, aiming to analyze the angle of inclination of leaves and their movement throughout the day. Given the importance of movement for the experiment, the system was able to process up to three images per second, recovering the needed 3D information for slope computation.

Depth data from ToF cameras can be fused to RGB data from common cameras to produce 3D reconstructions for leaves, despite the low resolution of ToF devices. Song *et al.* [50] fused data from a stereo RGB camera pair (480×1280 pixels) and a ToF camera (64×48 pixels) using the graph-cut energy minimization approach [7]. The stereo pair provided a higher resolution while the ToF information addressed disparity failures caused by occlusion and matching on textureless areas. Alenyà *et al.* [1] employed a simpler fusion approach: the 3D points from ToF data were transformed to the coordinates of the RGB camera reference frame, and then projected to the camera image plane - color points not having a 3D counterpart were discarded. Although simple, this approach was able to produce good results because (i) the employed ToF camera presents a greater resolution (200×200) and (ii) a robotic arm could move the cameras to new positions and acquire more data, under the *sensing-for-action* method proposed by the authors.

Under the stereo vision framework, a camera from the stereo pair can be replaced by a projector. The same ray intersection principle can be applied if the projector position and intrinsics are known and the pixel correspondences can be found. Bellasio *et al.* [5] used a calibrated camera-projector pair and a coded-light method to find pixel correspondences, recovering the 3D surface of pepper plant leaves. Chéné *et al.* [8] employed a RGB-D camera (a Microsoft Kinect device) to segment leaves and estimate their orientation and inclination. These

RGB-D devices are camera-projector triangulation-based systems assembled in a single device, also using coded-light to infer pixel correspondences [16].

Recently, multiple-view stereo (MVS) has been applied on plant digitizing to address the occlusion problems found in 3D plant reconstruction. Paproki *et al.* [35] employed the 3D S.O.M. software [3] to create 3D models for cotton plants and then estimate stem heights, leaf widths and leaf lengths. The cotton specimens were placed in a rotating tray presenting a calibration pattern used by the 3D S.O.M. software to estimate the camera relative position at each frame.

Santos and Oliveira [44] employed the structure from motion (SfM) framework [20] to recover the camera calibration data. SfM extends the stereo vision framework incorporating a step that simultaneously look for the best estimation for camera positions *and* 3D point locations. This process, called *bundle-adjustment* [20,51], is a global maximum-likelihood estimation process that evaluates all the multiple-views at the same time, minimizing the re-projection error for each view. Instead of using a calibration pattern, the authors employed a local feature detection and matching approach combined to bundle-adjustment to recover the camera parameters, as proposed by Snavely *et al.* [49] in the context of city architecture 3D modeling. This camera data and the initial sparse point cloud was employed as input for the patch-based MVS (PMVS) algorithm [18], which produced dense point clouds that represent the surface of leaves and internodes in experiments with basil, *Ixora* [44] and mint [43].

Sirault *et al.* [48] also reported 3D reconstruction results using the PMVS system. In their work, the calibration data came from a setting using fixed cameras and potted plants placed in a very precise turntable (2.5 million counts per revolution). Their digitizing platform, PlantScan^{TM}, is a chamber equipped with three RGB CCD cameras, a NIR camera and two LiDAR laser scanners, plus two termobolometer sensors that collect thermal information. Their stereo reconstruction fuses PMVS, voxel coloring [26] and LiDAR data using registration algorithms (RANSAC [13] and ICP [41]). The authors report their platform is able to digitize plants from a few centimeters up to two meters height and up to a meter thick, enabling the phenotyping of a broad range of different species.

Fixed camera settings can be cursed by occlusion problems. In contrast, a free-moving camera has more flexibility on getting images from different poses, adapting the acquisition to different plant architectures and sizes. A calibration artifact [3] could be used to provide the landmarks needed to camera localization. However, considering the diversity of plant architectures and sizes, the use of such artifacts would impose hard constraints in the camera acquisition, since they must be visible in every image. The present work relies on visual local features observed on the plant surface (and on objects nearby) to provide the landmarks for camera localization. A chessboard pattern is used just to normalize the scale and orientation of the final 3D model, and there is no need to observe such pattern in every image.

3   Method

The methodology starts with a computer-aided image acquisition step that helps the user on getting a set of images suitable for 3D reconstruction (Section 3.1). The images (video frames) and the local features acquired are employed in a localization and mapping step performed under the structure from motion framework, determining the camera parameters for each image and an initial 3D model for the scene (Section 3.2). A multiple-view stereo step takes the images and camera parameters for each pose to produce a dense 3D point cloud sampling the plant's surface (Section 3.3). Clustering is used to segment the point cloud, isolating the individual leaves, and then B-spline interpolation is employed to approximate the surface of each leaf (Section 3.4).

3.1   Computer-Aided Image Acquisition

A phenotyping setting employing a free moving camera is able to get poses that allow a better handling of occlusions and variations on plant size and morphology. The work of Alenyà *et al.* [1] illustrates this idea, showing how proper path-planning for a robotic arm can move the cameras to positions where occlusions can be easily solved (in their case, using ToF cameras and robot's positioning control).

In previous attempts on 3D plant modeling by SfM [43,44], hundreds of photographies were taken and used as input. This image capturing procedure was executed by human operators that spent up to 30 minutes on this acquisition step. Furthermore, the operator could discover some images out of focus or lacking local features, or even situations in which the wide-baseline between images produced poor feature matching, making the scene reconstruction impossible.

The aim of the proposed system for computer-aided image acquisition is to help the user to quickly produce an image set suitable for SfM-based 3D reconstruction using a video camera. This image set should present feature-rich images and good feature correspondence between them. Video streams produce thousands of frames in a few minutes, so the method automatically selects frames, ensuring a reasonable number of feature correspondences between the selected ones. There is a short-baseline/wide-baseline trade-off: too short baselines between successive frames would produce an enormous image set. However, too wide baselines would produce poor feature matching due to plant auto-similarity. Algorithm F describes the procedure.

Algorithm F (*Frame Selection*). This procedure produces a sequence of *keyframes* $\mathbf{K} = \langle K_1, K_2, \ldots K_n \rangle$ such that there is a proper local features matching between any pair of successive frames K_i and K_{i+1}. A feature matching is considered proper if (i) at least 10% of the found local features in K_{i+1} were properly matched to features in K_i and (ii) the estimated fundamental matrix F can properly map 70% of the matched features (inliers rate).

F1. [*Initialize.*] At the initialization, grab the first keyframe, K_1. Consider to select a frame presenting a large number of features.

F2. [*Frame process.*] Grab an input frame F. Detect local features using SURF [4] and compute their descriptors. Consider to use a GPU based implementation of SURF to ensure processing at the frame-rate.

F3. [*Feature matching to the last keyframe*]. Match the feature descriptors found in frame F to the ones in the last keyframe K_n, using the Lowe's criteria (see [28] and Section 3.2). Set r_{match} to the ratio of successfully matched features.

F4. [*Compute fundamental matrix.*] Compute the fundamental matrix $\mathbf{F}$ using RANSAC for robustness (see [20]). Set r_{in} to the ratio of inliers, i.e. the ratio of the points consistent to $\mathbf{F}^1$.

F5. [*Frame selection.*] If $r_{\text{match}} > 0.1$ and $r_{\text{in}} > 0.7$, then $F_{\text{last}} \leftarrow F$. Otherwise, if $F_{\text{last}} \neq \text{NIL}$, push F_{last} into $\mathbf{K}$ and set $F_{\text{last}} \leftarrow \text{NIL}$. Return to step F2. ∎

F_{last} is the last frame (i) presenting a good matching to the last keyframe (the test in step F5) and (ii) that is not yet a keyframe ($F_{\text{last}} \notin \mathbf{K}$). If the current frame F does not present a proper matching to the last keyframe and $F_{\text{last}} = \text{NIL}$, then the system is in *lost state*. The system will present the last keyframe to the user, who have to move the camera to new positions until a new grabbed frame F presents a good matching, turning the system back to a *tracking state*. The user can drop keyframes from $\mathbf{K}$, in an attempt to help on seeking a new frame that put the system in the tracking state again. Figure 1 (c) shows the acquisition user interface.

3.2   Visual Odometry

Visual odometry is the process of estimating the ego-motion of an agent [45], in this case a single hand-held camera. As the present work is concerned about 3D reconstruction of plants, global map consistency regarding the camera poses and the object is essential, so such an odometry is a simultaneous localization and mapping (SLAM) problem. The local features act as landmarks for the localization step, recovering the relative pose between two frames. The mapping step is performed registering the features in the current map, thus defining the absolute pose of the current frame. Global consistency can be enforced by bundle adjustment [20,51].

Windowed Feature Matching. As the local features are employed as landmarks, their positions in different frames have to be found. In the SfM framework [20], the feature correspondences between two frames K and K' allow a robust estimation of the fundamental matrix $\mathbf{F}$. Furthermore, $\mathbf{F}$ is used on the computation of the relative pose, in the form of two projection matrices $\mathbf{P}$ and $\mathbf{P}'$.

---

[1] $\mathbf{F}$ maps a point $\mathbf{x}$ in frame K to an *epipolar line* $\mathbf{l}' = \mathbf{Fx}$ in frame K'. A pair $\mathbf{x}, \mathbf{x}'$ is consistent to $\mathbf{F}$ iif the distance between $\mathbf{x}'$ and the line $\mathbf{l}$ is under a defined threshold. See [20] for details.

(a)   (b)

(c)

Fig. 1. Computer-aided image acquisition for structure from motion. (a) User freely moves a camera around the specimen, getting images from different poses to solve occlusions. (b) The employed machine-vision camera and a pattern used to recover the scale, essential to further metrology. (c) The acquisition system interface aids the user.

The local feature matching is performed using the stored SURF local features and their descriptors computed in the acquisition step, as presented in Algorithm F, step F2. The employed matching criteria is the one presented by Lowe [28]. For a feature descriptor f in K, its two nearest neighbors f'_1 and f'_2 are found in K', presenting Euclidean distances d_1 and d_2 respectively. A match (f, f'_1) is declared if $\frac{d_1}{d_2} < 0.6$ and if there is no other feature in K that matches f'_1 in K'.

For fast nearest neighbors searches, a KDTree is employed. Unfortunately, KDTree performance degenerates for large dimensions. Using PCA, the original SURF descriptors, which are 64-element vectors, are transformed into shorter vectors of dimension 16. Such dimensionality reduction did not degenerate the feature matching: just a few matches are lost if compared to the original 64-D descriptor space.

As discussed previously in Section 3.1, auto-similarity in plants can produce spurious matches between features from different frames in the wide-baseline case. Instead of looking for matches for each possible pair of frames, a *windowed matching* is employed: for each frame F_i, the matching is performed relative to frames $\langle F_{i-m}, ..., F_{i-2}, F_{i-1} \rangle$. An example of feature matching between two near frames is shown in Figure 2.

557 matches between K_{67} and K_{69}

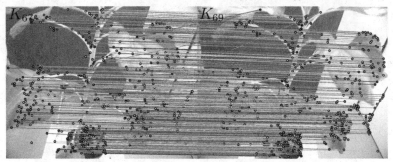

Fig. 2. Local feature matching between two keyframes K_{67} and K_{69} from the keyframes sequence produced for a sunflower specimen using Algorithm F. Local feature matching is performed using Lowe's method [28]. The robust RANSAC procedure can estimate the fundamental matrix F, considering wrong matches as outliers.

SfM. Considering the chain formed by the matches, $(f, f'), (f', f''), \ldots$, it is possible to define feature *tracks*. The localization and mapping procedure is performed by the SfM system called *Bundler*, developed by Snavely *et al.* [49]. At each step, Bundler selects the pose that observes the largest number of tracks whose 3D locations have already been estimated. This pose's extrinsic parameters are estimated by the direct linear transform (DLT) described by Hartley and Zisserman [20] under a RANSAC procedure for robustness. New 3D points are added to the map by triangulating the matching features between the new pose and the previous ones. After each pose estimation step, Bundler performs a bundle adjustment optimization, using the SBA package by Lourakis and Argyros [27].

Bundler's standard procedure employs David Lowe's SIFT implementation [28] for feature detection and matching. Matching is performed for *every combination of two frames*, and the intrinsic and extrinsic parameters for each pose are estimated. In this work, this procedure is modified: the windowed matching using SURF features is employed, and the intrinsic parameters are set to fixed values. If a pair of nearby frames (i.e., in a same window) presents less than 128 matches, it will not be considered for extrinsic parameters computation, since it could produce a poor estimation. In relation to the intrinsic parameters, Bundler was designed for SfM using pictures from different consumer cameras. In this work, the same fixed focus camera is moved around the plant, so the intrinsic parameters are the same for every camera pose.

In the experiments, Bundler produced some spurious camera poses. These wrong poses can affect the subsequent multiple-view stereo step, when a dense 3D model is computed. Fortunately, those wrong poses are detached from the right camera path. DBSCAN clustering [11] is employed to group camera locations in tracks. This clustering algorithm is able to group elongated clusters of points together, making it suitable to identify a long camera track and isolate spurious poses forming short tracks. Spurious camera positions and the 3D points triangulated from them are removed and a final bundle adjustment is performed for the remaining poses and points. The adjusted poses and the set of frames are then used as the input for the multiple-view stereo step.

Fig. 3. Structure from motion results for the *sunflower* sequence. The red and light green squares show the camera position for each input frame. The scene mapping is produced incrementally by the triangulation of the local features found, using the recovered pose information. Even in this sparse map, it is possible to see the plant's leaves, internodes and its pot.

3.3   Multiple-View Stereo

Camera poses retrieved in the previous step can be used by a multiple-view stereo (MVS) method to produce a dense 3D model. The method used here is the patch-based MVS (PMVS) proposed by Furukawa and Ponce [18]. This method produces a set of *surfels*, oriented 3D patches that cover a small area of an object surface (the surfel orientation should correspond to the surface normal vector). PMVS is composed by matching and expanding steps that create new patches and estimate their surface orientation while enforcing local photometric consistency, and a filtering step that removes erroneous patches, enforcing visibility consistency (exploring the camera poses and the patches projections). This point cloud (or surfels cloud) is used in the next step for segmentation.

Object Segmentation. No screen or shield was employed to form a standard background behind the plant during image acquisition. Such shields could constrain the user movement around the specimen. Furthermore, features identified on other objects in the scene actually help the SfM step, providing information from different depths that improves the pose estimation. However, after the 3D reconstruction, it is necessary to identify what elements of the point cloud that correspond to the objects of interest: the plant, its pot and the reference pattern (employed in a further step for scale correction). Again, DBSCAN clustering provides a proper solution: the objects of interest form a dense and possibly elongated cluster in the scene. Because the camera is always pointing to the plant, the objects of interest form the densest and largest cluster in the point cloud.

Scale Correction. To recover a proper scale for measurements and to place the model in a standard orientation, a chessboard-like pattern was inserted in the scene, near the plant. Two nearby frames where the pattern is visible are randomly selected. Eight reference points on the planar pattern are manually marked in each frame (Figure 4) and used to estimate a homography matrix H [20]. This matrix is able to transform points on the pattern plane in frame K to their corresponding ones in frame K'. The matrix H is used to find the points $\mathbf{x}'_i$ in K' corresponding to points $\mathbf{x}_i$ on the pattern in image K, ensuring the pairs $\mathbf{x}_i \leftrightarrow \mathbf{x}'_i$ are on the *same plane* in the scene. This is important because the method is relying on the 3D location of such reference points to properly align the model to a standard coordinate frame in millimeter scale.

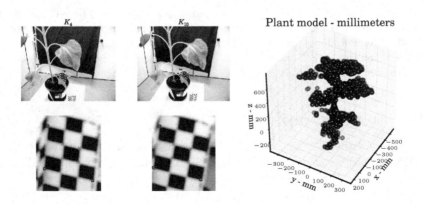

Fig. 4. Changing the model scale and orientation. Eight points on the pattern were marked in frames K_4 and K_{10}. The estimated homography ensures the points are in the same plane in both images. Three points (shown as circles) are used to define a new scale and orientation for the model. After the transformation (right image), measurements in the model can be performed in millimeters.

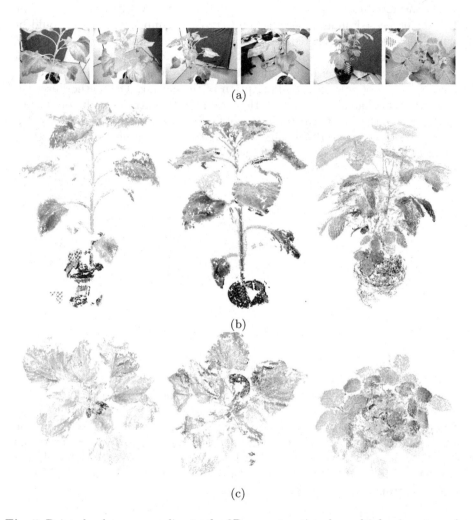

Fig. 5. Point clouds corresponding to the 3D reconstructions by multiple-view stereo for *sunflower* (left and middle) and *soybean* (right). (a) Examples of input frames, 1280 × 1024 pixels images captured by a machine vision camera (XIMEA model MQ013MG-E2). (b) 3D models: a 65,145 points model for the *sunflower/first take* data (left), a 48,974 points model for the *sunflower/second take* data (middle), and a 167,382 points model for the *soybean* data (right). (c) 3D models (top view). Point clouds are available in the supplementary material set as Stanford Triangle Format files – PLY.

3.4   Plant Segmentation

Segmentation is not just an essential part of the plant model analysis, but it can also be considered the *first* step. Once segmented and classified, each part can be further processed under a specific context. For example, internodes could be modeled by generalized cylinders and leaves by curve fitting.

The point cloud produced by the MVS step is segmented by *spectral clustering* [29,33,46]. Spectral clustering is a suitable option to problems where the centers and spreads are not an adequate description of the cluster. The method uses the top eigenvectors of an affinity matrix. Here, an affinity matrix is built computing, for each point in the cloud, the similarity to its 20 nearest neighbors (based on the Euclidean distance between the points' 3D locations). Examples of the clustering results can be seen in Figure 6 and Figure 7.

Fig. 6. Spectral segmentation for the *sunflower* model. Left: side view. Right: top view.

Surface Estimation. For each leaf point cloud, a surface is estimated using non-uniform rational B-splines (NURBS) [37]. As the leaf surface presents two main orientations, the B-spline surface is initialized using PCA to define such principal directions, adding few control points. In a refinement phase, new control points are added. Further, the surface is trimmed by a B-spline curve that encloses the points as proposed by Flóry and Hofer [14]. The entire procedure is described by Mörwald [30] in the Point Cloud Library documentation. Figure 7 shows some results for *soybean-leaves*.

4   Data and Results

Frame acquisition was performed using a XIMEA machine vision camera (model MQ013MG-E2) equiped with a EV76C560 sensor (resolution of 1280×1024 pixels), and 6 mm fixed focal length lenses (Fujinon model DF6HA-1B). Acquisitions were performed for a sunflower specimen (two takes), forming the *sunflower* dataset, and for a soybean specimen: a take covering the entire plant, the *soybean* dataset, and a second take, closing in a few leaves, the *soybean-leaves* dataset.

During the acquisition step, local feature detection, description and matching were performed using the GPU SURF implementation available in the OpenCV library (version 2.4). Structure from motion was performed using Bundler, version 0.4 [49] and multiple-view stereo using PMVS, version 2 [18]. DBSCAN and spectral clustering were performed using scikit-learn [36], version 0.14, and NURBS fitting using the Point Cloud Library (PCL) [42], version 1.7. All data (images, recovered camera poses, 3D models and segmentation) is publicly available[2]. The 3D models can be found in the supplementary material, as files in the Stanford Triangle Format (PLY)[3].

Figure 5 shows the 3D reconstructions for *sunflower* and *soybean*. Each plant presents height larger than 50 cm and, for each keyframe, just a part of the plant is visible. This contrasts with the small plant scenario found in previous works [43, 44], where the entire plant could be focused and placed in the camera field of view. The visual features detected in the plant surface were sufficient to recover the camera pose and map the entire specimen. Thin structures as the soybean internodes could be properly reconstructed (see supplementary data for a detailed view). The complexity and density of the soybean shoot demonstrates the advantages of a free-moving camera approach.

Figures 6 and 7 show the segmentation results. The graph-cuts performed by the spectral clustering are able to isolate the leaves, being effective for both soybean and sunflower plants. However, spectral clustering needs the desired number of segments be previously defined.

The 167,392 points model in Figure 5 and the 62,677 points model in Figure 7 correspond to the same soybean plant. Approximating the camera to the leaves produced a denser and more detailed 3D reconstruction. This means closer acquisitions could produce denser models for the full plants, however this would make the acquisition step longer and more tiresome for human operators.

Fig. 7. Leaf 3D modeling, segmentation and surface estimation using NURBS for the *soybean-leaves* dataset. Left: a 62,677 points model created by moving the camera near a set of 9 leaves in the sunflower specimen. Middle: segmented model. Right: trimmed NURBS surfaces.

---

[2] https://www.agropediabrasilis.cnptia.embrapa.br/web/plantscan/datasets
[3] PLY files can be visualized and manipulated using the open-source software Meshlab available at http://meshlab.sourceforge.net.

5 Conclusions

A single hand-held, free-moving camera can be used to create accurate three dimensional models for plants by using state-of-the-art structure from motion and multiple-view stereo techniques. This methodology is suitable for automatized plant phenotyping facilities or small laboratories with restricted resources.

The presented SfM methodology relies on local features detected in the plant surface acting as visual landmarks. Unfortunately, the lack of visual features in some plants can make camera localization unfeasible. Experiments with maize specimens, presenting almost featureless surfaces, were unsuccessful. Structured light approaches, that create "artificial features" using light patterns[4], or ToF cameras [15] would be more appropriated in those cases. For smaller plants, visual markers could be employed [3].

Better feedback could be provided in the acquisition step if real-time reconstruction was performed. Such information would let the user to evaluate model completeness and resolution level, allowing proper camera posing. Real-time reconstruction systems for RGB [32] and RGB-D [22,31] sensors are promising alternatives in this direction.

Systems based on monocular SfM, LiDAR, RGB-D and ToF cameras are providing lots of data and moving the computer vision field to the next step: the analysis of 3D point clouds for automatic scene understanding. This is also true for plant models, because phenotyping pipelines need to make sense of such 3D data for phenomic characterization. Automated segmentation, classification and metrology of each plant part are current research issues.

Acknowledgements. This work was supported by Brazilian Agricultural Research Corporation (Embrapa) under grants 03.11.07.007.00.00 (PLANTSCAN) and 05.12.12.00 1.00.02 (PHENOCORN). We would like to thank Katia de Lima Nechet (Embrapa Environment) for her support providing plant specimens.

References

1. Alenya, G., Dellen, B., Torras, C.: 3D modelling of leaves from color and ToF data for robotized plant measuring. In: 2011 IEEE International Conference on Robotics and Automation, pp. 3408–3414, May 2011
2. Alenya, G., Dellen, B., Foix, S., Torras, C.: Robotized Plant Probing: Leaf Segmentation Utilizing Time-of-Flight Data. IEEE Robotics & Automation Magazine **20**(3), 50–59 (2013)
3. Baumberg, A., Lyons, A., Taylor, R.: 3D S.O.M.A commercial software solution to 3D scanning. Graphical Models **67**(6), 476–495 (2005)
4. Bay, H., Ess, A., Tuytelaars, T., Van Gool, L.: Speeded-Up Robust Features (SURF). Computer Vision and Image Understanding **110**(3), 346–359 (2008)
5. Bellasio, C., Olejníčková, J., Tesa, R., Sebela, D., Nedbal, L.: Computer reconstruction of plant growth and chlorophyll fluorescence emission in three spatial dimensions. Sensors (Basel, Switzerland) **12**(1), 1052–1071 (2012)

---

[4] This is the method behind RGB-D devices as the Microsoft Kinect.

6. Biskup, B., Scharr, H., Schurr, U., Rascher, U.: A stereo imaging system for measuring structural parameters of plant canopies. Plant, Cell & Environment **30**(10), 1299–1308 (2007)
7. Boykov, Y., Veksler, O., Zabih, R.: Fast approximate energy minimization via graph cuts. IEEE Transactions on Pattern Analysis and Machine Intelligence **23**(11), 1222–1239 (2001)
8. Chéné, Y., Rousseau, D., Lucidarme, P., Bertheloot, J., Caffier, V., Morel, P., Belin, E., Chapeau-Blondeau, F.: On the use of depth camera for 3D phenotyping of entire plants. Computers and Electronics in Agriculture **82**, 122–127 (2012)
9. Dassot, M., Colin, A., Santenoise, P., Fournier, M., Constant, T.: Terrestrial laser scanning for measuring the solid wood volume, including branches, of adult standing trees in the forest environment. Computers and Electronics in Agriculture **89**, 86–93 (2012)
10. Delagrange, S., Rochon, P.: Reconstruction and analysis of a deciduous sapling using digital photographs or terrestrial-LiDAR technology. Annals of Botany **108**(6), 991–1000 (2011)
11. Ester, M., Kriegel, H.P., Sander, J., Xu, X.: A density-based algorithm for discovering clusters in large spatial databases with noise. In: KDD, vol. 96, pp. 226–231 (1996)
12. Fiorani, F., Schurr, U.: Future scenarios for plant phenotyping. Annual Review of Plant Biology **64**, 267–291 (2013)
13. Fischler, M.A., Bolles, R.C.: Random sample consensus: a paradigm for model fitting with applications to image analysis and automated cartography. Communications of the ACM **24**(6), 381–395 (1981)
14. Flöry, S., Hofer, M.: Constrained curve fitting on manifolds. Computer-Aided Design **40**(1), 25–34 (2008)
15. Foix, S., Alenya, G., Torras, C.: Lock-in Time-of-Flight (ToF) Cameras: A Survey. IEEE Sensors Journal **11**(9), 1917–1926 (2011)
16. Freedman, B., Shpunt, A., Machline, M., Arieli, Y.: Depth mapping using projected patterns. US Patent 8,493,496, July 23, 2013
17. Furbank, R.T., Tester, M.: Phenomics-technologies to relieve the phenotyping bottleneck. Trends in Plant Science **16**(12), 635–644 (2011)
18. Furukawa, Y., Ponce, J.: Accurate, dense, and robust multiview stereopsis. IEEE Transactions on Pattern Analysis and Machine Intelligence **32**(8), 1362–1376 (2010)
19. Godin, C., Costes, E., Sinoquet, H.: A Method for Describing Plant Architecture which Integrates Topology and Geometry. Annals of Botany **84**(3), 343–357 (1999)
20. Hartley, R., Zisserman, A.: Multiple View Geometry in Computer Vision, 2nd edn. Cambridge University Press, April 2004
21. van der Heijden, G., Song, Y., Horgan, G., Polder, G., Dieleman, A., Bink, M., Palloix, A., van Eeuwijk, F., Glasbey, C.: SPICY: towards automated phenotyping of large pepper plants in the greenhouse. Functional Plant Biology **39**(11), 870 (2012)
22. Henry, P., Krainin, M., Herbst, E., Ren, X., Fox, D.: RGB-D mapping: Using Kinect-style depth cameras for dense 3D modeling of indoor environments. The International Journal of Robotics Research **31**(5), 647–663 (2012)
23. Ivanov, N., Boissard, P., Chapron, M., Andrieu, B.: Computer stereo plotting for 3-D reconstruction of a maize canopy. Agricultural and Forest Meteorology **75**(1–3), 85–102 (1995)

24. Kaminuma, E., Heida, N., Tsumoto, Y., Yamamoto, N., Goto, N., Okamoto, N., Konagaya, A., Matsui, M., Toyoda, T.: Automatic quantification of morphological traits via three-dimensional measurement of Arabidopsis. The Plant Journal **38**(2), 358–365 (2004)
25. Lang, A.: Leaf orientation of a cotton plant. Agricultural Meteorology **11**(c), 37–51 (1973)
26. Leung, C., Appleton, B., Buckley, M., Sun, C.: Embedded voxel colouring with adaptive threshold selection using globally minimal surfaces. International Journal of Computer Vision **99**(2), 215–231 (2012)
27. Lourakis, M.I.A., Argyros, A.A.: SBA: A software package for generic sparse bundle adjustment. ACM Transactions on Mathematical Software **36**(1), 1–30 (2009)
28. Lowe, D.G.: Distinctive Image Features from Scale-Invariant Keypoints. International Journal of Computer Vision **60**(2), 91–110 (2004)
29. Luxburg, U.: A tutorial on spectral clustering. Statistics and Computing **17**(4), 395–416 (2007)
30. Mörwald, T.: Fitting trimmed B-splines to unordered point clouds. http://pointclouds.org/documentation/tutorials/bspline_fitting.php
31. Newcombe, R.a., Davison, A.J., Izadi, S., Kohli, P., Hilliges, O., Shotton, J., Molyneaux, D., Hodges, S., Kim, D., Fitzgibbon, A.: KinectFusion: Real-time dense surface mapping and tracking. In: 2011 10th IEEE International Symposium on Mixed and Augmented Reality, pp. 127–136. IEEE, October 2011
32. Newcombe, R.A., Lovegrove, S.J., Davison, A.J.: DTAM: dense tracking and mapping in real-time. In: 2011 International Conference on Computer Vision, pp. 2320–2327, November 2011
33. Ng, A., Jordan, M., Weiss, Y.: On spectral clustering: Analysis and an algorithm. Advances in neural information ... (2002)
34. Paproki, A., Fripp, J., Salvado, O., Sirault, X., Berry, S., Furbank, R.: Automated 3D segmentation and analysis of cotton plants. In: 2011 International Conference on Digital Image Computing: Techniques and Applications, pp. 555–560, December 2011
35. Paproki, A., Sirault, X., Berry, S., Furbank, R., Fripp, J.: A novel mesh processing based technique for 3D plant analysis. BMC Plant Biology **12**, 63 (2012)
36. Pedregosa, F., Varoquaux, G., Gramfort, A., Michel, V., Thirion, B., Grisel, O., Blondel, M., Prettenhofer, P., Weiss, R., Dubourg, V., Vanderplas, J., Passos, A., Cournapeau, D., Brucher, M., Perrot, M., Duchesnay, E.: Scikit-learn: Machine learning in Python. Journal of Machine Learning Research **12**, 2825–2830 (2011)
37. Piegl, L., Tiller, W.: The NURBS Book. Monographs in Visual Communication, U.S. Government Printing Office (1997)
38. Rakocevic, M., Sinoquet, H., Christophe, A., Varlet-Grancher, C.: Assessing the Geometric Structure of a White Clover (Trifolium repens L.) Canopy using3-D Digitising. Annals of Botany **86**(3), 519–526 (2000)
39. Rascher, U., Blossfeld, S., Fiorani, F., Jahnke, S., Jansen, M., Kuhn, A.J., Matsubara, S., Märtin, L.L.A., Merchant, A., Metzner, R., Müller-Linow, M., Nagel, K.A., Pieruschka, R., Pinto, F., Schreiber, C.M., Temperton, V.M., Thorpe, M.R., Dusschoten, D.V., Van Volkenburgh, E., Windt, C.W., Schurr, U.: Non-invasive approaches for phenotyping of enhanced performance traits in bean. Functional Plant Biology **38**(12), 968 (2011)

40. Reuzeau, C., Frankard, V., Hatzfeld, Y., Sanz, A., Camp, W.V., Lejeune, P., Wilde, C.D., Lievens, K., de Wolf, J., Vranken, E., Peerbolte, R., Broekaert, W.: Traitmill^{TM}: a functional genomics platform for the phenotypic analysis of cereals. Plant Genetic Resources 4(01), 20–24 (2006)
41. Rusinkiewicz, S., Levoy, M.: Efficient variants of the ICP algorithm. In: Proceedings Third International Conference on 3-D Digital Imaging and Modeling, pp. 145–152 (2001)
42. Rusu, R.B., Cousins, S.: 3D is here: point cloud library (PCL). In: IEEE International Conference on Robotics and Automation (ICRA), Shanghai, China, May 9–13 (2011)
43. Santos, T., Ueda, J.: Automatic 3D plant reconstruction from photographies, segmentation and classification of leaves and internodes using clustering 1. In: Sievänen, R., Nikinmaa, E., Godin, C., Anna Lintunen, P.N. (eds.) Proceedings of the 7th International Conference on Functional-Structural Plant Models, Saariselkä, Finland, pp. 95–97 (2013)
44. Santos, T.T., de Oliveira, A.A.: Image-based 3D digitizing for plant architecture analysis and phenotyping. In: Saúde, A.V., Guimarães, S.J.F. (eds.) Workshop on Industry Applications (WGARI) in SIBGRAPI 2012 (XXV Conference on Graphics, Patterns and Images). Ouro Preto (2012)
45. Scaramuzza, D., Fraundorfer, F.: Visual Odometry [Tutorial]. IEEE Robotics & Automation Magazine 18(4), 80–92 (2011)
46. Shi, J., Malik, J.: Normalized cuts and image segmentation. IEEE Transactions on Pattern Analysis and Machine Intelligence 22(8), 888–905 (2000)
47. Sinoquet, H., Moulia, B., Bonhomme, R.: Estimating the three-dimensional geometry of a maize crop as an input of radiation models: comparison between three-dimensional digitizing and plant profiles. Agricultural and Forest Meteorology 55(3–4), 233–249 (1991)
48. Sirault, X., Fripp, J., Paproki, A., Kuffner, P., Nguyen, C., Li, R., Daily, H., Guo, J., Furbank, R.: PlantScan: a three-dimensional phenotyping platform for capturing the structural dynamic of plant development and growth. In: Proceedings of the 7th International Conference on FunctionalStructural Plant Models, Saariselkä, Finland, pp. 45–48 (2013)
49. Snavely, N., Seitz, S., Szeliski, R.: Modeling the World from Internet Photo Collections. International Journal of Computer Vision 80(2), 189–210 (2008)
50. Song, Y., Glasbey, C.A., van der Heijden, G.W.A.M., Polder, G., Dieleman, J.A.: Combining stereo and time-of-flight images with application to automatic plant phenotyping. In: Heyden, A., Kahl, F. (eds.) SCIA 2011. LNCS, vol. 6688, pp. 467–478. Springer, Heidelberg (2011)
51. Triggs, B., McLauchlan, P.F., Hartley, R.I., Fitzgibbon, A.W.: Bundle adjustment – a modern synthesis. In: Triggs, B., Zisserman, A., Szeliski, R. (eds.) ICCV-WS 1999. LNCS, vol. 1883, p. 298. Springer, Heidelberg (2000)

W26 - Non-Rigid Shape Analysis and Deformable Image Alignment

Characterization of Partial Intrinsic Symmetries

Aurela Shehu[1,2]([⊠]), Alan Brunton[3], Stefanie Wuhrer[1], and Michael Wand[4]

[1] Cluster of Excellence MMCI, Saarland University, Saarbrücken, Germany
ashehu@mmci.uni-saarland.de
[2] Saarbrücken Graduate School of Computer Science, Saarbrücken, Germany
[3] Fraunhofer Institute for Computer Graphics Research IGD, Darmstadt, Germany
[4] Utrecht University, Utrecht, The Netherlands

Abstract. We present a mathematical framework and algorithm for characterizing and extracting partial intrinsic symmetries of surfaces, which is a fundamental building block for many modern geometry processing algorithms. Our goal is to compute all "significant" symmetry information of the shape, which we define as r-symmetries, i.e., we report all isometric self-maps within subsets of the shape that contain at least an intrinsic circle or radius r. By specifying r, the user has direct control over the scale at which symmetry should be detected. Unlike previous techniques, we do not rely on feature points, voting or probabilistic schemes. Rather than that, we bound computational efforts by splitting our algorithm into two phases. The first detects infinitesimal r-symmetries directly using a local differential analysis, and the second performs direct matching for the remaining discrete symmetries. We show that our algorithm can successfully characterize and extract intrinsic symmetries from a number of example shapes.

Keywords: Symmetry · Shape analysis · Shape matching · Intrinsic geometry · Slippability analysis

1 Introduction

Shape symmetry is beneficial for many applications such as shape segmentation, geometry completion, beautification, shape synthesis, scan denoising and shape matching. A symmetry, or symmetric mapping of a shape, refers to a self-mapping that does not alter the geometry of the shape. *Extrinsic geometry* refers to properties of the shape, which depend on the coordinate space in which the shape is embedded. *Intrinsic geometry* refers to properties that can be measured on the surface, which are invariant to the embedding.

To detect extrinsic symmetries, i.e. self-mappings that do not alter the extrinsic geometry of the shape, one looks for rigid transformations, which map the shape to itself. However, in many applications we are interested in shapes that deform non-rigidly such that the surface does not tear or stretch significantly, such as locomotion of humans and animals, or folding of cloth. The symmetries present in such shapes in general cannot be detected extrinsically due to

© Springer International Publishing Switzerland 2015
L. Agapito et al. (Eds.): ECCV 2014 Workshops, Part IV, LNCS 8928, pp. 267–282, 2015.
DOI: 10.1007/978-3-319-16220-1_19

asymmetry of the embedding. We can circumvent this problem by considering intrinsic geometry, which is invariant to isometric deformations. A self-mapping that does not alter the intrinsic geometry describes an *intrinsic symmetry*.

We can further distinguish between global and partial symmetries. A *global intrinsic symmetry* maps the entire shape to itself, whereas a *partial intrinsic symmetry* maps a part of the shape to another part of the shape, in a way that does not alter the intrinsic geometry of the part. In this work, we address the problem of detecting and characterizing partial intrinsic symmetries on a given shape. Shapes can be symmetric at various scales, and the desired symmetry scale may be application dependent. To model this, we use a symmetry scale r. For every geodesic disk of radius r on the shape, we aim to find whether there is a mapping of the disk on the shape, which does not induce any (significant) stretching. We call such a mapping an intrinsic r-symmetry.

The goal of our work is to report all r-symmetries, i.e., all mappings of large enough subsets of the shape to itself that are perfect isometries. The key challenge is that the space of partial intrinsic symmetries might be too large to systematically explore and report [24], [28]. Following Brunton et al. [6], we define partial correspondences by sets that are mapped with preservation of the local metric. Unlike Xu et al. [28], we do not require that the shortest geodesic paths to be maintained outside the mapped region, which leads to a much higher combinatorial complexity due to the global dependency on topology and boundaries of the subsets. In contrast, metric-preserving maps can be parametrized by only five degrees of freedom (two out of which do not even need fine sampling) [6], which makes an approximate enumeration of all isometries feasible in polynomial time. Our paper follows this idea but factors out infinitesimal symmetries, which dominate the run-time otherwise, and uses local descriptors to further narrow down the search.

Most methods that detect partial discrete intrinsic symmetries try to reduce the search space by computing features on the shape and further detect partial intrinsic symmetries in the feature space. While this approach reduces the complexity of the problem, it might miss some intrinsic r-symmetries. Further, existing methods have focused on either detecting partial infinitesimal symmetries [8], [26] or partial discrete symmetries [24], [28], [22], [13], [4], [12], [18], [23], [9], [15] but not both.

In contrast, we propose a method that finds discrete intrinsic r-symmetries and characterizes infinitesimal intrinsic r-symmetries of a shape in an efficient way. The search space is reduced by a mathematical analysis on infinitesimal r-symmetries, assuring that no information is thrown away, but simultaneously making the computations feasible. To our knowledge, this is the first method which provides a full characterization of intrinsic r-symmetries of a shape.

We provide a characterization of both infinitesimal and discrete partial pointwise intrinsic symmetries on 3D shapes, and present an algorithm for detecting such symmetries. Given as input a 3D shape and a radius r, our method tests first each point for infinitesimal r-symmetry and then for the ones with no infinitesimal r-symmetry it tests them for discrete r-symmetry since now we can enumerate the finite discrete r-symmetries. As a last step, for all the points that belong to discrete r-symmetries we compute approximate equivalence classes. We evaluate our method on a standard symmetry dataset.

1.1   Definitions and Problem Statement

We consider a shape to be a smooth, orientable 2-manifold $\mathcal{M} \subset \mathbb{R}^3$ embedded in three-dimensional space, and denote the tangent space of $\mathcal{M}$ at point $\mathbf{s} \in \mathcal{M}$ by $T_\mathbf{s}\mathcal{M}$. In practice, $\mathcal{M}$ is discretized by a set of points that are connected by a neighborhood graph. We denote the geodesic distance between two points $\mathbf{s}, \mathbf{t} \in \mathcal{M}$ by $d_\mathcal{M}(\mathbf{s}, \mathbf{t})$.

Definition 1. *The points $\mathbf{s}$ and $\mathbf{t}$ on $\mathcal{M}$ are called r-symmetric if there is a mapping function $f : \mathcal{U} \to \mathcal{M}$, where $\mathcal{U}$ is the geodesic disk of radius r centered at $\mathbf{s}$, with $f(\mathbf{s}) = \mathbf{t}$ such that for all point pairs $(\mathbf{x}_i, \mathbf{x}_j) \in \mathcal{U}$, it is*

$$|d_\mathcal{M}(\mathbf{x}_i, \mathbf{x}_j) - d_\mathcal{M}(f(\mathbf{x}_i), f(\mathbf{x}_j))| = 0. \tag{1}$$

Note that, for small enough r, $d_\mathcal{U}(\mathbf{x}_i, \mathbf{x}_j) = d_\mathcal{M}(\mathbf{x}_i, \mathbf{x}_j)$ as $\mathcal{U}$ is convex.

Consider mapping functions of the type $f : \mathcal{M} \to \mathcal{M}$. If Equation (1) is satisfied under such a mapping, then $\mathbf{s}$ and $\mathbf{t}$ define a *global intrinsic symmetry*. We consider *partial intrinsic symmetries* with mapping functions of the type $f : \mathcal{U} \to \mathcal{M}$, where parts are defined as geodesic neighborhoods of points with fixed radius. The set of r-symmetric points form an equivalence relation.

We have guarantees only for exact symmetries and as these occur rarely in practice, we relax the symmetry condition by allowing for a stretching up to a fixed threshold ϵ.

Definition 2. *The points $\mathbf{s}$ and $\mathbf{t}$ are called (ϵ, r)-symmetric if there is a mapping function $f : \mathcal{U} \to \mathcal{M}$ with $f(\mathbf{s}) = \mathbf{t}$ such that for all point pairs $(\mathbf{x}_i, \mathbf{x}_j) \in \mathcal{U}$, it is*

$$|d_\mathcal{M}(\mathbf{x}_i, \mathbf{x}_j) - d_\mathcal{M}(f(\mathbf{x}_i), f(\mathbf{x}_j))| \leq \epsilon. \tag{2}$$

The set of (ϵ, r)-symmetric points no longer form an equivalence relation.

When the mapping f encodes infinitesimal movements of points x_i in $\mathcal{U}$ and Equations (1) or (2) are satisfied, then $\mathbf{s}$ and $\mathbf{t}$ define an *infinitesimal (ϵ, r)-symmetry*. Note that in the literature, infinitesimal symmetries are often also called continuous symmetries because the isometries involved form a continuous set.

When the mapping f encodes movements by fixed geodesic distances of points x_i in $\mathcal{U}$ and Equations (1) or (2) are satisfied, then $\mathbf{s}$ and $\mathbf{t}$ define a *discrete (ϵ, r)-symmetry*. The reason for the term discrete is that the set of discrete global symmetries form a discrete set.

1.2   Overview

We now give a coarse outline of our algorithm for detecting intrinsic (ϵ, r)-symmetries. We start by detecting and factoring out all (possibly infinitely many)

Fig. 1. Illustrative example. Left to right: size of r, point slippability, symmetry-factored embedding distance from a corner of the cube.

infinitesimal (ϵ, r)-symmetries. We adapt methods that find infinitesimal symmetries in the extrinsic case [7], [10] to our scenario. Once the infinitesimal symmetries are factored out (e.g. leaving the white regions in Fig. 1, middle), there remain only a finite, and often manageable, number of discrete (ϵ, r)-symmetries. To extract these we use the fact that point-wise (ϵ, r)-symmetries arise from an ϵ-approximate isometric mapping (correspondence) between two regions $\mathcal{U}$ and $f(\mathcal{U})$, as defined in (2). Isometric mappings have a low number of degrees of freedom, which has been recently used to develop a direct region growing method for partial isometric correspondence [6]. We exploit this method, initialized with a sampling strategy based on spectral descriptors, to find the discrete symmetries. These steps are shown as illustration for a cube in Fig. 1, and explained in detail in the subsequent sections.

2   Related Work

There is a considerable amount of research on detecting extrinsic symmetry on 3D shapes and for an overview, we refer the reader to the survey from Mitra et al. [16]. Here we focus on research on detecting intrinsic symmetry.

To compute infinitesimal intrinsic symmetries, Ben Chen et al. [3] propose a method to compute approximate Killing vector fields on triangle meshes, which are tangent vector fields on the surface that generate isometric transformations. There are two methods that allow for the computation of partial infinitesimal symmetries. Solomon et al. [26] partition the shape into intrinsically symmetric building blocks and can be thought of as an extension of the method by Ben Chen et al. [3] to the partial case. While this method allows to "untangle" the global information into parts, it does not allow the detection of symmetries on a specific scale. Grushko et al. [8] find infinitesimal symmetries as the ones that lead to small stress of the generalized multi-dimensional scaling (MDS) energy [5]. It requires as input the target location of one point as boundary condition. Our method to detect infinitesimal partial symmetries can be seen as similar in spirit, but more general. We can find all directions by which a sample can move by an infinitesimal amount while its geodesic neighborhood stays symmetric, without the need for an initial target point location.

To compute global discrete intrinsic symmetries, several methods based on isometric invariants have been proposed. Kim et al. [11] use the average geodesic function to find feature points and compute global discrete symmetries as Möbius transformations generated by these feature points. Possible symmetries generated by non-feature points will not be reported. Methods that use the Laplace-Beltrami operator embed the surface into a space where the global discrete symmetry detection has a reduced search space. Ovsjanikov et al. [21] reduce the space further by only considering non-repeating eigenvalues and by finding global intrinsic symmetries by transforming the problem to extrinsic symmetry detection in the embedding space. Ovsjanikov et al. [20] identify and factor out symmetries before finding correspondences between a pair of near isometric shapes and require a symmetry map on one shape from the user.

After detecting approximate global symmetries, it remains to recover the symmetry group from the approximate information. Lipman et al. [13] propose an embedding where symmetry is factored out to recover approximate cliques in the embedding space, which correspond to equivalence classes of symmetric points. Wang et al. [27] extend this approach by introducing an embedding where repeating eigenvalues of the Laplace-Beltrami operator are used to capture symmetry transformations. In this work, we modify the method of Lipman et al. to find approximately equivalent parts for visualization purposes.

As the complexity of the space of all partial symmetries is believed to be large [24], [28], existing methods proceed by reducing the search space after sampling the surface.

Some methods find partial discrete symmetries by minimizing a MDS energy. Raviv et al. [24] define as partial discrete symmetry a self-isometric part that minimizes the generalized MDS energy, and find symmetries by comparing pairs of samples that pass a pruning method. Raviv et al. [23] extend the previous approach by using a diffusion distance metric. Mitra et al. [15] detect intrinsically symmetric blocks on a given surface by flattening the surface using MDS, by solving the problem on the embedded image, and by projecting the computed patterns back to the original surface. This method is restricted to surfaces that are topologically equivalent to a plane.

Berner et al. [4] reduce the search space of possible partial discrete symmetries by using features. This method might miss possible symmetry candidates because of the feature selection. To overcome this problem, Lasowski et al. [12] find partial intrinsic symmetries by modeling a probability distribution over all possible correspondences. This method is sensitive to topological noise.

Partial discrete symmetries can alternatively be detected by a voting procedure. Xu et al. [28] decouple the problem into the two problems of symmetric point pair detection and symmetry scale detection. The specific difficulty of this method is the preservation of all shortest geodesic paths after a partial mapping to a larger context. This makes the solution space too large for a low-level, systematic exploration. Our model avoids this by removing these global guarantees for indirect effects due to geometry outside the region identified as symmetric. Mukhopadhyay et al. [18] detect overlapping intrinsically symmetric regions by a voting procedure of symmetric point pairs and characterize the computed symmetries. Jiang et al. [9] extend this type of voting procedure by coupling it with a robust skeleton extraction method. All of these methods require complex optimizations before the voting step, and are sensitive to topological noise.

Furthermore, in all of these methods, the scale(s) of the detected symmetries cannot be controlled by the user. Our method gives direct control of the scale of symmetry to be detected to the user.

To summarize, existing methods reduce the resulting search space, commonly using features, pruning, or voting techniques. In contrast, we observe that the space of all partial symmetries can be modeled explicitly as follows. There may be infinitely many infinitesimal partial symmetries, and points that have infinitesimal partial symmetries need to be detected and factored out to make partial symmetry detection feasible. Additionally, there may be finitely many discrete partial symmetries, each of which can be parameterized by a pair of point and tangent direction matches in a low-dimensional search space. This observation allows us to systematically detect infinitesimal and discrete partial symmetries in a way that is similar in spirit to work on detecting extrinsic partial symmetries for a micro-tile decomposition of a shape [10].

3   Infinitesimal r-Symmetry Detection

This section presents our approach to detect and characterize infinitesimal (ϵ, r)-symmetries.

3.1   Detecting r-Symmetries

We aim to find all directions $\mathbf{d}$, such that all points $\mathbf{x}_i \in \mathcal{U}$ can move by an infinitesimal amount in direction $\mathbf{d}$ without inducing any stretching. In contrast to the method of Ben-Chen et al. [3], we constraint the measured stretching to the shape part $\mathcal{U}$ instead of the entire shape. Here, $\mathbf{d} = [\delta_1^T \ \ldots \ \delta_n^T]^T$ is a vector of length $2n$ that defines how each point $\mathbf{x}_i$ moves in its local tangent plane $T_{\mathbf{x}_i}\mathcal{M}$. We extend the notation from works on extrinsic symmetry detection [7] and call the directions $\mathbf{d}$ r-slippage directions.

To find the r-slippage directions $\mathbf{d}$, we construct a matrix $\mathbf{A}$ that has all r-slippage directions as eigenvectors with corresponding eigenvalue zero. This can be seen as a direct extension of the extrinsic slippage analysis of Gelfand and Guibas [7] to the intrinsic case. The main challenge in extending the slippage analysis to the intrinsic case is that the degrees of freedom that control the movement a part $\mathcal{U}$ increases from 6 in the extrinsic case (3 for rotation, 3 for translation) to $2n$ in the intrinsic case, where n denotes the number of samples in $\mathcal{U}$ (2 to indicate the movement of each sample in its tangent plane).

We start by considering the stretching of a mapping $f : \mathcal{U} \rightarrow \mathcal{M}$. Given a uniform sampling of the manifold $\mathcal{M}$, the stretching is

$$E_{SD}(f) = \frac{1}{n^2} \sum_{i=1}^{n} \sum_{j=1}^{n} (d_{\mathcal{M}}(f(\mathbf{x}_i), f(\mathbf{x}_j)) - d_{\mathcal{M}}(\mathbf{x}_i, \mathbf{x}_j))^2, \tag{3}$$

where n is the number of samples in $\mathcal{U}$ and serves as an approximation of the area $A_{\mathcal{U}}$ of $\mathcal{U}$.

The energy expressed in Equation (3) is similar to the energy used in Generalized Multi-Dimensional Scaling (GMDS) [5]. GMDS tries to fit a surface $\mathcal{X}$ to a surface $\mathcal{Y}$ without distorting the intrinsic metric of $\mathcal{X}$. In our case, we try to fit the geodesic disk $\mathcal{U}$ to $f(\mathcal{U})$ without distorting the intrinsic metric of $\mathcal{U}$.

To find the r-slippage directions, we aim to minimize the energy given in Equation (3). Consider the identity mapping $f_0(\mathbf{x}) = \mathbf{x}$, $\mathbf{x} \in \mathcal{U}$. This mapping obviously minimizes $E_S(f_0) = 0$ and $E_{SD}(f_0) = 0$. Since f_0 minimizes E_{SD}, the gradient $\nabla_{f_0} E_{SD}(f)$ is zero as well. We write the gradient with respect to the mapping $f(\mathbf{x}_k)$ of a particular sample $\mathbf{x}_k$ as

$$\nabla_{f(\mathbf{x}_k)} E_{SD}(f) = \frac{\partial E_{SD}}{\partial f(\mathbf{x}_k)} = \frac{4}{n^2} \sum_{i=1}^{n} (d_{\mathcal{M}}(f(\mathbf{x}_k), f(\mathbf{x}_i)) - d_{\mathcal{M}}(\mathbf{x}_k, \mathbf{x}_i)) \nabla_k \mathbf{p}_{ik}, \qquad (4)$$

with $\nabla_k \mathbf{p}_{ik} = \frac{\partial}{\partial f(\mathbf{x}_k)} (d_{\mathcal{M}}(f(\mathbf{x}_i), f(\mathbf{x}_k)))$, which, from the Eikonal equation, is a unit-vector in $T_{f(\mathbf{x}_k)} \mathcal{M}$.

Consider updating f_0 by an infinitesimal amount in direction $\mathbf{d}$. We are interested in finding directions $\mathbf{d}$, such that the mapping $f_0 + \mathbf{d}$ has a gradient of zero, which means $\nabla_{f(\mathbf{x}_k)} E_{SD}(f_0 + \mathbf{d}) = 0$.

The second derivative of E_{SD} with respect to the mapping f gives the rate of change of the first derivative under the mapping. Let $\mathbf{A}$ denote the second-order derivative matrix of f_0 that contains the block matrices

$$\mathbf{A}_{ki} = \nabla_{f(\mathbf{x}_k)} \nabla_{f(\mathbf{x}_i)} E_{SD}(f_0)$$
$$\mathbf{A}_{kk} = \nabla_{f(\mathbf{x}_k)} \nabla_{f(\mathbf{x}_k)} E_{SD}(f_0). \qquad (5)$$

For small $\mathbf{d}$, we can find the r-slippage directions $\mathbf{d}$ of $\mathcal{U}$ as the eigenvectors of $\mathbf{A}$ with corresponding eigenvalues zero, which means vectors $\mathbf{d}$ with

$$\nabla_{f(\mathbf{x}_k)} E_{SD}(f_0 + \mathbf{d}) \approx \mathbf{A}\mathbf{d} = \mathbf{0}. \qquad (6)$$

The matrix $\mathbf{A}$ is symmetric, which implies that all its eigenvalues are real.

It remains to compute the second derivatives of E_{SD} with respect to the mapping. Taking the derivative of $\nabla_{f(\mathbf{x}_k)} E_{SD}(f)$ with respect to $f(\mathbf{x}_k)$ we get

$$\nabla_{f(\mathbf{x}_k)} \nabla_{f(\mathbf{x}_k)} E_{SD}(f) = \frac{4}{n^2} \sum_{i=1}^{n} \left(\nabla_k \mathbf{p}_{ik} \nabla_k \mathbf{p}_{ik}^T + (d_{\mathcal{M}}(f(\mathbf{x}_k), f(\mathbf{x}_i)) - d_{\mathcal{M}}(\mathbf{x}_k, \mathbf{x}_i)) \nabla_k \nabla_k \mathbf{p}_{ik}^T \right).$$
$$(7)$$

Taking the derivative of $\nabla_{f(\mathbf{x}_k)} E_{SD}(f)$ with respect to $f(\mathbf{x}_i)$, $i \neq k$, we get

$$\nabla_{f(\mathbf{x}_k)} \nabla_{f(\mathbf{x}_i)} E_{SD}(f) = \frac{4}{n^2} \left(\nabla_i \mathbf{p}_{ik} \nabla_k \mathbf{p}_{ik}^T + (d_{\mathcal{M}}(f(\mathbf{x}_k), f(\mathbf{x}_i)) - d_{\mathcal{M}}(\mathbf{x}_k, \mathbf{x}_i)) \nabla_i \nabla_k \mathbf{p}_{ik}^T \right). \qquad (8)$$

In the following, we make the assumption that $\mathcal{M}$ is approximated locally by its tangent planes, which causes the second order derivative terms $\nabla_k \nabla_k \mathbf{p}_{ik}$ and $\nabla_i \nabla_k \mathbf{p}_{ik}$ in Equations (7) and (8) to vanish and lead to the following simplified derivatives

$$\nabla_{f(\mathbf{x}_k)} \nabla_{f(\mathbf{x}_k)} E_{SD}(f) = \frac{4}{n^2} \sum_{i=1}^{n} \nabla_k \mathbf{p}_{ik} \nabla_k \mathbf{p}_{ik}^T$$
$$\nabla_{f(\mathbf{x}_k)} \nabla_{f(\mathbf{x}_i)} E_{SD}(f) = \frac{4}{n^2} \nabla_i \mathbf{p}_{ik} \nabla_k \mathbf{p}_{ik}^T. \qquad (9)$$

3.2 Detecting (ϵ, r)-Symmetries

We now aim to compute all directions, by which a sample **s** can move by an infinitesimal amount while staying (ϵ, r)-symmetric. We call these directions (ϵ, r)-*slippage directions* in the following.

From the previous section (Equation (6)) we know that for $\epsilon = 0$, the r-slippage directions can be found by finding all eigenvectors **d** of the second derivative matrix **A** of f_0 with associated eigenvalues zero. In this section, we show that the (ϵ, r)-slippage directions of **s** can be found by finding all eigenvectors **d** of the second derivative matrix **A** of f_0 with associated eigenvalues λ with $|\lambda| \leq (\frac{2}{n^2}\epsilon^2)$. Note that there is no derivation of an upper bound in previous work related to slippage analysis [7].

In practice, we are not looking for the null space of A, but we consider all eigenvectors **d** with associated eigenvalues λ with $|\lambda|$ at most some threshold to be (ϵ, r)-slippage directions.

By integrating both sides of Equation 6, and using that the eigenvector **d** of **A** has at most unit length, we obtain

$$\int_{\mathbf{x}=0}^{\mathbf{d}} \nabla_{f(\mathbf{x}_k)} E_{SD}(f_0 + \mathbf{x})dx = \int_{\mathbf{x}=0}^{\mathbf{d}} \mathbf{A}\mathbf{x}dx$$

$$E_{SD}(f_0 + \mathbf{d}) \leq \frac{1}{2}|\lambda| \tag{10}$$

Hence, using Equation 3, we can obtain the following loose upper bound on any individual stretch $|d_{\mathcal{M}}(\mathbf{x}_i + \delta_i, \mathbf{x}_j + \delta_j) - d_{\mathcal{M}}(\mathbf{x}_i, \mathbf{x}_j)| \leq \frac{n}{\sqrt{2}}\sqrt{|\lambda|}, \forall i, j$, where δ_i is the part of the offset vector **d** in the tangent space of $\mathbf{x}_i$. This implies that by finding all eigenvectors **d** of **A** with associated eigenvalues λ with $|\lambda| \leq (\frac{2}{n^2}\epsilon^2)$, we can find the (ϵ, r)-slippage directions.

3.3 Characterization of Samples

With the results from the previous section, we can find all linearly independent (ϵ, r)-slippage directions for a sample **s** on $\mathcal{M}$. It is known that $\mathcal{M}$ can have at most three linearly independent (global) slippage directions [25]. Hence, we can characterize the sample **s** according to how many linearly independent (ϵ, r)-slippage directions **s** has. In the following, we call **s** t-*slippable* for $t = 0, 1, 2, 3$ if **s** has t linearly independent (ϵ, r)-slippage directions. Furthermore, we call **s** *slippable* if it has at least one (ϵ, r)-slippage direction, and *non-slippable* otherwise. Consider the illustrative example of a cube shown in the middle of Fig. 1, where white is 0-slippable, red 1-slippable, green 2-slippable and blue 3-slippable. A disk of radius r is shown in blue in the left of Fig. 1. As shown, a cube is 3-slippable almost everywhere except at the corners, where it is 0-slippable.

4 Discrete r-Symmetry Detection

In the previous section we presented our approach to detect infinitesimal (ϵ, r)-symmetries. In the following, we can factor out slippable points from further analysis, thereby reducing the search space for discrete discrete (ϵ, r)-symmetries to all oriented matches of only the non-slippable points.

4.1   Discrete r-Symmetries by Isometric Region Growing

To test if two points have a discrete (ϵ, r)-symmetry, we use the method proposed by Brunton et al. [6]. Based on the observation that a map of a single point pair and its tangent space is sufficient to recover an isometry, they propose a low-dimensional representation to efficiently compute a mapping $f : \mathcal{V} \to \mathcal{M}$ that minimizes the stretch given in Equation (3). Here, $\mathcal{V}$ is grown to the largest possible size that allows a mapping with metric stretching at most ϵ.

From a conceptual point of view, detecting all discrete (ϵ, r)-symmetries would involve trying all possible point pairs with all possible direction alignments, and to check if the tangent spaces are related by an isometry up to a threshold ϵ. As suggested by Brunton et al. [6], one may compute features in order to reduce the search space. However, feature detection methods may miss certain symmetries. To reduce this risk, we sample a subset of the surface points that are left after removing all slippable points, and we test all pairs of samples.

To reduce the search space, we do not test point pairs that are close-by in terms of geodesic distance for symmetry. Furthermore, we prune the remaining point pairs and directions using an isometry-invariant shape descriptor. We choose the state of the art Wave Kernel Signature (WKS) [2] as descriptor, and disregard point pairs whose WKS do not agree up to a threshold τ. Computing the WKS globally over the entire surface is not consistent with our partial symmetry model. To remedy this, we compute the WKS over the geodesic r-neighborhood $\mathcal{U}$ of a point. This step is to speed up on exact data, i.e. shapes that contain exact isometric parts. In this case, all r-symmetries will be discovered but the method will try not to investigate the least promising ones.

For every point pair that passed the point pruning step, we proceed by pruning the direction pairs. Direction pairs pruning is done with the help of a descriptor, which we call *Wave Kernel Map* (WKM) in the following and is defined based on the wave kernel signature [2] in a similar way that the heat kernel map is defined based on the heat kernel signature [19]. Given that the wave kernel signature is defined as $\mathrm{WKS}_e(\mathbf{x}, \mathbf{x}) = C_e \sum_k \phi_k^2(\mathbf{x}) e^{-\frac{(e - \log E_k)^2}{2\sigma}}$, we define the wave kernel map as

$$\mathrm{WKM}_e(\mathbf{x}, \mathbf{y}) = C_e \sum_k \phi_k(\mathbf{x}) \phi_k(\mathbf{y}) e^{-\frac{(e - \log E_k)^2}{2\sigma}}. \tag{11}$$

Let $\mathbf{s}, \mathbf{t} \in \mathcal{M}$ be a point pair which passed the point pruning step, where $\mathcal{U}$ is a geodesic disk centered at $\mathbf{s}$, $f(\mathcal{U})$ is the corresponding patch of $\mathcal{U}$ under the mapping function f and $f(\mathbf{s}) = \mathbf{t}$. For all $\mathbf{x} \in \mathcal{U}$ we compute $\mathrm{WKM}_e(\mathbf{s}, \mathbf{x})$ and for all $\mathbf{y} \in f(\mathcal{U})$ we compute $\mathrm{WKM}_e(\mathbf{t}, \mathbf{y})$. Let $\mathbf{s}_{max}$ and $\mathbf{t}_{max}$ be

$$\mathbf{s}_{max} = \max_x \mathrm{WKM}_e(\mathbf{s}, \mathbf{x})$$

$$\mathbf{t}_{max} = \max_y \mathrm{WKM}_e(\mathbf{t}, \mathbf{y}). \tag{12}$$

We consider as direction pairs the union of the direction matches dir_s based on s_{max} and the direction matches dir_t based on t_{max} where

$$\text{dir}_s = \{(s_{max}, t_{\text{dir}}) | t_{\text{dir}} : |\text{WKM}_e(t, t_{\text{dir}}) - \text{WKM}_e(s, s_{max})| \leq \tau_d\}$$
$$\text{dir}_t = \{(t_{max}, s_{\text{dir}}) | s_{\text{dir}} : |\text{WKM}_e(s, s_{\text{dir}}) - \text{WKM}_e(t, t_{max})| \leq \tau_d\} \tag{13}$$

and where τ_d is a direction pair threshold. These point pairs are used to encode the direction pairs from the point pair s, t. By disregarding all other possible direction matches, we can eliminate alignments that are not near-isometric.

After pruning the point and direction pairs, we use the method proposed by Brunton et al. [6] for each pair of points plus directions to find a mapping $f : \mathcal{V} \rightarrow \mathcal{M}$ that is isometric up to threshold ϵ. From this output, we can detect all points that are (ϵ, r)-symmetric by reporting every point $s \in \mathcal{V}$ whose geodesic r-neighborhood $\mathcal{U}$ is entirely contained in $\mathcal{V}$ along with its corresponding point t and vice versa.

4.2 Approximate Equivalence Classes

Finally, we would like to detect classes of equivalent points under (ϵ, r)-symmetries. In the case of exact data, we look for r-symmetries ($\epsilon = 0$) and this step is not necessary since we can directly find exact equivalence classes. Considering $\epsilon > 0$, this problem is ill-posed as the set of all (ϵ, r)-symmetries do not form equivalence classes in general. However, since we assume that a threshold of ϵ is only required to counteract noise, there is an underlying equivalence class. To find this, we detect fuzzy equivalence classes of (ϵ, r)-symmetries using an approach similar to the one proposed by Lipman et al. [13]. In this way, transition consistencies will be amplified and everything else diminished.

We use our detected discrete (ϵ, r)-symmetries to construct a dissimilarity matrix $\mathbf{S} \in \mathbb{R}^{n \times n}$ as

$$\mathbf{S}_{ij} = \min\{\min_{i'} d_{\mathcal{M}}(i, i'), \min_{j'} d_{\mathcal{M}}(j, j')\}, \tag{14}$$

where (i, j') and (j, i') define a discrete (ϵ, r)-symmetry and n is the number of samples on $\mathcal{M}$. We now can compute the symmetry correspondence matrix $\mathbf{C}$ as proposed by Lipman et al. [13] as $\tilde{\mathbf{C}}_{ij} = e^{-\left(\frac{S_{ij}}{\sigma \, diam}\right)^2}$, where $diam$ is twice the intrinsic radius of the manifold $\mathcal{M}$. The symmetry correspondence matrix is derived from $\tilde{\mathbf{C}}$ by making each row sum up to one. After applying eigendecomposition to the matrix $\mathbf{C}$, we compute the symmetry factored embedding by using the eigenvalues and the eigenvectors of $\mathbf{C}$.

To visualize the approximate equivalence classes, we compute the symmetry-factored embedding (SFE) distance as Euclidean distance in embedding space and color the points based on the distance, where blue is small and red is large. Consider again the illustrative example of a cube in Fig. 1. The right of Fig. 1 shows the SFE distance from one of the corners of the cube. All of the corners have a small SFE distance to each other, and are therefore colored blue. The farther away a point is from the corner, the more red is its color.

5 Experiments

We evaluate our method on a common intrinsic symmetry dataset that is available from Xu et al. [28]. Our method requires as input a uniformly sampled manifold mesh. Therefore, as a preprocessing step, we resample the meshes uniformly using ReMesh [1]. Since most models do not consist of a single mesh, we assemble them into a single manifold mesh. We simplify scale invariance for our algorithm by normalizing the surface area to $A_{\mathcal{M}} = 100$.

5.1 Implementation Details

In our implementation, we encode the tangent directions in an arbitrary but fixed coordinate system in $\mathbb{R}^3$. Hence, the matrix $\mathbf{A}$ used in Equation (6) has dimensionality $3n \times 3n$, and we encode $\nabla_i \mathbf{p}_{ik}$ and $\nabla_k \mathbf{p}_{ik}$ in $\mathbb{R}^3$. To prevent non-tangent directions to show up as (ϵ, r)-slippage directions, we add quadratic-constraints in the normal direction to the blocks of $\mathbf{A}$.

Both infinitesimal and discrete r−symmetry detection algorithms require geodesic distance information and we compute them as in Brunton et al. [6]. For efficiency, we detect symmetry on a subset of the vertices computed using Poisson disk sampling. The sample spacing s is fixed as $0.1r$ in our experiments.

In our experiments, the threshold used to characterize slippability is fixed to $0.03A_{\mathcal{M}}$ for $r = 0.1R$, where $R = \sqrt{A_{\mathcal{M}}/\pi}$ is the intrinsic radius of the surface. As r increases, we decrease the threshold quadratically to account for the change in area $A_{\mathcal{U}}$ (as in Fig. 2). Note that the threshold can be updated interactively.

Discrete symmetry characterization includes the computation of the wave kernel descriptor in order to prune out points which might not lead to symmetric parts. The parameters used for the wave kernel descriptor computations are $M = 100$ energy scales and number of eigenvalues equal to the rank of matrix being decomposed. To compute the discrete Laplace-Beltrami operator, the approach by Meyer et al. [14] is adopted resulting in a generalized eigenvalue problem which is solved with the Arnoldi method of ARPACK. To project original to subsampled mesh points, an approximate nearest neighbor search [17] is used.

5.2 Infinitesimal Symmetry

We color-code the slippability as follows: white is 0-slippable, red 1-slippable, green 2-slippable and blue 3-slippable. Fig. 2 shows the influence of r on point slippability. As expected, for larger r, points become less slippable.

Fig. 3 shows the influence of the threshold used to characterize slippability. As expected, for larger thresholds, points become more slippable. Note that for all thresholds, some points near the tips of all tentacles are found to be non-slippable, while the eyes are only classified as non-slippable for smaller thresholds. Consider for example a geodesic disk centered at a point between the octopus eyes. It can be thought of as topologically equivalent to a flat plane with two bumps. When big threshold is used then the stretching induced from the bumps is tolerated and therefore is evaluated by the method as a flat plane and colored hence blue. As we

Fig. 2. Each pair shows symmetry size and resulting slippability. From left to right: $r = 0.1R$, $0.2R$ and $0.3R$ with thresholds $0.03A_{\mathcal{M}}$, $0.0075A_{\mathcal{M}}$ and $0.0033A_{\mathcal{M}}$, respectively. Color scheme: white (0), red (1), green (2), blue (3).

decrease the threshold, the stretching is tolerated less and the eyes start getting colored white and characterized as non-slippable.

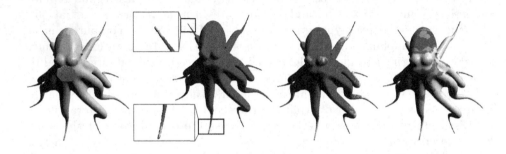

Fig. 3. Left to right: symmetry size r, point slippability for thresholds $0.03A_{\mathcal{M}}$, $0.003A_{\mathcal{M}}$ and $0.0003A_{\mathcal{M}}$. Color scheme: white (0), red (1), green (2), blue (3).

Fig. 4 shows infinitesimal symmetry detection results for different meshes for $r = 0.1R$. Note that symmetric parts receive the same color and that at this scale, very smooth surfaces only contain slippable points (see top left), while fine scale details of size below r result in 0-slippable points (see palm leaves).

5.3   Discrete Symmetry

We color-code the discrete symmetry results using the symmetry factored embedding distance from a marked point from blue (small distance) to red (large distance). For all of the following experiments, the symmetry radius is $r = 0.1R$, and the threshold for the infinitesimal symmetries is set to $0.03A_{\mathcal{M}}$. The thresholds used to prune point and direction pairs using the wave kernel descriptor were set manually per model to ensure that not too many point and direction matches are processed. We set the thresholds to $\tau = 1e - 3$ and $\tau_d = 1e - 3$ for the octopus model and to $\tau = 1e - 18$ and $\tau_d = 1e - 10$ for the ballet model.

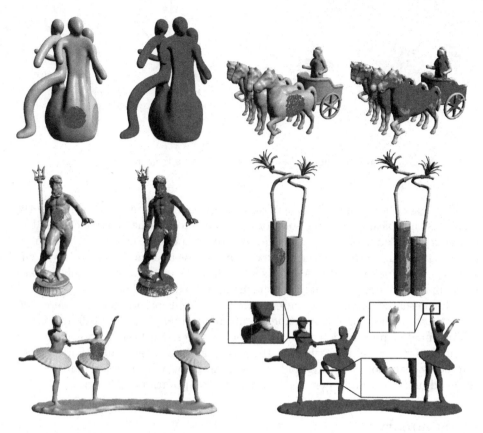

Fig. 4. For each model, left: symmetry size r, and right: point slippability. Color scheme: white (0), red (1), green (2), blue (3).

Fig. 5 shows the symmetry-factored embedding distance from the marked point on the octopus and the ballet models. For the octopus model, the non-slippable points are all near the tips of the tentacles, as shown in Fig. 3 (second from left). Note that for the discrete symmetry result, pairs of points close to the tips of all pairs of tentacles are correctly found to be (ϵ, r)-symmetric and hence, parts of all tentacle tips are shown in blue. For the ballet model, all dancer limbs that are not attached to other parts of the ballet model are found to be non-slippable, as shown in Fig. 4 (last row). Note that for the discrete symmetry result, pairs of points close to the tips of limbs that are not attached to other parts are correctly found to be (ϵ, r)-symmetric and shown in blue.

5.4   Discussion

Our method aims to detect partial infinitesimal and discrete symmetries and hence has different characteristics and applications than prior work that detects

Fig. 5. Symmetry factored embedding distances from marked points.

such symmetries globally [3], [20]. Considering partial symmetries significantly increases the space of possible solutions. We have found that intrinsic slippability is an ill-posed problem, and even more so than extrinsic slippability: Small perturbations in the intrinsic geometry do not cause a large change in the eigenvalues of the corresponding matrix of second derivatives. This in particular makes the slippability results strongly dependent on the threshold.

The presented algorithm requires a number of input parameters. We were able to fix most parameters for our experiments by normalizing the mesh areas. For infinitesimal symmetry detection, the slippage threshold needed to be adjusted manually for few models, which is supported at interactive rates. For discrete symmetry detection, the thresholds for pruning point and direction pairs needed to be adjusted manually per model to ensure computational efficiency.

6   Summary

For an orientable surface in $\mathbb{R}^3$, intrinsic r-symmetries are partial intrinsic symmetries: mappings of geodesic disks of radius r to other parts of the surface, which do not distort the intrinsic geometry of the disk. We have presented a method to extract discrete intrinsic (ϵ, r)-symmetries and characterize the infinitesimal intrinsic (ϵ, r)-symmetries of a shape. The algorithm is motivated by the observation that in the ideal case (no approximation), the set of symmetries can be exhaustively computed by direct sampling. Such symmetries are invariant to isometric deformations of the shape and topological changes such as contacts or holes, which are recognized as boundaries of partiality (see Fig. 5, right).

We have shown that our method can extract discrete intrinsic (ϵ, r)-symmetries and characterize infinitesimal (ϵ, r)-symmetries at each point on a standard symmetry dataset. We leave a large scale evaluation for future work.

Acknowledgments. We thank Tino Weinkauf for helpful discussions. This work has partially been funded by the Cluster of Excellence on *Multimodal Computing and Interaction* within the Excellence Initiative of the German Federal Government.

References

1. Attene, M., Falcidieno, B.: Remesh: An interactive environment to edit and repair triangle meshes. In: Shape Modeling and Applications (2006)
2. Aubry, M., Schlickewei, U., Cremers, D.: The wave kernel signature: A quantum mechanical approach to shape analysis. In: International Conference on Computer Vision Workshops (2011)
3. Ben-Chen, M., Butscher, A., Solomon, J., Guibas, L.: On discrete killing vector fields and patterns on surfaces. Computer Graphics Forum 25, 1701–1711 (2010)
4. Berner, A., Bokeloh, M., Wand, M., Schilling, A., Seidel, H.P.: Generalized intrinsic symmetry detection. Tech. rep, Max-Planck Institute for Informatics (2009)
5. Bronstein, A., Bronstein, M., Kimmel, R.: Numerical Geometry of Non-Rigid Shapes. Springer (2008)
6. Brunton, A., Wand, M., Wuhrer, S., Seidel, H.P., Weinkauf, T.: A low-dimensional representation for robust partial isometric correspondences computation. Graphical Models 76, 70–85 (2014)
7. Gelfand, N., Guibas, L.: Shape segmentation using local slippage analysis. In: Symposium on Geometry Processing (2004)
8. Grushko, C., Raviv, D., Kimmel, R.: Intrinsic local symmetries: A computational framework. In: Eurographics Workshop on 3D Object Retrieval (2012)
9. Jiang, W., Xu, K., Chang, Z.Q., Zhang, H.: Skeleton-based intrinsic symmetry detection on point clouds. Graphical Models 75, 177–188 (2013)
10. Kalojanov, J., Bokeloh, M., Wand, M., Guibas, L., Seidel, H.P., Slusallek, P.: Microtiles: Extracting building blocks from correspondences. In: Symposium on Geometry Processing (2012)
11. Kim, V.G., Lipman, Y., Chen, X., Funkhouser, T.: Möbius transformations for global intrinsic symmetry analysis. Computer Graphics Forum 29, 1689–1700 (2010)
12. Lasowski, R., Tevs, A., Seidel, H.P., Wand, M.: A probabilistic framework for partial intrinsic symmetries in geometric data. In: International Conference on Computer Vision (2009)
13. Lipman, Y., Chen, X., Daubechies, I., Funkhouser, T.A.: Symmetry factored embedding and distance. ACM Transactions on Graphics 29(103), 1–12 (2010)
14. Meyer, M., Desbrun, M., Schröder, P., Barr, A.H.: Mathematics and Visualization 3, chap. Discrete Differential-Geometry Operators for Triangulated 2-Manifolds. Springer (2002)
15. Mitra, N., Bronstein, A., Bronstein, M.: Intrinsic regularity detection in 3d geometry. In: European Conference on Computer Vision (2010)
16. Mitra, N., Pauly, M., Wand, M., Ceylan, D.: Symmetry in 3d geometry: Extraction and applications. In: Eurographics State of the Art Report (2012)
17. Mount, D., Arya, S.: ANN: A library for approximate nearest neighbor searching (2010). http://www.cs.umd.edu/mount/ANN/
18. Mukhopadhyay, A., Bhandarkar, S., Porikli, F.: Detection and characterization of intrinsic symmetry. Tech. rep., arXiv 1309.7472 (2013)
19. Ovsjanikov, M., Mérigot, Q., Mmoli, F., Guibas, L.: One point isometric matching with the heat kernel. Computer Graphics Forum 29, 1555–1564 (2010)
20. Ovsjanikov, M., Mrigot, Q., Patraucean, V., Guibas, L.: Shape matching via quotient spaces. Computer Graphics Forum 32, 1–11 (2013)
21. Ovsjanikov, M., Sun, J., Guibas, L.: Global intrinsic symmetries of shapes. In: Symposium on Geometry Processing (2008)

22. Raviv, D., Bronstein, A., Bronstein, M., Kimmel, R.: Symmetries of non-rigid shapes. In: International Conference on Computer Vision (2007)
23. Raviv, D., Bronstein, A., Bronstein, M., Kimmel, R.: Diffusion symmetries of non-rigid shapes. In: International Symposium on 3D Data Processing, Visualization and Transmission (2010)
24. Raviv, D., Bronstein, A., Bronstein, M., Kimmel, R.: Full and partial symmetries of non-rigid shapes. International Journal of Computer Vision **89**, 18–39 (2010)
25. Rinow, W.: Über Zusammenhänge zwischen der Differentialgeometrie im Großen und im Kleinen. Mathematische Zeitschrift **35**, 512–528 (1932)
26. Solomon, J., Ben-Chen, M., Butscher, A., Guibas, L.: Discovery of intrinsic primitives on triangle meshes. In: Eurographics (2011)
27. Wang, H., Simari, P., Su, Z., Zhang, H.: Spectral global intrinsic symmetry invariant functions. Graphics Interface (2014)
28. Xu, K., Zhang, H., Jiang, W., Dyer, R., Cheng, Z., Liu, L., Chen, B.: Multi-scale partial intrinsic symmetry detection. ACM Transactions on Graphics **31**(181), 1–11 (2012)

Supervised Descriptor Learning for Non-Rigid Shape Matching

Étienne Corman[1,2], Maks Ovsjanikov[1($\boxtimes$)], and Antonin Chambolle[2]

[1] LIX, École Polytechnique, Palaiseau, France
`maks@lix.polytechnique.fr`
[2] CMAP, École Polytechnique, CNRS, Palaiseau, France

Abstract. We present a novel method for computing correspondences
between pairs of non-rigid shapes. Unlike the majority of existing techniques that assume a deformation model, such as intrinsic isometries,
a priori and use a pre-defined set of point or part descriptors, we consider the problem of *learning* a correspondence model given a collection
of reference pairs with known mappings between them. Our formulation
is purely intrinsic and does not rely on a consistent parametrization or
spatial positions of vertices on the shapes. Instead, we consider the problem of finding the optimal set of descriptors that can be jointly used to
reproduce the given reference maps. We show how this problem can be
formalized and solved for efficiently by using the recently proposed functional maps framework. Moreover, we demonstrate how to extract the
functional subspaces that can be mapped reliably across shapes. This
gives us a way to not only obtain better functional correspondences, but
also to associate a confidence value to the different parts of the mappings.
We demonstrate the efficiency and usefulness of the proposedapproach
on a variety of challenging shape matching tasks.

Keywords: Shape matching · Correspondences · Feature learning

1 Introduction

Finding high quality correspondences is a key component in many tasks including statistical shape analysis [12], deformation transfer [30] and interpolation
(morphing) [16] among others. While a number of efficient techniques have been
proposed to address the problem of rigid alignment [32], the problem of general
non-rigid shape matching remains difficult.

Most existing methods for finding correspondences between non-rigid shapes
rely on an *a priori* deformation model, which specifies the space of "reasonable"
maps between shapes. Perhaps the most popular and widely used such model is
that of approximate intrinsic isometries [5,21], where the mapping is assumed
to preserve geodesic distances between all pairs of points on the shapes. A more
general possibility is to consider conformal deformations, which are only assumed
to preserve angles [17,19] or to parameterize the space of possible maps using

© Springer International Publishing Switzerland 2015
L. Agapito et al. (Eds.): ECCV 2014 Workshops, Part IV, LNCS 8928, pp. 283–298, 2015.
DOI: 10.1007/978-3-319-16220-1_20

a fixed deformation model [36]. Although these techniques can produce good results when the deformation satisfies the *a priori* model, they can fail badly as soon as even moderate deviations from the model are introduced. This is especially critical since many natural deformations, such as articulated motion of humans or animals are known to induce potentially significant geodesic distortion [27]. Incorporating the possibility for such distortion into a deformation model is challenging especially using a purely axiomatic (theoretical) approach.

Rather than trying to devise a theoretical deformation model capable of adapting to known deformations, several communities have tackled this challenge by using a data-driven approach, where the space of "reasonable" maps or deformations is learned from a set of examples, e.g. [8]. Since obtaining example deformations is often significantly easier than devising a unified theoretical deformation model, such an approach allows the resulting techniques to remain flexible yet efficient in the particular settings where they are applied.

Most data-driven approaches for devising a deformation model, however, rely heavily on a consistent parametrization of the deformation domain (e.g. on a fixed grid in Euclidean space), and perform statistical analysis on the positions of vertices of the shapes [4, 9–11]. When computing correspondences between pairs of surfaces in 3D, such parametrization is often unavailable and moreover, shapes can undergo severe deformations which are difficult to capture using purely extrinsic approaches.

In this paper, we propose a purely intrinsic method for exploiting prior correspondence information between pairs of shapes to find better correspondences between a reference shape and a new previously unseen instance. Rather than doing the learning over, e.g., the positions of the vertices on the shapes, we propose to find the optimal set of *point descriptors* that can be jointly used to reproduce the given reference maps. While such an optimization is, in general, very complicated, since even to evaluate how well the descriptors can reproduce a given map would require a full solution of the shape matching problem, we show how this problem can be formalized and solved for efficiently by using the recently proposed functional maps framework [22]. Moreover, we demonstrate how to extract the functional subspaces that can be mapped reliably across shapes. This gives us a way to not only obtain better functional correspondences, but also to associate a confidence value to the different parts of the mappings. Our approach is also quite general since it can be used as a preprocessing step of other methods using functional maps [3, 14, 24] in order to improve the quality of the results and help to handle difficult deformation. Note that in this paper we focus on the shape matching problem which is the most developed application of the functional maps.

1.1   Related Work

Non-rigid shape matching is a very-well developed area and its complete overview is beyond the scope of this paper (see, e.g., [6, 35] for recent surveys of this field). We therefore concentrate on the work directly related to ours, namely near-isometric shape matching with special emphasis on approaches that utilise prior knowledge for establishing correspondences between pairs of shapes.

The vast majority of techniques for non-rigid shape matching implicitly make use of a deformation model for finding correspondences between geometric shapes. Perhaps the most common model in the context of intrinsic (i.e., not relying on vertex positions and not assuming approximate alignment) approaches is approximate isometries, introduced by Bronstein et al. [5] and Mémoli [21]. This model has been used by a large number of methods, (e.g., [13,22,23,28,33] among many others) that all assume that the sought correspondences must approximately preserve pairwise geodesic distances. Another set of approaches is based on a more relaxed model, conformal mappings, used by, e.g., [17,19] where only angles are assumed to be preserved. Other techniques, such as the one used by Zhang et al. [36] explicitly deform a shape using a fixed deformation model to find correspondences between non-rigid shapes.

All of these approaches use a model given *a priori* to find correspondences, which can be problematic if the real deformations do not agree with the given model. Interestingly, it has recently been observed [27] that even articulated motion of humans can induce noticeable isometric distortion, which could explain some of the difficulties encountered by previously proposed techniques.

In contrast, other works have proposed to *learn* an appropriate deformation model from a set of examples, and then use this model for shape matching. Perhaps the best-known example of this approach are Active Shape and Active Appearance Models [8,9] and their variants (see, e.g., [11]) used widely in Computer Vision. In a similar vein, techniques in Statistical Shape Analysis [10] use the distribution of positions of pre-specified landmark points in 3D to learn a statistical deformation model over which inference can be made. Related techniques are commonly used in medical imaging and Morphometrics [4] and in Geometry Processing communities, e.g. [1,12] among many others. However, all of these methods assume the existence of a common domain over which learning can be made, and which most often is done using vertex coordinates of either landmark points or all points on a fixed reference shape. In the context of intrinsic shape matching, where shapes lack labeled landmark points and can undergo severe deformations, vertex coordinates are often not relevant, limiting the applicability of such techniques.

Rather than relying on vertex positions, recent methods have considered using derived properties such as point or triangle *descriptors* for learning. Thus, Kalogerakis et al. [15] and Van Kaick et al. [34] have proposed using a set example shape to train classifiers for part segmentation and labeling, which can then be used to establish part-level correspondences. Similarly, Chen et al. [7] explore the predictive power of various descriptors for detecting distinctive landmark (schelling) points identified by users. These methods, while similar to ours in learning on the level of descriptors do not, however, specifically address the shape matching problem.

Perhaps most closely related to ours are recent works by Litman et al. [20] and Rodolà et al. [26], where the authors use a set of examples to learn the most informative descriptors that are used directly in the context of shape matching. Our approach is fundamentally different, however, since rather than trying to identify descriptors that can distinguish different points, we propose to find the optimal *descriptor set* that can be used to *jointly produce the entire map across shapes*. We thus avoid the problem of obtaining *consistent* correspondences present in these approaches (and obtained during post-processing), since consistency is incorporated directly in the learning stage. Crucially, we use the recently proposed functional map representation [22] that allows us to formulate the learning problem purely intrinsically, while permitting to directly control and optimize for the influence of descriptors on the quality of the final map.

Goals. Given a collection of (training) shapes with known correspondences our goal is to identify the most informative descriptor set that can be used to solve the non-rigid shape matching problem on new (test) instances. Besides we want to learn where are the most stable correspondences.

2   Consistent Functional Maps

Our method is based on the functional map representation introduced in [22]. In this section, we give a brief overview of the representation and the method used in [22] to construct a functional map for a given pair of shapes.

While our method is general, throughout the paper we assume that all shapes are represented as triangle meshes, and all functions are expressed as vectors in the basis of the eigenfunctions of the Laplace-Beltrami operator. This basis needs to be computed beforehand on each shape. The objective is to output a uniquely defined functional map.

2.1   Functional Map Representation

The functional map representation is based on the observation that given two surfaces S_0 and S_i, a point-to-point map $T_i : S_i \rightarrow S_0$ induces a map between function spaces $C_i : L^2(S_0) \rightarrow L^2(S_i)$, where $L^2(S)$ is the set of square integrable functions defined on the surface S. The functional map C_i is defined by composition with T_i as $C_i f = f \circ T_i$. The operator C_i is a linear transformation and given a basis it can be represented as a matrix in the discrete setting. This matrix can be easily computed if the map T is known.

The basic method described in [22] approximates the functional map C_i using a set of linear constraints. The first type of constraints is given by a set of pairs of functions, which we refer to below as "probe functions", that are expected to be preserved by the deformation. The second is a regularization term coming from the deformation model. This leads to the least square problem:

$$X_i = \underset{C}{\arg\min} \, \|CG_0 - G_i\|_F^2 + \alpha \|C \odot W\|_F^2, \tag{1}$$

where $\|.\|_F$ denotes the Frobenius norm. The use and meaning of each term will be detailed in the following paragraphs.

Probe Functions. The probe functions can be represented by two matrices G_0 and G_i, where each pair of corresponding columns represents a pair of functions g_0, g_i such that $C_i g_0 \approx g_i$ is expected to hold for the unknown C_i. In practice we normalize the corresponding column so that each column has the same L^2 norm. Thus, the functional map should verify $C G_0 \approx G_i$. In the context of isometric matching the probe functions are given by classical descriptors, such as the HKS [31], or WKS [2].

Regularization. The existence of intrinsic symmetries can lead to an ambiguity between two equally good solutions. In general, the probe functions do not resolve the symmetry ambiguity, that is G_0 and G_i are composed only of symmetric functions. So, in addition to the probe function constraints, the authors of [22] have proposed a regularization using the assumption that the deformation is nearly isometric. This assumption is equivalent to the commutativity of C_i with the Laplace-Beltrami operator, namely $C_i \Delta_0 = \Delta_i C_i$. In the discrete setting the eigenfunctions of the Laplace-Beltrami operator are used as function basis. Thus, this equation can be written as $C_i \odot W = 0$ where "$\odot$" denotes the component-wise multiplication and the matrix W is defined by $W_{kl} = \lambda_k^i - \lambda_l^0$ with λ_k^i the kth eigenvalue of the Laplace-Beltrami operator on the surface S_i.

Uniqueness of the Solution. In practice the eigenvalues of the Laplace-Beltrami operator of two different shapes are always numerically different except for the zero eigenvalues. Thus, the only zero coefficient of W is $W_{1,1}$ which weights the coefficient $C_{1,1}$ of the functional map. Since the corresponding eigenfunctions are constant, $C_{1,1}$ maps the constant functions of $L^2(S_0)$ into the constant functions of $L^2(S_i)$. The coefficient $C_{1,1}$ should always be one. Therefore, since W is non zero everywhere, the solution of (1) is unique without any assumptions on G_0.

2.2   Main Challenge

In the original article [22] the probe functions are assumed to be given, so how to choose them was not discussed. As mentioned in introduction, this choice can already be challenging. For example in Figure 1a the smoothed Gaussian curvature computed on two different meshes provides a decent functional correspondence. At the same time, in Figure 1b the logarithm of the Gaussian curvature, while intrinsic in theory, does not result in a useful correspondence.

One option to identify the best descriptors would be to simply find the most stable probe functions in the example (training) set, by learning spectral descriptors [20] for example. However, some descriptors (e.g., the constant function) can be stable without at all being informative. More importantly, however, as can be seen from Equation (1), the descriptors influence the resulting functional maps X_i *jointly*. As an example, if a correspondence is described by several probe functions the resulting functional map will tend to respect this constraint while other meaningful correspondences will be arbitrarily put aside due to their low redundancy. So picking the best descriptors independently will not necessarily result in high quality maps.

(a) Smoothed Gaussian curvature   (b) Logarithm of the absolute value of
                                              Gaussian Curvature

Fig. 1. Probe functions computed independently on two shapes. One carries meaningful information (a) and the other is misleading (b).

Thus, the key idea developed in this paper is to introduce weights for probe functions, over which learning can be made. As explained below, the probe function constraint will be replaced by: $\|CG_0D - G_iD\|_F^2$. The weights D will be optimized so that the weighted descriptors are jointly as informative as possible. This will allow us to improve the quality of the functional maps and to extract the most stable functional subspaces.

2.3   Algorithm Outline

We propose a two-step method described in following two sections and summarized in Figure 2. Given collection of shapes, we learn the most informative set of weight D by solving an optimization problem. We then extract a function basis whose components are ordered by quality of correspondence. When given a previously unseen shape, we use this information to compute a high-quality functional map using the optimal weights and to discard the badly mapped functions by reducing the functional space.

3   Selection of the Best Functional Correspondences

The idea developed here is to assign a weight to each pair of probe functions. These weights can then be tuned according to their consistency in the matching. Since *a priori* there is no reason to choose one probe function over another, we propose to learn the optimal weights given a training set of shapes.

As input we need a set of N triangulated meshes with known correspondences representing the same object undergoing a set of deformations. Our main assumption is that the optimal weights on the probe functions should be stable across the shapes in the collection. Thus, if we are given a new deformation of the same shape, the learned weight should also select the consistent probe functions. The output of our algorithm will be a set of weights for the probe functions, which, as we will show below, can then be used to find correspondences between new, unseen shape instances.

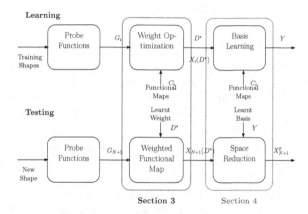

Fig. 2. Pipeline of the proposed algorithm with the corresponding section. Top: learning from a given collection. Bottom: processing a new shape.

3.1 Weighting the Probe Functions

As described above, our main idea is to introduce a set of weights on the functional correspondences to measure their usefulness in finding a relevant map by using a diagonal matrix D. For a given weight matrix D, the linear constraints given by the probe functions become $CG_0D = G_iD$. We can then define the function $X_i(D)$, which maps a given sets of weight to the corresponding functional map, via the solution of the optimization problem:

$$X_i(D) = \arg\min_{C} \|CG_0D - G_iD\|_F^2 + \alpha\|C \odot W\|_F^2 \qquad (2)$$

We choose here to fix α and tune D. We could also try to tune all the parameters (α and D) but the coefficients would be defined up to a multiplicative constant and $C(D)$ may no longer be well-defined when α is equal to zero.

Since all the functional map start from the reference shape S_0, this shape obviously plays special role in our method. Ideally we would like to take as reference the most "average" shape of the collection. Following this idea, a simple procedure is presented in [29] to find the shape of the collection which minimizes the average isometric distortion. However, in our experiments we chose the symmetric standing pose as reference.

As discussed in the previous section $X_i(D)$ is well-defined and differentiable.

3.2 Finding the Best Weights

Learning from a Given Collection. We assume we are given a collection of N nearly isometric deformations of the same object with known functional maps C_i. The optimal weights $D^\star$ are the ones that produce an approximation $X_i(D)$ that is closest to the ground truth C_i. Thus, we want to solve the following optimization problem:

$$D^\star \in \arg\min_D \sum_{i=1}^N \|X_i(D) - C_i\|, \tag{3}$$

where the sum is over the set of given training maps C_i.

Note that the choice of the norm is important. We would like the functional map $X_i(D)$ to match C_i over as-large-as possible functional subspace. This is equivalent to minimizing the rank of the difference $X_i(D) - C_i$. Thus, the important quantities are the singular values of the differences $X_i(D) - C_i$.

The naive choice of the squared Frobenius norm is not well suited for our problem since $\|A\|_F^2 = \|\sigma(A)\|_2^2$ where $\sigma(A)$ is the vector containing the singular values of the matrix A. Therefore this norm would give a large weight to the biggest singular values, which correspond to the worst-matched functional subspaces. Among these subspaces is the space of antisymmetric functions that we have no hope of mapping since the probe functions give us very little information about this subspace. At the same time, the small singular values have little influence on the minimization whereas they are the ones we would like to optimize.

The Choice of the Norm. To tackle the rank minimization problem , we choose the following norm which a regularization of the l^0-norm:

$$\|A\|_\epsilon = \sum_{i=1}^N \frac{\sigma(A)_i^2}{\sigma(A)_i^2 + \epsilon}. \tag{4}$$

Note that the problem (3) is differentiable as long as $\|.\|_\epsilon$ is differentiable. The gradient can be computed efficiently using the Jacobian matrix of the singular values as expressed in [25]. In practice, we solve this optimization problem using a standard L-BFGS algorithm.

The choice of ϵ can have a big impact on the results. In fact since we are using a gradient descent method the big singular values are in the flat part of $\|.\|_\epsilon$ therefore their gradient will be granted a small weight. On the contrary the singular values in the slope will have a big influence on the minimization. So with an ϵ too small only a few singular values will be minimized but with an ϵ too big a lot of singular values will be minimized not well.

We chose the parameter ϵ such that at the initialization 80 percent of the singular values satisfy $\frac{\sigma_i^2}{\sigma_i^2 + \epsilon} \leq 0.9$.

4   Basis Function Extraction

Since the probe functions can give redundant information in some shape parts and incomplete information in others, our functional map will map some subspaces of $L^2(S_0)$ with more confidence than others. Using a collection of shapes we would like to extract the most stable subspaces.

For this purpose we propose to use the learned optimal weights D and the resulting estimated functional maps $X_i(D)$ and to identify stably mapped functional subspaces by comparing $X_i(D)$ to the reference maps C_i. The output will be Y an orthonormal basis of $L^2(S_0)$ ordered with decreasing confidence. As we demonstrate in Section 5, in most cases this order remains stable even for maps that are estimated to previously unseen shapes.

4.1 Identifying Stable Subspaces

The most well-mapped function $y_0 \in L^2(S_0)$ is such that $X_i y_0$ is the closest to $C_i y_0$ for all i. Such function is solution of the problem:

$$y_0 \in \underset{y \in L^2(S_0), \|y\|=1}{\arg\min} \sum_{i=1}^{N} \|(X_i - C_i)y\|_F^2$$

We can then iteratively define an orthonormal basis of $L^2(S_0)$ ordered by decreasing accuracy in the mapping, by solving the following problem:

$$y_{n+1} \in \underset{y \in L^2(S_0), (y,y_j)=0 \, \forall j \leq n}{\arg\min} \sum_{i=1}^{N} \|(X_i - C_i)y\|_F^2$$

Such a basis can be efficiently computed by considering the singular value decomposition of the matrix:

$$X = \begin{pmatrix} X_1 - C_1 \\ \dots \\ X_N - C_N \end{pmatrix} = U\Sigma V^t.$$

It is well-known that y_j must be equal to singular vectors corresponding to the jth smallest singular value of X. We can, therefore, form a new orthonormal basis Y of $L^2(S_0)$ composed of the singular vectors of X by increasing singular values. This allows us to quantify the quality of the mapping of a functional subspace just by looking at the singular values of X: the smaller the singular values are, the better the mapping.

4.2 Functional Map to a Test Shape Using a Reduced Basis

Now if we are given an extra shape S_{N+1} that does not belong to the training set, we first compute its probe functions and store them in a matrix G_{N+1}. We then compute the functional map X_{N+1} by using the previously solved for weight matrix D. Finally, since we know that X_{N+1} contains some badly mapped subspaces (for example the antisymmetric functions), by using Y_p the p first column of Y, we compute the reduced map X_{N+1}^p

$$X_{N+1}^p = X_{N+1}Y_p : L^2(S_0) \cap L^2(\text{Im}(Y_p)) \to L^2(S_{N+1})$$

5   Experimental Results

5.1   Functional Correspondences

The probe functions used to solve the problem in Eq. (2) are given by various descriptors computed on each shape:

- Heat Kernel Signature [31]
- Wave Kernel Signature [2] at three different variances
- Gaussian and Mean Curvature
- Logarithm of the absolute value of Gaussian and Mean Curvature
- Mesh Saliency [18]

The HKS, WKS and Mesh Saliency are computed at various scales to ensure a wide variability. The curvatures are processed in order to obtain a family of functions. Since the curvatures can have very high peaks we take the logarithm of their absolute value to put more weight on the small curvatures areas. The family of functions is then created by considering the solution of the Heat Diffusion Equation at various times when each function is used as initial heat distribution over the surface.

5.2   Isometric Shape Matching

TOSCA Dataset. We have evaluated our method on the shape matching benchmark TOSCA [6]. For each shape class we use all the available shapes for training, except one for testing and we choose the standard standing pose as shape S_0. We compare three ways of weighting the probe functions: a unique weight for all the functions, a weight per category of descriptors and one weight per probe function.

For all the experiments we express all functions in the basis given by the first 50 eigenfunctions of the Laplace-Beltrami operator. We compute 50 probe functions divided in 9 categories (WKS is divided in three categories with tree different variances) of descriptors. We take 5 functions per category except for the Mesh Saliency where 10 functions are computed. Since all the shapes in TOSCA have an internal symmetry, we cannot hope to recover the entire functional map, and thus Eq. (4) is a reasonable choice of norm.

The experiments follow the pipeline shown in Figure 2. First we learn the optimal weights and extract the ordered basis using the training set of shapes. Second we are given an unknown shape. We use the optimal weights to compute the functional map and the extracted basis to suppress the badly mapped function subspaces. The L-BFGS algorithm used to solve the optimization problem in Eq. (3) is initialized with the naive functional maps solution of (1) with $\alpha = 10^{-3}$. As several methods using functional maps [22,24] have been proved to be more efficient than the state-of-the-art methods, we compare all of the functional maps and subspaces computed with our method to the baseline "naive" map, obtained using the identity matrix D, which correspond to the original method described in [22].

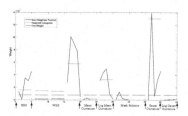 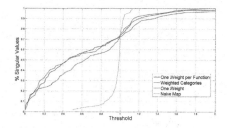

Fig. 3. Left: Optimal weights for different strategies after training with 9 cats. Right: Effect of the different weights on the distribution of the singular value of the difference $X_{N+1}(D) - C_{N+1}$.

Performance. The proposed approach was implemented in MATLAB. Note that the number of vertices of each shape has no effect on the performance since all the functions are expressed in a reduced function basis. The most time consuming task in our pipeline is the training part which requires to solve a difficult non-linear optimization problem (3). The processing cost is dominated by the computation of the gradient of the energy, which is done by solving two linear systems for each shape of the training set at each iteration. However, the contributions of each shape to the gradient are independent so this can be done in parallel. The learning process with a training set of 10 shapes took about 45 min on an Intel i7 processor without parallelization.

Optimal Weights. Figure 3 (left) shows the weights obtained after solving the problem in Eq. (3) with a training set composed of 9 cats. To demonstrate the importance of weighting the probe functions on the quality of the functional map, we study the distribution of the singular values of the difference $X_{N+1}(D) - C_{N+1}$ for the different learned weights. In Figure 3 (right) each curve depicts the percentage of singular values below the threshold given on the x-axis. For the perfect map, all singular values would be zero. As can be seen, the functional maps with the optimal weights have a bigger concentration of small singular values than the naive functional map. Therefore there exists a bigger functional subspace on which these functional maps provide a good approximation of the ground truth. Note that the naive map has no small singular values and is indeed a very bad approximation.

Stable Subspaces. From the naive maps and functional maps with optimal weights, we extract four function bases ordered by decreasing stability. The most stable functions for each case are shown in Figure 4. Even the most stable functions from the naive maps are not mapped very accurately since they are very bad approximation of the truth. For the other bases the functions seem consistent with the information we would expect from descriptors as HKS and WKS: a distinction between flat area (body) and salient area (legs, tail, head). Note that even with only one weight we are able to retrieve meaningful stable areas.

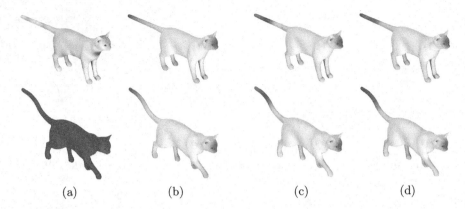

(a)   (b)   (c)   (d)

Fig. 4. Visualization of the first component of the extracted basis. First row: the reference shape. Second row: transfer using different functional maps: (4a) naive map, (4b) unique weight, (4c) one weight per category of function, (4d) one weight per functions.

We also evaluate the extracted functional basis by computing the difference between the ground truth map and our approximation on the unseen shape:

$$\epsilon_i = \|(X_{N+1}(D) - C_{N+1})y_i\|_2, \tag{5}$$

where y_i is the ith function of the extracted basis. We compare this error for the three weighting strategies with the naive map in Figure 5 (left). The extracted basis was ordered by decreasing quality on the training set. Note that this order is still preserved on the unknown shape for the 25 first functions of the basis. Most of all we are able to identify the worst mapped subspaces, which can be safely removed.

Despite only estimating the functional maps on a subspace of the full functional space, we converted them to point-to-point correspondences using the method described in [22]. Figure 5 right compares the quality of the correspondences before and after reducing the space dimension from 50 to 25. We obtain better results with our learned weight than with the naive map. For the weighted maps, the reductions perform better or similarly than the full maps. Thus our basis extraction manages to identify correctly the most stable subspaces. For the naive map our reduction space strategy fails as there is no well-mapped subspace.

5.3   Non-Isometric Shape Matching

Until now we have assumed the deformation to be nearly isometric. Our algorithm to find the optimal set of probe functions and the extraction of the most stable subspaces do not contain any explicit knowledge of the type of deformation. In fact, this assumption is only used to construct the least-square problem (1). Which means that our framework can be adapted to any kind of deformation model as long as we have a consistent way of computing a functional map form probe functions.

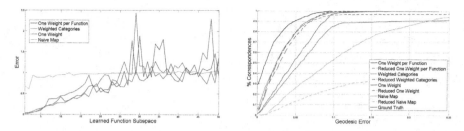

Fig. 5. Left: Accuracy of the extracted function basis measured with Eq. (5). Right: Comparison between full map (plain lines) and reduced map (dash lines). Symmetric correspondences are considered correct.

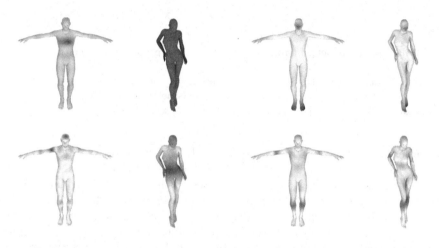

Stable functions before training   Stable functions after training

Fig. 8. Visualization of the first two components of the extracted basis on the reference shape (man) then mapped to the unseen shape (woman) using the functional map without optimization (left) and with the learned weight (right)

To test this case, we consider a man or a gorilla and 12 women in different poses from the TOSCA dataset. The ground truth functional maps are computed using a thousand user-picked correspondences. The meshes have different number of vertices and different connectivity. We train our method on 10 poses and use the last for testing.

The resulting problem is very noisy for two reasons. First, the ground truth functional maps are computed from sparse correspondences, and therefore can be inaccurate on some functional subspace. However, the use of a collection of shape for training allows us to remove this noise. Second, since all the probe functions used are designed for isometric deformation, few are going to contain useful information.

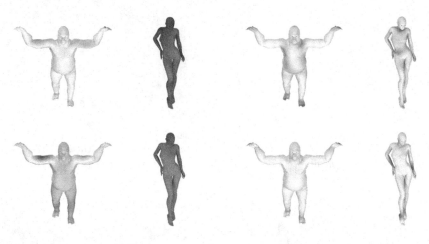

Stable functions before training   Stable functions after training

Fig. 11. Visualization of the first two components of the extracted basis on the reference shape (gorilla) then mapped to the unseen shape (woman) using the functional map without optimization (left) and with the learned weight (right)

In order to introduce a wide variability of functions we pre-compute on each shape 50 basis functions, 310 probe functions and we put a weight on each probe function. The descent algorithm is initialized as in the previous experiment. Figure 11 (left) shows the most stable functions learned from the training maps. Each of these functions is also mapped to a previously unseen pose using the "ground truth" map converted to a functional map. Note that the functions are badly transferred, due to the incompatibility of the LB basis and the noise in the input maps. Compare this with Figure 11 (right) where the probe functions have been weighted using our method. The stable functions indicate the head, the hands and the feet to be the most stable area. Besides, these functions are correctly mapped on a new shape using *a computed* functional map with the learned weights. Clearly, the fact that we use a collection helps removing the noise of the input data. Thus, our method is able to correctly identify the most stable functional subspace with mild assumptions on the underlying deformation.

6   Conclusion

In this work, we presented a method to learn the most informative descriptors for non-rigid shape matching, from a given set of shape correspondences. Our method is purely intrinsic and allows us to obtain high quality *consistent* correspondences to new, unseen shapes, and to identify the most reliably mapped functional subspaces. The approach is flexible and can potentially be applied to scenarios that lack a good theoretical deformation model, as demonstrated by meaningful even non isometric deformation. One of its weaknesses is a relatively high cost for the training, and in the future, we plan to explore more efficient optimization strategies.

Acknowledgments. The authors would like to acknowledge the support of the French Direction Générale de l'Armement (DGA), the CNRS chaire d'excellence, Marie Curie CIG-334283-HRGP, a Google Faculty Research Award, and the "EANOI" joint FWF n. I1148 / ANR-12-IS01-0003 project.

References

1. Anguelov, D., Srinivasan, P., Koller, D., Thrun, S., Rodgers, J., Davis, J.: Scape: shape completion and animation of people. In: ACM Transactions on Graphics (TOG) **24**, pp. 408–416. ACM (2005)
2. Aubry, M., Schlickewei, U., Cremers, D.: The wave kernel signature: A quantum mechanical approach to shape analysis. In: Computer Vision Workshops (ICCV Workshops), pp. 1626–1633. IEEE (2011)
3. Azencot, O., Ben-Chen, M., Chazal, F., Ovsjanikov, M.: An operator approach to tangent vector field processing. Computer Graphics Forum **32**(5), 73–82 (2013)
4. Bookstein, F.L.: Landmark methods for forms without landmarks: morphometrics of group differences in outline shape. Medical image analysis **1**(3), 225–243 (1997)
5. Bronstein, A.M., Bronstein, M.M., Kimmel, R.: Generalized multidimensional scaling: a framework for isometry-invariant partial surface matching. PNAS **103**(5) (2006)
6. Bronstein, A.M., Bronstein, M.M., Kimmel, R.: Numerical geometry of non-rigid shapes. Springer (2008)
7. Chen, X., Saparov, A., Pang, B., Funkhouser, T.: Schelling points on 3d surface meshes. ACM Trans. Graph. (TOG) **31**(4), 29 (2012)
8. Cootes, T.F., Taylor, C.J., Cooper, D.H., Graham, J.: Training models of shape from sets of examples. In: BMVC 1992, pp. 9–18 (1992)
9. Cootes, T.F., Taylor, C.J., Cooper, D.H., Graham, J.: Active shape models-their training and application. Computer Vision and Image Understanding **61**(1), 38–59 (1995)
10. Dryden, I.L., Mardia, K.V.: Statistical shape analysis, vol. 4. John Wiley & Sons, New York (1998)
11. Gao, X., Su, Y., Li, X., Tao, D.: A review of active appearance models. IEEE Transactions on Systems, Man, and Cybernetics, Part C: Applications and Reviews **40**(2), 145–158 (2010)
12. Hasler, N., Stoll, C., Sunkel, M., Rosenhahn, B., Seidel, H.P.: A statistical model of human pose and body shape. In: Computer Graphics Forum **28**, pp. 337–346. Wiley Online Library (2009)
13. Huang, Q.X., Adams, B., Wicke, M., Guibas, L.J.: Non-rigid registration under isometric deformations. CGF (Proc. SGP) **27**(5), 1449–1457 (2008)
14. Huang, Q., Wang, F., Guibas, L.: Functional map networks for analyzing and exploring large shape collections. ACM Trans. Graph. **33**(4), 36:1–36:11 (2014)
15. Kalogerakis, E., Hertzmann, A., Singh, K.: Learning 3d mesh segmentation and labeling. ACM Trans. Graph. **29**(4), 102 (2010)
16. Kilian, M., Mitra, N.J., Pottmann, H.: Geometric modeling in shape space. ACM Transactions on Graphics (TOG) **26**, 64 (2007)

17. Kim, V.G., Lipman, Y., Funkhouser, T.: Blended intrinsic maps. ACM TOG (Proc. SIGGRAPH) **30**(4) (2011)

18. Lee, C.H., Varshney, A., Jacobs, D.W.: Mesh saliency. In: ACM Transactions on Graphics (TOG) **24**, pp. 659–666. ACM (2005)

19. Lipman, Y., Funkhouser, T.: Mobius voting for surface correspondence. ACM Transactions on Graphics (Proc. SIGGRAPH) 28(3), August 2009

20. Litman, R., Bronstein, A.: Learning spectral descriptors for deformable shape correspondence (2013)

21. Mémoli, F.: On the use of gromov-hausdorff distances for shape comparison. In: Symposium on Point Based Graphics, pp. 81–90 (2007)

22. Ovsjanikov, M., Ben-Chen, M., Solomon, J., Butscher, A., Guibas, L.: Functional maps: a flexible representation of maps between shapes. ACM Trans. Graph. **31**(4), 30:1–30:11 (2012). http://doi.acm.org/10.1145/2185520.2185526

23. Ovsjanikov, M., Mérigot, Q., Mémoli, F., Guibas, L.: One point isometric matching with the heat kernel. CGF **29**(5), 1555–1564 (2010)

24. Ovsjanikov, M., Mérigot, Q., Pătrăucean, V., Guibas, L.: Shape matching via quotient spaces. Computer Graphics Forum **32**(5), 1–11 (2013)

25. Papadopoulo, T., Lourakis, M.I.A.: Estimating the jacobian of the singular value decomposition: Theory and applications. In: Vernon, D. (ed.) ECCV 2000. LNCS, vol. 1842, pp. 554–570. Springer, Heidelberg (2000)

26. Rodolà, E., Bulò, S.R., Windheuser, T., Vestner, M., Cremers, D.: Dense non-rigid shape correspondence using random forests. In: Proc. CVPR (2014)

27. Rustamov, R.M., Ovsjanikov, M., Azencot, O., Ben-Chen, M., Chazal, F., Guibas, L.: Map-based exploration of intrinsic shape differences and variability. ACM Transactions on Graphics (TOG) **32**(4), 72 (2013)

28. Sahillioğlu, Y., Yemez, Y.: Coarse-to-fine combinatorial matching for dense isometric shape correspondence. Computer Graphics Forum **30**(5), 1461–1470 (2011)

29. Shapira, N., Ben-Chen, M.: Cross-collection map inference by intrinsic alignment of shape spaces. In: Computer Graphics Forum. Wiley Online Library (2014)

30. Sumner, R.W., Zwicker, M., Gotsman, C., Popović, J.: Mesh-based inverse kinematics. In: ACM SIGGRAPH, pp. 488–495 (2005)

31. Sun, J., Ovsjanikov, M., Guibas, L.: A concise and provably informative multiscale signature based on heat diffusion. In: Computer Graphics Forum **28**, pp. 1383–1392. Wiley Online Library (2009)

32. Tam, G.K., Cheng, Z.Q., Lai, Y.K., Langbein, F.C., Liu, Y., Marshall, D., Martin, R.R., Sun, X.F., Rosin, P.L.: Registration of 3d point clouds and meshes: A survey from rigid to nonrigid. IEEE Transactions on Visualization and Computer Graphics **19**(7), 1199–1217 (2013)

33. Tevs, A., Bokeloh, M., Wand, M., Schilling, A., Seidel, H.P.: Isometric registration of ambiguous and partial data. In: Proc. CVPR, pp. 1185–1192 (2009)

34. Van Kaick, O., Tagliasacchi, A., Sidi, O., Zhang, H., Cohen-Or, D., Wolf, L., Hamarneh, G.: Prior knowledge for part correspondence. Computer Graphics Forum (Proc. Eurographics) **30**(2), 553–562 (2011)

35. Van Kaick, O., Zhang, H., Hamarneh, G., Cohen-Or, D.: A survey on shape correspondence. Computer Graphics Forum **30**(6), 1681–1707 (2011)

36. Zhang, H., Sheffer, A., Cohen-Or, D., Zhou, Q., Van Kaick, O., Tagliasacchi, A.: Deformation-driven shape correspondence. In: Proc. SGP, pp. 1431–1439 (2008)

Anisotropic Laplace-Beltrami Operators for Shape Analysis

Mathieu Andreux[1]([✉]), Emanuele Rodolà[2], Mathieu Aubry[3],
and Daniel Cremers[2]

[1] École polytechnique, Palaiseau, France
andreux@in.tum.de
[2] Technische Universität München, Munich, Germany
[3] Université Paris Est LIGM - École des Ponts Paristech, Champs-sur-Marne, France

Abstract. This paper introduces an *anisotropic* Laplace-Beltrami operator for shape analysis. While keeping useful properties of the standard Laplace-Beltrami operator, it introduces variability in the directions of principal curvature, giving rise to a more intuitive and semantically meaningful diffusion process. Although the benefits of anisotropic diffusion have already been noted in the area of mesh processing (*e.g.* surface regularization), focusing on the Laplacian itself, rather than on the diffusion process it induces, opens the possibility to effectively replace the omnipresent Laplace-Beltrami operator in many shape analysis methods. After providing a mathematical formulation and analysis of this new operator, we derive a practical implementation on discrete meshes. Further, we demonstrate the effectiveness of our new operator when employed in conjunction with different methods for shape segmentation and matching.

Keywords: Shape analysis · Anisotropic diffusion · Curvature · Non-rigid matching · Segmentation · Laplace-Beltrami operator

1 Introduction

Over the last decade, tools derived from harmonic analysis have been successfully used in three-dimensional computer vision for numerous tasks such as shape segmentation, classification, or matching.

The Laplace-Beltrami (LB) operator, or Laplacian, is the natural operator to introduce when studying diffusion processes on shapes. The study of heat diffusion led, for instance, to the definition of the Heat Kernel Signature (HKS) [24], one of the most relevant shape signatures to date. Since the theoretical guarantees of this signature come from the operator itself and its eigen-decomposition, subsequent studies have tried to use the same analytical objects to model different physical phenomena. These include the definition of new signatures such as the Wave Kernel Signature (WKS) [1], learning combinations of LB eigenfunctions to deal with more general classes of deformations [13], or directly employing the eigen-functions themselves for segmentation tasks [21]. However, all these works rely on the notion of an *isotropic* LB operator.

© Springer International Publishing Switzerland 2015
L. Agapito et al. (Eds.): ECCV 2014 Workshops, Part IV, LNCS 8928, pp. 299–312, 2015.
DOI: 10.1007/978-3-319-16220-1_21

Fig. 1. Example of stable regions detected via consensus segmentation [21] using the standard Laplacian (first row) and the proposed anisotropic operator (second row). Notice how the local changes in curvature directly affect the detected regions in the second case, giving rise to a more stable and semantically meaningful segmentation. Corresponding regions are colored consistently for visualization purposes.

On the other hand, anisotropic diffusion processes have provided interesting results for shape regularization tasks by taking into account *local* details, but to the best of our knowledge, an anisotropic LB operator by itself has not been used in three-dimensional shape analysis.

In this paper, we propose to study an anisotropic LB operator in the context of shape segmentation and matching. More precisely, we change the diffusion speed along the directions of principal curvature on the surface. Intuitively, this anisotropy can lead to more *semantically consistent* shape segmentations, and can improve the accuracy of point signatures.

1.1   Related Work

3D Shape Analysis: Sometimes called the "swiss army knife" of 3D shape analysis, the Laplacian is used for matching, segmentation and classification. Computing the LB operator directly on meshes with approaches such as [15,18,20], numerous works exploit the information contained in its eigen-decomposition to build a new representation of a shape, either by explicit formulas [1,23,24] or by learning [13,22]. Based on these descriptors, several methods have been developed for segmentation purposes, for instance [14,21]. Recently, Kovnatsky *et al.* [12] modified the metric tensor of the manifold to take into account photometric information: they build another isotropic LB operator upon it and subsequently use the same techniques as presented above.

Anisotropic Denoising and Regularization: All the previously mentioned applications are based on the isotropic LB operator. On the other hand, anisotropic phenomena, such as diffusion, have been analyzed in the fields of image restoring and geometry processing. From the seminal work of Perona *et al.* [16] to the ameliorations of Black *et al.* on 2D images [2], there have been multiple extensions to three-dimensional smoothing and fairing, see *e.g.* [6,8,25]. In all cases, these methods do not compute an anisotropic Laplacian but rather solve the associated anisotropic heat equation.

Medical Image Analysis: Several approaches have also used anisotropic diffusion either on textures or directly on the surface in order to analyze MRI data [3,9]. However, as for denoising and regularization, these methods focus on computing the solutions of the associated anisotropic heat diffusion, without computing the anisotropic LB operator *per se*.

High Dimensional Data Analysis: Spectral clustering based on the LB operator is also a tool used for the analysis of high dimensional data, for instance sets of images. Recently, Kim *et al.* [11] have extended these methods by approximating an anisotropic LB operator in point clouds of high dimension using graph reweighting.

1.2 Contributions

In this work, we propose to transfer the use of anisotropic LB operators to the analysis of 3D shapes. The operator we introduce has a simple mathematical formulation, it can be straightforwardly discretized and provides better results in our experiments than existing alternatives. The key contributions of our work can be summarized as follows:

– We introduce an anisotropic LB (ALB) operator for shape analysis: it preserves the key properties of the isotropic Laplacian, while taking into account extrinsic geometric information;
– We derive a discrete version of this operator for 3D meshes: it can be implemented efficiently and boils down to a simple matrix multiplication;
– We perform an experimental evaluation of the impact of this operator for several standard shape analysis methods.

2 Anisotropic Diffusion on Surfaces

In this section, we introduce the general framework of anisotropic LB operators based on curvature for smooth surfaces, analyze their mathematical properties and derive a discrete version of our selected ALB operator for a 3D mesh.

2.1 Continuous Formulation

We consider a smooth, compact surface $S \subset \mathbb{R}^3$. After briefly recalling some notions of Riemannian geometry, we introduce an anisotropic LB operator on the surface which takes into account its extrinsic curvature.

Mathematically, we model S as a Riemannian manifold of dimension 2. This implies that locally around each point $p \in S$, the surface is very close to the tangent plane at p, which we denote by T_pS. The way in which S differs by bending from T_pS is encoded in the second fundamental form, represented by

Fig. 2. Representation of the maximal principal curvature κ_M at each point of two shapes from the TOSCA dataset. Blue parts correspond to regions of low maximal curvature.

at 2×2 matrix. The eigenvalues of this matrix are called *principal curvatures*, noted κ_m and κ_M where $\kappa_m \leq \kappa_M$. The corresponding normalized eigenvectors v_m, v_M are called directions of principal curvature, and form a basis of $T_p\mathcal{S}$. Intuitively, in the direction v_M the surface $\mathcal{S}$ bends the most around p, and conversely for v_m. See Figure 2 for a depiction of the maximal curvature κ_M on two shapes. The quantities κ_m and κ_M are called *extrinsic* since they encode the relationship between $\mathcal{S}$ and its embedding space $\mathbb{R}^3$. Moreover, since $\mathcal{S}$ looks locally like a plane, we are able to import most of the calculus known in $\mathbb{R}^2$ onto $\mathcal{S}$; in particular, the gradient (∇) and divergence (div) operators carry the same properties as in the Euclidean case.

Several important results and tools in the field of shape analysis are based on the Laplace-Beltrami operator Δ, defined as:

$$\Delta f = \mathrm{div}(\nabla f). \tag{1}$$

The Laplace-Beltrami operator is an *intrinsic* quantity of the surface, *i.e.* it is invariant under isometric deformations of the manifold. It is also *isotropic*: the corresponding diffusion process does not depend on the direction.

More generally, in this paper we are interested in *anisotropic* LB operators of the form

$$\Delta_D f = \mathrm{div}(D\,(\nabla f)), \tag{2}$$

where D is a 2×2 matrix acting on tangent vectors. We call D the *anisotropic tensor*, since its deviation from the identity encodes deviation from the isotropic case. In the case of a diffusion process, D controls both the *direction* and the *magnitude* of the diffusion on the surface $\mathcal{S}$, as shown in Figure 3.

Inspired by successful applications of curvature-aware anisotropic diffusion to denoising of images and surfaces [2,6,8,16,25], and by recent advances in the analysis of high-dimensional data [11], we attempt to incorporate *extrinsic* information into the anisotropic tensor D for shape analysis purposes. We do so by introducing the following generic linear operator, defined in the orthonormal basis (v_m, v_M):

$$D_\alpha = \begin{pmatrix} \Psi_\alpha^m(\kappa_m, \kappa_M) & 0 \\ 0 & \Psi_\alpha^M(\kappa_M, \kappa_m) \end{pmatrix}. \tag{3}$$

Fig. 3. Solutions of the heat equation $\Delta u = \frac{\partial}{\partial t} u$ computed at time $t = 3 \cdot 10^{-3}$, with a highly peaked Gaussian on the back of the horse as initial condition. We show the isotropic case (middle), anisotropic case favoring high curvature (left), and deflecting high curvature (right).

By choosing appropriate functions Ψ_α^m and Ψ_α^M, it is possible to favor directions of high curvature or directions of low curvature. In our experiments, we set $\Psi_\alpha^m(\kappa_m, \kappa_M) = \psi_\alpha(\kappa_M)$ and $\Psi_\alpha^M(\kappa_m, \kappa_M) = \psi_\alpha(\kappa_m)$, where ψ_α is defined as:

$$\psi_\alpha(x) = \frac{1}{1 + \alpha |x|} . \tag{4}$$

In the equation above, $\alpha > 0$ directly controls deviation from isotropy, whereas $\alpha \to 0$ leads to the common LB operator.

In general, operator D_α modifies both the direction and the norm of a given input vector. This differentiates our approach from the anisotropic LB operator $\tilde{\Delta}_{\tilde{D}}$ introduced in [11], where the anisotropic factor $\tilde{D}$ only modifies the norm of a given input vector, but not its direction (see Eq. (5) below).

2.2 Mathematical Analysis

In this section we state the general properties of the ALB operator Δ_{D_α}. Essentially, Δ_{D_α} conserves the strong analytical properties of the conventional Laplace-Beltrami operator Δ. This is in contrast with the previous proposal of [11]; in the following, we will also provide a brief comparison of the two variants.

Our operator has all the key properties of the isotropic case: $-\Delta_{D_\alpha}$ is linear, *symmetric, positive semi-definite* and therefore has a *discrete spectrum* $0 = E_0 \leq E_1 \leq \ldots \leq E_k \leq \ldots$, with associated eigenfunctions $\phi_0, \phi_1, \ldots$, and $E_k \to +\infty$. These properties simply stem from the divergence theorem and the symmetry of D_α (3). However, our operator is *not isometry-invariant*. Indeed, although the product of the principal curvatures, or Gaussian curvature, is preserved under such deformations, it is not the case for each of the principal curvatures. Let us imagine for instance a surface initially planar, and then folded across a line in an isometric fashion: a non-zero principal curvature will appear along the folding line, although the Gaussian curvature will remain equal to zero there. Since our operator directly depends on these extrinsic quantities, it is not in general

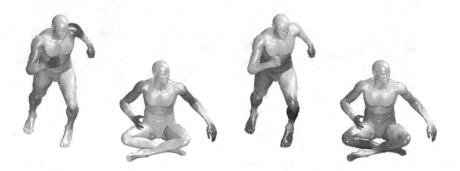

Fig. 4. The tenth eigenfunction of Δ (shapes on the left) and Δ_{D_α} (on the right, here $\alpha = 10$). We observe that while the LB operator is invariant under near-isometries, this property is lost for the ALB operator: the eigenfunction is preserved more accurately in the first case.

invariant under isometries. This phenomenon is reflected on the eigenfunctions of Δ_{D_α}, as showed in Figure 4.

It should be noted that the operator $\tilde{\Delta}_{\tilde{D}}$ as defined in [11] is also not invariant to isometries, furthermore it loses other key properties of Δ. In particular, the anisotropic factor $\tilde{D}$ has the form:

$$\tilde{D}(v) = \left\| Q\left(\frac{v}{\|v\|}\right) \right\| v, \tag{5}$$

where $Q : T_p\mathcal{S} \to T_p\mathcal{S}$ is a linear application acting on tangent vectors, also depending on the second fundamental form in a similar manner as D_α.

We remark that if D_α itself is plugged into (5) as the matrix Q, it follows that D_α and $\tilde{D}$ roughly have the same qualitative properties, apart from the fact that $\tilde{D}$ does not modify the direction of input vectors. Nevertheless, $\tilde{D}$ is not linear, hence the loss of linearity of $\tilde{\Delta}_{\tilde{D}}$. Moreover, in this case Green's theorem leads to the non-symmetric expression:

$$\langle -\tilde{\Delta}_{\tilde{D}}f, g\rangle = \int_{\mathcal{S}} \left\| Q\left(\frac{\nabla f}{\|\nabla f\|}\right) \right\| \nabla f \cdot \nabla g \neq \langle f, -\tilde{\Delta}_{\tilde{D}}g\rangle. \tag{6}$$

The difference between the mathematical properties of Δ_{D_α} and $\tilde{\Delta}_{\tilde{D}}$ also becomes evident in our evaluation: in most of our experiments, Δ_{D_α} performs better than $\tilde{\Delta}_{\tilde{D}}$, although the effect of curvature on the diffusivity factors is the same.

2.3   Numerical Implementation

In this part, we use a finite-element method to derive a numerical scheme for Δ_D, where in all generality D is a symmetric matrix, allowing us to compute this operator on triangulated meshes. While more sophisticated approaches using discrete exterior calculus may be employed for this step [10], finite elements are a common tool to discretize differential operators, and have been applied with success to anisotropic operators [6]. In the following, we first recall the basics of finite elements, then provide the formula for our discretized operator in this framework, and finally prove it.

Throughout this discretization, we consider a triangulated mesh consisting of nodes $(z_i)_{1 \leq i \leq N}$, seen as a sample of a surface $\mathcal{S}$. Any scalar function f on $\mathcal{S}$ can be represented by a vector $\underline{f} = (f_i)$, where $f_i = f(z_i)$. Our goal is to express $\Delta_D f$ in terms of geometric values related to the mesh and the vector $\underline{f}$. In other words, by linearity, we need to find a matrix L_D acting on $\underline{f}$ and representing the anisotropic operator Δ_D by the relation $\underline{\Delta_D f} = L_D \underline{f}$.

For this purpose, we use finite elements of the first order : the approach consists in approximating f by a piecewise affine version of it taking the same values at the vertices z_i. Formally, we define "hat" functions Φ_i satisfying: $\Phi_i(z_j) = \delta_{ij}$, where Φ_i is affine on each triangle of the mesh, and write $f \approx \sum_i f_i \Phi_i$. Further, we assume that D is constant on each triangle. The weak formulation of the operator Δ_D boils down by linearity to $C\underline{f} = A\left(\underline{\Delta_D f}\right)$ where the symmetric *mass matrix* A and *stiffness matrix* C are defined as:

$$A_{ij} = \langle \Phi_i, \Phi_j \rangle \;,\; C_{ij} = -\langle D(\nabla \Phi_i), \nabla \Phi_j \rangle \,. \tag{7}$$

Inverting A, our discretized operator L_D finally reads:

$$L_D = A^{-1}C \,. \tag{8}$$

We now state the following results:

$$A_{ij} = \mathcal{A}_i^{\text{Vor}} \delta_{ij} \tag{9}$$

$$C_{ij} = \begin{cases} \frac{1}{2}\left(\Gamma_{ij} \frac{\cos(\gamma_{ij})}{\sin(\alpha_{ij})} + \Xi_{ij} \frac{\cos(\xi_{ij})}{\sin(\beta_{ij})}\right) & i \neq j \\ -\sum_{T \ni z_j} I(T)_j & i = j \end{cases}, \tag{10}$$

where $\mathcal{A}_i^{\text{Vor}}$ denotes the Voronoi area around z_i. Symbols Γ_{ij} and γ_{ij} are defined as in Figure 5, and Ξ_{ij}, ξ_{ij} are their counterparts in the triangle (z_i, z_j, z_p). For all triangles $T = (z_k, z_j, z_i)$, we write $I(T)_j = \frac{1}{2}\frac{D^\perp e_j}{\|e_j\|} \cdot \frac{e_j}{\|e_j\|}(\cot(\alpha_{ij}) + \cot(\theta_{jk}))$ with $D^\perp$ defined in (12) and α_{ij}, θ_{ij} as in Figure 5.

Note that whenever $D \equiv Id$, this scheme boils down to the popular cotangent scheme [8,15,18]. Moreover, the matrices involved are sparse, which makes their computation simple and efficient.

In order to express numerically the anisotropic tensor D, we computed at each vertex of the mesh the principal curvatures and corresponding directions using the method described in [7] as implemented in [17], and then averaged over each triangle to obtain a constant operator.

In the remainder of this section, we derive the results stated in (9), (10). We fix j and compute C_{ij}, A_{ij} for all i. Clearly, we have $C_{ij}, A_{ij} = 0$ if z_i, z_j are not neighbors. We now assume that this is the case, with $i \neq j$, and decompose the integral over the surface on the different triangles containing the edge (z_i, z_j).

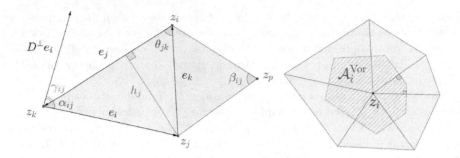

Fig. 5. Left: Adjacent edges and angles. Right: Voronoi area around z_i, *i.e.* the area of the set of points such that their closest point among the vertices of mesh is z_i. $\Gamma_{ij} = \frac{\|D^\perp e_i\|}{\|e_i\|}$ and $\gamma_{ij} = -\arccos\left(\frac{D^\perp e_i \cdot e_j}{\|D^\perp e_i\| \cdot \|e_j\|}\right)$.

Let us be given a triangle $T = (z_k, z_j, z_i)$, and let $e_i = \overrightarrow{z_k z_j}$, $e_j = \overrightarrow{z_i z_k}$, $e_k = \overrightarrow{z_j z_i}$. We refer to the heights of the triangle to the points z_p as h_p. Finally, let $\alpha_{ij} = \widehat{z_j z_k z_i}$. It is straightforward that $\nabla\Phi_i = \frac{1}{h_i \|e_i\|} R_{\frac{\pi}{2}} e_i$ and $\nabla\Phi_j = \frac{1}{h_j \|e_j\|} R_{\frac{\pi}{2}} e_j$ where $R_{\frac{\pi}{2}}$ denotes the rotation of angle $\frac{\pi}{2}$. Therefore:

$$D\nabla\Phi_i \cdot \nabla\Phi_j = \frac{1}{h_i \|e_i\|} DR_{\frac{\pi}{2}} e_i \cdot \frac{1}{h_j \|e_j\|} R_{\frac{\pi}{2}} e_j = \frac{1}{4A_T{}^2} D^\perp e_i \cdot e_j, \qquad (11)$$

where

$$D^\perp = R_{\frac{\pi}{2}}^T D R_{\frac{\pi}{2}}. \qquad (12)$$

Furthermore, if $i \neq j$, we also know that the area A_T of the triangle T satisfies $A_T = \frac{1}{2} \|e_i\| \|e_j\| \sin(\alpha_{ij})$. Consequently, when integrating the constant value $D\nabla\Phi_i \cdot \nabla\Phi_j$ over the whole triangle T, we get:

$$\int_T D\nabla\Phi_i \cdot \nabla\Phi_j dS = \frac{1}{4A_T} D^\perp e_i \cdot e_j = -\frac{1}{2}\Gamma_{ij} \frac{\cos(\gamma_{ij})}{\sin(\alpha_{ij})}, \qquad (13)$$

where γ_{ij} is the angle between the $D^\perp e_i$ and $-e_j$ and $\Gamma_{ij} = \frac{\|D^\perp e_i\|}{\|e_i\|}$. Summing up over the two triangles sharing the edge (z_i, z_j), we obtain

$$C_{ij} = \langle D\nabla\Phi_j, \nabla\Phi_i \rangle = -\frac{1}{2}\left(\Gamma_{ij}\frac{\cos(\gamma_{ij})}{\sin(\alpha_{ij})} + \Xi_{ij}\frac{\cos(\xi_{ij})}{\sin(\beta_{ij})}\right), \qquad (14)$$

where Ξ_{ij} and ξ_{ij} are the counterparts of Γ_{ij} and γ_{ij} on the other triangle adjacent to the edge (z_i, z_j).

For the diagonal coefficient C_{jj}, when considering any triangle $T = (z_k, z_j, z_i)$ containing z_j, the same reasoning as above leads to:

$$I(T)_j := \int_T D\nabla\Phi_j \cdot \nabla\Phi_j dS = \frac{1}{4A_T} D^\perp e_j \cdot e_j = \frac{1}{2}\frac{D^\perp e_j}{\|e_j\|} \cdot \frac{e_j}{\|e_j\|}\frac{\|e_j\|}{h_j}. \qquad (15)$$

Fig. 6. Maximally stable components detected on a horse shape equipped with our linear anisotropic LB operator Δ_{D_α}. From left to right, we use $\alpha = 0$ (corresponding to the standard LB operator), $\alpha = 5$ and $\alpha = 10$.

From the relation $\frac{\|e_i\|}{h_j} = \cot(\alpha_{ij}) + \cot(\theta_{jk})$, where α_{ij} and θ_{jk} are the two base angles corresponding to z_j (see Figure 5), we get:

$$I(T)_j = \frac{1}{2}\frac{D^\perp e_j}{\|e_j\|} \cdot \frac{e_j}{\|e_j\|}\left(\cot(\alpha_{ij}) + \cot(\theta_{jk})\right). \tag{16}$$

When $\alpha = 0$, we simply have $D^\perp = Id$, and once again we fall back to the cotangent scheme.

Finally, $\langle D\nabla\Phi_j, \nabla\Phi_j\rangle$ is nothing but the sum of (16) over all triangles T involved in z_j. Combining (7),(14) and (16), the result (10) comes easily. Regarding the expression for the mass matrix A (9), we refer to [15,20]. In practice, we used the method described in [8] to compute the Voronoi areas.

3   Experiments

In this section we investigate the practical benefits of adopting the proposed operator in two problems commonly arising in shape analysis, namely stable region detection and matching of deformable shapes, using the datasets [4,5].

3.1   Segmentation and Region Detection

Recent state-of-the-art approaches in deformable shape matching rely on the ability to detect repeatable regions on the given shapes [19]. In these experiments, we employ the anisotropic Laplacian within two different frameworks for detecting region-based features.

The first approach follows the consensus segmentation technique of [21]. The region detection process operates as follows. First, given a shape $\mathcal{S}$, several segmentations are produced by a clustering method (k-means) over an intrinsic embedding of the shape points. Different segmentations are obtained by

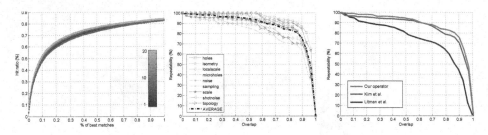

Fig. 7. Left: Hit ratio for isotropic (red curve) and anisotropic HKS (α varying from blue to green) on nearly-isometrically deformed shapes (*michael* class from the TOSCA dataset). Middle: Repeatability curves of MSER detection [14] using our anisotropic operator, for all deformations over the SHREC'10 dataset. Right: Repeatability averaged over all deformations of the SHREC'10 dataset, for our anisotropic operator (green), Kim *et al.*'s (red), and the standard Laplace-Beltrami operator (blue).

initializing the clustering process with different randomized seeds. The intrinsic embedding is provided by the simple mapping

$$p \mapsto \left(\frac{\phi_1(p)}{\sqrt{E_1}}, \frac{\phi_2(p)}{\sqrt{E_2}}, \frac{\phi_3(p)}{\sqrt{E_3}}, \cdots \right) \tag{17}$$

for each $p \in \mathcal{S}$, where ϕ_k are the eigenfunctions and E_k the corresponding eigenvalues of the Laplace-Beltrami operator on $\mathcal{S}$. The mapping above is commonly referred to as the Global Point Signature embedding of $\mathcal{S}$ [23]. Given this initial collection of segmentations, the corresponding *Fréchet mean* (according to an appropriate notion of distance among segmentations) is then solved for in a robust manner (we refer to [21] for the technical details). Intuitively, this process attempts to achieve an "agreement" between the several segmentations constituting the initial putative set; being based entirely on quantities directly derived from the eigenfunctions of Δ (17), regions produced by the consensus approach tend to reflect the overall trend of the eigenfunctions themselves. As such, apart from yielding a stable segmentation of the shape, this approach can easily provide a visual clue on the general behavior of a given operator.

In Figure 1 we show the regions detected on two nearly-isometric shapes via consensus segmentation, when the two manifolds are equipped with the standard LB operator Δ and our proposed anisotropic variant Δ_{D_α}. Notice how, although the regions resulting from the consensus process are repeatable across the two operators, the outcome of the anisotropic case is more stable (two different poses produce the same regions) and more semantically meaningful (no cross-regions covering semantically different parts).

The second experiment is aimed at providing a quantitative comparison between the segmentations produced when employing the two operators Δ and Δ_{D_α}. For these comparisons we adopted a different region detection technique, namely the Maximally Stable Extremal Regions (MSER) approach of [14]. Note that, differently from the consensus approach, the MSER technique is based on the *diffusion process* induced by the different operators rather than their simple eigen-decomposition. Thus, this experiment is aimed at evaluating our operator from a diffusion-geometric perspective, when put in comparison to the standard Laplacian within a common segmentation pipeline.

The comparisons were performed on the SHREC'10 benchmark. The dataset consists of three different shape classes (*dog, horse, man*) undergoing 9 different types of deformation (including *e.g.*, topological changes, downsampling, and local changes in scale), each at 5 intensity levels. To measure the stability of a given segmentation, we evaluated its *repeatability* curve across the whole dataset [14]. In particular, let $\mathcal{M}_0$ be a "null" (*i.e.*, in a canonical pose) and $\mathcal{M}$ be a deformed shape respectively. Given the ground-truth correspondence $g : \mathcal{M}_0 \to \mathcal{M}$, we can compute the *overlap* between two regions $\mathcal{A}_0 \subset \mathcal{M}_0$ and $\mathcal{B} \subset \mathcal{M}$ as the area ratio:

$$O(\mathcal{B}, \mathcal{A}_0) = \frac{|g^{-1}(\mathcal{B}) \cap \mathcal{A}_0|}{|g^{-1}(\mathcal{B}) \cup \mathcal{A}_0|} , \tag{18}$$

where $| \cdot |$ denotes the surface area. Note that

$$0 \leq O(\mathcal{B}, \mathcal{A}_0) \leq 1 , \tag{19}$$

the last inequality being attained if and only if $g^{-1}(\mathcal{B}) = \mathcal{A}_0$. For a fixed overlap value ν, the *repeatability* at ν is defined as the percentage of regions in $\mathcal{M}$ having an overlap greater than ν with regions in $\mathcal{M}_0$. For any given segmentation, the repeatability at overlap 0 is 100%, and the more stable the segmentation is, the higher the repeatability remains as ν increases.

In Figure 7 (last two columns) we show the repeatability curves obtained by MSER detection using our linear anisotropic operator Δ_D (green curve), the non-linear variant $\tilde{\Delta}_{\tilde{D}}$ (red curve), and the standard LB operator Δ_α (blue curve). Both anisotropic operators (here computed with $\alpha = 10$) outperform the standard Laplacian by a large margin, while there is only a minor difference in performance between them. This result directly confirms the observation (Section 2.2) that the two operators carry similar qualitative properties, with our linear proposal demonstrating overall better behaviour on the dataset considered. Finally, in Figure 6 we show some examples of MSER segmentations produced with our operator for different values of α.

3.2 Shape Matching

As observed in Section 2.2, the proposed anisotropic Laplacian is not an isometry invariant; hence, its direct application in the computation of intrinsic descriptors [1, 13] may not lead to an increase of performance in typical non-rigid matching scenarios.

Quantitative comparisons among the matching results obtained with a standard HKS implementation [24] and its anisotropic variant are shown in Figure 7 (left). In this experiment, we first performed a (Euclidean) farthest point sampling of a shape in the standard "null" pose; we computed a descriptor for each of the sampled points, and then looked for its closest matches (in descriptor space) on several nearly-isometric deformations of the shape. We did this for the standard HKS descriptor (red curve), and for the anisotropic HKS with α ranging uniformly between 1 (blue) and 20 (green). Each curve depicts the percentage of points in the null shape having their *exact* correspondence in the first $0 - 1\%$ of all shape points, sorted according to descriptor similarity.

As it can be seen from the plot, the advantage brought by the direct adoption of anisotropic diffusion for shape matching is only minimal. This is to be expected, since as shown in Figure 3, solutions to the heat equation will tend to evolve differently along regions of different curvature. However, as seen in the previous section, when used in conjunction with appropriate stability criteria, this property can become very useful for tasks of segmentation of deformable shapes.

4   Conclusions

In this paper we introduced the use of an *anisotropic* Laplace-Beltrami operator for shape analysis, and we derived a numerical scheme that allows to compute it easily for a triangulated mesh. In extensive evaluations, we showed that the proposed operator can improve either quantitatively or qualitatively several shape analysis methods initially developed with the standard Laplace-Beltrami operator in mind. These include the definition of shape signatures and the detection of stable regions following different approaches. Based on these promising results, we believe that the adoption of anisotropic Laplace-Beltrami operators for three-dimensional shape analysis constitutes a valid future direction of research.

Acknowledgments. This work is supported by an Alexander von Humboldt Fellowship and ANR Project SEMAPOLIS (ANR-13-CORD-0003).

References

1. Aubry, M., Schlickewei, U., Cremers, D.: The wave kernel signature: A quantum mechanical approach to shape analysis. In: ICCV Workshops, pp. 1626–1633 (2011)
2. Black, M.J., Sapiro, G., Marimont, D.H., Heeger, D.: Robust anisotropic diffusion. Trans. Img. Proc. **7**(3), 421–432 (1998)
3. Boucher, M., Evans, A., Siddiqi, K.: Anisotropic Diffusion of Tensor Fields for Fold Shape Analysis on Surfaces. In: Székely, G., Hahn, H.K. (eds.) IPMI 2011. LNCS, vol. 6801, pp. 271–282. Springer, Heidelberg (2011)
4. Bronstein, A.M., Bronstein, M.M., Castellani, U., Dubrovina, A., Guibas, L.J., Horaud, R.P., Kimmel, R., Knossow, D., von Lavante, E., Mateus, D., Ovsjanikov, M., Sharma, A.: Shrec 2010: robust correspondence benchmark. In: Proc. EUROGRAPHICS Workshop on 3D Object Retrieval, EG 3DOR 2010 (2010)

5. Bronstein, A., Bronstein, M., Kimmel, R.: Numerical Geometry of Non-Rigid Shapes, 1st edn. Springer Publishing Company, Incorporated (2008)
6. Clarenz, U., Diewald, U., Rumpf, M.: Anisotropic geometric diffusion in surface processing. In: Proc. of the Conference on Visualization 2000, VIS 2000, pp. 397–405 (2000)
7. Cohen-Steiner, D., Morvan, J.M.: Restricted delaunay triangulations and normal cycle. In: Proc. of the Nineteenth Annual Symposium on Computational Geometry, SCG 2003, pp. 312–321 (2003)
8. Desbrun, M., Meyer, M., Schröder, P., Barr, A.H.: Implicit fairing of irregular meshes using diffusion and curvature flow. In: Proc. of the 26th Annual Conference on Computer Graphics and Interactive Techniques. pp. 317–324. SIGGRAPH '99 (1999)
9. Fillard, P., Arsigny, V., Ayache, N., Pennec, X.: A Riemannian Framework for the Processing of Tensor-Valued Images. In: Fogh Olsen, O., Florack, L.M.J., Kuijper, A. (eds.) DSSCV 2005. LNCS, vol. 3753, pp. 112–123. Springer, Heidelberg (2005)
10. de Goes, F., Liu, B., Budninskiy, M., Tong, Y., Desbrun, M.: Discrete 2-tensor fields on triangulations. Computer Graphics Forum 33(5) (2014)
11. Kim, K., Tompkin, J., Theobalt, C.: Curvature-aware regularization on Riemannian submanifolds. In: Proc. of the IEEE International Conference on Computer Vision, ICCV 2013, pp. 881–888 (2013)
12. Kovnatsky, A., Raviv, D., Bronstein, M.M., Bronstein, A.M., Kimmel, R.: Geometric and photometric data fusion in non-rigid shape analysis. Numerical Mathematics: Theory, Methods and Applications (NM-TMA) 6(1), 199–222 (2013)
13. Litman, R., Bronstein, A.: Learning spectral descriptors for deformable shape correspondence. IEEE Transactions on Pattern Analysis and Machine Intelligence 36(1), 171–180 (2014)
14. Litman, R., Bronstein, A.M., Bronstein, M.M.: Diffusion-geometric maximally stable component detection in deformable shapes. Computers & Graphics 35(3), 549–560 (2011)
15. Meyer, M., Desbrun, M., Schröder, P., Barr, A.H.: Discrete differential-geometry operators for triangulated 2-manifolds. Visualization and Mathematics III, pp. 35–57 (2003)
16. Perona, P., Malik, J.: Scale-space and edge detection using anisotropic diffusion. IEEE Trans. Pattern Anal. Mach. Intell. 12(7), 629–639 (1990)
17. Peyré, G.: Toolbox graph - a toolbox to process graph and triangulated meshes. (2008) https://www.ceremade.dauphine.fr~peyre/matlab/graph/content.html
18. Pinkall, U., Polthier, K.: Computing discrete minimal surfaces and their conjugates. Experimental Mathematics 2(1), 15–36 (1993)
19. Pokrass, J., Bronstein, A.M., Bronstein, M.M., Sprechmann, P., Sapiro, G.: Sparse modeling of intrinsic correspondences. Computer Graphics Forum 32(2pt. 4), 459–468 (2013)
20. Reuter, M., Biasotti, S., Giorgi, D., Patanè, G., Spagnuolo, M.: Discrete laplace-beltrami operators for shape analysis and segmentation. Computers & Graphics 33(3), 381–390 (2009)
21. Rodolà, E., Rota Bulò, S., Cremers, D.: Robust region detection via consensus segmentation of deformable shapes. Computer Graphics Forum 33(5) (2014)

22. Rodolà, E., Rota Bulò, S., Windheuser, T., Vestner, M., Cremers, D.: Dense non-rigid shape correspondence using random forests. In: IEEE Conference on Computer Vision and Pattern Recognition (CVPR) (2014)
23. Rustamov, R.M.: Laplace-beltrami eigenfunctions for deformation invariant shape representation. In: Proc. of the Fifth Eurographics Symposium on Geometry Processing, SGP 2007, pp. 225–233 (2007)
24. Sun, J., Ovsjanikov, M., Guibas, L.: A concise and provably informative multi-scale signature based on heat diffusion. In: Proc. of the Symposium on Geometry Processing, SGP 2009, pp. 1383–1392 (2009)
25. Tasdizen, T., Whitaker, R., Burchard, P., Osher, S.: Geometric surface smoothing via anisotropic diffusion of normals. In: Proc. of the Conference on Visualization 2002, VIS 2002, pp. 125–132 (2002)

A Bioinformatics Approach
to 3D Shape Matching

Manuele Bicego(✉), Stefano Danese, Simone Melzi, and Umberto Castellani

Dipartimento di Informatica, University of Verona,
Strada le Grazie 15, 37134 Verona, Italy
manuele.bicego@univr.it

Abstract. In this paper we exploit the effectiveness of bioinformatics tools to deal with 3D shape matching. The key idea is to transform the shape into a biological sequence and take advantage of bioinformatics tools for sequence alignment to improve shape matching. In order to extract a reliable ordering of mesh vertices we employ the spectral-based sequencing method derived from the well known *Fiedler Vector*. Local geometric features are then collected and quantized into a finite set of discrete values in analogy with *nucleotide* or *aminoacid* sequence. Two standard biological sequence matching strategies are employed aiming at evaluating both local and global alignment methods. Preliminary experiments are performed on standard non-rigid shape datasets by showing promising results in comparison with other methods.

Keywords: Non-rigid shape matching · Biological sequence alignment · Spectral mesh processing · Local geometry

1   Introduction

The research in Computational Biology and Bioinformatics experienced an unprecedented growth in recent years, tying together many disciplines and fields of computer science. In particular, very often Pattern Recognition/Machine Learning techniques are used to solve problems and extract knowledge from biological data [2]. There are lots of motivations for exploiting these disciplines: it is possible to "learn from examples", derive quantitative models, handle non vectorial data, and deal with many classification, clustering and detection problems commonly encountered in the life sciences. In many cases, Pattern Recognition techniques can not be applied "as they are"; researchers spent large efforts to tailor and adapt techniques, so that biological constraints and needs are taken into account. Sometimes, this led very far away from the original methodology, with a clear example in the profile-HMMs [10].

Provocatively speaking, this tight interaction is mainly unidirectional, with the biology/life science side earning the largest benefit. Very recently, an alternative way of interaction has started to be investigated [3,6,21,22]: translate advanced bioinformatics solutions into ideas and methodologies useful to solve

© Springer International Publishing Switzerland 2015
L. Agapito et al. (Eds.): ECCV 2014 Workshops, Part IV, LNCS 8928, pp. 313–325, 2015.
DOI: 10.1007/978-3-319-16220-1_22

a pattern recognition problem. The main goal in such contexts is to answer to the following intriguing question: *can we reverse the way of interaction?*, or, in other words, *can we exploit advanced bioinformatics models and solutions to solve pattern recognition tasks?* This perspective is rather new in the literature, with only few relevant examples [3,6,21,22]: in particular, in the video genome project[1] [6], aimed at analysing video sequences, authors established an analogy between biological sequences and videos: in particular, the authors defined the so called "video-DNA", a way to map features extracted from video frames into nucleotidic biological sequences: given the analogy, many different video analysis problems can be faced using the huge range of effective, optimised, and interpretable bioinformatics tools derived from more than 40 years of research. For example authors were able to search for videos using the famous BLAST [1] – a surprisingly fast and effective heuristic-driven algorithm for biological sequence retrieval. In [3,21,22], authors exploited the analogies which can be established between the contour of a 2D shape and a biological sequence to face the 2D shape classification problem with biological sequence alignment tools. They show in [3,22] that, even if employing very basic matching techniques, really promising results can be obtained on different datasets. Moreover, in [21] authors demonstrated that a careful and context-aware setting of the parameters of the biological sequence alignment tools permit to improve even more the obtained accuracies.

This paper is inserted in the above-described context, and explores the possibility of exploiting bioinformatics solutions to face the 3D shape matching problem. Matching of 3D shapes represents an important field in Pattern Recognition and Computer vision research, with various efficient approaches (see [7,14,17,20] for recent surveys). In general ideal shape matching methods should be highly discriminative and invariant to pose and shape deformations [27]. The majority of methods are focused on effective shape representation aiming at compactly characterizing the shape by a *signature* (or shape *descriptor* [12,20,30]). A large class of methods are based on the matching between the whole shapes by defining a *global* shape descriptor [12,27,30]. Conversely, many approaches are exploiting *local* signatures by leading to a point-to-point matching [8,28]. Recently a lot of work has been proposed to combine *local* and *global* methods by extending the so called *Bag of Words* paradigm to 3D shapes [5,31].

In this paper rather than focusing on the kind of descriptor we propose to pay more attention on the matching phase by facing the 3D shape matching problem with biological sequence analysis tools. The key idea consists of encoding the 3D shape as a biological sequence and employing tailored bioinformatics tools to perform the matching. In order to extract the biological sequence from a 3D shape we exploit spectral-based mesh sequencing methods. As proposed for streaming mesh [13] or mesh partitioning [18] we used the order provided by the second eigenvector of the Laplace operator, usually referred to as *Fiedler Vector*. Then, we collect the shape index [16] at each vertex of the shape as local geometric feature. The ordered sequence of local geometry features is then mapped

---

[1] See http://v-nome.org/about.html

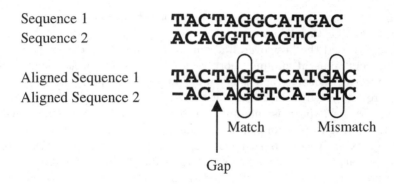

Fig. 1. Alignment of two sequences

into a biological sequence with two simple mappings, one leading to a nucleotide sequence, the other leading to an aminoacid sequence. Once encoded 3D shapes in biological sequences, we employed standard sequence alignment tools (like the Smith-Waterman [29] and the Needleman-Wunch [24] algorithms) to devise a sequence similarity measure. Such similarity is finally used in a standard nearest neighbour classification scenario. Moreover, the alignment procedure provides us a robust estimation of corresponding points among shape pairs.

We tested our approach in matching non-rigid shapes with strong pose variations from two standard datasets: Tosca [4] and Shape Google [5]. Even if we applied a very simple mapping as well as the basic standard bioinformatics solutions to this problem, we obtained very promising results, also in comparison with the state of the art.

2   Background: Biological Sequence Alignment

Analysis of biological sequences is of paramount importance in biology and medicine, very often representing the basic operation in many computational biology and bioinformatics analyses. Broadly speaking, biological sequences are of two types: nucleotide sequences – i.e. strings made with the 4 symbols of DNA, namely $ATCG$ – and aminoacid sequences – i.e. strings with symbols coming from a 20 letters alphabet. Intuitively, the alignment of two sequences is aimed at finding the best registration between them (namely the best way of superimposing one sequence on the other). From a practical point of view, alignment is obtained by inserting spaces inside the sequences (the so called *gaps*) in order to maximize the point to point similarity between them – see Fig. 1. A huge amount of approaches have been proposed in the past to face this problem (see [15,19] for recent reviews and perspectives on the topic), with already effective methods aged in the seventies or early eighties [24,29]. Broadly, we can classify them into pairwise and multiple alignment approaches, with the former devoted at finding the best registration of two sequences and the latter aimed ad finding a simultaneous alignment of more than two sequences. Another interesting classification is among global or local alignment approaches: global methods try to find the best overall alignment between sequences, whereas the local alignment aims at finding short regions of highly similar sequences. A thorough treatment of this topic is of course out of the scope of this paper. Here, since we are interested in investigating the basic potentialities of our ideas, we chose two very basic pairwise alignment tools (namely the Needleman-Wunsch [24] and the Smith-Waterman [29] algorithms), representing the reference in this field – being extensively employed since their proposal in the seventies/eighties.

In particular, the NeedlemanWunsch algorithm [24] is a dynamic programming method for finding the best *global* alignment between two sequences – it represents the first application of dynamic programming to biological sequence comparison. The basic idea is to maximize the similarity between two sequences by *i)* making use of a similarity matrix (also called Scoring Matrix) which defines the similarity between every pair of symbols in the alphabet and *ii)* by taking into account penalty values for gap opening and extension. There are many possible scoring matrices, which are typically built on the basis of biological knowledge[2].

On the other side, the Smith-Waterman algorithm [29] is a dynamic programming method for local alignment, which identifies homologous regions (i.e., roughly speaking, similar regions) between sequences by searching for optimal local alignments. Instead of looking at an entire sequence at once, the S-W algorithm compares multi-lengthed segments, looking for whichever segment maximizes the scoring measure. A scoring system is used, which includes a set of specified gap penalties.

3   The Proposed Method

The main steps of our proposed pipeline are i) spectral-based shape sequencing, ii) local feature extraction, iii) mapping into biological sequences, and iv) shape matching by sequence alignment. Figure 2 shows the scheme of proposed method. In order to highlight the effectiveness of proposed pipeline we show in Figure 3 the geometric processing of two shapes of the same class in two different poses (i.e., strong isometric transformation). It is interesting to observe that Fiedler vector defines a vertex ordering that goes from the tip of the tail to the head of the cat for both the shapes. Moreover, the extracted local geometric features, namely the Shape index, highlights coherently the semantic components of the cat (see for example the eyes, the ears, and the paws). In the following we introduce more theoretical details of the proposed approach.

3.1   Spectral-Based Shape Sequencing

Let $\mathcal{M}$ be a mesh with N-vertices. A function on $\mathcal{M}$ has a discrete representation specified by a vector with N components. A Mesh Laplacian is a linear operator

---

[2] For example, in the nucleotide case, it is known from the chemical composition of DNA basis that it is more difficult to have a change from an Adedine to a Thymine rather than to a Guanine.

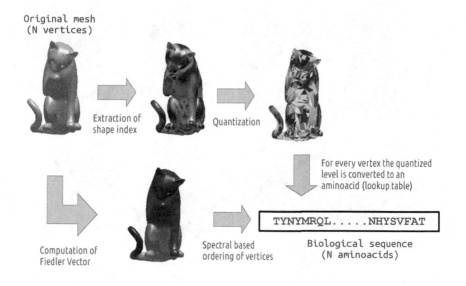

Original mesh
(N vertices)

Extraction of
shape index

Quantization

For every vertex the quantized
level is converted to an
aminoacid (lookup table)

TYNYMRQL.....NHYSVFAT

Computation of
Fiedler Vector

Spectral based
ordering of vertices

Biological sequence
(N aminoacids)

Fig. 2. Scheme of proposed method

L defined by a $N \times N$ matrix [32]:

$$(\mathbf{L}\mathbf{f})_i = b_i^{-1} \sum_{j \in N(i)} w_{ij}(f_i - f_j), \tag{1}$$

and it can be factored into the product of a diagonal and a symmetric matrix

$$L = B^{-1}S, \tag{2}$$

where B^{-1} is a diagonal matrix whose diagonal entries are b_i^{-1} and S is a symmetric matrix whose diagonal entries are given by $s_{ii} = \sum_{j \in N(i)} w_{ij}$ and whose off diagonal entries are $-w_{ij}$. A particular class of mesh Laplacians is defined by the discrete Laplace-Beltrami operator for Riemannian manifold. Here, we use the so called *cotangent* weighting scheme [23,26]. It is well known that from the Laplace Beltrami mesh operator it is possible to obtain an ordering of its vertices. Consider the problem of embedding vertices in the line. This problem is mathematically equivalent to seek a permutation $\pi : V \longrightarrow \{1, 2, ..., n\}$ of the vertices of a mesh $\mathcal{M} = (V, E)$. A solution to this problem can be given by the so called *Fiedler Vector* [11], i.e., the eigenvector associated with the smallest non-zero eigenvalue of L. In other words, the Fiedler vector provides a way to order the vertices of the mesh: by following this order we can derive a sequence of vertices, to be characterized via local geometric properties (i.e., shape index) and translated into biological symbols.

Fig. 3. Geometric processing of two isometric shapes. From left to right: original shapes, Fiedler vector, Shape Index, and shape quantization.

3.2 Local Feature Extraction

We encode local geometric properties of the surface using the *Shape Index* [16], which is defined as:

$$si = -\frac{2}{\pi}\arctan\left(\frac{k_1 + k_2}{k_1 - k_2}\right) \quad k_1 > k_2,$$

where k_1, k_2 are the principal curvatures of a generic vertex. The Shape Index varies in $[-1, 1]$ and provides a local categorization of the shape into primitive forms such as spherical cap and cup, rut, ridge, trough, or saddle [16]. Shape index is scale invariant [16] and it has already been successfully employed for surface matching [8].

3.3 Mapping Into Biological Sequences

Once obtained from the mesh, the ordered sequence of shape indeces should be converted into a biological sequence, in order to permit the mapping. It is interesting to note that there is a strict parallelism between this sequence-based encoding of 3D surfaces and the protein: in both cases the matching is based on the sequences, which are determining the 3D shape (proteins are sequences of aminoacids folded in 3D).

Even if different schemes for mapping shape indeces to aminoacids can be adopted, here we investigated two very simple schemes, both having pros and cons:

- *DNA-mapping*: in this case the shape index is directly mapped to the ATCG alphabet of DNA sequences. We divided the [-1:1] interval into 3 zones ([-1:-0.3], (-0.3:0.3), [0.3 1]), which roughly correspond to values indicating concavity, convexity and saddle characteristics of the surface. Then, each zone is mapped to a different nucleotide (with one character left out), thus transforming the 3D shape into a sequence of highly identifiable geometric characteristics, which are directly mapped into nucleotides. The disadvantage of this encoding scheme is that the quantization is rather heavy (only three symbols), this possibly leading to a loss of details.
- *Protein-mapping*: this method tries to overcome the problems of the previous scheme by exploiting the aminoacid alphabet, which is composed by 20 symbols. Againg we split the shape index range into 20 equally spaced intervals, each one corresponding to an aminoacid. In this way the loss of details derived from the quantization may be less crucial; on the other side, the geometric interpretation can be partially lost.

3.4   Shape Matching by Sequence Alignment

Given the encoding, the alignment of the two obtained biological sequences straightforwardly permits to define a classification strategy based on standard Nearest Neighbour (NN) classifier [9]. We are aware that, given a similarity matrix, interesting alternatives to NN exist (e.g. the dissimilarity-based representation paradigm [25]). However, NN remains rather accurate, still being enough simple to demonstrate the suitability of our proposed approach. Note that in this paper we are more interested in showing the feasibility of our perspective, rather than reaching state of the art results. Moreover, this technique is really interpretable, since it gives an intuitive motivation of the assigned class label by showing the nearest neighbour to the user. In more detail, NN classifier, given an unknown object X and a distance, finds the point in the training set which is nearest to X, assigning X to the class of that point. This is a natural choice, since given our framework it is straightforward to define a distance between 2D shapes: after encoding the two 3D shapes into biological sequences, we can align them and use the alignment error as a measure of distance.

In our experiments we used both local and global alignment tools: in particular, again for being as basic as possible, we employed the two historical approaches described in previous section, namely the Needleman-Wunsch [24] and the Smith-Waterman [29] algorithms. Moreover, we normalize the alignment score by the averaged length of the two involved sequences.

4   Experiments

We evaluated the proposed approach on two 3D shape matching scenarios. We exploited the following variants of the matching algorithm:

- SW / NW: the two alignment algorithms used: SW stands for Smith-Waterman, NW for Needleman-Wunch

- AA / NT: the two coding strategies employed: AA represents the protein coding (i.e. using 20 aminoacids), NT represents the DNA coding (i.e. using the four nucleotides)
- Basic / Advanced: this option refers to the alignment parameters. Actually two are the parameters that should be defined when aligning two biological sequences: the scoring matrix and the gap opening/extending penalty. As explained in the previous Sections, the former defines the price of every substitution in the matrix, whereas the latter defines the penalty in the similarity got while opening (or extending) a gap region. These two parameters typically have a clear biological meaning, and can change drastically the final result. In this preliminary evaluation, we performed two sets of experiments: in the former (referred to as "Basic") we tried to keep as easiest as possible the scheme, leaving such parameters as set by default in the Matlab implementation (Matlab bioinformatics toolbox); in the latter (referred to as "Advanced") we relaxed one biological assumption which does not hold in the shape classification case – this being of course only the first step through the tailoring of the sequence alignment tools to our problem. In particular we observe that in biology the gap penalty is typically high: it is not really desirable to break a biological sequence. In the shape case, nevertheless, such a strong constraint does not hold: actually, gaps can really help in dealing with occlusions and – mainly – scale changes.

We compared the best results of our approach with the following methods:

- Shape DNA method [27] as gold standard for non-rigid shape matching.
- DTW: Dynamic Time warping distance between the Shape Index sequences ordered with the Fiedler Vector. We used a 10% warping window constraint, which is the customary setting in the speech recognition community.
- Histogram of Shape Index as basic shape descriptor. We considered 20, 50, 100, 150, 200, 300 bins, reporting in the table only the best result.

In our first experiment we employed the Tosca *non-rigid world* dataset [4] composed of 10 classes of non-rigid objects: cat, centaur, man1, dog, gorilla, man2, horse, lioness, seahorse, and woman (see Figure 4). For each class there are different number of samples by leading to a total of 143 models. Table 1 reports classification errors obtained using the Leave One Out (LOO) protocol. Our approach reaches the best classification score with several sequence matching approaches by outperforming in particular Shape DNA method. DTW performed better than simple Shape Index histogram by confirming the reliability of the ordering extracted from the Fiedler vector.

As mentioned before, the advantage of the proposed biologically inspired method consists of performing a robust alignment of the input sequences that leads in our case to the estimation of an (incomplete) point-to-point matching. In order to visually evaluate this procedure we plotted the estimated matching among some pairs of shapes from Tosca dataset. Figure 5 shows the estimated correspondences where only fully matched pairs of points are highlighted. It is interesting to observe that correspondences are quite convincing. For instance

Fig. 4. Tosca non-rigid objects: cat, centaur, man1, dog, gorilla, man2, horse, lioness, seahorse, and woman

Table 1. Results with Tosca dataset

Method	AA	NT
NW (Basic)	**0.0000**	0.0350
SW (Basic)	0.0629	0.1189
NW (Advanced)	**0.0000**	0.1888
SW (Advanced)	0.0629	0.2308

Method	Error LOO
Shape DNA	0.0070
Shape Index Hist (100 bin)	0.0839
DTW	0.0420
Proposed approach (best)	**0.0000**

the paws of the cats or the heads of the horses are correctly matching. Note that due to the symmetry of the shapes some correspondences are switched from left to right side (see for example the fingers or right and left hands of man pair). Finally, it is worth noting that the alignment fails in presence of strong shape partiality like in the case of matching between man and centaur (see Figure 5 bottom right). Clearly this aspect has to be investigated more thoroughly in our future research, as done for example in the 2D shape classification case in [21].

The second experiment is evaluated on a subset of the Shape Google dataset [5]. The dataset is composed of 10 classes of non-rigid objects: dog, cat1, cat2, woman, man, dromedary, elephant, flamingo, horse, cougar. Each object appeared with multiple modifications and transformations of the original shape. Here we evaluated isometry and isometry-topology transformations with five different strength levels (see isometry-topology transformations in Figure 6).

Tables 2 and 3 show classification results. Our approach showed the best results also in this case by confirming the robustness of the proposed methods

Fig. 5. Point to point matching

Fig. 6. ShapeGoogle dataset: null shape (left) and five different strength levels of topological and isometric transformation

against strong shape deformations. In particular, zero error is observed for several configurations. Here, it seems evident that errors introduced by topological noise are compensated by the robustness of the biological sequence matching algorithms.

As a final observation, let us try to understand the behaviour of the different variants of the proposed approach. Concerning the alignment algorithm, it seems that the global method (NW) performs better than the local one (SW): actually local methods can be more useful when trying to match objects with occlusions, not present in the analysed dataset. Concerning the encoding methods, the AA version seems to be more adequate, especially in the ShapeGoogle dataset: probably the quantization derived from the NT scheme is too strong in this case, destroying information which is useful for matching.

Table 2. Results with ShapeGoogle-isometry dataset

Method	AA	NT
NW (Basic)	0.0408	0.1224
SW (Basic)	0.0612	0.1429
NW (Advanced)	**0.0000**	0.1020
SW (Advanced)	**0.0000**	0.1020

Method	Error LOO
Shape DNA	0.1020
Shape Index Hist (20 bin)	0.1837
DTW	0.0408
Proposed approach (best)	**0.0000**

Table 3. Results with ShapeGoogle-isometry-topology dataset

Method	AA	NT
NW (Basic)	**0.0000**	0.1837
SW (Basic)	**0.0000**	0.2245
NW (Advanced)	**0.0000**	0.1224
SW (Advanced)	**0.0000**	0.1224

Method	Error LOO
Shape DNA	0.3469
Shape Index Hist (20 bin)	0.2041
DTW	0.1224
Proposed approach (best)	**0.0000**

5   Conclusions

In this paper we focus on the matching phase in non-rigid 3D shape comparison problems. We show how bioinformatics methods can be useful to cope with shape alignment by encoding a 3D mesh as a discrete biological sequence. A well defined pipeline is introduced to address the problems of vertex sequences, local shape description and quantization, and shape classification by sequence alignment. Despite the fact that each single step is simple and well known, the overall method has shown promising results and encourages us to further exploit the idea of 3D matching approaches with established bioinformatics tools. Once a correspondence between 3D shapes and biological sequences is defined, many other interesting information can be extracted (to detect interesting parts, or to do mesh segmentation), by exploiting the huge amount of bioinformatics tools developed in more than 40 years of research.

References

1. Altschul, S.F., Gish, W., Miller, W., Myers, E.W., Lipman, D.J.: Basic local alignment search tool. Journal of Molecular Biology **215**(3), 403–410 (1990)
2. Baldi, P., Brunak, S.: Bioinformatics: the machine learning approach, 2nd edn. MIT Press, Cambridge (2001)
3. Bicego, M., Lovato, P.: 2d shape recognition using biological sequence alignment tools. In: ICPR, pp. 1359–1362 (2012)
4. Bronstein, A.M., Bronstein, M.M., Kimmel, R.: Numerical geometry of non-rigid shapes. Springer (2008)
5. Bronstein, A.M., Bronstein, M.M., Guibas, L.J., Ovsjanikov, M.: Shape google: Geometric words and expressions for invariant shape retrieval. TOG **30**(1), 1–20 (2011)
6. Bronstein, A.M., Bronstein, M.M., Kimmel, R.: The video genome. CoRR abs/1003.5320 (2010)
7. Castellani, U., Bartoli, A.: 3D shape registration. In: 3D Imaging, Analysis, and Applications. Springer (2012)
8. Castellani, U., Cristani, M., Murino, V.: Statistical 3D shape analysis by local generative descriptors. IEEE Transaction on Pattern Analysis and Machine Intelligence (PAMI) **33**, 2555–2560 (2011)
9. Duda, R., Hart, P., Stork, D.: Pattern Classification (2nd edn.). Wiley Interscience (2001)
10. Eddy, S.R.: Profile hidden markov models. Bioinformatics **14**(9), 755–763 (1998)
11. Fiedler, M.: Algebraic connectivity of graphs. A property of eigenvectors of non-negative sym- metric matrices and its application to graph theory **25**(4), 619–633 (1975)
12. Funkhouser, T., Kazhdan, M., Min, P., Shilane, P.: Shape-based retrieval and analysis of 3D models. ACM Comm. **48**, 58–64 (2005)
13. Isenburg, M., Lindstrom, P.: Streaming meshes. In: Proceedings of Visualization, pp. 231–238 (2005)
14. Kaick, O.V., Zhang, H., Hamarneh, G., Cohen-Or, D.: A survey on shape correspondence. Computer Graphics Forum **30**, 1681–1707 (2011)
15. Kemena, C., Notredame, C.: Upcoming challenges for multiple sequence alignment methods in the high-throughput era. Bioinformatics **25**(19) (2009)
16. Koenderink, J., van Doorn, A.: Surface shape and curvature scales. Image and Visual Computing **10**, 557–565 (1992)
17. Li, C., Hamza, A.B.: Spatially aggregating spectral descriptors for nonrigid 3d shape retrieval: a comparative survey. Multimedia Systems **20**, 253–581 (2014)
18. Li, C., Hamza, A.: Intrinsic spatial pyramid matching for deformable 3d shape retrieval. J. Multimedia Information Retrieval **2**(4), 261–271 (2013)
19. Li, H., Homer, N.: A survey of sequence alignment algorithms for next-generation sequencing. Briefings in Bioinformatics **11**(5), 473–483 (2010)
20. Lian, Z., et al.: A Comparison of Methods for Non-rigid 3D Shape Retrieval. Pattern Recognition **46**(1), 449–461 (2013)
21. Lovato, P., Milanese, A., Centomo, C., Giorgetti, A., Bicego, M.: S-BLOSUM: classification of 2d shapes with biological sequence alignment. In: Proc. Int. Conf on Pattern Recognition (ICPR 2014) (2014)
22. Lovato, P., Bicego, M.: 2d shapes classification using blast. In: Gimel'farb, G., Hancock, E., Imiya, A., Kuijper, A., Kudo, M., Omachi, S., Windeatt, T., Yamada, K. (eds.) SSPR & SPR 2012. LNCS, vol. 7626, pp. 273–281. Springer, Heidelberg (2012)

23. Meyer, M., Desbrun, M., Schröder, P., Barr., A.H.: Discrete differential-geometry operators for triangulated 2-manifolds. In: Proc. of VisMath, pp. 35–57 (2002)
24. Needleman, S., Wunsch, C.: A general method applicable to the search for similarities in the amino acid sequence of two proteins. Journal of Molecular Biology **48**, 443–453 (1970)
25. Pekalska, E., Duin, R.P.: The dissimilarity representation for Pattern Recongition - Foundations and Applications. World Scientific (2005)
26. Pinkall, U., Polthier, K.: Computing discrete minimal surfaces and their conjugates. Experimental Mathematics **1**(2), 15–6 (1993)
27. Reuter, M., Wolter, F.E., Peinecke, N.: Laplace-Beltrami spectra as 'Shape-DNA' of surfaces and solids. Computer-Aided Design **38**, 342–366 (2006)
28. Ruggeri, M., Patane, G., Spagnuolo, M., Sauper, D.: Spectral-driven isometry-invariant matching of 3d shapes. International Journal of Computer Vision **89**, 248–265 (2010)
29. Smith, T., Waterman, M.S.: Identification of common molecular subsequences. Journal of Molecular Biology **147**(1), 195–197 (1981)
30. Tangelder, J.W., Veltkamp, R.C.: A survey of content based 3D shape retrieval methods. In: Proc. Conf. Shape Modelling and Applications, pp. 145–156 (2004)
31. Toldo, R., Castellani, U., Fusiello, A.: The bag of words approach for retrieval and categorization of 3D objects. The Visual Computer **26**, 1257–1268 (2010)
32. Zhang, H., van Kaick, O., Dyer, R.: Spectral mesh processing. Eurographics, 1–29 (2009)

A Grassmannian Framework for Face Recognition of 3D Dynamic Sequences with Challenging Conditions

Taleb Alashkar[1], Boulbaba Ben Amor[1],
Mohamed Daoudi[1], and Stefano Berretti[2]([✉])

[1] Télécom Lille/LIFL (UMR CNRS/Lille1 8022), Lille, France
[2] University of Florence, Florence, Italy
stefano.berretti@unifi.it

Abstract. Modern face recognition approaches target successful person identification in challenging scenarios, where uncooperative subjects are captured under unconstrained imaging conditions. With the introduction of a new generation of 3D acquisition devices capable of dynamic acquisitions, this trend is now emerging also in 3D based approaches. Motivated by these considerations, in this paper we propose an original and effective framework to address face recognition from 3D temporal sequences acquired in adverse conditions, including internal and external occlusions, pose and expression variations, and talking. Due to the novelty of the proposed scenario, a new database has been collected using a single-view structured light scanner with a large field of view, which allows free movement of the acquired subjects. The 3D temporal sequences are divided into fragments each modeled as a linear subspace in order to embody the shape and the motion of the facial surfaces. In virtue of the Riemannian geometry of the space of real k-dimensional linear subspaces, called Grassmann manifold, a new formulation of the matching between 3D temporal sequences has been developed. An unsupervised clustering over the Grassmann manifold is also introduced for efficient recognition. The proposed approach achieves promising results, without requiring any prior training or manual intervention.

Keywords: Face recognition · 3d dynamic face sequences · Grassmann manifold

1 Introduction

Early biometric solutions using the face for recognizing persons' identity were based on the face appearance in 2D still images acquired in controlled ambient, with ideal illumination conditions and with cooperative subjects. However, these over constrained solutions are of limited utility in real contexts, such as law enforcement, surveillance systems and access control, where occlusions, pose variation, illumination changes and facial expressions are present. Limitations of methods based on 2D still images have stimulated the investigation of

© Springer International Publishing Switzerland 2015
L. Agapito et al. (Eds.): ECCV 2014 Workshops, Part IV, LNCS 8928, pp. 326–340, 2015.
DOI: 10.1007/978-3-319-16220-1_23

new solutions, which also exploit the temporal dimension of 2D-videos acquired with 2D cameras. In fact, it is a shared conviction that motion information can improve the recognition rate, especially under uncontrolled viewing conditions [1,5,10]. However, evaluations on unconstrained face recognition (FR) from 2D still images and videos, such as the Multiple Biometric Grand Challenge [16] showed that FR under pose variations is still a distant goal [1]. This boosted a large corpus of ongoing work focusing on FR in the "wild" [19,21,23].

Recently, the availability of 3D acquisition systems opened the way to 3D face recognition solutions. Since these approaches use the 3D geometry of the face, they have the advantage of being robust against illumination and pose variations [2,3]. However, most of the existing solutions are tested on datasets collected under well-controlled settings using static acquisition systems [17], though some methods have recently appeared that account for pose variation, facial expressions and occlusions [7,15]. Most recent advancements of 3D technologies, like structured-light and time-of-flight scanners, made 3D dynamic acquisition systems available in the market at lower cost. These devices have still optical capabilities that are far from those exhibited by 2D cameras and often differ in terms of operating distance and resolution (for example, Kinect-like devices operate up to some meter, but with low resolution). Despite of these limitations, they make possible real-time capturing of a continuous flow of 3D scans, thus opening the way to solutions capable of performing face and facial expression recognition from dynamic sequences of 3D face scans. Apart for its technical practicability, adding the temporal dimension to 3D acquisitions is motivated by the observation that the face is a deformable 3D surface changing over time, so that using the temporal component can be essential to improve recognition, especially under adverse acquisition conditions. A clear example of this is given by spoofing attacks that can be difficult to detect in 2D still images or even in 2D videos, but result much more evident when the 3D temporal component is considered.

Works addressing FR from temporal sequences of 3D scans are still a few, with some of them restricted to RGB-D Kinect-like sensors [12,14]. For example, Min et al. [14] proposed a real-time 3D face recognition system using multiple RGB-D instances. The approach does not exploit temporal correlation; however, it shows that exploiting majority voting between multiple instances provides better recognition rate than using static scans. Similarly, working on RGB-D acquisitions, Li et al. [12] proposed an algorithm for face recognition under varying poses, expressions, illumination and disguise. To the best of our knowledge, the only approach addressing FR from dynamic sequences of 3D face scans is that proposed by Sun et al. [20], where a 3D dynamic spatio-temporal approach is derived by computing a local descriptor based on the curvature values at vertices of 3D faces. Spatial and temporal Hidden Markov Models are used for the recognition process, using 22 landmarks manually annotated and tracked over time. As an important achievement of this work it is also evidenced that 3D face dynamics provides better results that 2D videos and 3D static scans. However, the applicability of this work remains limited, since it requires 3D high resolution scans in the sequences. In addition, the method requires scans in frontal pose, without pose variation or occlusions.

In this work, a new FR approach from temporal sequences of 3D scans acquired in adverse conditions, including internal and external occlusions, large and free pose variations, facial expressions and talking is proposed. To the best of our knowledge, this is the first work proposing this new paradigm to overcome the 2D video and 3D static based limitations. A subspace-based modeling approach is introduced, where the spatial-temporal data are modeled as a finite-dimensional linear subspace. Thus, each linear subspace is considered as an element on a Grassmann manifold. This formulation has some interesting aspects: *(i)* Comparing two subspaces is cheaper than comparing two 3D dynamic fragments; *(ii)* It is more robust to noise and missing data, which are common in realistic scenarios. In addition, this approach uses a holistic descriptor based on shape normals, without requiring any manual/automatic landmarking. The facial motion is also modeled and exploited in the recognition process.

According to the proposed representation, each subject in the gallery is represented by several 3D subsequences as instances, thus resulting in a large gallery set. Therefore, to optimize the efficiency of recognition, an unsupervised clustering approach over the Grassmannian of the gallery instances is applied. Due to the absence of databases collecting 3D dynamic sequences for FR under adverse conditions, we constructed a new database, which includes scans exhibiting free pose variations, facial expressions, talking, internal and external occlusions. In so doing, our dataset differs from the few existing 3D dynamic face databases (also called 4D datasets) [6,13,24], which are collected for facial expressions and/or action units recognition under highly conditioned settings and using high-resolution 3D acquisition.

In summary, the main contributions of this work are:

- A new FR scenario, where 3D dynamic sequences of the face are compared in order to permit FR under occlusions, pose variations and expressions;
- A new representation of 3D dynamic face sequences, which exploits relevant geometry tools on Grassmannian manifold, and unsupervised clustering of 3D temporal sequences;
- A new 3D dynamic face database, which includes well-known FR challenges in realistic scenarios.

The rest of the paper is organized as follows: Our FR approach between 3D dynamic sequences is presented in Sect. 2; In Sect. 3, the gallery clustering strategy for optimizing the efficiency of recognition is described; Experiments on the BU-4DFE database and the new 3D dynamic face dataset we collected are reported in Sect. 4; Discussion and conclusions are given in Sect. 5.

2   Face Recognition From 3D Temporal Sequences

In the proposed scenario, we consider 3D scans of the face that are acquired continuously through a 3D camera, thus constituting a temporal 3D sequence with dynamic variations of the geometry of the face. Using these data, the proposed approach is designed to exploit the spatio-temporal information available in 3D dynamic sequences of the face. To achieve this goal, a subspace modeling framework is applied. The basic idea of this solution is to extract a set of 3D temporal subsequences (fragments) from each 3D full temporal sequence, each constituted by a predefined number of 3D frames, and model each fragment f as a linear subspace $\mathcal{P}_f$, which can be represented as an element on a Grassmann manifold. According to this, given a 3D temporal sequence G in the gallery constituted by the concatenation of N 3D temporal fragments g_i indexed by i, so that $G = \{g_{i,(i=1,...,N)}\}$, and a probe 3D temporal fragment f with m successive frames $f_{probe} = [f_1, \ldots, f_m]$, the process of comparing a probe fragment with a gallery sequence can be formulated as follows:

$$g^* = \arg\min_i \ d(\mathcal{P}_{f_{probe}}, \mathcal{P}_{g_i}) \,, \tag{1}$$

where $d(.,.)$ denotes the geodesic distance between two linear subspaces, and g^* is the 3D temporal fragment of the gallery closer to the probe fragment according to the used distance. The complete recognition process is then obtained by extending this analysis to all the gallery sequences.

In order to apply the above representation and matching strategy, several steps are required for the scan preprocessing and subspace modeling, as illustrated in Fig. 1. After the acquisition, the face region of each frame in a 3D temporal sequence is cropped. Due to pose variations and the scanner technology, the number of vertices representing the surface of the face mesh varies in the same session and from one session to another. For the subspace modeling approach, it is important to have the same number of vertices representing the face in each frame of a sequence. To this end, a down-sampling is applied to each frame, so as to produce a constant number of n vertices per frame. Then, the normal at each vertex is estimated based on the neighborhood vertices included in a sphere of radius R around the vertex [18]. The set of estimated normals at the vertices of each frame capture the shape of the face, and is used as a spatial holistic descriptor of the face surface.

However, 3D frames constituting the 3D temporal sequences do not show a correspondence between their respective vertices, which is indeed necessary to develop the proposed linear subspace representation. In order to establish a rough and fast correspondence between frames, a normal shooting technique [4] is used between each two successive frames. As a result of this process, each 3D temporal fragment can be modeled as a matrix $\mathcal{S}$ of size $n \times \omega$, where n is the number of vertices, and ω is the number of frames in the 3D temporal fragment. Each column of $\mathcal{S}$ is given by the z component of the estimated normals at each vertex of one frame, so that each row embodies the motion information originated from the variability over time of the z component of the normal of one vertex of the face surface. The main reason for using only the z component, rather than x and/or y of the estimated normal is that z provides a discriminative signature between faces of different subjects, whereas the other two components are more similar in inter-class cases, thus leading to less discrimination in the

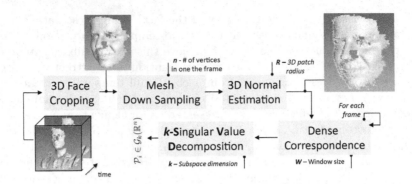

Fig. 1. Overview of the proposed approach

feature vector. Finally, a k-Singular Value Decomposition of the obtained matrix is performed $S = U\Sigma V^t$. The eigenvectors matrix U is an orthonormal basis of the subspace $\mathcal{P} = \text{span}(U)$, which is an element on the Grassman manifold $\mathcal{G}_k(\mathbb{R}^n)$. As a result of this pipeline, each 3D temporal fragment is viewed as an element of the Grassmannian manifold, and the original problem of comparing temporal sequences of 3D face scans is turned into a distance measurement between the elements over the Grassmannian manifold corresponding to the 3D temporal fragments.

2.1 Matching of 3D Temporal Fragments on the Grassmann Manifold

Let $\mathcal{G}_k(\mathbb{R}^n)$ be the Grassmann manifold of a set of k-dimensional linear subspaces of $\mathbb{R}^n$, and $\mathcal{X}$, $\mathcal{Y}$ denote a pair of subspaces on $\mathcal{G}_k(\mathbb{R}^n)$. Formally, the Riemannian distance between $\mathcal{X}$ and $\mathcal{Y}$ is the length of the shortest path connecting the two points on the manifold (i.e., the geodesic distance), as it is depicted in Fig. 2.

Golub and Loan [9] introduced an intuitive and computationally efficient way of defining the distance between two linear subspaces using the principal angles. In fact, there is a set of principal angles $\Theta = [\theta_1, \ldots, \theta_k]$ $(0 \leq \theta_1, \ldots, \theta_k \leq \pi/2)$, between the subspaces $\mathcal{X}$ and $\mathcal{Y}$ of size $n \times k$, recursively defined as follows:

$$\theta_k = \cos^{-1} \left(\max_{u_k \in \mathcal{X}} \max_{v_k \in \mathcal{Y}} \langle u_k^t, v_k \rangle \right), \tag{2}$$

where u_k and v_k are the vectors of the basis spanning, respectively, the subspaces $\mathcal{X}$ and $\mathcal{Y}$, subject to the additional constraints: (1) $\langle u_k^t, u_k \rangle = \langle v_k^t, v_k \rangle = 1$, being $\langle ., . \rangle$ the inner product in $\mathbb{R}^n$; and (2) $\langle u_k^t, u_i \rangle = \langle v_k^t, v_i \rangle = 0$ $(i = 1, \ldots, k-1)$. In other words, the first principal angle θ_1 is the smallest angle between all pairs of unit basis vectors in the two subspaces. The rest of the principal angles are defined in a similar manner.

Based on the definition of the principal angles, the geodesic distance between $\mathcal{X}$ and $\mathcal{Y}$ can be defined as [8]: $d^2(\mathcal{X}, \mathcal{Y}) = \sum_i \theta_i^2$. This distance is used to measure the similarity between two 3D temporal fragments, permitting to smooth

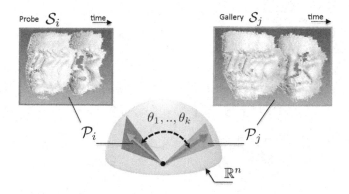

Fig. 2. Principal angles $\Theta = [\theta_1, .., \theta_k]$ computed between two linear subspaces $\mathcal{P}_i$ and $\mathcal{P}_j$ of the Grassmannian manifold $\mathcal{G}_k(\mathbb{R}^n)$

the effect of noisy data, at the same time showing robustness with respect to acquisition variations.

However, the combination of free pose variations of the subjects, and the use of a single-view 3D scanner for acquisition can result in many frames with missing parts of the face due to self occlusions. As a consequence, it is not possible to find correspondence and track vertices throughout successive frames of the whole 3D video. The proposed solution for this problem is to consider a sliding window of size ω containing an affordable pose variation. According to this, each subsequence of size ω, called 3D temporal fragment, represents approximately one pose of the moving face. In this way, each subject in the gallery is represented by multiple instances. Besides, this step helps to solve the problem of pose variation, in that it keeps the motion information coming from the variability of the face surface embodied in the linear subspace of each instance. The same procedure is applied to the probe sequence, where each ω successive frames are modeled as one probe to be recognized. According to this, the matching between probe and gallery is modeled as a multiple instance matching, with the final recognition decision based on majority voting. Figure 3 summarizes this process, showing how each subject in the gallery can be represented by several instances. In addition, it is also shown how using majority voting to accumulate the recognition decision coming from several successive instances can improve the accuracy of the final recognition decision. In particular, the recognition rate increases over time since more instances from the probe session give more chance to find similar poses in the gallery session of the subject.

3   Gallery Clustering for Efficient Recognition

As it is mentioned in Sect. 2, to solve the problem of pose variations the sequence of each subject in the gallery is divided into multiple instances over time. The same procedure is applied to probe sequences. So, each 3D temporal fragment

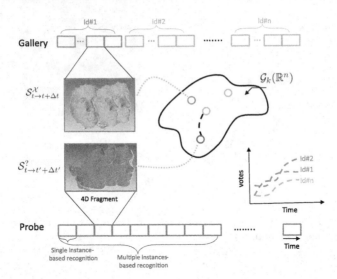

Fig. 3. Face recognition based on the match of multiple 3D temporal fragments derived from gallery and probe sequences: The sequences in the gallery (top of the figure) and the probe sequence (bottom of the figure) are divided into multiple 3D temporal fragments; each 3D temporal fragment is then regarded as a point on the Grassmannian manifold (mapping on $\mathcal{G}_k(\mathbb{R}^n)$, in the middle of the figure); the geodesic distance on the manifold is computed between every pair of fragments; the final recognition decision exploits majority voting over the time of successive instances (2D plots on the right)

of a probe is compared with all the 3D temporal fragments in the gallery. This exhaustive search can be avoided by clustering gallery instances according to the main pose of the 3D frames. After applying this unsupervised clustering, each cluster uses the *Karcher* mean [11] of the final elements included in the cluster as representative element. In this way, each probe sequence is compared just with the clusters' representative in order to recognize to which cluster it belongs to. Then, the comparison is extended to the instances that belong to this cluster in the gallery. This method significantly reduces the recognition time by avoiding the comparison of the probe instance with all the gallery instances.

The proposed clustering is performed using the K-means algorithm on the Grassmann manifold [22], as reported in Algorithm 1. This directly descends from the modeling of each 3D temporal fragment as a linear subspace (that is, an element on the Grassmann manifold with a well defined geodesic distance between any two elements). Let us consider a set of points on the Grassmann manifold $\mathcal{P} = \{\mathcal{P}_i\}_{i=1}^n$. They should be clustered in k clusters $\mathcal{C} = \{\mathcal{C}_i\}_{i=1}^k$. Each cluster has a mean on the Grassmann manifold $(\mu_1, \mu_2, \ldots, \mu_k)$. Each mean point should satisfy this condition: the sum of geodesic distances between the class mean and its elements is minimized. To solve this problem, an expectation maximization (EM) method is used. First, k points from $\mathcal{P}$ are initialized at random as cluster centers $(\mu_1^0, \mu_2^0, \ldots, \mu_k^0)$. Each point in $\mathcal{P}$ is then assigned to the nearest center in the E-step. Then, in the M-step, the cluster centers

---

Algorithm 1. Intrinsic K-means clustering on $\mathcal{G}_k(\mathbb{R}^n)$

Require: $\mathcal{P}_{i(1 \leq i \leq m)} \in \mathcal{G}_k(\mathbb{R}^n)$, N: Number of iterations,
    Initialize cluster centers $(\mu_1^0, \ldots, \mu_k^0)$ at random
    $j \leftarrow 0$
    while $(j < N)$ **do**
        Assign each $\mathcal{P}_i$ to the nearest cluster $\mathcal{C}_t$ by computing $d^2(\mathcal{P}_i, \mu_t) \leftarrow |exp_{\mu_t}^{-1}(\mathcal{P}_i)|^2$,
        being μ_t the center of $\mathcal{C}_t$
        Recompute cluster centers $(\mu_1^j, \ldots, \mu_k^j)$ using Algorithm 2
        $j \leftarrow j + 1$
    end while
Ensure: $\mathfrak{C} = \mathcal{C}_{t(1 \leq t \leq K)}$ the obtained clusters

---

are recomputed using the Karcher mean algorithm described in Algorithm 2 as detailed in [22]. Applying this clustering procedure to the gallery instances results in aggregations, which are produced according to the instance poses. As a consequence, instances from the same subject or from different subjects that have similar poses fall in the same cluster.

Algorithm 2. Computation of Karcher Mean on $\mathcal{G}_k(\mathbb{R}^n)$

Require: $\mathcal{P}_{i(0 \leq i \leq n)} \in \mathcal{G}_k(\mathbb{R}^n)$, $\epsilon > 0$
    Initialize $\mu_0 \leftarrow \mathcal{P}_0$, $i \leftarrow 0$,
    repeat
        Compute $\nu_i \leftarrow exp_{\mu_i}^{-1}(\mathcal{P}_j)$ for $j = 0, \ldots, n$
        Compute the average tangent vector $\bar{\nu} \leftarrow \frac{1}{n} \sum \nu_i$
        Move μ_i according to $\mu_{i+1} \leftarrow exp_{\mu_i}(\epsilon \bar{\mu})$
        $i \leftarrow i + 1$
    until $(\|\bar{\nu}\| \neq \epsilon)$
Ensure: μ: Karcher Mean of $\{\mathcal{P}_i\}$

---

4 Experimental Results

The proposed approach for face recognition from 3D dynamic sequences has been evaluated on the BU-4DFE dataset, in order to compare our solution with results reported by state of the art solutions, and on a new 3D dynamic face database that we present in Sect. 4.2.

4.1 Evaluation on BU-4DFE Database

Binghamton University 4D Facial Expression (BU-4DFE) database [24] is a 3D dynamic facial expression public database containing 101 subjects. For each subject there are 6 different facial expression sessions. Each session lasts about 4 seconds containing approximately 100 3D scans (frames). The number of vertices in each 3D frame is between 35,000 to 40,000. All the frames show a frontal pose without any kind of occlusion. The same evaluation protocol used in [20] for expression dependent experiment is followed to validate our framework on the same database and to compare the performances, even though it is not the best settings for face recognition challenges. The six sessions of each subject are divided into two halves, each comprising 50 frames: the first half is used for training and the second for testing. For each subject there are 6 instances in the gallery, each of them belonging to one of the different basic expression session (i.e., angry, disgust, fear, happy, sad and surprise), and the same as probe. For this experiment, 60 subjects are selected as in [20]. Each instance in the gallery and the probe are modeled as a 10-dimensional linear subspace. The number of vertices in each scan is downsampled to $n = 10,000$. Comparison is performed over the Grassmann manifold by finding the smallest geodesic distance between the probe instance and gallery instances. The achieved recognition rate using single-based method is 92%. In [20], Sun et al. achieved 97.5%. However, 22 facial landmarks are manually annotated for vertex flow tracking, while the proposed approach uses an automatic tracking method. In [20], a training stage is also applied on the gallery data before recognition. Table 1 reports a comparison of the two approaches by considering efficiency and effectiveness aspects.

Table 1. Performance analysis and comparison

	Sun et al. [20]	This work
One frame processing	15 sec	3 sec
One probe recognition	5 sec	3 sec
CPU used	3.2 GHz	2.66 GHz
FR rate	97.5%	92%

4.2   Experimental Results on a New 3D Dynamic Face Dataset

Few 3D dynamic face databases, such as the BU-4DFE [24], D3DFACS [6], Hi4D-ADSIP [13] have recently appeared for the purpose of facial expressions and/or action units recognition. However, other FR challenges, like pose variation and occlusion are not considered. As an additional contribution of this work, we constructed a 3D dynamic face database, which presents the following features: (1) It includes most of the FR challenges that occur in realistic scenarios, like pose variation, facial expressions, talking, internal and external occlusions, which are not considered in current 3D dynamic databases; (2) The collected scans have low resolution, which is more convenient for real-world applications (for example, the number of vertices in each scan is about 4,000, which is 10 times less than BU-4DFE); (3) The field of view of the used 3D scanner is wide enough to permit non-cooperative free movement of the subject; (4) A single-view structured light system is used for 3D dynamic sequence acquisition, which permits

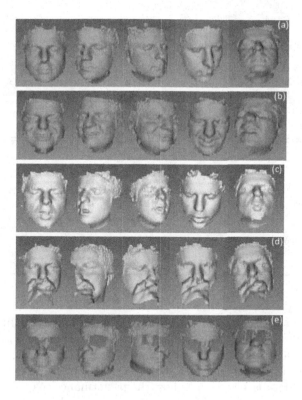

Fig. 4. Example 3D dynamic sequences from our face database acquired under unconstrained conditions: (a) neutral; (b) expressive; (c) talking; (d) internal occlusions (hand, hair); (e) and external occlusions (glasses, scarf)

real time capturing. Such system is more convenient in real world applications than multiple view systems used for current dynamic databases, which need long offline registration stages and highly conditioned acquisition environments.

In the proposed database, for each subject we have: *(i)* A full 3D static model with texture acquired using the *Artec* MHT 3D scanner, without any kind of occlusion or expression in the daylight with closed eyes; *(ii)* Six 3D dynamic sessions recorded using the *Artec* L 3D scanner. Each session lasts over 20 seconds, with 15fps as a temporal resolution (i.e., 300 frames in each session). These sessions represent five different unconstrained scenarios, namely: *neutral* (Ne), *facial expression* (Fe), *talking* (Tk), *external occlusion* (Eo) by scarf or sun glasses, and *internal occlusion* (Io) by hand or hair (examples are shown in Fig. 4). Two sessions are acquired for the neutral case, and one session for the other four scenarios. All the six 3D dynamic sessions are acquired under uncontrolled pose variations around pitch and yaw axes, where subjects are free to move at normal speed. So far, 58 subjects have been collected, 23 females and 35 males. The average number of vertices is about 4,000 per frame (or mesh) for 3D dynamic videos, and around 50,000 for 3D models. The dataset is made freely available by request. Comparison with other existing 3D dynamic face datasets is given in Table 2.

Table 2. Comparison between existing 3D dynamic face datasets

Dataset	#subjects	Temporal resolution	Spatial resolution	Illumination conditions	Pose changes
Posed BU-4DFE [24]	101	25	35,000	controlled	No
Spontaneous BU-4DFE [25]	41	25	40,000	controlled	Limited
D3DFACS [6]	10	60	30,000	controlled	No
Hi4D-ADSIP [13]	80	60	20,000	controlled	No
Our Database	58	15	4,000	un-controlled	Free

Evaluation on the Proposed 3D Dynamic Face Dataset. In a first experiment, we considered a subset of 13 subjects, with one of the two neutral sessions used as gallery and four sessions (i.e., neutral, facial expression, talking, and external occlusion) as probes. The goal behind doing these experiments on a small set of our database is to show how the performance of our framework vary according to different settings. This allows us to select the best setting to run on the whole subjects as it is reported in the next experiment. In so doing, we down sampled the 3D scans to $n = 3,500$ vertices, with a radius of $R = 15mm$ for the neighborhood sphere in the 3D normal estimation. The effect of varying the window size ω used to derive the 3D temporal fragment is explored by repeating the experiment for $\omega = \{5, 10, 15, 20\}$. This value is also used to change the number of eigenvectors which are considered after applying k-SVD (i.e., the obtained basis of a subspace). Each session contains about 300 frames, and the number of instances in the gallery differs according to ω (e.g., for $\omega = 15$ each subject has 20 instances, with 260 total instances in the gallery). In the testing, the four different testing sessions (i.e., Ne, Fe, Tk, Eo) for each subject are divided into multiple instances too. Each instance in the probe sessions is considered as a separate probe and is compared against the 260 instances of a neutral session in the gallery. The Nearest-Neighbor (NN) classifier given in Eq. (1) is applied to find the identity of the probe instances.

Recognition rates are reported in Fig. 5(a), for the four scenarios and the different window size. The best recognition rate is obtained for $\omega = 15$, confirming the intuition that embodying motion information, coming from the temporal variability on the face surface, provides additional discriminative features for face recognition. For $\omega = 20$ and greater values, this approach scores lower recognition rate due to large pose variations, which make no more possible to track all the vertices from the first to the last frame of a 3D temporal fragment.

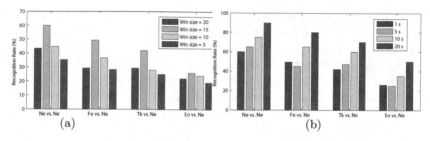

Fig. 5. (a) Single-instance based FR results as a function of the window size ω; (b) Multiple-instances based recognition rates

It also results that the most challenging problem is the occlusion by glasses, where the facial shape is corrupted and presents missing data in the eyes region, as illustrated in Fig. 4(e).

In the previous experiment, only one instance out of the probe session is used for recognition. Due to noise and low resolution of the 3D videos this can be not effective. Using multiple instances of the probe session it is expected to improve the performance. To verify this intuition, the effect on the recognition rate deriving by the application of majority voting is investigated. In this case, the recognition rate is evaluated by combining decisions of multiple successive instances (5, 10 and 20, in addition to the single instance) of the probe session and considering them as one probe. Then, the majority voting is applied to determine which subject in the gallery obtains more votes from the successive probe instances. Figure 5(b) shows the results, where the whole session over 20 seconds and 20 instances are considered ($\omega = 15$ frames per instance are used). It clearly emerges that using more instances as one probe for voting provides better recognition rate in all the investigated scenarios.

Clustering Based Face Recognition. The matching approach proposed above is based on an exhaustive comparison of the 3D temporal fragments constituting a probe against all the gallery 3D temporal fragments, which results in a time con-suming recognition process. To optimize the recognition time, the unsupervised clustering method described in Sect. 3 is applied. The 260 instances in the gallery are clustered into five clusters representing the main poses of the face. Experi-mentally, this number of classes gives better recognition rate than others. The results of clustering based 3D dynamic FR are reported for both single instance and multiple-instances based methods. In Fig. 6, exhaustive vs. clustering based recognition rates are presented for all the five scenarios. For the solution using a 3D single-instance (i.e., in the figure it corresponds to the required time of 1s, since this includes the 15 3D frames of a fragment), the clustering-based approach gives lower recognition rate than exhaustive search for all the cases, since the gallery neutral sessions are acquired under unconstrained random pose variations. Thus, it is not necessary to find the pose of each probe instance in the gallery session of this subject. Nevertheless, after applying majority voting on multiple-instances based results, the recognition rates start to converge to exhaustive search rates when using 5 and 10 instances for voting. When the whole session, i.e., 20 instances is used as one probe, the clustering based recognition rate overcomes the exhaustive search method for the Ne scenario and they are comparable for the other three scenarios (Fe, Tk and Eo). The number of comparisons needed in the Ne scenario with clustering is 4 times less than in the exhaustive search method.

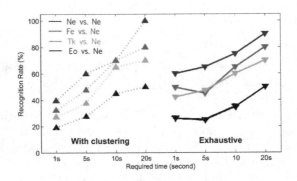

Fig. 6. Clustering-based vs. exhaustive recognition results for each test scenario, when the time required for recognition (i.e., number of 3D temporal fragments in majority voting) is varied

Results of these pilot experiments, have been used to set the best parameters for the approach (i.e., window size ω=15, that is 20 instances are used for each subject, with majority voting applied using all the instances). Using this setting, an experiment on all the 58 subjects of the dataset has been conducted. The recognition rate for the four scenarios (Ne, Fe, Tk, and Eo) resulted equal to 72%, 62%, 65%, and 36%, respectively. Compared to the results reported in Fig. 5 for the train sample of the dataset, and for the same number of instances used in the majority voting (i.e., 20), it can be observed just a small decrease in the performance for the Tk case. A more marked decrease is observed instead in the cases of neutral (Ne), facial expressions (Fe), and external occlusion (Eo).

5   Conclusions

In this work, a geometric framework based on Grassmann manifold representation for face recognition is proposed, which exploits the advantages of 3D dynamic faces. This approach allows us to compare two 3D face videos and to compute statistics (e.g., mean, clustering of a set of 3D face videos). Applying our approach on BU-4DFE [24] database, we have obtained a recognition rate of 92%. The proposed approach does not require to manually annotate landmarks of the face for vertex tracking, and can naturally handle several challenges, like large pose variations, facial expressions, talking and external occlusions. In order to address face recognition in such challenging conditions, a 3D dynamic face recognition database has been also constructed and made publicly available. Single and multiple-instances based recognition results are reported on this new dataset, showing that a majority voting strategy improves the performance in all the scenarios.

References

1. Barr, J., Bowyer, K., Flynn, P., Biswas, S.: Face recognition from video: a review. International Journal of Pattern Recognition and Artificial Intelligence **26**(5) (2012)
2. Berretti, S., Del Bimbo, A., Pala, P.: 3D face recognition using iso-geodesic stripes. IEEE Transaction on Pattern Analysis and Machine Intelligence **32**(12), 2162–2177 (2010)
3. Bowyer, K., Chang, K., Flynn, P.: A survey of approaches and challenges in 3D and multi-modal 3D + 2D face recognition. Computer Vision and Image Understanding **101**(1), 1–15 (2006)
4. Chen, Y., Medioni, G.: Object modeling by registration of multiple range images. Robotics and Automation. **3**, 2724–2729 (1991)
5. Chen, Y.C., Patel, V., Phillips, P., Chellappa, R.: Dictionary-based face recognition from video. In: European Conf. on Computer Vision, pp. 766–779 (2012)
6. Cosker, D., Krumhuber, E., Hilton, A.: A facs valid 3D dynamic action unit database with applications to 3D dynamic morphable facial modeling. In: Int. Conf. on Computer Vision, pp. 2296–2303 (2011)
7. Drira, H., Ben Amor, B., Srivastava, A., Daoudi, M., Slama, R.: 3D face recognition under expressions, occlusions, and pose variations. IEEE Transaction on Pattern Analysis and Machine Intelligence **35**(9), 2270–2283 (2013)
8. Edelman, A., Arias, T., Smith, S.: The geometry of algorithms with orthogonality constraints. Siam J. Matrix Anal. Appl. **20**(2), 303–353 (1998)
9. Golub, G., Van Loan, C.: Matrix computations, 3rd edn. Johns Hopkins University Press, Baltimore (1996)
10. Hadid, A., Pietikäinen, M.: Manifold learning for video-to-video face recognition. In: Fierrez, J., Ortega-Garcia, J., Esposito, A., Drygajlo, A., Faundez-Zanuy, M. (eds.) BioID MultiComm2009. LNCS, vol. 5707, pp. 9–16. Springer, Heidelberg (2009)
11. Karcher, H.: Riemannian center of mass and mollifier smoothing. Communications on Pure and Applied Mathematics **30**, 509–541 (1977)
12. Li, B., Mian, A., Liu, W., Krishna, A.: Using kinect for face recognition under varying poses, expressions, illumination and disguise. In: 2013 IEEE Workshop on Applications of Computer Vision (WACV), pp. 186–192, January 2013
13. Matuszewski, B., Quan, W., Shark, Lk, McLoughlin, A., Lightbody, C., Emsley, H., Watkins, C.: Hi4d-adsip 3D dynamic facial articulation database. Image and Vision Computing **30**(10) (2012)
14. Min, R., Choi, J., Medioni, G., Dugelay, J.L.: Real-time 3D face identification from a depth camera. In: Int. Conf. on Pattern Recognition, pp. 1739–1742 (2012)

15. Passalis, G., Perakis, P., Theoharis, T., Kakadiaris, I.: Using facial symmetry to handle pose variations in real-world 3D face recognition. IEEE Transaction on Pattern Analysis and Machine Intelligence **33**(10), 1938–1951 (2011)
16. Phillips, P., Flynn, P., Beveridge, J., Scruggs, W., O'Toole, A., Bolme, D., Bowyer, K., Draper, B., Givens, G., Lui, Y., Sahibzada, H., Scallan, J., Weimer, S.: Overview of the multiple biometrics grand challenge. In: IAPR/IEEE Int. Conf. on Biometrics, pp. 705–714 (2009)
17. Phillips, P., Flynn, P., Scruggs, W., Bowyer, K., Chang, J., Hoffman, K., Marques, J., Min, J., Worek, W.: Overview of the face recognition grand challenge. In: Int. Conf. on Computer Vision and Pattern Recognition, pp. 947–954 (2005)
18. Rusu, R.: Semantic 3D Object Maps for Everyday Manipulation in Human Living Environments. Ph.D. thesis, Computer Science department, Technische Universitaet Muenchen, Germany (2009)
19. Simonyan, K., Parkhi, O.M., Vedaldi, A., Zisserman, A.: Fisher vector faces in the wild. In: British Machine Vision Conference (2013)
20. Sun, Y., Chen, X., Rosato, M., Yin, L.: Tracking vertex flow and model adaptation for three dimensional spatiotemporal face analysis. IEEE Transaction on Systems, Man, and Cybernetics, Part A **40**(3), 461–474 (2010)
21. Taigman, Y., Yang, M., Ranzato, M., Wolf, L.: Deepface: Closing the gap to human-level performance in face verification. In: Int. Conf. on Computer Vision and Pattern Recognition (2014)
22. Turaga, P., Veeraraghavan, A., Srivastava, A., Chellappa, R.: Statistical computations on grassmann and stiefel manifolds for image and video-based recognition. IEEE Transaction on Pattern Analysis and Machine Intelligence **33**(11), 2273–2286 (2011)
23. Wang, H., Kang, B., Kim, D.: Pfw: A face database in the wild for studying face identification and verification in uncontrolled environment. In: IAPR Asian Conf. on Pattern Recognition (ACPR), pp. 356–360 (2013)
24. Yin, L., Chen, X., Sun, Y., Worm, T., Reale, M.: A high-resolution 3D dynamic facial expression database. In: Face and Gesture Recognition, pp. 1–6 (2008)
25. Zhang, X., Yin, L., Cohn, J., Canavan, S., Reale, M., Horowitz, A., Liu, P.: A high-resolution spontaneous 3d dynamic facial expression database. In: 10th IEEE Int. Conf. on Automatic Face and Gesture Recognition (FG'10), pp. 1–6, April 2013

A Novel Graph Embedding Framework
for Object Recognition

Mario Manzo[1], Simone Pellino[1], Alfredo Petrosino[1 (✉)],
and Alessandro Rozza[2]

[1] University of Naples Parthenope, Naples, Italy
petrosino@uniparthenope.it
[2] Research Team - Hyera Software, Coccaglio, Italy

Abstract. A great deal of research works have been devoted to understand image contents. In this field many well-known methods exploit Bag of Words (BoW) features describing image contents as appearance frequency histogram of visual words. These approaches have a main drawback, the location information and the relationships between features are lost. To overcame this limitation we propose a novel methodology for the Object recognition task. A digital image is described as a feature vector computed by means of a new graph embedding paradigm on the Attributed Relational SIFT Regions Graph. The final classification is performed by using Logistic Label Propagation classifier. Our framework is evaluated on standard databases (such as ETH-80, COIL-100 and ALOI) and the achieved results compared with those obtained by well-known methodologies confirm its quality.

Keywords: Image classification · Object recognition · Graph based image representation · Graph embedding

1 Introduction

In the last decade a great deal of research has been devoted to 3D object recognition. In order to capture distinctive details of the images, most of the image representation techniques leverage local features, such as SIFT [15] and HOG [18]. Unfortunately, local features would require to solve an assignment problem between every image pair, thus making it unfeasible to use them in real world scenarios. For this reason, a common strategy to integrate the local features into a fixed length global representation is to use the Bag Of Words approach. This technique is roughly composed of three steps: the local features extraction, the codebook generation and local features encoding, and the code pooling to generate the global image representation [5].

Despite the promising results achieved employing this kind of features, the main problem of this approach is due to the fact that the location and spatial information between local features are not considered. In order to solve this problem some research works exploit local and structural information of the image

© Springer International Publishing Switzerland 2015
L. Agapito et al. (Eds.): ECCV 2014 Workshops, Part IV, LNCS 8928, pp. 341–352, 2015.
DOI: 10.1007/978-3-319-16220-1_24

by employing graphs to model it in order to add some high level information (relations) to the low-level representation of the individual parts [19,30].

In this work, we propose an object recognition framework that is able to represent images in order to capture local and structural information. First of all an image is represented by the ARSG structure, as proposed in [16]. This structure encodes the SIFT features extracted from the image in a hierarchical fashion by considering both the individual image features and more global image regions. Pairwise relationships between features and regions are encoded in an incidence graph, which serves as a reduced representation for the entire image.

Originally, in [16] image comparison was performed through the direct comparison of the derived graphs. Since direct comparison to each image in the database becomes infeasible in this setting, we propose to extract a set of sample graphs and characterize each image through a feature vector (graph embedding), whose i-th coordinate is the similarity of ARSG graph of the given image to the i-th sample graph. This embedding paradigm, as proposed in [24], was efficiently experienced for non rigid scene recognition showing state-of-the-art results on datasets like SUN 397 [31] and KTH-IDOL 2 [10]. The main idea of this paper is to adapt this representation to the context of 3D object recognition in the presence of a potentially large image database. A semi-supervised learning approach, by means of a Logistic Label Propagation (LLP, [13]) algorithm, is adopted to accurately estimate the label values as the posterior probabilities. The results achieved on standard datasets compared with those obtained by well-known approaches confirm the quality of the proposed framework.

The paper is organized as follows: Section 2 summarizes the related works; Section 3 introduces the proposed object recognition framework; Section 4 describes the experimental results; Section 5 presents our conclusions and future works.

2   Related Works

The Object recognition is the task of finding and identifying objects in a video sequence or image. Given an image containing objects of interest and a set of labels, corresponding to a set of known models, the aim is to assign correct labels to regions that contains the objects of interest. This task is very difficult particularly if we consider the design of the recognition system. The main problems concern the object representations and their classifications. The goal is to emulate human system, which performs efficiently and dynamically the Object recognition task.

To capture distinctive details of the images, many image representation techniques leverage local features, such as SIFT [15] and HOG [18]. We recall that, unfortunately, the usage of local features as they are would require to solve an assignment problem between every image pair, thus making it unfeasible to use them in real world scenarios. For this reason, a common strategy to integrate the local features into a fixed length global representation is to use the Bag Of Words approach [5].

In [29] an Mth order tensor discriminant analysis approach for object categorization and recognition is described. This tensor approach avoids to transform 3D color images or 2D grayscale images into high dimensional feature vectors. The method represents a color image as a Mth order tensor and the original tensor objects are mapped into a low dimensional feature space where nearest neighbor classifiers and AdaBoost (hereinafter DTROD-AdaBoost) are employed to perform the final classification.

In [23] an approach to object recognition is described. It is based on matching of local image features. Precisely, the method recognizes objects under very different viewing conditions. The main idea concerns several affine-invariant constructions of Local Affine Frames (LAFs) for local image patches extraction. The robustness of the matching procedure is performed by giving multiple frames to each image region detected, and selecting the most discriminative ones. Matching score is estimated as the number of established local correspondences, without enforcing a global model consistency.

Despite the quality of the results obtained by employing the aforementioned approaches the location and spatial information between local features are not considered. In this context, graph structures can be a great help in order to reduce the gap between the location and spatial information of local features. Graphs are adopted in application domains where relations among data (edges) must be highlighted. Image processing [1,16], pattern recognition [7,11,25], and many other fields benefit from data graph representations and related manipulation algorithms.

The most used graph-based image representation is the Region Adjacency Graph (RAG) [27] in which a node represents a region of the image and an edge exists between two nodes if the underlying regions are adjacent. Despite this representation is widely used, there are other interesting alternatives in literature. Among them, in [9] a method for generic object recognition through graph structural expression using SIFT features is described. This approach creates a graph structure that connects the SIFT keypoints. This formulation reduces the computation complexity and, at same time, improves the detection performance.

In [7] a graph mining algorithm, called gdFil, is described. This work exploits two novel properties that allow to remove all duplicate candidates in Frequent Connected Subgraph (FCS) before support calculation. Support calculation task is addressed through a strategy based on embedding structures.

In [11] a graph mining framework called APproximate Graph Mining (APGM) is proposed. The framework is designed to identify approximate matched FCSs and to mine useful patterns from noisy graph database.

In [1] another graph mining algorithm for FCSs over undirected and labeled graph collections (called Vertex and Edge Approximate graph Miner, VEAM) is presented. VEAM addresses the approximate matching problem using both vertex and edge label sets during the mining process. The framework is tested in the context of graph-based image classification.

Considering the Object recognition task, in [30] an object is represented by means of SIFT features selected by an approach based on visual saliency.

Precisely the objects are modelled by a Class Specific Hyper-Graphs (CSHG) by exploiting Delaunay graphs and considering the SIFT keypoints as nodes.

In [19] another graph mining technique for object recognition is proposed. In this work an image is represented by an irregular pyramid. Each level of the structure is a RAG and the whole pyramid is built from bottom to top, where the base level is the entire image. Image regions are represented by different basic low-level descriptors to add context information and the structure is captured by employing a Frequent Approximate Subgraph (FAS).

In [20] a graph matching scheme that involves Visual Features (color, texture and shape) and Spatial Relations (VFSR) to detect similar objects is described. The goal is to show that the combination of visual and spatial features is a promising approach to improve the object recognition task. The spatial descriptors proposed are easy to build, store and manipulate, and can be employed to explicitly represent many possible spatial configurations between pairs of image regions, considering several basic orientation and topological relationships.

In [17] an object recognition approach based on hierarchical features is proposed(hereinafter RSW+Boosting) to capture local and structural information. This method employs a combination of decision trees to classify the objects.

In literature other approaches that capture local and spatial information without employing graph structures are presented. Among them, in [21] a temporal approach based on local features (hereinafter Sequential Patterns) is presented. The temporal information captures the spatial relations between local features. The problem of object recognition is seen as a sequential prediction task. A Discriminative Variable Memory Markov model, which captures multiple statistical sources features generating sequential patterns in a stochastic manner, is adopted.

3   Overview of our Framework

Our object recognition framework, called LLP + ARSRGemb, is composed by three different modules (the complete flowchart is shown in figure 1). In the first module each image is converted in an Attributed Relational SIFT-based Graph (ARSRG, [16]). This structure is able to capture local information preserving the spatial relationships between them (see Section 3.1). In the second module the set of ARSRGs is split in two subsets: training and prototypes. Each training ARSRG is embedded into an n-dimensional vector space (where n is the cardinality of prototypes set) by means of a novel graph embedding paradigm (see Section 3.2). Each component of this vector encodes the distance between the described structure and one of the prototypes. This distance is computed by an efficient graph matching algorithm proposed in [16]. Finally, a Logistic Label Propagation classifier (see Section 3.3) is trained on the n-dimensional vectors. Notice that, the computational complexity depends on the graph embedding of the

ARSRGs that is $O(N * M * K)$, where N are the number of ARSRG to encode into vector space, M are the ARSRG prototypes, and K is the time complexity of the ARSRG computation.

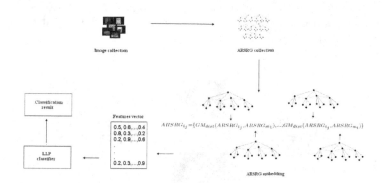

Fig. 1. Overview of the Object recognition framework

3.1 Graph Based Image Representation

In this section we describe the graph based image representation employed. This representation, called Attributed Relational SIFT-based Regions Graph (ARSRG), was proposed by Manzo et al. in [16]. The structure is composed by three different levels of nodes: the *Root node*, the *RAG Nodes*, and the *Leaf nodes*. The *Root node* represents the whole image and is linked with all the *RAG Nodes*[27] of the second level. *RAG Nodes* represent image regions, extracted by means of a segmentation technique, and encode adjacency relationships between them. At this level, adjacent regions in the image are represented by connected nodes. Finally, the *Leaf nodes* represent the set of SIFT [15] descriptors extracted from the image. Employing these descriptors invariance to the view-point, to the illumination, and to the scale is guaranteed. Precisely, a descriptor is associated to a region based on its spatial coordinates and the descriptors belonging to the same region are connected by edges. Figure 2 shows an example of ARSRG construction.

The choice of ARSRG for objects representation arises from an important property of the graph structure. This property concerns relations established among local features and structural information of the object encoded into the RAG configuration located at second level. It has been demonstrated that global configuration and local information of scene play a key role in the human recognition task. In this context, relations can be distinguished in: horizontal and vertical. Horizontal relations provide information about spatial closeness between image regions (level two) or SIFT features (level three). Vertical relations concern connections among image regions (level two) and SIFT features (level three). Using this type of configuration invariance to changes, such as viewpoints, illuminations, scale, is ensured which are often the reason of poor performance in the task of objects recognition.

Compared to the approach proposed in [16], in which the ARSRG structures are adopted to calculate distances between images in order to solve a retrieval problem, we employ ARSRG structures to map image features, through the ARSRG embedding procedure described in the next section, in a space that can be easily managed during the classification stage.

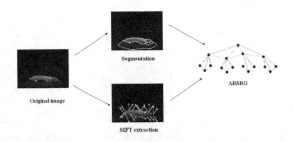

Fig. 2. An example of ARSRG construction

3.2 ARSRG Embedding

In literature many approaches have been proposed for dimensionality reduction. Among them, the most popular are Principal Component Analysis (PCA, [12]), Linear Discriminant Analysis (LDA, [2]), and Kernel variants of this techniques [2]. The main goal of these approaches is to derive lower dimensional representation from the original higher dimensional feature space preserving some properties of the data.

These techniques works on unstructured data. To overcome this limitation and handle structured data, such as graphs, we report the graph embedding approach, as proposed in [24] for non rigid scene recognition, with the purpose to provide a fixed-dimensional vector representation of an ARSRG structure.

Consider a labeled set of sample graphs $\mathcal{S} = \{\mathcal{G}_1, \ldots, \mathcal{G}_n\}$ and a graph similarity measure $s(\mathcal{G}_i, \mathcal{G}_j)$, where $\mathcal{S}$ can be any kind of graph set and $s(\mathcal{G}_i, \mathcal{G}_j)$ can be any kind of graph similarity measure. Moreover consider a set $\mathcal{P} = \{\mathcal{P}_1, \ldots, \mathcal{P}_m\}$ of $m <= n$ prototypes extracted from $\mathcal{S}$, and compute the similarities of a given input graph $\mathcal{G}_j$ with each prototype $\mathcal{P}_k \in \mathcal{P}$. This leads to m similarities, $s_1 = s(\mathcal{G}_j, \mathcal{P}_1), \ldots, s_m = s(\mathcal{G}_j, \mathcal{P}_m)$, which can be represented in an m-dimensional vector $(s_1, \ldots, s_m)$. Employing this approach any graph can be transformed into a vector of real numbers. Precisely, consider a graph domain $\mathcal{G}$, the training set of graphs $\mathcal{S} = \{\mathcal{G}_1, \ldots, \mathcal{G}_n\} \subseteq \mathcal{G}$, and a set of prototype graphs $\mathcal{P} = \{\mathcal{P}_1, \ldots, \mathcal{P}_m\} \subseteq \mathcal{S}$, the vector of mapping between $\mathcal{S}$ and $\mathcal{P}$ is defined as follows:

$$\Phi_m^{\mathcal{P}}(\mathcal{G}_m) = (s(\mathcal{G}_m, \mathcal{P}_1), \ldots, s(\mathcal{G}_m, \mathcal{P}_m)) \tag{1}$$

where $s(\mathcal{G}_m, \mathcal{P}_i)$ is a graph similarity measure between graph $\mathcal{G}_m$ and the ith prototype. This paradigm can be applied to ARSRG structures

obtaining a vector for each training ARSRG whose components encode the distance between the considered graph and all the ARSRG prototypes. Distance values are obtained through an iterative and efficient graph matching algorithm proposed in [16]. Precisely, this matching algorithm measures regions similarity among the ARSRG structures exploiting the topological relation information.

The matching phase is handled through a hierarchical exploration of ARSRG, that can be roughly divided in two steps: filtering of regions based on their size; subgraph matching performed by matching features belonging to single regions located at the third level of ARSRG.

The algorithm can be also seen as an image matching (retrieval) procedure, which works on two levels. The first level exploits global features, that are the regions extracted through a segmentation algorithm called JSEG [6], which performs a segmentation of color-texture regions in images through a first color quantization followed by a spatial segmentation; the second level explores local invariant region features. In this way, both local and structural image features are analyzed during the matching process.

The combination of graph embedding and graph based SIFT structures has already been proposed in the literature. In [9], graph based SIFT structures are embedded into a vector space according to the graph edit distance operations for generic object recognition application. Also, in [4] the graphs are mapped into a vector space by means of graph embedding, for representing human's shapes with purpose of action recognition. Differently from the aforementioned approaches, our algorithm is designed to solve more efficiently and effectively the graph embedding problem. Indeed our approach performs the matching phase employing the subgraphs representing image regions instead of the overall graphs representing the entire image, greatly reducing the time complexity. Moreover, since our approach considers local and structural information during the graph matching comparison the robustness to light, scale, and viewpoint changes is ensured (this does not happen for the aforementioned approaches that use edit operations). This is a key aspect that can strongly improve the object recognition performance.

3.3   Classification Phase

The final classification phase is managed by employing a semi-supervised learning technique called logistic label propagation (LLP, [13]) algorithm. This method employs the logistic function to classify input data, similarly to logistic regression. To deal with unlabeled samples as well as labeled ones, the logistic functions are learnt by using similarities between samples as proposed in [32]. Precisely, the learning problem is formulated as Gaussian random fields on graphs, where a field is described in terms of harmonic functions, and is efficiently solved using matrix methods or belief propagation. Note that, in this technique the logistic regression is effectively incorporated in terms of posterior probabilities.

4   Experimental Results

In this section we analyze the results achieved by our framework on three popular datasets. For each database we adopt the experimental settings proposed in well-known object recognition papers, especially the selection of graphs prototype crucial in the representation of objects-classes, thus to further assess our results. Moreover, we compare the achieved results with those obtained by a baseline approach that employs the same classifier used in our framework (Logistic Label Propagation classifier) applied on Bag of Words (LLP + BoW) to highlight the quality of our features. This section is organized as follows: in Section 4.1 the databases employed are summarized, while in Section 4.2 the results achieved are presented.

4.1   Datasets

The experiments have been performed on three datasets that differs in size, design, and topic. Precisely, we have employed the following databases:

1. The Columbia Image Database Library (COIL-100, [22]), which consists of 100 objects. Each object is represented by 72 colored images that show it under different rotation point of view.
2. The Amsterdam Library Of Images (ALOI, [8]) is a color image collection of 1000 small objects. We used the Object Viewpoint Collection. In contrast to COIL-100, where the objects are cropped to fill the full image, in ALOI the images contain the background and the objects in their original size.
3. The ETH-80 Image Set [14], which contains 80 objects from 8 categories and each object is represented by 41 different views, thus obtaining a total of 3280 images.

(a)   (b)   (c)   (d)   (e)   (f)

Fig. 3. Example images from the COIL-100 dataset (first 2 images), ALOI dataset (second 2 images) and from the ETH-80 dataset (last 2 images)

4.2   Discussion

Table 1 summarizes the accuracy results of the proposed framework on ETH-80 database. In order to perform a direct comparison with the methods employed in [19], the same setup is adopted. Precisely, we took the same 6 categories (*apples, cars, cows, cups, horses,* and *tomatoes*). For each category 4 objects are taken and for each object 10 different views are considered thus obtaining a total of 240 images. From the remaining images, 60 per category (15 views per object) are used as testing examples. We reported the results achieved by our baseline (LLP+BoW), and those obtained in [19] by employing the approaches proposed in [7] (gdFil), in [11] (APGM), and in [1] (VEAM). As can be seen in Table 1, our method outperforms the results obtained by the other approaches. These results confirm that our framework correctly deals with object view changes.

Table 1. Recognition accuracy on the ETH-80 database

Method	Accuracy
LLP+ARSRGemb	**89.26%**
LLP+BoW	58.83%
gdFil	47.59%
APGM	84.39%
VEAM	82.68%

Table 2 summarizes the results achieved by LLP + ARSRG*emb* on COIL-100 database. In order to perform a direct comparison with the methods employed in [19,20], the same setup is adopted. Precisely, we have randomly selected 25 objects and we have employed the 11% of the images as training set and the remaining ones as testing set. We have reported the results achieved by our baseline (LLP + BoW), and those obtained in [19,20] by employing their approach (VFSR) and the approaches proposed in [7] (gdFil), in [11] (APGM), in [1] (VEAM), in [29] (DTROD-AdaBoost), in [17] (RSW+Boosting), in [21] (Sequential Patterns), and in [23] (LAF). The results are presented in terms of accuracy and the best performance is highlighted in bold face. Our approach confirms its qualities also employing this database. Indeed our approach obtained the best overall accuracy.

Table 2. Recognition accuracy on the COIL-100 database

Method	Accuracy
LLP+ARSRGemb	**99.55%**
LLP+BoW	51.71%
gdFil	32.61%
VFSR	91.60%
APGM	99.11%
VEAM	99.44%
DTROD-AdaBoost	84.50%
RSW+Boosting	89.20%
Sequential Patterns	89.80%
LAF	99.40%

Table 3 summarizes the accuracy results obtained by LLP + ARSRGemb on the ALOI database. As can be see, the experiments have been performed by increasing the number of images thus to assess the robustness of the proposed framework. In order to perform a direct comparison with the methods employed in [28], the same setup is adopted; precisely, only the first 100 objects are employed. Color images have been converted to gray level and second image of each class was adopted for training and the remaining for testing. Two images of each class are considered, having a total of 200 images. Subsequently, at each iteration for each class one additional training image is attached. In Table 3 we have only shown the results by considering batch of 400 images since the intermediate results did not provide great differences. We have reported the results achieved by our baseline (LLP + BoW), and those obtained in [28] by employing some variants of Linear Discriminant Analysis (ILDAaPCA,batchLDA, ILDAonK, and ILDAonL). ILDAaPCA works first creating a PCA subspace by augmenting the k dimensional reconstructive subspace with additional $c - 1$ vectors containing discriminative information. Those additional vectors are created from vectors that would be discarded when truncating the subspace to k-dimensions. In this way, the full discriminative information is included. Subsequently, the actual LDA representation from the obtained augmented subspace is built. batchLDA builds a new model in each update step using the same number of images as the incremental algorithms. ILDAonK updates a PCA basis truncated to the size $\hat{k} = k + c - 1$. The parameter k encodes the 80% of the energy, in term of fraction of the total variance, of the starting model constant during the experiment. ILDAonL updates the $(c - 1)$-dimensional LDA basis directly and only discriminative information is used. These results show that our framework is able to obtain good results with a small amount of training set and that it is little affected by overfitting problems.

Table 3. Recognition accuracy on the ALOI database

Method	200	400	800	1200	1600	2000
LLP+ARSRGemb	86.00%	90.00%	93.00%	96.00%	95.62%	96.00%
LLP+BoW	49.60%	55.00%	50.42%	50.13%	49.81%	48.88%
batchLDA	51.00%	52.00%	62.00%	62.00%	70.00%	71.00%
ILDAaPCA	51.00%	42.00%	53.00%	48.00%	45.00%	50.00%
ILDAonK	42.00%	45.00%	53.00%	48.00%	45.00%	51.00%
ILDAonL	51.00%	52.00%	61.00%	61.00%	65.00%	69.00%

As can be noticed from the reported results, our framework is able to provide good overall performances for the Object recognition task, confirming its quality and its robustness. Moreover, this work confirms that capture local information preserving the spatial relationships between them can strongly improve the performance in the Object recognition field.

It is important to highlight that, thanks to the graph embedding paradigm, the main computational overhead only concerns the extraction of graph-based representation in the training stage, while the classification can be performed very quickly. This is particularly important since it was not possible to obtain results in a reasonable time when we tried to compare our framework with two state-of-the-art kernel graph approaches [3, 26] on RAG structures.

5   Conclusions and Future Works

In this paper, we have proposed a framework to embed graph structures into vector spaces in order to improve object recognition. In this paper we have shown that representing images to efficiently capture global and local features improves the quality of the object recognition task and reduces the overfitting problems. Consequently, the achieved results compared to those obtained by well-known methodologies have shown that our approach is promising. Testing on larger and more complex databases such as Pascal VOC, Caltech 256, as well as the employment of different graph matching algorithms in order to improve the system performance are issues under exam.

References

1. Acosta-Mendoza, N., Gago-Alonso, A., Medina-Pagola, J.E.: Frequent approximate subgraphs as features for graph-based image classification. Knowledge-Based Systems **27**, 381–392 (2012)
2. Bishop, C.: Pattern Recognition and Machine Learning. Springer (2006)
3. Borgwardt, K.M., Kriegel, H.P.: Shortest-path kernels on graphs. In: Fifth IEEE International Conference on Data Mining, p. 8. IEEE (2005)
4. Borzeshi, E.Z., Piccardi, M., Xu, R.: A discriminative prototype selection approach for graph embedding in human action recognition. In: 2011 IEEE International Conference on Computer Vision Workshops (ICCV Workshops), pp. 1295–1301. IEEE (2011)
5. Chatfield, K., Lempitsky, V., Vedaldi, A., Zisserman, A.: The devil is in the details: an evaluation of recent feature encoding methods. In: BMVC (2011)
6. Deng, Y., Manjunath, B.: Unsupervised segmentation of color-texture regions in images and video. IEEE Transactions on Pattern Analysis and Machine Intelligence **23**(8), 800–810 (2001)
7. Gago-Alonso, A., Carrasco-Ochoa, J.A., Medina-Pagola, J.E., Martínez-Trinidad, J.F.: Full duplicate candidate pruning for frequent connected subgraph mining. Integrated Computer-Aided Engineering **17**(3), 211–225 (2010)
8. Geusebroek, J.M., Burghouts, G.J., Smeulders, A.W.: The amsterdam library of object images. International Journal of Computer Vision **61**(1), 103–112 (2005)
9. Hori, T., Takiguchi, T., Ariki, Y.: Generic object recognition by graph structural expression. In: 2012 IEEE International Conference on Acoustics, Speech and Signal Processing (ICASSP), pp. 1021–1024. IEEE (2012)
10. Luo, J., Pronobis, A., Caputo, B., Jensfelt, P.: The kth-idol2 database. Technical Report CVAP304, Kungliga Tekniska Hoegskolan, CVAP/CAS (2006)
11. Jia, Y., Zhang, J., Huan, J.: An efficient graph-mining method for complicated and noisy data with real-world applications. Knowledge and Information Systems **28**(2), 423–447 (2011)
12. Jollife, I.T.: Principal Component Analysis. Springer Series in Statistics. Springer, New York (1986)
13. Kobayashi, T., Watanabe, K., Otsu, N.: Logistic label propagation. Pattern Recognition Letters **33**(5), 580–588 (2012)
14. Leibe, B., Schiele, B.: Analyzing appearance and contour based methods for object categorization. In: Proceedings. 2003 IEEE Computer Society Conference on Computer Vision and Pattern Recognition, vol. 2, pp. II-409. IEEE (2003)

15. Lowe, D.G.: Distinctive image features from scale-invariant keypoints. International Journal of Computer Vision **60**(2), 91–110 (2004)
16. Manzo, M., Petrosino, A.: Attributed relational sift-based regions graph for art painting retrieval. In: Petrosino, A. (ed.) ICIAP 2013, Part I. LNCS, vol. 8156, pp. 833–842. Springer, Heidelberg (2013)
17. Marée, R., Geurts, P., Piater, J., Wehenkel, L.: Decision trees and random subwindows for object recognition. In: ICML Workshop on Machine Learning Techniques for Processing Multimedia Content (MLMM2005) (2005)
18. Mikolajczyk, K., Schmid, C.: A performance evaluation of local descriptors. IEEE Transactions on Pattern Analysis and Machine Intelligence **27**(10), 1615–1630 (2005)
19. Morales-González, A., Acosta-Mendoza, N., Gago-Alonso, A., García-Reyes, E.B., Medina-Pagola, J.E.: A new proposal for graph-based image classification using frequent approximate subgraphs. Pattern Recognition **47**(1), 169–177 (2014)
20. Morales-González, A., García-Reyes, E.B.: Simple object recognition based on spatial relations and visual features represented using irregular pyramids. Multimedia Tools and Applications **63**(3), 875–897 (2013)
21. Morioka, N.: Learning object representations using sequential patterns. In: Wobcke, W., Zhang, M. (eds.) AI 2008. LNCS (LNAI), vol. 5360, pp. 551–561. Springer, Heidelberg (2008)
22. Nayar, S.K., Nene, S.A., Murase, H.: Columbia object image library (coil 100). Department of Comp. Science, Columbia University, Tech. Rep. CUCS-006-96 (1996)
23. Obdrzalek, S., Matas, J.: Object recognition using local affine frames on distinguished regions. In: BMVC, vol. 2, pp. 13–122 (2002)
24. Pellino, S., Petrosino, A.: Bag of graph words for scene recognition. Pattern Recognition Letters p. submitted (2014)
25. Rozza, A., Manzo, M., Petrosino, A.: A novel graph-based fisher kernel method for semi-supervised learning. In: Submitted to ICPR 2014 (2014)
26. Shervashidze, N., Schweitzer, P., Van Leeuwen, E.J., Mehlhorn, K., Borgwardt, K.M.: Weisfeiler-lehman graph kernels. The Journal of Machine Learning Research **12**, 2539–2561 (2011)
27. Tremeau, A., Colantoni, P.: Regions adjacency graph applied to color image segmentation. IEEE Transactions on Image Processing **9**(4), 735–744 (2000)
28. Uray, M., Skocaj, D., Roth, P.M., Bischof, H., Leonardis, A.: Incremental lda learning by combining reconstructive and discriminative approaches. In: BMVC, pp. 1–10 (2007)
29. Wang, Y., Gong, S.: Tensor discriminant analysis for view-based object recognition. In: 18th International Conference on Pattern Recognition, ICPR 2006, vol. 3, pp. 33–36. IEEE (2006)
30. Xia, S., Hancock, E.: 3d object recognition using hyper-graphs and ranked local invariant features. Structural, Syntactic, and Statistical Pattern Recognition, 117–126 (2008)
31. Xiao, J., Hays J., Ehinger, K., Oliva, A., Torralba, A.: Sun database: Large-scale scene 488 recognition from abbey to zoo. In: IEEE Conference on Computer Vision and Pattern 489 Recognition (CVPR), pp. 3485–3492 (2010)
32. Zhu, X., Ghahramani, Z., Lafferty, J., et al.: Semi-supervised learning using gaussian fields and harmonic functions. In: ICML, vol. 3, pp. 912–919 (2003)

Multiple Alignment of Spatiotemporal Deformable Objects for the Average-Organ Computation

Shun Inagaki[1], Hayato Itoh[1], and Atsushi Imiya[2]([⊠])

[1] Graduate School of Advanced Integration Science, Chiba University,
Yayoi-cho 1-33, Inage-ku, Chiba 263-8522, Japan
[2] Institute of Management and Information Technologies, Chiba University,
Yayoi-cho 1-33, Inage-ku, Chiba 263-8522, Japan
imiya@faculty.chiba-u.jp

Abstract. We deal with multiple image warping, which computes deformation fields between an image and a collection of images, as an extension of variational image registration. Using multiple image warping, we develop a variational method for the computation of average images of biological organs in three-dimensional Euclidean space. The average shape of three-dimensional biological organs is an essential feature to discriminate abnormal organs from normal organs. There are two kinds of volumetric image sets in medical image analysis. The first one is a collection of static volumetric data of an organ and/or organs. The other is a collection of temporal volumetric data of an organ and/or organs. A collection of temporal volumetric beating hearts is an example of temporal volumetric data. For spatiotemporal volumetric data, we can compute (1) the temporal average, which is the average of a heart during a cycle, (2) the frame average, which is the average of hearts at a frame, and (3) the temporal average of frame averages.

1 Introduction

In this paper, we deal with multiple image warping, which computes deformation fields between an image and a collection of images. This collection of multiple deformation fields provides the average image and shape of a collection of volumetric images and objects.

In medical diagnosis, the average shape of individual organs provides essential properties for the general expression of organs [20]. In computational anatomy, the statistical average shape, which is computed using principal component analysis of a shape descriptor, is well defined [12].

There are two kinds of volumetric image sets in medical image analysis. The first one is a collection of static volumetric data of an organ. The other is a collection of temporal volumetric data of an organ. A sequence of images of beating volumetric hearts is an example of temporal volumetric data. For spatiotemporal volumetric data, we can compute (1) the temporal average, which is the average of a heart during a cycle, (2) the frame average, which is the

© Springer International Publishing Switzerland 2015
L. Agapito et al. (Eds.): ECCV 2014 Workshops, Part IV, LNCS 8928, pp. 353–366, 2015.
DOI: 10.1007/978-3-319-16220-1_25

average of hearts at a frame, and (3) the temporal average of frame averages. The first, second and third averages derive the standard shape of the organ of a human, the standard shape of a frame of beating hearts and the standard shape of a collection of beating hearts, respectively. Therefore, the second average detects abnormalities of a heart from a collection of hearts. Moreover, the third average derives a standard static heart for computational anatomy.

2 Related Works

In both structure pattern recognition [9,19] and variational registration [20], the average shape among a collection of given shapes is of interest. Some pioneering works demonstrated a registration process achieved by pattern matching based on dynamic programming [22,23], which is a fundamental idea in pattern recognition. These approaches involve the matching and retrieval of occluded shapes, and they are intended for the global alignment of planar shapes.

The shape-matching algorithm observes a collection of given shapes, detects the contours and then computes (1) distances among them and (2) point correspondences between the contours [10]. However, it tends to be less accurate in the representation of local structures because the point correspondences are computed without preserving the geometric local structure of the shapes. In structure pattern recognition [9,19], the average of a collection of combinatorial structures such as strings and graphs is of interest. Multiple alignment of strings, which is achieved by dynamic programing, is a fundamental tool for motif search in bioinformatics. For multiple alignment of volumetric data, we apply variational method, since these data are not expressed as strings.

Warping and morphing are fundamental techniques in computer graphics to interpolate and generate shapes and objects. In medical applications, morphing is used for the description of the deformation process of biological organs. This process predicts the deformable motion of biological organs in the human torso such as the beating heart, and the deformation of lungs during breathing. In medical image diagnosis and retrieval [2,20], average images and shapes of individual organs provide essential properties for the general expression of organs. Shape retrieval categorises and classifies shapes, and finds shapes from portions of shapes. In shape retrieval, the matching of shapes based on the diffeomorphism of shapes [5,6] and the descriptor of shape boundary contours [10] are used. In the matching process for discrete shapes, the string edit distance [7,9] computed by dynamic programming is a fundamental tool. Moreover, in the matching process of images, the variational registration strategy [2,3,20] is a typical tool. In computational anatomy, the statistical average shape, which is computed using principal component analysis of the shape descriptor, is well defined [11,12]. In both structure pattern recognition [7,8] and variation registration [4,20], the average shape of a collection of given shapes is of interest.

There are various methods for computing the average shape [4,21]. These methods are based on the mathematical definition that shapes are the boundary contours of physical objects [13,14]. This definition is suitable for dealing with highly nonlinear geometric variations. Furthermore, in the comparative reading of medical images, image registration is the main method used to classify the differences among the images. In particular, the establishment of local deformations between a collection of given shapes has attracted researchers of medical image analysis for decades.

3   Variational Average Computation

We define a variational average image g of volumetric images $\{f_i\}_{i=1}^m$ in the three-dimensional Euclidean space $\mathbf{R}^3$ as the minimiser of the variational problem

$$J(\{u_k\}_{k=1}^m) = \sum_{k=1}^m \int_{\mathbf{R}^3} (g(x - u_k) - f_k(x))^2 dx + \lambda \int_{\mathbf{R}^3} |\nabla g|^2 dx$$

$$+ \mu \sum_{k=1}^m \int_{\mathbf{R}^3} |\nabla u_k|^2 dx + \sigma \int_{\mathbf{R}^3} \left(\sum_{k=1}^m u_k\right)^2 dx \tag{1}$$

where

$$\Gamma = \int_{\mathbf{R}^3} |\nabla g|^2 dx, \; U_k = \int_{\mathbf{R}^3} |\nabla u_k|^2 dx, \; S = \sum_{k=1}^m u_k, \tag{2}$$

are regularisers for g and deformation fields $\{u_k\}_{k=1}^n$. The constraints Γ and U_k imply that the average g and the deformation fields are smooth, respectively. The constraint S implies that the average image exists at the median point of the deformation fields. We set the solution of the variational problem of eq. (1) as

$$g = \text{VA}_k(\{f_k\}_{k=1}^m). \tag{3}$$

For a collection of spatiotemporal functions $\{h_i(x, t)\}_{i=1}^m$ defined in the interval $0 \le t \le T$, we define a collection of temporally sampled data as

$$h_{ij}(x) = h_i(x, (j-1)\Delta), i = 1, 2, \cdots, m, j = 1, \cdots, n \tag{4}$$

for $(n-1)\Delta = T$. For $\{h_{ij}\}_{i=1\,j=1}^{m\,n}$, we define a pair of collections of averages as

$$\{g_i(x)\}_{i=1}^m = \text{VA}_j(\{h_{ij}\}_{i=1\,j=1}^{m\,n}), \; \{g(x, j)\}_{j=1}^n = \text{VA}_i(\{h_{ij}\}_{i=1\,j=1}^{m\,n}). \tag{5}$$

Here, $g_i(x)$ and $g(x, j_0)$ are the temporal average of a sequence $h_i(x, t)$ and the frame average of $h_i(x, j_0\Delta)$ for a fixed j_0 such that $1 \le j \le n$, respectively.

Moreover, these two averages derive

$$\bar{g}(x) = \text{VA}_i(\{g_i\}_{i=1}^m), \; \underline{g}(x) = \text{VA}_j(\{g(x, j)\}_{j=1}^n). \tag{6}$$

Here, $\bar{g}$ and $\underline{g}$ is the spatial average of the temporal averages and the temporal average of the spatial averages, respectivly. Figure 1 shows the relations among these four averages for temporal volumetric image data. For these two averages $\bar{g}$ and $\underline{g}$, we have the following property.

Property 1. *The spatial average of the temporal averages $\bar{g}$ and the temporal average of the spatial averages $\underline{g}$ generally satisfy the irequality $\bar{g}(x) \ne \underline{g}(x)$.*

This property implies that the order of operations for average computation affects the results.

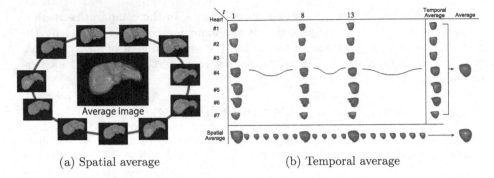

(a) Spatial average   (b) Temporal average

Fig. 1. Average image. (a) The average shape of usual organs is computed by the uni-step method. (b) The average shape of temporal organs, such as beating hearts, is computed by the bi-step method. First, we compute the temporal average of an organ. Then, the spatial average is computed from individual temporal averages.

4   Fast Numerical Computation

We derive a numerical method for solving eq. (1). From eq. (1), for the variational average image g and deformation fields u_k we derive the Euler-Lagrange equations

$$\alpha \Delta g(x) - G = 0, \quad \beta \Delta u_k(x) - U_k = 0, \tag{7}$$

where

$$G = \sum_{k=1}^{m} (g(x) - f_k(x - u_k)), \tag{8}$$

$$U_k = \gamma(\sum_{k=1}^{m} u_k + (g(x) - f_k(x - u_k))\nabla(g(x) - f_k(x - u_k))). \tag{9}$$

Next, we convert the elliptic partial differential equations in eq. (7) to the diffusion equations

$$\frac{\partial g}{\partial t} = \Delta g(x) - \frac{1}{\alpha}G, \quad \frac{\partial u_k}{\partial t} = \Delta u_k(x) - \frac{1}{\beta}U_k, \tag{10}$$

and discretise them as

$$\frac{g^{(n+1)} - g^{(n)}}{\tau} = Lg^{(n+1)} - \frac{1}{\alpha}G^{(n)}, \tag{11}$$

$$\frac{u_k^{(n+1)} - u_k^{(n)}}{\tau} = Lu_k^{(n+1)} - \frac{1}{\beta}U_k^{(n)}, \tag{12}$$

where L is the discrete Laplacian operation. Therefore, we obtain the iteration forms [18]

$$(I - \tau L)g^{(n+1)} = g^{(n)} - \frac{\tau}{\alpha}G^{(n)}, \tag{13}$$

$$(I - \tau L)u_k^{(n+1)} = u_k^{(n)} - \frac{\tau}{\beta}U_k^{(n)}. \tag{14}$$

For three-dimensional problems, L are described as

$$L = D \otimes I \otimes I + I \otimes D \otimes I + I \otimes I \otimes D, \tag{15}$$

for

$$D = \begin{pmatrix} -1 & 1 & 0 & \cdots & 0 & 0 & 0 \\ 1 & -2 & 1 & \cdots & 0 & 0 & 0 \\ 0 & 1 & -2 & \cdots & 0 & 0 & 0 \\ \vdots & \vdots & \vdots & \ddots & \vdots & \vdots & \vdots \\ 0 & 0 & 0 & \cdots & 1 & -2 & 1 \\ 0 & 0 & 0 & \cdots & 0 & 1 & -1 \end{pmatrix}, \tag{16}$$

where $A \otimes B$ is the Kronecker product of matrices A and B, assuming the von-Neumann condition on the boundary. The eigenvalues of D are $\lambda_k = -4\sin^2\frac{\pi k}{2M}$ for the $M \times M$ matrix [17], and the eigenmatrix [16] of D, is

$$\Phi = \left(\left(\epsilon \cos\frac{(2j+1)i}{2\pi}\pi M \right) \right), \quad \epsilon = \begin{cases} 1 & \text{if } j = 0 \\ \frac{1}{\sqrt{2}} & \text{otherwise.} \end{cases} \tag{17}$$

Φ is the matrix of the DCT-II transform. Therefore, the matrix L is decomposed as

$$\begin{aligned} L &= (\Phi \otimes \Phi \otimes \Phi)(\Lambda \otimes I \otimes I + I \otimes \Lambda \otimes I + I \otimes I \otimes \Lambda)(\Phi \otimes \Phi \otimes \Phi)^\top \\ &= U\Sigma U^\top \end{aligned} \tag{18}$$

and the eigenvalues of L are $\lambda_i + \lambda_j + \lambda_k$.

In each step of the iteration, the results are expressed on the Euler frame. Images sampled by the Lagrange frame do not guarantee correspondence between points. Therefore, we resample the results using the Lagrange frame [1]. In the Lagrange-frame-sampled images, we use Delaunay-triangle-based interpolation [1] since the method satisfies the minimum gradient property.

Setting $g^{(n)}$ to be the vector expression of the sampled $g^{(n)}$, we have the iteration form

$$g^{(n+1)} = UM^nU^\top(1 - \frac{m\tau}{\alpha})g^{(1)} + b^{(n)}, \tag{19}$$

where $b^{(n)} = \sum_{k=1}^{m}\frac{\tau}{\alpha}f_k(x - u_k^{(n)})$. For sufficiently large n, we can replace $b^{(n)}$ with a constant vector c. Therefore, we analyse the convergence condition of

$$g^{(n+1)} = UM^nU^\top(1 - \frac{m\tau}{\alpha})g^{(1)} + c, \tag{20}$$

---

[1] There are two reference frames, the Euler frame and Lagrange frame [3]. When we have an image B and an invertible transform φ, the frames are described as $B^{Lagrange}(\varphi(i,j,k)) := B(i,j,k)$ and $B^{Euler}(i,j,k) := B(\varphi^{-1}(i,j,k))$.

where c is a constant vector with the property $|c - b^{(N)}| < \varepsilon \ll 1$ for a sufficiently large integer N.

Since the matrix U is a unitary matrix, the convergence property of the algorithm depends on the spectral radius of the matrix M. Therefore, $g^{(n)}$ converges if the relation

$$\max\left(\left|\frac{1}{1 - \tau(\lambda_i + \lambda_j + \lambda_k)}\left(1 - \frac{m\tau}{\alpha}\right)\right|\right) < 1, \tag{21}$$

is satisfied for $0 < \alpha$, $0 < \tau$ and $0 < m$. The inequality $-12 < (\lambda_i + \lambda_j + \lambda_k) \le 0$ implies that the value of $\frac{1}{1 - \tau(\lambda_i + \lambda_j + \lambda_k)}$ becomes maximum for $\lambda_i + \lambda_j + \lambda_k = 0$. Therefore, from the inequality

$$\max\left(\left|\left(1 - \frac{m\tau}{\alpha}\right)\right|\right) < 1, \tag{22}$$

for $-1 < 1 - \frac{m\tau}{\alpha} < 1$, if $\tau < \frac{2\alpha}{m}$ is satisfied, the iteration form converges to the unique solution.

For the computation of u_k, setting $|d - \frac{\tau}{\beta}(\gamma \sum_{j=1, j\neq k}^{m} u_j^{(N)})| < \varepsilon \ll 1$ for a sufficiently large N, we have the relation

$$u_k^{(n+1)} = \left(1 - \frac{(1 + \epsilon)\gamma\tau}{\beta}\right) U M^n U^\top u_k^{(n)} + d, \tag{23}$$

where ϵ is a small perturbation caused by warping of data in each step of the iteration. The spectral radius of the matrix $\left(1 - \frac{(1+\epsilon)\gamma\tau}{\beta}\right) U M^n U^\top$ derives the convergence condition,

$$\max\left(\left|\frac{1}{1 - \tau(\lambda_i + \lambda_j + \lambda_k)}\left(1 - \frac{\tau(1 + \epsilon)\gamma}{\beta}\right)\right|\right) < 1. \tag{24}$$

Equation (24) leads to the convergence condition $\tau < \frac{2\beta}{(1+\epsilon)\gamma}$.

5   Numerical Examples

For numerical examples we computed averages of seven hearts with 20 frames. These images show renders surfaces of volumetric grey valued images in the three dimensional Euclidean space. The numerical results show the rendered surfaces. The resolution of each volumetric heart is Grey-value × Horizontal × Vertical × Depth $= 256 \times 128 \times 128 \times 15$. In total, the size of data is $256 \times 128 \times 128 \times 15 \times 20 \times 7$. Figures 2 and 3 show 20 frames of temporal volumetric images a couple of beating heart sequences. These figures show that shapes f heart depend on the frames and individuals.

We evaluate the warp image error WIE, the total deformation norm FNS, the volume V_i and the deformation energy DE_k which are defined as

$$\text{WIE}(\boldsymbol{x}) = \int_{\mathbf{R}^3} \|g(\boldsymbol{x}) - f_i(\boldsymbol{x} - \boldsymbol{u}_k)\|_2 d\boldsymbol{x}, \tag{25}$$

$$\text{FNS}(\boldsymbol{x}) = \|\sum_{i=1}^{n} \boldsymbol{u}_i\|_2, \tag{26}$$

$$V_k = \int_{\mathbf{R}^3} f_k(\boldsymbol{x} - \boldsymbol{u}_k) d\boldsymbol{x}, \tag{27}$$

$$DE_k = \int_{\mathbf{R}^3} \|\boldsymbol{u}_k(\boldsymbol{x})\|_2^2 d\boldsymbol{x}. \tag{28}$$

For the numerical computation, we adopt the regularisation parameters $\alpha = 10^{-1}$, $\beta = 10^2$ and $\gamma = 10^4$.

Figures 4 (a), (b) and (c) show rendered shapes of the spatial average of the temporal averages, the eigenorgan of the temporal averages and the arithmetic average with respect to time, respectively. For the eigenorgan, see Appendix. Figures 4 (b), (d) and (f) show radar charts of the total deformation norms of cycle of a volumetric beating-heart for the variational temporal average, the temporal eigenorgan and the arithmetic average with respect to time, respectively.

In the radar charts, 20 frames of a volumetric beating-heart sequence are shown on the circle and the arrow from the origin of the circle is the deformation energy required to deform the temporal average, which is shown in the centre of the chart, to the volumetric image at each frame. The arrows show the total difference between the average and each shape on the circle. These charts show that the variational average is a stable shape with respect to the cyclic deformation because the deformations on the chart are symmetric. However, the eigenorgan of the beating volumetric heart is unstable against cyclic motion because the deformation on the chart is asymmetric.

Figures 5(a) and (b) show the total of deformation norms and the warp image errors, respectively for the three averages.

Figures 6(a) and (b) show the spatial average of the temporal averages of the seven beating hearts. and the eigenorgan of the temporal averages of the seven beating volumetric hearts, respectively. The boundary of the spatial average of the temporal averages is smooth, although that of the eigenorgan contains small vibrations. These results show the variational average of the variational temporal averages is suitable for the construction of the model of the stationary heart of a human. Figure 6(c) shows the graphical expression of multidimensional scaling of 7 hearts. Figure 6(c) shows the graphical expression of multidimensional scaling of 7 hearts. This graph clarifies that both averages exist in a neighbour area of the median shape.

6   Validation of the Results

Tables 1 and 2 evaluate the WIE and FN, respectively, of temporal average of a volumetric beating-heart sequence. Tables 3 and 4 evaluate the WIE and

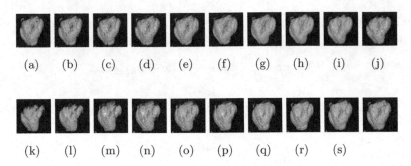

Fig. 2. Sequence of volumetric beating-heart images I. (a)-(t) are a sequence of 20 input temporal images. These images show renders surfaces of volumetric grey valued images in the three dimensional Euclidean space.

FN, respectively, of spatial average of volumetric beating-hearts of a frame 20 sequences. These results show that our method achieves multiple alignment of temporal volumetric data for the computation of the average of a beating-heart image sequence and the temporal average of beating-heart sequence occupies the mean region of a volumetric beating-heart sequence, respectively.

Figure 8 shows the distance between the average heart and each frame of seven hearts for arithmetic average, eigenorgan and variational average computed by the proposed method, respectively. For the distance between a pair of volumetric images, see Appendix. In this figure, the top, middle and bottom rows are the temporal arithmetic average, the temporal eigenorgan and the temporal variational average, respectively. Figures 9(a) and 9(b) show radar charts of the spatial temporal averages and the temporal spatial averages of a collection of heart sequences, respectively. In these evaluations, the volumetric centroids of the average and each frame are aligned as the pre-processing

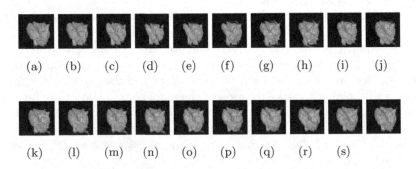

Fig. 3. Sequence of volumetric beating-heart images II. (a)-(t) are a sequence of 20 input temporal images. These images show renders surfaces of volumetric grey valued images in the three dimensional Euclidean space.

Table 1. WIE of each heart

data number		1	2	3	4	5	6	7
arithmetic average	average	1.326	1.950	2.111	2.699	3.250	2.284	1.505
	variance	0.045	0.160	0.142	0.191	0.322	0.139	0.036
eigenorgan	average	1.522	2.434	2.706	3.236	4.102	2.826	1.774
	variance	0.507	1.368	1.047	1.000	4.296	1.172	0.966
variational average	average	0.622	1.090	1.069	1.555	1.891	0.529	0.631
	variance	0.008	0.050	0.027	0.095	0.133	0.010	0.008

Table 2. FIN of individual heart

data number	1	2	3	4	5	6	7
average of deformation vector norms	0.014	0.022	0.031	0.028	0.043	0.146	0.015
variance of deformation vector norms	0.000	0.000	0.000	0.000	0.000	0.001	0.000
deformation energy	0.000	0.001	0.001	0.001	0.001	0.002	0.000

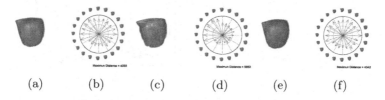

(a)   (b)   (c)   (d)   (e)   (f)

Fig. 4. Comparison of the three averages of a beating heart. (a) Arithmetic average of a beating-heart sequence. (b) Radar chart of the total deformation norms for the arithmetic average. (c) Eigenorgan of a beating-heart sequence. (d) Radar chart of the total deformation norms for the eigenorgan of a sequence of a beating heart. (e) Variational average of a beating-heart sequence. (f) Radar chart of the total deformation norms for the variational temporal average of a beating heart. In the radar charts, 20 frames of a volumetric beating-heart sequence are shown on the circle and the arrow from the origin of the circle is the deformation energy required to deform the temporal average, which is shown in the centre of the chart, to the volumetric image at each frame. The arrows show the total difference between the average and each shape on the circle.

In the radar charts, the arrows show the volumetric difference between the average at the centre and each frame of motion. The variational temporal average processes geometrical properties that the difference between the average and each frame expresses the geometrical and volumetric differences caused by deformation in a beating-heart sequence.

Table 3. WIE for frames

data number		1	2	3	4	5	6	7	8	9	10
arithmetic average	average	6.251	6.092	5.975	5.502	5.085	4.736	4.252	4.223	4.051	4.351
	variance	1.575	1.433	0.785	0.431	0.396	0.336	0.356	0.607	0.759	1.141
eigenorgan	average	10.700	10.488	10.125	9.303	8.626	8.006	7.182	6.869	6.802	7.247
	variance	14.230	13.814	13.104	11.065	10.178	7.922	4.868	5.429	6.220	8.269
variational average	average	2.672	2.671	2.576	2.331	2.180	2.111	1.999	1.900	1.876	1.996
	variance	0.264	0.300	0.249	0.163	0.174	0.143	0.136	0.150	0.150	0.188
data number		11	12	13	14	15	16	17	18	19	20
arithmetic average	average	4.762	5.109	5.309	5.461	6.058	6.318	6.433	6.620	6.627	6.496
	variance	1.329	1.483	1.523	1.326	1.344	1.544	1.978	2.103	1.795	1.496
eigenorgan	average	8.124	9.670	9.060	9.591	10.227	10.804	11.197	11.226	10.979	10.679
	variance	9.639	8.846	12.372	13.613	14.197	15.423	16.549	17.201	15.505	14.022
variational average	average	2.166	2.357	2.368	2.402	2.527	2.565	2.697	2.778	2.795	2.750
	variance	0.208	0.238	0.244	0.221	0.205	0.252	0.347	0.375	0.327	0.239

(a)   (b)

Fig. 5. Comparison of the three averages for a beating-heart sequence. (a) Total deformation norms $\mathrm{FNS}(\boldsymbol{x}) = \|\sum_{i=1}^{m} \boldsymbol{u}_i\|_2$. (b) Warp errors $\mathrm{WIE}(\boldsymbol{x}) = \|g(\boldsymbol{x}) - f_i(\boldsymbol{x} - \boldsymbol{u}_i)\|_2$.

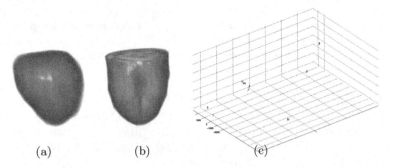

(a)   (b)   (c)

Fig. 6. Comparison of the averages of a beating heart. (a) Spatial average of the temporal averages of 7 beating hearts. (b) Eigenorgan of the temporal averages of 7 beating hearts. (c) The graphical MDS of two types of variational averages.

Table 4. FEN of the spatial averages

frame number	1	2	3	4	5	6	7	8	9	10
average of deformation vector norms	0.162	0.164	0.158	0.149	0.136	0.119	0.108	0.107	0.104	0.115
variance of deformation vector norms	0.002	0.001	0.001	0.000	0.000	0.000	0.000	0.001	0.001	0.001
deformation energy	0.002	0.002	0.002	0.002	0.002	0.002	0.002	0.002	0.002	0.002
frame number	11	12	13	14	15	16	17	18	19	20
average of deformation vector norms	0.129	0.141	0.150	0.148	0.164	0.172	0.173	0.175	0.174	0.169
variance of deformation vector norms	0.001	0.001	0.001	0.001	0.001	0.001	0.002	0.002	0.002	0.001
deformation energy	0.002	0.002	0.002	0.002	0.003	0.003	0.003	0.003	0.003	0.003

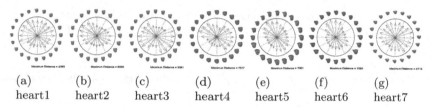

(a)	(b)	(c)	(d)	(e)	(f)	(g)
heart1	heart2	heart3	heart4	heart5	heart6	heart7

Fig. 7. Distances between arithmetic average heart and inputs

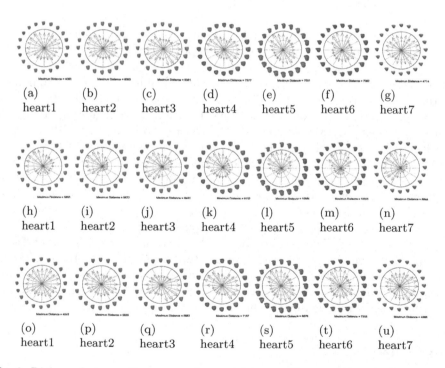

(a)	(b)	(c)	(d)	(e)	(f)	(g)
heart1	heart2	heart3	heart4	heart5	heart6	heart7

(h)	(i)	(j)	(k)	(l)	(m)	(n)
heart1	heart2	heart3	heart4	heart5	heart6	heart7

(o)	(p)	(q)	(r)	(s)	(t)	(u)
heart1	heart2	heart3	heart4	heart5	heart6	heart7

Fig. 8. Distance between the average heart and inputs. Top, middle and bottom rows are the temporal arithmetic average, the temporal eigenorgan and the temporal variational average, respectively.

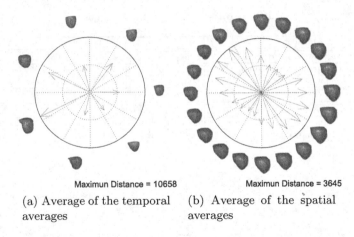

(a) Average of the temporal averages   (b) Average of the spatial averages

Fig. 9. Spatial temporal averages and temporal spatial averages of a collection of heart sequences

7   Conclusions

Using multiple image warping, which computes deformation fields between an image and a collection of images, we developed a variational method for the computation of the average images and the average shapes of both static and temporal biological organs in three-dimensional Euclidean space. We combined the diffusion registration technique and optical-flow computation for the computation of spatial deformation field between the average image and input organs.

For spatiotemporal volumetric data, (1) the temporal average is the average of a heart during a cycle, (2) the frame average is the average of hearts at a frame, and (3) the temporal average of frame averages. The first, second and third averages derive the standard shape of the organ of a human, the standard shape of a frame of beating hearts and the standard shape of a collection of beating hearts, respectively.

This research was supported by the "Computational Anatomy for Computer-Aided Diagnosis and Therapy: Frontiers of Medical Image Sciences" and "Multidisciplinary Computational Anatomy and Its Application to Highly Intelligent Diagnosis and Therapy" projects funded by a Grant-in-Aid for Scientific Research on Innovative Areas from MEXT, Japan, and by Grants-in-Aid for Scientific Research funded by the Japan Society for the Promotion of Science.

Appendix

Let

$$\int_{\mathbf{R}^3} f^2 d\boldsymbol{x} \leq \infty$$

for a function $f(\boldsymbol{x})$ defined on $\mathbf{R}^3$. Since

$$f(\boldsymbol{x} + \boldsymbol{\delta}) = f(\boldsymbol{x}) + \boldsymbol{\delta}^\top \nabla f$$

and

$$\int_{\mathbf{R}^3} f f_x d\boldsymbol{x} = 0, \quad \int_{\mathbf{R}^3} f_x f_y d\boldsymbol{x} = 0, \quad \int_{\mathbf{R}^3} f f_y d\boldsymbol{x} = 0,$$

$$\int_{\mathbf{R}^3} f_y f_z d\boldsymbol{x} = 0, \quad \int_{\mathbf{R}^3} f f_z d\boldsymbol{x} = 0, \quad \int_{\mathbf{R}^3} f_z f_x d\boldsymbol{x} = 0$$

in the neighbourhood of the point $\boldsymbol{x}$, the local dimension of the volumetric-image space is four. Therefore, using the local orthogonal base, the volumetric eigenimage is expressed as

$$f(\boldsymbol{x}) = \sum_{k=1}^{4} \alpha_k \boldsymbol{u}_k(\boldsymbol{x}),$$

where $\{\boldsymbol{u}_i\}_{i=1}^{4}$ are the first four principal components of the covariance kernel $K(\boldsymbol{x}, \boldsymbol{y}) = \sum_{i=1}^{n} f(\boldsymbol{x}) f(\boldsymbol{y})$.

Setting

$$f_a(\boldsymbol{x}) = \frac{1}{n} \sum_{i=1}^{n} f_i(\boldsymbol{x} - \boldsymbol{g}_i), \quad \boldsymbol{g}_i = \frac{1}{\Omega} \int_{\mathbf{R}^3} f_i(\boldsymbol{x}) d\boldsymbol{x}$$

the volumetric distance is computed as

$$D(f, g) = \min_{\boldsymbol{R}} \int_{\mathbf{R}^3} |f_a(\boldsymbol{x}) - g_a(\boldsymbol{R}\boldsymbol{x})|^2 d\boldsymbol{x}.$$

References

1. Hjelle, Ø., Dæhlen, M.: Triangulations and Applications. Mathematics and Visualization Series. Springer (2006)
2. Fischer, B., Modersitzki, J.: Ill-posed medicine- an introduction to image registration. Inverse Prob. **24**, 1–17 (2008)
3. Modersitzki, J.: Numerical Methods for Image Registration, OUP (2004)
4. Rumpf, M., Wirth, B.: A nonlinear elastic shape averaging approach. SIAM J. Imaging Sci. **2**, 800–833 (2009)
5. Arrate, F., Ratnanather, J.T., Younes, L.: Diffeomorphic active contours. SIAM J. Imaging Sci. **3**, 176–198 (2010)
6. Sharon, E., Mumford, D.: 2D-shape analysis using conformal mapping. IJCV **70**, 55–75 (2006)
7. Sebastian, T.B., Klein, P.N., Kimia, B.B.: On aligning curves. IEEE PAMI **25**, 116–125 (2003)
8. Baeza-Yates, R., Valiente, G.: An image similarity measure based on graph matching. In: Proc. 7th Int. Symp. String Processing and Information Retrieval, pp. 8–38 (2000)
9. Riesen, K., Bunke, H.: Approximate graph edit distance computation by means of bipartite graph matching. Image Vision Comput. **27**, 950–959 (2009)

10. Tanase, M., Veltkamp, R.C., Haverkort, H.J.: Multiple polyline to polygon matching. In: Deng, X., Du, D.-Z. (eds.) ISAAC 2005. LNCS, vol. 3827, pp. 60–70. Springer, Heidelberg (2005)
11. Stegmann, M.B., Gomez, D.D.: A brief introduction to statistical shape analysis, Informatics and Mathematical Modelling, Technical University of Denmark (2002). http://www2.imm.dtu.dk/pubdb/p.php?403
12. Srivastava, A., Joshi, S., Mio, W., Liu, X.: Statistical shape analysis: Clustering, learning, and testing. IEEE PAMI **27**, 590–602 (2005)
13. Rumpf, M., Wirth, B.: An elasticity-based covariance analysis of shapes. IJCV **92**, 281–295 (2011)
14. Wirth, B., Bar, L., Rumpf, M., Sapiro, G.: A continuum mechanical approach to geodesics in shape space. IJCV **93**, 293–318 (2011)
15. Strang, G.: Computational Science and Engineering. Wellesley-Cambridge Press (2007)
16. Strang, G., Nguyen, T.: Wavelets and Filter Banks. Wellesley-Cambridge Press (1996)
17. Demmel, J.W.: Applied Numerical Linear Algebra. SIAM (1997)
18. Varga, R.S.: Matrix Iterative Analysis, 2nd edn. Springer (2000)
19. Sebastian, T.B., Klein, P.N., Kimia, B.B.: On aligning curves. IEEE PAMI **25**, 116–125 (2003)
20. Hill, D.L.G., Batchelor, P.G., Holden, M., Hawkes, D.J.: Medical image registration. Physics in Medicine and Biology **46**, R1–45 (2001)
21. Avants, B., Gee, J.C.: Geodesic estimation for large deformation anatomical shape averaging and interpolation. NeuroImage **23**, S139–S150 (2004)
22. Milios, E., Petrakis, E.G.M.: Shape retrieval based on dynamic programming. IEEE IP **9**, 141–147 (2000)
23. Grigorescu, C., Petkov, N.: Distance sets for shape filters and shape recognition. IEEE IP **12**, 1274–1286 (2003)

Refining Mitochondria Segmentation in Electron Microscopy Imagery with Active Surfaces

Anne Jorstad$^{(\boxtimes)}$ and Pascal Fua

Ecole Polytechnique Fédérale de Lausanne, Lausanne, Switzerland
anne.jorstad@epfl.ch

Abstract. We present an active surface-based method for refining the boundary surfaces of mitochondria segmentation data. We exploit the fact that mitochondria have thick dark membranes, so referencing the image data at the inner membrane can help drive a more accurate delineation of the outer membrane surface. Given the initial boundary prediction from a machine learning-based segmentation algorithm as input, we compare several cost functions used to drive an explicit update scheme to locally refine 3D mesh surfaces, and results are presented on electron microscopy imagery. Our resulting surfaces are seen to fit very accurately to the mitochondria membranes, more accurately even than the available hand-annotations of the data.

1 Introduction

Meaningful statistics regarding the volumes, surface areas, and lengths of subcellular structures such as mitochondria and synapses in the brain are key to allowing neuroscientists to compare these objects in healthy people and those with degenerative brain diseases and to understand brain connectivity. These statistics require not just object detection, but also very accurate surface structure delineation.

State-of-the-art image segmentation algorithms such as [1,6,7,10] produce reasonably good localization results, in that they are able to detect most instances of the object they are searching for, and provide a rough outline. However, they often fail to accurately define the detailed boundary surface of the object in question to the precision required for accurate geometric measurements, especially surface area. In this paper, we propose an explicit active surface scheme to improve the precision of segmentation results in the case of mitochondria in 3D electron microscopy (EM) imaging. To this end, we take into account their thick membranes, as seen in Figure 1, and compare several cost functions used to drive the local surface refinement.

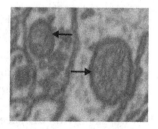

Fig. 1. Mitochondria have thick membranes

Our method models the outer and inner membrane boundaries as active surfaces [5] in a 3D volume. Tied together by a spring-like proximity energy

© Springer International Publishing Switzerland 2015
L. Agapito et al. (Eds.): ECCV 2014 Workshops, Part IV, LNCS 8928, pp. 367–379, 2015.
DOI: 10.1007/978-3-319-16220-1_26

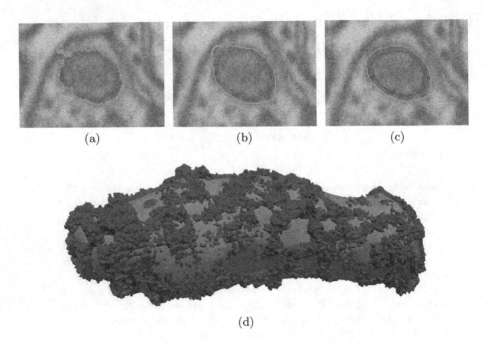

(a)   (b)   (c)

(d)

Fig. 2. Surface refinement process. (a) Cross section of 3D input segmentation before smoothing. (b) After Gaussian smoothing. (c) After running our algorithm. (d) Resulting 3D surface shown in blue with 3D input shown in red.

function, the surfaces are updated by minimizing energy terms defined by the image data at the outer and inner surfaces. The initial input to our algorithm is the output segmentation results from methods that use feature-based machine learning to predict whether or not a given voxel is contained within a structure of interest. As these objects are generally computed on supervoxels, the resulting output segmentations tend to be noisy and coarse, as shown in Figure 2. Often times, the final step of these algorithms involves simply smoothing the results so that they appear more visually pleasing, but this does not capture many of the fine surface details. Computing the correct 3D surfaces, whose surface areas will be meaningful for neuroscience applications, requires returning to the image data to perform further local surface updates, as we propose.

Related work includes [12], which searches for membranes in medical images, but works only on 2D slices. The cost function in this model defines a minimum and maximum membrane thickness in 2D, between which there is no penalty, whereas we know a precise value of mitochondria membrane thickness in 3D, and perform our calculations accordingly in 3D. In [11], the best fit to a deformable membrane template of a certain topology is sought, but in our case a single or double surface update scheme that allows each surface to align with small detailed gradients in the image is sufficient. Shape priors are used successfully in [8], but in this work we focus on surface image information alone.

2 Method

Our goal is to precisely capture the true 3D boundaries of mitochondria surfaces, starting from the well-localized but rough binary segmentation data provided by [10]. The initial rough surfaces are Gaussian smoothed, but the resulting objects do not capture fine surface detail. We use an explicit active surface method that starts from an initialization of surface points as a 3D mesh and iterates in a gradient descent energy minimization scheme until either a local minimum is reached or a maximum number of iterations has been computed. We define energy functions that are based on the gradients of the image data near the membrane boundaries, and is also dependent on the proximity to a second surface tracing the inner boundary of the membrane.

The boundary of a mitochondrion is defined by a thick dark membrane. The most discriminatory image data exists at the outside boundary of this membrane, which is a local image gradient maximum, and can be found by minimizing $\frac{1}{1+\|\nabla I\|}$, as in [3]. The inner boundary of the membrane is also a local minimum of this function, but is a much weaker boundary than the outer membrane, as can be seen in Figure 1. Although it is weaker, considering image data from the inner surface can contribute to defining a more robust final outer surface. We will compare active surface schemes that jointly update both an inner and an outer surface, where each surface incorporates varying amounts of information from the current position of the other.

It is known from biology that organelles are generally smooth objects, and it is important that the final surfaces be smooth so that accurate surface areas of the objects can be computed and compared. We achieve this objective by a standard application of Laplacian smoothing as in [13], which minimizes the curvature of the surface, and where at each update, every point is redefined to be a weighted average of itself and its neighbors. At each iteration k over the mesh of 3D points X, we update

$$X^{k+1} = A^{-1}\left(\gamma X^k - w \nabla E^{\mathrm{sum}}(X^k)\right),\tag{1}$$

where $E^{\mathrm{sum}}(X) = \sum_{\mathbf{x}} E(\mathbf{x})$ is the cost function defined at each point to be minimized as described below, the matrix $A = \gamma I + \alpha L_n$, for relative weighting parameters γ and α, and L_n is the normalized graph Laplacian ($L(i,i) = 1$, $L(i,j) = \frac{-1}{\|\mathcal{N}_{v_i}\|_0}$, where $\|\mathcal{N}_{v_i}\|_0$ is the number of neighbors of vertex v_i). The multiplication by A^{-1} is performed in practice by LU decomposition. This smoothing operation is applied at the end of each iteration, updating the new point locations relative to those of their neighbors.

The directional force of each iteration is defined by an energy function depending on the image data, and also on the proximity between the inner and outer membrane surfaces. We will compare four energy functions E_I based on the image data at each surface point $\mathbf{x}$, one of which iterates towards regions of large image gradient (Eq. 2), while the others additionally take into consideration the direction of the image gradient:

$$E_I^1(\mathbf{x}) = \frac{1}{1 + \|\nabla I(\mathbf{x})\|}, \tag{2}$$

$$E_I^2(\mathbf{x}) = \frac{1}{1 + \|\nabla I(\mathbf{x})\|} \left(\arccos\left(\hat{n}(\mathbf{x}) \cdot \widehat{\nabla I}(\mathbf{x}) \right) + \delta \right), \tag{3}$$

$$E_I^3(\mathbf{x}) = -\hat{n}(\mathbf{x}) \cdot \nabla I(\mathbf{x}), \tag{4}$$

$$E_I^4(\mathbf{x}) = \frac{1}{1 + \|\nabla I(\mathbf{x})\|} \left(1 - \left(\hat{n}(\mathbf{x}) \cdot \widehat{\nabla I}(\mathbf{x}) \right) * \left(\widehat{\nabla I}(\mathbf{x}) \cdot -\widehat{\nabla I}(\mathbf{x}_{\text{clspt}}) \right) \right). \tag{5}$$

Here $\hat{n}(\mathbf{x})$ is the surface normal vector at $\mathbf{x}$ with unit length, $\widehat{\nabla I}(\mathbf{x})$ is the normalized image gradient direction vector, and $\mathbf{x}_{\text{clspt}}$ is the closest point on the second surface to point $\mathbf{x}$ on the first surface. As described above, minimizing Equation (2) updates the surface towards local image gradient maxima. Equations (3), (4), and (5) additionally encourage surfaces whose normal vectors point in the direction of dark to light in the image. The intuition behind Equation 3 is that when the surface normal is in line with the image gradient, $\hat{n}(\mathbf{x}) \cdot \widehat{\nabla I}(\mathbf{x}) \approx 1$, when they are perpendicular $\hat{n}(\mathbf{x}) \cdot \widehat{\nabla I}(\mathbf{x}) \approx 0$, and when they are pointing in opposite directions, $\hat{n}(\mathbf{x}) \cdot \widehat{\nabla I}(\mathbf{x}) \approx -1$, so $\cos^{-1}$ of this dot product is 0 when the vectors are aligned, with values up to π when they are pointing in opposite directions. Using the $\cos^{-1}$ means that the true angle between the two vectors is measured and penalized linearly. This value is then offset by δ so that it is never 0 and the other term encouraging large gradient magnitudes can still direct the surface updates even when the surface is aligned with the image gradient. In Eq. 4, the image gradient is not normalized, resulting in the simplest expression that penalizes a surface normal that is not aligned with the image gradient, while also progressing towards a large image gradient. From the first dot product of Equation 5, the surface is encouraged to align with the image gradient, while the second dot product encourages the inner and outer surfaces to be locally parallel; this quantity is again scaled by the image gradient magnitude term.

We want to take advantage of the fact that the membrane has both an outer and an inner boundary, so we will consider a cost function that optimizes the two surfaces together. Mitochondria membranes are known to have a very consistent thickness, so we add to the energy function a term that penalizes points on the surfaces that are not the known distance r apart. For each point x_i on surface S_1, the closest point $\mathbf{x}_{\text{clspt}}$ is found on surface S_2 (and vice versa), and for convenience of notation we define the closest point to $\mathbf{x}_i$ as

$$\mathbf{x}_{\text{clspt}} = \arg\min_{\mathbf{x}_j \in S_2} \|\mathbf{x}_i - \mathbf{x}_j\|. \tag{6}$$

The distance $\|\mathbf{x}_i - \mathbf{x}_{\text{clspt}}\|$ is penalized via a Gaussian centered at the standard membrane thickness, resulting in the proximity cost function:

$$E_P(\mathbf{x}_i \in S_1) = \left(\frac{\|\mathbf{x}_i - \mathbf{x}_{\text{clspt}}\| - r}{\sigma} \right)^2. \tag{7}$$

In order to understand the influence of tracing the inner membrane surface in addition to the outer one, we will also consider a weighting between the inner and outer energies

$$E_I^{\text{total}}(\mathbf{x}_i \in S_1) = (1 - w_{\text{other}})E_I(\mathbf{x}_i) + w_{\text{other}}E_I(\mathbf{x}_{\text{clspt}}) \tag{8}$$

where the weight w_{other} is a value between 0 and 0.5. We note that even if $w_{\text{other}} = 0$ the locations of the two membranes influence each other via the proximity term E_P.

The resulting function to be optimized is therefore

$$E(\mathbf{x}_i \in S_1) = w_I E_I^{\text{total}}(\mathbf{x}_i) + w_P E_P(\mathbf{x}_i), \tag{9}$$

for relative weighting parameters w_I and w_P (and similarly for points on the second surface S_2). In order to calculate the minimizing surface, the gradient descent scheme from Equation 1 is applied, where the gradient term is defined to be

$$\nabla E(\mathbf{x}_i^k) = w_I \widehat{\nabla E_I}^{\text{total}}(\mathbf{x}_i^k) + w_P \widehat{\nabla E_P}(\mathbf{x}_i^k). \tag{10}$$

We note that all energy gradients in our algorithm are normalized so that their relative influence can be adjusted explicitly using the weights w_I, w_P and w_{other}.

3   Discussion

Electron Microscopy data is notoriously difficult to work with, because the texture and intensity variations across all parts of the images are so similar. If the initial segmentation that our algorithm is given is not within a reasonably small radius of the true surface boundary, there is nothing an active surface algorithm making only local updates can do to progress to the true boundary, such as in Figure 3. There are far too many local gradient maxima between the found object segmentation and the true boundary, even after significant smoothing, and these cases are beyond the scope of the local update routines using only image data that are being compared in this study. This type of error must be fixed by a stronger initial segmentation algorithm, and for the purposes of this study, we remove the found mitochondria whose volumes are less than half of the true objects, so that we can understand the strengths of the methods being presented.

The update schemes presented in this work rely on having reasonably strong image gradients to iterate towards. While the outer mitochondria membrane boundaries do have acceptably strong image gradients, so do many other nearby structures that can easily distract from the organelle in question. This is why referencing the inner membrane can help. However, the gradients at the inner membrane boundaries are weak. Instead of using gradients, the proposed method can further benefit from an inner boundary delineation defined by a statistical model based on region texture, such as in [4]. This will be a focus of future work.

The bottleneck of the presented methods is the computation required to find the closest points between surfaces. We use an axis-aligned bounding box tree to speed up the search, and the operations can be done in parallel, but this remains the most computationally intensive piece of our algorithm.

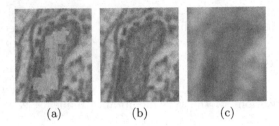

(a)   (b)   (c)

Fig. 3. (a) Example of an erroneous input segmentation that is too far from (b) the true surface boundaries for the local surface refinements based on the gradients of (c) smoothed images presented in this paper to overcome.

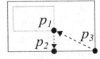

It is important to note that the membrane proximity term we use is not symmetric. Take the simple example of two concentric rectangles, as in Figure 4. The closest point to the corner of the inside rectangle (p_1) on the outside rectangle

Fig. 4.

(p_2) is significantly closer than the closest point to the corner of the outside rectangle (p_3) to the inside one (p_1). This means that the proximity gradient of the outside surface tends to be stronger than that of the inside surface, and the outside surface is therefore more prone to moving inward than the inside surface is to moving outward. We can handle this size discrepancy numerically by using normalized gradient vectors in our calculations. This does not address the lack of symmetry in the directions of the gradients, but because we are able to initialize the surfaces relative to each other, this discrepancy does not usually significantly affect the surface updates. However, due to this inconsistency, we observed that if the weight w_{other} from Equation (8) is too high the accuracy of the method decreases.

Most of the gradient calculations required to update Equation 1 are straightforward to compute, and the image gradients can be pre-calculated. However, the last term in Eq. 8 depends on data from the closest point to $\mathbf{x}_i \in S_1$ on the other surface. To calculate the gradient of this term finite differences must be used, which requires performing the closest point search three separate times to compute the energy at small offsets in the x-, y-, and z- directions. The $\frac{\partial}{\partial x}$ term is computed as follows:

$$\frac{E_I\left(\arg\min_{\mathbf{x}_j \in S_2}\|(\mathbf{x}_i + [\Delta x, 0, 0]) - \mathbf{x}_j\|\right) - E_I\left(\arg\min_{\mathbf{x}_j \in S_2}\|\mathbf{x}_i - \mathbf{x}_j\|\right)}{\Delta x}. \tag{11}$$

4   Experiments

Our algorithm has been developed to perform local refinements to the surfaces of segmented structures in 3D electron microscopy medical image stacks. For testing we used a publicly available dataset[1] that consists of a $1024 \times 768 \times 165$

---

[1] http://cvlab.epfl.ch/data/em

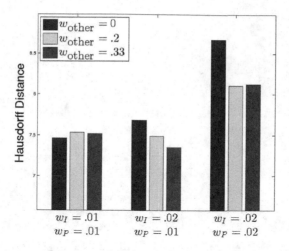

Fig. 5. For parameter verification, Hausdorff Distance results are presented for varying values of w_I, w_P, and w_{other}. All tests are performed using E_I^1.

image stack. We obtained from the authors the output of their algorithm [10], which correctly finds most mitochondria in the stack albeit with fairly rough boundaries. These boundaries were Gaussian smoothed before processing, and our method is then meant to update these smoothed surfaces to capture fine surface details. We first used the standard Marching Cubes algorithm of [9] to generate a 3D mesh corresponding to the outer boundary of each mitochondrion. We then initialized the inner membrane surface by eroding the initial segmentation by the expected membrane thickness. The mesh surfaces are defined by 50,000 vertices on average, but this quantity varies considerably, ranging from 10,000 to 114,000 vertices depending on the size of each mitochondrion and how much of it is contained within the image stack.

Parameter ranges were tuned on an artificial 3D image of a smoothed black ball with a thick boundary on a white background. The fixed parameters used in our experiments are as follows: segmentation smoothing $\sigma = 5$, smoothing for image gradients $\sigma = 5$, membrane thickness $r = 4, \sigma = 1$, Laplacian parameters $\gamma = 1$ and $\alpha = .5$, and the number of iterations is 100. In Figure 5 we present a range of results for a single cost function (E_I^1) as the weighting parameters are varied over a small range of values found to perform well. Observing that w_P should be no greater than 0.01, we present the rest of our experiments using the parameters $w_I = 0.01$ and $w_P = 0.01$, but as all nearby parameter values produce similar final results, the methods are seen to be stable. In future work better optimization schemes can be derived that modify the weights throughout the optimization.

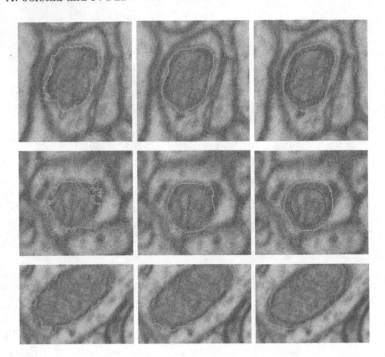

Fig. 6. From noisy initial segmentations (left), we observe that incorporating an outer and inner membrane proximity term (right) into the surface refinement energy function results in a more precise surface extraction than when it is not used (center). See also Figure 2. This result is the primary contribution of this work.

4.1   Qualitative Evaluation

A cross-section of the full segmentation surface refinement results is presented in Figure 10 along with the final surfaces of the whole image stack. The smooth surfaces our method produces are seen to be very consistent with the image data. At this scale, the differences between the four energy function compared is visibly negligible.

We observe that performing surface updates that track both the inner and outer membranes together, and penalizes discrepancies between them, results in more accurate final surface reconstructions. For several examples see Figures 2 and 6. This is the fundamental contribution of this work.

Of the four energy functions we propose, the most basic function E_I^1 performs remarkably well considering that it only depends on the magnitude and not the direction of the image gradients. This function cannot in principle distinguish between the inner and outer membranes, and so should be more prone to iterating towards false membranes. However, it is interesting to note that the other cost functions, which were designed to improve upon E_I^1, do not appear to perform substantially better. It is observed that E_I^2 and E_I^3 provide very similar results, in spite of the fact that E_I^2 depends on more meaningful quantities. This is likely due to the fact that EM imagery is so noisy that precise numerical

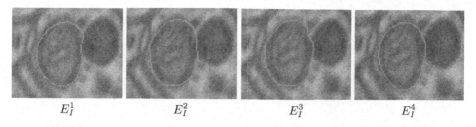

$$E_I^1 \qquad\qquad E_I^2 \qquad\qquad E_I^3 \qquad\qquad E_I^4$$

Fig. 7. Example surface refinements from each of the energy functions considered. We find that the function that does not take any directional term into account (E_I^1) and the function that encourages the two surfaces to point in opposite directions (E_I^4) are typically the most accurate.

relations between pixels is not as meaningful as in other contexts. The final energy function E_I^4 that also enforces that the two surfaces should be locally parallel, in addition to being aligned with the image data, performs somewhat better than E_I^2 and E_I^3. For an example visual comparison of the four energy functions, see Figure 7.

4.2   Quantitative Evaluation

The dataset we use includes hand-annotations provided by an expert that roughly denote the voxels that correspond to mitochondria in the images. As is fairly common in such annotations created frame-by-frame, noticeable jumps can often be observed between consecutive frames because the human annotator was not consistent in deciding from one frame to the next where a mitochondrion boundary ended, for example see Figure 8. This implies that, while sufficient for large-scale coarse mitochondria segmentation, the hand annotations are not perfectly accurate. We attempted to improve the hand annotations by going through each frame of a mitochondrion and carefully marking each boundary pixel, a process that takes about two minutes per frame, or about five hours per mitochondrion. This process is not tenable for a data set of any reasonable size. We also attempted to obtain more precise segmentations using the 3D carving tool provided in ilastik 1.0[2], the Interactive Learning and Segmentation Toolkit, which implements the seeded watershed algorithm to perform interactive image segmentation. Extracting the object boundaries in 3D instead of going through individual 2D frames alleviates the problem of frame-by-frame discrepancies that were demonstrated in Figure 8. Unfortunately, this tool, similar to any automatic segmentation tool, relies on object boundaries having strong image gradients, which is simply not always the case in EM imagery, as described above. The resulting "carved out" objects include sections of smooth boundaries as desired, but also large regions of grossly incorrect surfaces where the segmentation has ballooned into the surrounding regions, or been caught significantly inside the mitochondrial structure where a stronger gradient has been found, as

---

[2] www.ilastik.org

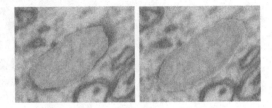

Fig. 8. Two adjacent image slices from the reference hand-annotations. The inconsistency between images slices that comes from labling each slice independently leads to locally inaccurate surfaces. The surfaces constructed by the methods presented in this paper are seen to be more accurate than the provided hand annotations.

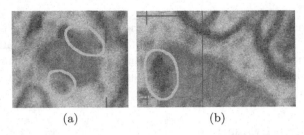

(a)   (b)

Fig. 9. Examples of the ilastik carving tool (a) oversegmenting and (b) undersegmenting a mitochondrion object. Note that these images are from the same segmentation, and it tends to be impossible to correct the error in one direction without further exacerbating the error in the other. (The red lines are part of the ilastik interface and can be ignored.)

in Figure 9. These segmentations must then be hand-corrected frame-by-frame as before, and the overall processing time at over two hours per mitochondrion is still unmanageable on a large scale.

It is therefore understandable that the precise surface refinements we compute in this work are often visually better than the noisy hand annotations available for reference, yet can be penalized numerically when compared against them. To attempt to alleviate the discrepancy between image frames, the hand annotations are smoothed with the same Gaussian smoothing σ as the images. This means, however, that the initial smoothed segmentations and the hand annotations are both highly smoothed blobs, and are often closer to each other than they are to the fine surface details that they have smoothed across. We find that while our method is observed to consistently arrive at accurate image boundaries, as seen above, comparing our results to the hand annotations does not result in solutions that are numerically as much stronger than the smoothed initial segmentations as we would expect. Nevertheless, for general verification purposes we compare our results with the provided hand annotations.

Image segmentation accuracy is often measured by the Jaccard index, but as we are interested in surface precision and not the volume overlap that the Jaccard index quantifies, we will instead perform our numeric evaluations using a measure

Table 1. Surface refinement results for each of the energy functions E_I compared to the provided hand annotations, where the values presented represent the average Hausdorff Distance over all mitochondria in the image stack. It is again observed that E_I^1 and E_I^4 perform more strongly than the other two energy functions described.

Method	Hausdorff Distance		
Input segmentation	12.518		
Smoothed input segmentation	8.144		
	$w_{other} = 0$	$w_{other} = .2$	$w_{other} = .33$
E_I^1	**7.460**	7.530	7.518
E_I^2	8.054	8.012	8.017
E_I^3	8.006	8.028	8.071
E_I^4	7.713	7.991	7.987

of surface similarity. The Hausdorff Distance measures how close two surfaces are in space by finding the minimum distance from each point on one surface to the other surface, and vice versa, and then returns the maximum of these minimum distances. The Hausdorff Distance is computed for each mitochondrion in the image stack separately, and the average result is presented in Table 1. We also provide these measurement results on the input data and the Gaussian smoothed version of the input data, which is what we use to initialize our algorithm. These results show that our proposed method does produce an improvement, albeit not as large as visual inspection would indicate. As discussed above, this is essentially an artifact of the inaccuracy of the hand annotations, which are highly smoothed, and therefore very similar to the smoothed input segmentation, while often penalizing our results when they are *more* accurate than those provided. This phenomenon has been previously observed in [2], where in order to avoid the inaccuracies at the boundaries of hand-annotated EM data the authors ignore all voxels near the structure boundaries when comparing segmentations. What we can say from the numerical results is that our method does reduce outliers. We refer back to the qualitative results above for further verification of the accuracy of the presented method.

We observe both qualitatively and quantitatively that the cost functions E_I^1 and E_I^4 perform better than the others. While E_I^1 compares the most positively with the hand annotations, qualitatively it appears that E_I^4 performs at least as well. Numerically it also appears that making use of $w_{other} > 0$ actually hurts the process. This means that while using the proximity term from Equation 7 is helpful, using the current gradient values of both surfaces to define the direction in which each individual surface should step is actually confusing the process. This is likely due to the fact that the point proximity is not symmetric, and so the corresponding surface points are not always jointly meaningful, as discussed in Section 3.

The original goal of this work was to construct more accurate surfaces so that analyses involving their surface areas can be as precise as possible for biological applications. Unfortunately, the "ground truth" surface area of a mitochondrion simply cannot be obtained, and so we must instead focus on refining surfaces to be as accurate as possible given the image data.

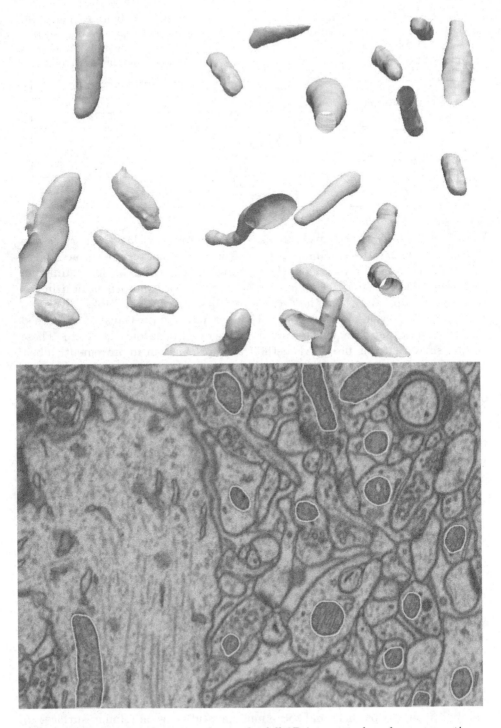

Fig. 10. Final surface fitting results on the full 3D image stack and a cross section

5 Conclusion

We have compared several energy functions used to drive an explicit surface refinement algorithm, with the goal of making local adjustments to the output of mitochondria segmentation algorithms in challenging EM imagery. The well-localized but rough initial segmentation is smoothed, and the methods then update the surfaces towards local surface details. Qualitative and quantitative results are provided that demonstrate the effectiveness of the method. We observe that our method is able to provide mitochondria surface segmentation results that are more accurate than the available hand annotations. The resulting smooth surfaces can be used in biological applications where it is important to be able to accurately calculate and compare the surface areas of mitochondria.

Acknowledgments. This work was supported in part by the MicroNano ERC project.

References

1. Becker, C., Ali, K., Knott, G., Fua, P.: Learning context cues for synapse segmentation in EM volumes. In: Ayache, N., Delingette, H., Golland, P., Mori, K. (eds.) MICCAI 2012, Part I. LNCS, vol. 7510, pp. 585–592. Springer, Heidelberg (2012)
2. Becker, C., Ali, K., Knott, G., Fua, P.: Learning Context Cues for Synapse Segmentation. TMI **32**(10), 1864–1877 (2013)
3. Caselles, V., Kimme, R., Sapiro, G.: Geodesic active contours. In: Proceedings Fifth International Conference on Computer Vision, pp. 694–699 (1995)
4. Chan, T.F., Vese, L.A.: Active contours without edges. In: TIP, pp. 266–277 (2001)
5. He, L., Peng, Z., Everding, B., Wang, X., Han, C.Y., Weiss, K.L., Wee, W.G.: A Comparative Study of Deformable Contour Methods on Medical Image Segmentation. Image and Vision Computing **26**(2), 141–163 (2008)
6. Kreshuk, A., Straehle, C.N., Sommer, C., Koethe, U., Knott, G., Hamprecht, F.: Automated segmentation of synapses in 3D EM data. In: ISBI (2011)
7. Laptev, D., Vezhnevets, A., Dwivedi, S., Buhmann, J.M.: Anisotropic ssTEM image segmentation using dense correspondence across sections. In: Ayache, N., Delingette, H., Golland, P., Mori, K. (eds.) MICCAI 2012, Part I. LNCS, vol. 7510, pp. 323–330. Springer, Heidelberg (2012)
8. Leventon, M.E., Grimson, W.E., Faugeras, O.: Statistical shape influence in geodesic active contours. In: CVPR, pp. 316–323 (2000)
9. Lorensen, W., Cline, H.: Marching cubes: a high resolution 3D surface construction algorithm. In: SIGGRAPH, pp. 163–169 (1987)
10. Lucchi, A., Li, Y., Fua, P.: Learning for structured prediction using approximate subgradient descent with working sets. In: CVPR, June 2013
11. Prevost, R., Cuingnet, R., Mory, B., Cohen, L.D., Ardon, R.: Incorporating shape variability in image segmentation via implicit template deformation. In: Mori, K., Sakuma, I., Sato, Y., Barillot, C., Navab, N. (eds.) MICCAI 2013, Part III. LNCS, vol. 8151, pp. 82–89. Springer, Heidelberg (2013)
12. Vazquez-Reina, A., Miller, E., Pfister, H.: Multiphase geometric couplings for the segmentation of neuronal processes. In: CVPR, pp. 2020–2027 (2009)
13. Vollmer, J., Mencl, R., Mueller, H.: Improved laplacian smoothing of noisy surface meshes. Computer Graphics Forum. **18**, 131–138 (1999). Wiley Online Library

W27 - Video Segmentation

First International Workshop on Video Segmentation - Panel Discussion

Thomas Brox[1], Fabio Galasso[2,3]([✉]), Fuxin Li[4], James Matthew Rehg[4], and Bernt Schiele[2]

[1] University of Freiburg, Freiburg im Breisgau, Germany
[2] Max Planck Institute for Informatics, Saarbrücken, Germany
fabio.galasso@gmail.com
[3] OSRAM Corporate Research, Munich, Germany
[4] Georgia Institute of Technology, Atlanta, GA, USA

Abstract. Interest in video segmentation has grown significantly in recent years, resulting in a large body of works along with advances in both methods and datasets. Progress in video segmentation would enable new approaches to building 3D object models from video, understanding dynamic scenes, robot-object interaction and several other high-level vision tasks. The workshop brought together a broad and representative group of video segmentation researchers working on a wide range of topics. This paper summarizes the panel discussion at the workshop, which focused on three questions: (1) Why does video segmentation currently not meet the performance of image segmentation and what difficulties prevent it from leveraging motion? (2) Is video segmentation a stand-alone problem or should it rather be addressed in combination with recognition and reconstruction? (3) Which are the right video segmentation subtasks the field should focus on, and how can we measure progress?

Keywords: Video segmentation · Computer vision

1 The State of Video Segmentation

While early works on motion segmentation date back to the 1970s, video segmentation has received especially growing interest in computer vision for the last few years, as is witnessed by its increasing presence in mainstream journal and conference publications [1–3,5–18,20–25,28–31]. This interest has led to diverse definitions of the video segmentation problem: some researchers see it as the problem of separating foreground from background while taking into account a potentially moving camera [3,13,22,31]; some see it as identification of moving objects [6,15,20], some as a data simplification method that yields an over-complete supervoxel representation of a video [5,23,29,30], creates and ranks segmentation proposals [2,13,31], or computes hierarchical sets of coarse-to-fine video segmentations [11,21,30].

As a consequence of such diversity, different datasets have been proposed. These include Hopkins 155 on motion segmentation [26], GT-SegTrack (v1 [27]

© Springer International Publishing Switzerland 2015
L. Agapito et al. (Eds.): ECCV 2014 Workshops, Part IV, LNCS 8928, pp. 383–388, 2015.
DOI: 10.1007/978-3-319-16220-1_27

and v2 [16]), INRIA-video [15], Youtube segment annotation [25], the Freiburg-Berkeley Motion Segmentation Dataset (FBMS-59) [19], and VSB-100 [8]. The datasets come with different evaluation metrics and annotation standards, reflecting the diverse problem statements: supervoxels, video object proposals, motion segmentation, unsupervised general video segmentation.

2   The Panelists

- Michael Black, MPI for Intelligent Systems
- Irfan Essa, Georgia Institute of Technology
- Vittorio Ferrari, University of Edinburgh
- Cristian Sminchisescu, Lund University
- René Vidal, Johns Hopkins University
- Jue Wang, Adobe Systems

3   Three Open Questions to Initiate the Discussion

- The first open problem stems from a recent observation in Galasso et al. [8] that a relatively *simple* propagation of state-of-the-art image segments over time with a good optical flow method outperforms the tested video segmentation algorithms. Furthermore, almost all tested methods drop significantly in performance when the general video segmentation task (including also non-moving objects) is reduced to a subtask, where only moving objects are required to be segmented (motion subtask [8]). Common sense would expect the segmentation of moving objects to be better defined and *easier* than segmentation of static objects.
- Second, the panelists were asked for their opinion on whether video segmentation should be addressed as a standalone problem or studied in relation with recognition and reconstruction computer vision tasks.
- The third proposed discussion point regarded the particular tasks which video segmentation should address to meet the requirements of potential applications and to serve as intermediate problems that would likely advance progress. What is a good way to measure progress?

4   Panel Discussion

Michael Black suggested looking at the persistent properties of objects in a video, such as material properties of surfaces and object identity. He proposed to consider the recent contributions on intrinsic videos and albedo and to delve into the physical properties of objects in order to characterize them. In a short presentation before the panel discussion he had referred to the recent efforts of his group to introduce a segmentation benchmark based on the open movie Sintel [4], where labels are based on object identity and those parts of an object that differ in material. Michal Irani from the audience expressed doubts that this would lead to a good definition of the problem. She points out that the annotation was per-frame, thus would not differ if the frames of the video were put in a different order. She compares this with an image that is interpreted just as a set of independent rows, undergoing row-based segmentation, row by row. Michael Black emphasized that the kind of annotation he mentioned *is* temporally coherent. Whether one would use motion segmentation to find such temporally coherent segmentations or some other way to localize the surfaces of the objects, in his opinion, does not change the definition of the problem. Shai Avidan from the audience proposed a stronger three-dimensional reasoning about objects, a suggestion that was later seconded by Cristian Sminchisescu. In contrast, Michael Black was sceptical on whether the reward of this would vanish due to the additional complexity which could introduce new problems.

Irfan Essa commented on the additional difficulties which video segmentation faces when compared to image segmentation. Temporal persistence of the provided segments, occlusions and disocclusions of objects over time especially as objects rotate in space, their appearance and disappearance, the varying size of regions over time are just a few examples he named. He recommended the use of metrics and observations which allow for progress in such tasks, looking beyond the frame-to-frame causality. He added that there is more to the definition of a segment, naming research on perceptual grouping and efforts to understand segments across scales alongside characteristics such as texture. In this respect, he believes that motion or the definition of a temporal tube, are probably not simplifying this complex problem.

The discussion on the task led to the question whether video segmentation is a stand-alone problem or whether it should be addressed alongside reconstruction and recognition tasks. Giving a first introductory statement on this question, Cristian Sminchisescu pointed out that certain problems could definitely be defined as stand-alone problems. Such problems include simple segmentation objectives enforcing continuation properties or forms of spatial layout loss, which could serve the definition of a fine-level detailed segmentation. On similar notes, motion segmentation may find justifications in the biological development of children, who first learn to distinguish to discern motion, and later Gestalt principles such as symmetry and continuity, before they understand the characteristics of simple objects. More generally, however, he believes that interaction with reconstruction and recognition might be essential, one such example being a 3D or 2.5D reconstruction to understand occlusion as opposed to simply tracking superpixels.

With respect to this interplay, Vittorio Ferrari introduced the term "Vision complete". In reference to terms like "NP-complete" and "AI complete", he uses this terminology for problems that require the whole vision problem to be solved before we will see satisfactory solutions. According to him, video segmentation will only be solved once also the other "vision" tasks are solved. He specifically underlined the interplay between segmentation and recognition, which builds upon the human capacity to segment objects from the background thanks to their prior knowledge on object appearance. In this respect, reconstruction may come into play at a more mature stage of understanding of these problems. In his opinion, a 3D reconstruction of complex videos such as the Sintel movie will definitely come from such virtuous interplay.

Triggered from a comment from the audience, Cristian Sminchisescu said that it is desirable to be robust to different tasks, but he thinks there is a lesson that can be learned from biological systems, which rather aim for sufficiency rather than completeness. A video segmentation approach may not be required to work in all cases as long as it works reliably for the setting it is applied to. That going beyond a single task is desirable is agreed by Vittorio Ferrari.

As the discussion had turned to tasks, Jue Wang made a statement on the third suggested discussion theme: what to evaluate segmentation on. From his point of view, a number of tasks are currently relevant to industry, including video understanding, object extraction and video segmentation for composition. In particular, regarding composition, one important feature to benchmark is temporal consistency independent of accuracy. Supposedly, consistency becomes more difficult when both the object and background move. According to Jue Wang, it is desirable to have different sets of ground truth for different tasks. As an example, video segmentation for recognition could be tested on the base of the final recognition rate.

Picking up on the first question, René Vidal pointed out that judging image segmentation better than the video counterpart could as well be a problem of annotations and metrics, as both are prone to mistakes. One such example is the relevance of the pixel count in most metrics, which clearly favors larger objects. In his opinion, there should be research on metrics and a universal metric is not desirable. Evaluating tasks such as motion segmentation or high precision boundaries for medical imaging in isolation is meaningful as it helps make progress and understand the limits of that task in isolation, a desirable research question. According to him, there is value in addressing tasks both jointly and one-at-a-time.

A further point in the discussion concerned terminology. While terms such as image, motion and video segmentation should be used carefully in their own domain, there is agreement that these concepts can be intended as supersets, with the video segmentation one including the previous two.

Michal Irani suggested video compression as an additional valuable task since video segments should provide the elementary components to best describe the video. Another important related task is action recognition. Cristian Sminchisescu added that intending video segmentation as a layered process might lead to the necessity of different layers for different tasks.

As a final suggestion, Vittorio Ferrari proposed to evaluate video segmentation methods by a relative metric, where humans are asked which of two segmentations is better. The motivation for this is that humans are good at relative assessment compared to absolute ones. In the same the Turing test might not be the perfect indication of machine intelligence, he added, getting the best numbers on a video segmentation benchmark might not indicate the best practical performance.

References

1. Badrinarayanan, V., Budvytis, I., Cipolla, R.: Mixture of trees probabilistic graphical model for video segmentation. IJCV (2013)
2. Banica, D., Agape, A., Ion, A., Sminchisescu, C.: Video object segmentation by salient segment chain composition. In: International Conference on Computer Vision, IPGM Workshop (2013)
3. Bergh, M.V.D., Roig, G., Boix, X., Manen, S., Gool, L.V.: Online video seeds for temporal window objectness. In: ICCV (2013)
4. Butler, D.J., Wulff, J., Stanley, G.B., Black, M.J.: A naturalistic open source movie for optical flow evaluation. In: Fitzgibbon, A., Lazebnik, S., Perona, P., Sato, Y., Schmid, C. (eds.) ECCV 2012, Part VI. LNCS, vol. 7577, pp. 611–625. Springer, Heidelberg (2012)
5. Chang, J., Wei, D., Fisher, J.W.: A video representation using temporal superpixels. In: CVPR (2013)
6. Dragon, R., Rosenhahn, B., Ostermann, J.: Multi-scale clustering of frame-to-frame correspondences for motion segmentation. In: Fitzgibbon, A., Lazebnik, S., Perona, P., Sato, Y., Schmid, C. (eds.) ECCV 2012, Part II. LNCS, vol. 7573, pp. 445–458. Springer, Heidelberg (2012)
7. Fragkiadaki, K., Shi, J.: Video segmentation by tracing discontinuities in a trajectory embedding. In: CVPR (2012)
8. Galasso, F., Nagaraja, N.S., Cardenas, T.J., Brox, T., Schiele, B.: A unified video segmentation benchmark: Annotation, metrics and analysis. In: ICCV (2013)
9. Godec, M., Roth, P.M., Bischof, H.: Hough-based tracking of non-rigid objects. In: ICCV (2011)
10. Grundmann, M., Kwatra, V., Han, M., Essa, I.: Efficient hierarchical graph-based video segmentation. In: CVPR (2010)
11. Jain, A., Chatterjee, S., Vidal, R.: Coarse-to-fine semantic video segmentation using supervoxel trees. In: ICCV (2013)
12. Lee, J., Kwak, S., Han, B., Choi, S.: Online video segmentation by bayesian split-merge clustering. In: Fitzgibbon, A., Lazebnik, S., Perona, P., Sato, Y., Schmid, C. (eds.) ECCV 2012, Part IV. LNCS, vol. 7575, pp. 856–869. Springer, Heidelberg (2012)
13. Lee, Y.J., Kim, J., Grauman, K.: Key-segments for video object segmentation. In: ICCV (2011)
14. Levinshtein, A., Sminchisescu, C., Dickinson, S.: Spatiotemporal closure. In: Kimmel, R., Klette, R., Sugimoto, A. (eds.) ACCV 2010, Part I. LNCS, vol. 6492, pp. 369–382. Springer, Heidelberg (2011)
15. Lezama, J., Alahari, K., Sivic, J., Laptev, I.: Track to the future: Spatio-temporal video segmentation with long-range motion cues. In: CVPR (2011)
16. Li, F., Kim, T., Humayun, A., Tsai, D., Rehg, J.M.: Video segmentation by tracking many figure-ground segments. In: ICCV (2013)
17. Ma, T., Latecki, L.J.: Maximum weight cliques with mutex constraints for video object segmentation. In: CVPR (2012)
18. Maire, M., Yu, S.X.: Progressive multigrid eigensolvers for multiscale spectral segmentation. In: ICCV (2013)
19. Ochs, P., Malik, J., Brox, T.: Segmentation of moving objects by long term video analysis. PAMI (2014)
20. Ochs, P., Brox, T.: Object segmentation in video: a hierarchical variational approach for turning point trajectories into dense regions. In: ICCV (2011)

21. Palou, G., Salembier, P.: Hierarchical video representation with trajectory binary partition tree. In: CVPR (2013)
22. Papazoglou, A., Ferrari, V.: Fast object segmentation in unconstrained video. In: ICCV (2013)
23. Reso, M., Jachalsky, J., Rosenhahn, B., Ostermann, J.: Temporally consistent superpixels. In: ICCV (2013)
24. Sundaram, N., Keutzer, K.: Long term video segmentation through pixel level spectral clustering on gpus. In: ICCV Workshops (2011)
25. Tang, K., Sukthankar, R., Yagnik, J., Fei-Fei, L.: Discriminative segment annotation in weakly labeled video. In: CVPR (2013)
26. Tron, R., Vidal, R.: A benchmark for the comparison of 3-D motion segmentation algorithms. In: CVPR (2007)
27. Tsai, D., Flagg, M., Rehg, J.M.: Motion coherent tracking with multi-label mrf optimization. In: BMVC (2010)
28. Vazquez-Reina, A., Avidan, S., Pfister, H., Miller, E.: Multiple hypothesis video segmentation from superpixel flows. In: Daniilidis, K., Maragos, P., Paragios, N. (eds.) ECCV 2010, Part V. LNCS, vol. 6315, pp. 268–281. Springer, Heidelberg (2010)
29. Xu, C., Corso, J.J.: Evaluation of super-voxel methods for early video processing. In: CVPR (2012)
30. Xu, C., Xiong, C., Corso, J.J.: Streaming hierarchical video segmentation. In: Fitzgibbon, A., Lazebnik, S., Perona, P., Sato, Y., Schmid, C. (eds.) ECCV 2012, Part VI. LNCS, vol. 7577, pp. 626–639. Springer, Heidelberg (2012)
31. Zhang, D., Javed, O., Shah, M.: Video object segmentation through spatially accurate and temporally dense extraction of primary object regions. In: CVPR (2013)

Author Index

Printed in the United States
By Bookmasters